PENGUIN BOOKS

THE PORTABLE
AGE OF REASON READER

Each volume in The Viking Portable Library either presents a representative selection from the works of a single outstanding writer or offers a comprehensive anthology on a special subject. Averaging 700 pages in length and designed for compactness and readability, these books fill a need not met by other compilations. All are edited by distinguished authorities, who have written introductory essays and included much other helpful material.

"The Viking Portables have done more for good reading and good writers than anything that has come along since I can remember."
—Arthur Mizener

The Portable
AGE OF REASON
Reader

❖ ❖ ❖

Edited, and with an Introduction, by

CRANE BRINTON

PENGUIN BOOKS

Penguin Books Ltd, Harmondsworth,
Middlesex, England
Penguin Books, 625 Madison Avenue,
New York, New York 10022, U.S.A.
Penguin Books Australia Ltd, Ringwood,
Victoria, Australia
Penguin Books Canada Ltd, 2801 John Street,
Markham, Ontario, Canada L3R 1B4
Penguin Books (N.Z.) Ltd, 182–190 Wairau Road,
Auckland 10, New Zealand

First published in the United States of America
by The Viking Press 1956
Paperbound edition published 1962
Reprinted 1962 (twice), 1963, 1964, 1966 (twice),
1968, 1969, 1972, 1973 (twice), 1975
Published in Penguin Books 1977

LIBRARY OF CONGRESS CATALOGING IN PUBLICATION DATA
Brinton, Clarence Crane, 1898–1968, ed.
The portable age of reason reader.
First published in 1956.
1. Enlightenment—Addresses, essays, lectures.
2. Philosophy, Modern—18th century—Addresses, essays, lectures.
I. Title.
[B802.B7 1977]   808.8   77-1505
ISBN 0 14 015.063 3

Printed in the United States of America by
Kingsport Press, Inc., Kingsport, Tennessee
Set in Linotype Caledonia

Contents

Prologue: The Birth of Reason

I. Proper Studies: Manners, Morals, Politics

MORALS AND MANNERS

v

EDUCATION

POLITICS AND ECONOMICS

CONTENTS

THE PRINCIPLES OF 1776 AND 1789

THE HEAVENLY CITY

II. The Ways of Reason: Philosophy and Natural Science

III. Nature and Nature's God: Religion

IV. Sense and Sensibility: Literature

V. Self-Revelation: Memoirs and Letters

Epilogue: Reason Becomes Revolution

Introduction

The Age of Reason is sometimes taken as synonymous with the Enlightenment of the eighteenth century. The ideas, tastes, and attitudes of men and women of the eighteenth century, though in part derived from the Greeks, and sharpened and refurbished in the Renaissance, begin to take firm shape early in the seventeenth century. For those who like a dramatic and specific date, the simple but far-reaching phrase of Descartes, "I think, therefore I am," will do very well for a beginning: 1637. The generation that grew up in the first half of the seventeenth century, though they gave full credit to the thinkers of the Renaissance for beginning the emancipation of the European mind, inclined to the belief that they themselves were the first to be *fully* emancipated. Descartes clearly felt this way. Dryden expressed the feeling neatly when he wrote in the 1660s that Bacon, Gilbert, Harvey, and the other "natural philosophers" had at last dealt the *coup de grâce* to Aristotle:

> The longest tyranny that ever sway'd,
> Was that wherein our ancestors betray'd
> Their free-born reason to the Stagirite,
> And made his torch their universal light.

Our Age of Reason will then be, roughly, the period of nearly two centuries from about 1630 to the end of the eighteenth century, when the Romantics took over.

Reason in the Age of Reason was no simple thing. Along with "nature," "reason" was a word of all work, a semanticist's despair, but an indispensable cluster of ideas for the men and women who created and sustained our civilization. For most people in that age, reason was the way the human mind—all human minds—naturally worked. In their opinion this natural working was indeed, as matters then stood, seriously impeded in the great majority of human beings by ignorance, superstition, preconceptions, errors, by bad laws and bad institutions—in short, by bad environment. But the capacity for reason was there in all men, like a seed deprived of good soil and water. Give it good soil and water—give it a good environment—and it will flower as nature meant it to flower.

The central concern of the Age of Reason was the problem, or rather, series of related political and moral problems, we have just outlined summarily: how to insure the rule of right reason here on earth. But the spectrum of human thought and feeling in the seventeenth and eighteenth centuries was by no means a narrow one. You can find almost all varieties of human experience in these centuries. The age of wit, epigram, polished decorum saw—and in Paris, capital city of the Enlightenment—crowds of miracle-seekers trying to carry off the sacred dirt from the tomb of a recently deceased Jansenist priest. Wit indeed got its revenge here, but wryly, and somewhat against itself. When royal officials barred off the graveyard entirely, the couplet ran through Paris:

> De par le roi défense à Dieu
> De faire miracle en ce lieu.[1]

---

[1] By royal command God is forbidden to commit miracles in this place. [C.B.'s note.]

In the oversimple and basically false view held in the nineteenth century, philosophy in the Age of Reason was one-sidedly rationalist, this-worldly, utilitarian; indeed, in medieval terms, nominalist. Actually the age produced, in Spinoza and Berkeley, not to mention Kant, "rationalists" indeed of a sort, but rationalists who climbed as high into the rarefied air of the Ideal as any philosopher ever has. The age produced one very great formal philosopher who really deserves to be called a skeptic—David Hume. It produced formal philosophers, not indeed rated very high in the usual manuals of history of philosophy, who claimed to base philosophy on common sense—the Scottish school of Thomas Reid and his followers. Locke no doubt set the philosophic tone for the Enlightenment, and Locke is certainly no Platonic idealist but very much a this-worldly empiricist. But even Locke is no extreme nominalist, no anti-intellectualist, but a moderate in all things. Even Locke's God is a Whig.

The Age of Reason was also an Age of Faith. For the enlightened, faith in reason, of course; did not the article on *philosophe* in the great Encyclopedia itself state that what grace is to the theologian, reason is to the *philosophe*? But for the rest, the spectrum of attitudes toward religion is extraordinarily complete and extraordinarily modern. There was always a numerous traditional Catholic, Anglican, and Lutheran religious Right, which refused to be seduced by fashion. Within the Catholic Church itself, these years saw the growth and spread, to an enlightened bourgeoisie in France and other countries, of Jansenism, sometimes called the "Puritanism of the Roman Catholic Church," and illustrated by the genius of Pascal and Racine. Within Protestantism, these years saw the rise of the last of the great sects, those of German Pietism and the closely related Anglo-American Methodism. Though the Pietists and Methodists do not look in retrospect quite as wild as they looked to the respectable and well-behaved religious moderates of the time, it must be admitted that they had a touch of holy-rolling. Next, as we move along the religious spectrum from ultra-violet to infra-red, there is a whole series of phases of what the age liked to call "natural" or "rational" religion, in contrast to "revealed" religion or just plain "superstition." The roots of Unitarianism in its modern form are clearly in the Age of Reason; and Unitarianism is furthest to the Left among those who call themselves Christians.

Most of the very enlightened, by 1750 or so, preferred not to call themselves Christians, though they admired the Christian ethical ideal. The best blanket-word for these believers is "deist"; both Voltaire and Rousseau, exceedingly different temperaments, can take the label. Voltaire was a cool deist; his famous epigram, of which he himself was very fond, really gives the show away: "If God did not exist, it would be necessary to invent him." For deists of this stamp, religion was at bottom necessary for the sheep—and perhaps in a disciplinary sense, for the shepherds. Rousseau was a warm deist; he could, strange though it seems, be moved by a God who did no more than design and start the universe, but never interfered with its running. Finally, at the extreme are the materialists, the outright atheists, never numerous, always in much disrepute, and publishing with some difficulty in defiance of the laws. By no mere quibble must these men, for the most part, be listed on the religious spectrum. They really *believed* in the marvelous machine this material universe seemed to them to be; they understood it, felt themselves a part of it. Diderot, who began as a deist but was converted to atheism, is a superior specimen; more conventional and much duller are men like the Baron d'Holbach and La Mettrie— the last the author of the characteristic *Man a Machine*. It is quite typical of the Age of Reason that one of its favorite topics of debate was: Can the open atheist be a good citizen? The prevailing opinion, even among the enlightened, was that he cannot. Morality, they held, needs some kind of religious sanction.

Along this spectrum, it seems fair to single out some form of deism as the typical religious outlook of the Age of Reason. This is no statistical average, certainly not for whole populations even in England and France. But deism was, to use a contemporary term of our own age, the belief of the "intellectuals." It was held not infrequently by men who never formally gave up conventional Christianity. Thus Pope, whose *Essay on Man* is a neat summary of deist commonplaces, was born into the English Catholic minority and remained a kind of Catholic all his life; on the Continent the philosophic priest was a familiar figure. The Italian abbé Galliani was accepted in the inner circle of the *philosophes*.

It should be clear that in the strict sense of the word the age was not skeptical, though in Christian polemics against the characteristic figures of the Enlightenment the word has often been used. From Locke and Bayle on, there were numerous very well-known thinkers who were skeptics in the sense that they did not "believe in" miracles, or the Real Presence, or the divinity of Christ; they were *not* skeptics, for the most part, in the sense of holding that no certain knowledge in such fields as theology, metaphysics, or epistemology is possible. Hume indeed will do as a skeptic; his demonstration—or if you prefer, attempted demonstration—that cause-and-effect is a mental construct, and not a verifiable "fact" or even "law" of a universe external to the human mind, fluttered the philosophic dovecotes and set Kant on his way to rescue faith in objective knowledge. But even Hume, after all a Scot, could not resist the temptation to believe in certain respects at least in something like the universe of common sense.

The seventeenth and eighteenth centuries are the great creative centuries of modern natural science. Though we now know that the foundations on which Galileo, Newton, Harvey, Huygens, Lavoisier, and their colleagues built go far back *through* the Middle Ages (*not* just skipping them) to Greece and the ancient Near East, it is still true that these men of the Age of Reason built the building as we know it. And more important for the student of the master ideas about the universe and man's place in it that have been held in Western culture, these centuries of the Age of Reason are the years in which many of the attitudes, or mental constructs, developed by practicing scientists in their work were taken over by the enlightened and developed into a cosmology, into a *Weltanschauung* or world-view, into an ethics. To deal briefly with a very big subject indeed: the contemporary twentieth-century position, clear in such philosophers of science as Von Mach and Henri Poincaré, that science does not even ask questions about the ultimate or absolute, would have been unintelligible to most of the enlightened—always excepting the prescient Diderot, Hume, and a few similar spirits. The others, generally speaking, believed that the science they loved to dabble in gave answers superior to those formerly given by

Jesus, St. Paul, or even Confucius and Mahomet, to the puzzle of man's fate in this universe. Their conception of the universe, and man in it—as J. H. Randall, Jr., shows in his *Making of the Modern Mind* —was in terms of what he there calls "the Newtonian world-machine." Newton had made clear to us the *true* workings of the planetary system and thus enabled us to adapt ourselves to it; clearly what remained was to find the *true* workings of society, the state, the family; the laws, so to speak, of human or social gravity. We could then adapt ourselves to these laws; meanwhile, the less systematic achievements of Right Reason would certainly be better than superstition and fanaticism. Here is one of the important focal points in the growth of modern "liberalism," ethical culture, positivism, and free-thinking, which, it must be repeated, is not a form of skepticism but a form of religion.

In these years what are still hopefully called the social sciences grew out of this matrix of natural science and cosmological belief. Economics, indeed economic statistics, go back at least to the seventeenth century. With Adam Smith's *Wealth of Nations* (1776) the discipline of economics comes of age. The *philosophes* might also be called *sociologues,* though the inventor of that barbarous Greco-Latin hybrid, Auguste Comte, was a belated child of the eighteenth century who flourished in the nineteenth. Psychology as a formal discipline may be said to begin in this age with Locke, Condillac, Hartley, though as a "proper study" the study of man's behavior surely goes back as far as any of our records go. Anthropology, however, will do as a sample of the modern social sciences. It has some of its roots in the Age of Discovery, but by the eighteenth century it had begun to take on its modern form. There is indeed in the eighteenth century a good deal of bastard anthropology—deliberate use of invented Chinese, Persians, Red Indians, South Sea Islanders to attack Western institutions and ways of life, bad reporting by prejudiced travelers, theorizing about a primitive state of nature (Rousseau, in spite of what his defenders say, was a very bad anthropologist). But there is also a great deal of careful amassing of facts, and in thinkers like Montesquieu the beginnings of an attempt to organize those facts into tentative uniformities. De Brosses, with some indebtedness to Hume, concludes his study of fetish-gods (1760) with words that still sound fitting for the "behavioral sciences": "It is not through his possibilities, but through his behavior, that man must be studied; it is not a matter of imagining what he might have done, or ought to have done, but of seeing what he does." History must be studied that way too; and if the study was often made for polemic purposes (nothing new), and if it tended to produce grander generalizations than historians since the Age of Reason have considered quite decent, still there were in these years many patient, careful searchers into "what really happened."

History, however, seemed to the Age of Reason not a science but an art, or at worst, as Voltaire put it, "a pack of tricks played on the dead"; at best, as Bolingbroke put it, "philosophy teaching by examples." Some of the greatest men of the time—Voltaire, Hume, Gibbon, Robertson—wrote history. With the writing of history we are in the midst of the literary and artistic phase of the Age of Reason. That phase has been at least as much subject to misunderstanding and polemical attack as the philosophical and ethical phase; and the mid-twentieth-century historian of ideas is at least as tempted in this field as in the other to react too violently against nineteenth-century critical stereotypes. It is not fair to describe Pope as a shallow optimist, a glib but shockingly unsystematic popularizer of fashionable deism, a versifier—horrid word—but not as a poet. But he was certainly no Blake, or even a Wordsworth. The fine arts are not fairly described as formal, pretentious, academic, aristocratic in a bad sense—one thinks of both Chardin (good) and Greuze (bad)—but Delacroix could not have painted as he did had he been born a few years earlier; and though in its love of *chinoiseries* and the like the eighteenth century marks the beginning of the fatal eclecticism which was to ruin so much of nineteenth-century architecture and its train of decorative arts, it is hard to imagine Whistler, for example, doing his Peacock Room in the eighteenth century.

For the fact is that the arts—in the widest sense of the word, which includes literature—were in the Age of Reason "classical" or even "neo-classical," and in the age that followed "romantic." We come once more to those worn old words, those chestnuts of criticism. They are unavoidable, but perhaps they may now be used without praise or blame—well, without much praise or blame—simply as convenient but of course inadequate attempts to do the cataloguing the human mind has to do, even when it concerns itself with the Beautiful and the Good.

The contrast between the Age of Reason and the Romantic Age has its dangers, which become clear when one gets down to cases. Set up your pairs as you will—classic love of form, romantic love of color; classic appeal to the head, romantic appeal to the heart; classic didacticism, romantic lyricism; classic belief in an ordered "nature," romantic belief in disordered, indeed chaotic, "nature." Better yet, take all these contrasts and many others and try to set up in your mind a complex pattern for each of these class terms. Then try to decide just when Romanticism begins—with the *Lyrical Ballads* (1798) or *Atala* (1801) or "Sturm und Drang" (as early as the 1780s)? But what will you do with Rousseau, surely in part a romantic? You are already back in mid-eighteenth century, and if you are not careful you will find yourself coming out, via the early enthusiasts for Gothic, the Wartons, the Countess of Winchilsea, the Duc de Saint-Simon (whose style at least is almost Proustian), and Pascal, at the other end of the Age of Reason, which will not, however, thereby be telescoped out of existence.

For the fact is that some of what we are trying to pin down in these old terms of classic and romantic are abiding elements in human nature. There are always romantics, there are always classicists; and indeed every human being is both a romanticist and a classicist —though in some, no doubt, one element hardly amounts to more than what the chemist calls a "trace." The historian of culture can only note, as far as possible, just how the mixture varies in place and in time. On the whole, for the years with which we are here concerned, the classical prevails—and prevails to the extent that even the work of the rebels, those out of tune with their age, cannot quite escape its stamp. All the rebels against reason, for instance, write with admirable clarity, write a good rational prose. Law, the English "mystic," writes as clearly as an Addison. Rousseau does more; he attacks the rationalist *philosophes* with their own weapons of paradox.

Some positive generalizations about the art and letters of the age are worth making. First of all, in the two centuries or so with which we are concerned, there is certainly change, development. If one takes a specific form of art—say, French tragedy—then the great achievement, that of Corneille and Racine, comes early and the rest of the period is a very good example of the exhaustion of an art form. It is, however, a great mistake to catalogue the seventeenth century as "creative," the "century of genius," and the eighteenth century as "imitative," the "century of propaganda." What happens to the art of the word, at least, is rather a shift from concern with the lofty and dramatic to a concern with ordinary human behavior, a shift in which tragedy and lyric and epic poetry suffer, but comedy, the novel, and the essay gain. The fine arts are more complex, but not even the overtones of the term "rococo" should suggest exhaustion and decay. Finally, there is that characteristic achievement of the eighteenth century, which we have rather tamely catalogued as the beginnings of the social sciences, but which from another point of view is best described as a turning of great creative literary minds to the problems of man as—in the full Aristotelian sense—a political animal.

The ideal remains, however, in spite of all the talk about the common man and the noble savage, an aristocratic humanism. No doubt a kindly soul like Condorcet may be described as a "democratic humanist," but the two words go badly together, and most democrats, who hardly appear until late in the eighteenth century, reject the traditional ideal of the gentleman. Something indeed happens in these centuries to the humanism of the Renaissance. Especially in the eighteenth century, the Christian humanist tends to be—and with reason—less serene and more moody, worried. He is Samuel Johnson, no longer St. Thomas More. As for the non-Christian or secular humanist, he comes to be, for one thing, a vehement anti-Christian, which on the whole he is not in the sixteenth century; and he is vastly less robust. The eighteenth century is not an athletic century; its Cellinis turn into Casanovas. But the humanist ideal is there, perhaps too polished, too formalized, into something rather exhausting to live up to, at the court of the young Louis XIV, in the England of Queen Anne and George I. And the literary men are right in the midst of it all, still gentlemen in the face of the growing threat of Grub Street, still dependent on kings, noblemen, and really rich merchants in the face of the growing threat of a mass market for literary wares, still Bossuets, Boileaus, Addisons, Popes, and, yes, Voltaires. Defoe is there, however, with the future before him—no elegant subscription lists running to the thousands of pounds, as for Pope's translations from Homer, but just over-the-counter sales to ordinary people.

This is indeed an age of formal art. Not even the French Revolution broke for the arts the prestige of "those rules of old discover'd, not deviz'd." Yet here we need least of all to listen to the complaints of the first generation of Romantics. The alexandrine and the heroic couplet did indeed wear out, but so does any form of poetry in this world of fashion—including the form innocently called *vers libre*. In themselves and at their best in these years, with Racine or with Pope, the alexandrine and the heroic couplet are admirably fitted for the job they have to do, may seem even to the convinced relativist to have deserved Pope's characteristic assertion that they and the other rules of "classical" art are not just "deviz'd" by the determined, inventive individual. So at least the Age of Reason believed; the rules of art, like the rules of morals, politics, science, and the other activities of the human mind, are "out there," lands to be discovered, settled, and lived in and cultivated, even in a modest sense to be changed by this cultivation; but not to be escaped—not, at least, by the sane.

Of course the rules were not rigidly adhered to, not often and not for very long. The famous three unities of classic French tragedy will do as a sample. Time —twenty-four hours; place—not just one city or town but one central palace, hall, or such public place, with anterooms or corridors for the sole change; action—just one thread of plot, or at least with no really distracting minor characters and sub-plots. Racine observed these rules quite as naturally and successfully as Shakespeare observed his rules; but hardly anyone else did. Corneille had a hard time. His Roderick in the *Cid* lived about the fullest twenty-four hours in literature.

Even granting the Victorians that some of the art forms of the Age of Reason proved often straitjackets, the fact remains that one of the great achievements of the age is the novel, a genre that certainly has not run to the three or any other unities. The modern novel, after confused and long-winded beginnings, really comes of age in the eighteenth century. It is still often long-winded, a term that seems understatement now when applied, say, to Richardson's *Sir Charles Grandison*. But it is no longer confused. With Fielding and his fellows, in France with Rousseau, Laclos, Prévost, in Germany with Goethe, it begins its modern reign. Now the novel is not an aristocratic genre. To tie its rise to the rise of a middle class is at least a half-truth, perhaps even a nine-tenths-truth. Those incurable aristocrats, the liberally educated and the learned, looked down in the eighteenth century on the novel as vulgar and designed for females; in a sense the novel was born on the wrong side of the tracks. But the tracks then did not so much separate the rich and the poor as they did the purists, the "classicists," who might have been born quite humbly, and the curious-minded and unconventional, who might have been born ladies, or even gentlemen.

The novel is one of the characteristic genres of the Age of Reason because it is the best literary form for the study of men in all their variety. We come again to the vast curiosity the seventeenth and eighteenth centuries had for all the range of human experience. Taine could hardly have been more wrong than when he accused the writers of the classical age of obsession with an unreal, abstract, "perfect" natural man, of failing to understand *men* in their preoccupation with *man*. The second- and third-raters of the generation just before the French Revolution, a Helvetius, a Holbach, sometimes sound as if they did believe in such an abstract man. There are in this as in all ages philosophers so engaged that they really do not see much of the external world they write about in their theory of knowledge. But for the most part even the rationalists, the kindly rationalists who would like men not to be wolves, or pigs, or parrots, or tomcats, are fully aware that in fact they often are. Hume's famous statement that reason is, and ought to be, the slave of the passions is not in the least out of tune with the times. Adam Smith even found that Hume rather overestimated human rationality. This is in Western literature the great age of the aphorism. Not even in Franklin, let alone in La Rochefoucauld or Vauvenargues, is the aphorism a form of silly optimism about human nature. It is, in fact, the hardest-boiled of all the genres; sentimental optimism simply doesn't get ex-

pressed in aphorisms. So too the dark and twisted, the
cruel, the obscene, and the perverted, are all there in
the Age of Reason; there are fine Freudian depths
not only in the lives but in the works of Swift, Diderot,
Rousseau, Sterne, Restif de la Bretonne, de Sade, and
surely both those immortal correspondents, Voltaire
and Frederick the Great. In short, the age was by no
means naïve about the facts of life as it is now lived;
if some writers—a Bernardin de Saint-Pierre, a Godwin,
a Condorcet, indeed in a sense most of the enlightened
—now seem naïve about life as it might be, or as it
was at other points in space-time, then surely the age
was less rationalist, more idealistic, than our textbooks
commonly admit.

Many of these writers report on much of human
behavior in a way that really did shock the Victorians,
and that of course cannot shock us today but does
seem pretty lighthearted—to some of us, enviably so.
From the English Restoration comedy of the second
half of the seventeenth century right through to Restif
de la Bretonne's *Le Pornographe* on the eve of the
French Revolution, there is a great deal of the spice
of sex. Diderot wrote a potboiler, the *Bijoux Indiscrets*,
which even today is kept by discreet librarians under
lock and key. Voltaire clearly relished, in a literary
way, the difference between men and women. Gibbon
appeared to the nineteenth-century French critic,
Sainte-Beuve, addicted to "coldly erudite obscenity" in
the footnotes of his great *Decline and Fall*. With the
Marquis de Sade—from whom our overworked *sadism,
sadistic*—at the end of the Age of Reason the light-
heartedness disappears, and we begin to feel very close
to home. In most of these writers, however, the pursuit of the opposite sex seemed part of the pursuit of
happiness. Charles Lamb was of course wrong in his

famous dictum that the English Restoration comedy does not really deal with living creatures but only with a play world, "innocent" at heart. But Lamb's instincts in this matter were sound. The men of the Age of Reason were as reasonable about sex as it is possible to be; on the whole they enjoyed it, both vicariously and directly.

This capacity for enjoyment, indeed this gusto, is one of the two big generalizations about the Age of Reason worth holding on to. There are of course exceptions; but even in the unhappy, the tortured, the spirit of the age leaves its mark. Unreason takes on some of the marks of reason, so that a Rousseau does not sound like a Nietzsche. Even the possessed are, if by no means sane, at any rate never feeble, feverish in their behavior. Swift and Samuel Johnson suffer vigorously; neither ever sounds at all like a Kierkegaard. The gusto of the *philosophes,* as we have noted, is not quite like that of the Renaissance. It is less robust but quite as real. It is in many of the writers of the Age of Reason expressed as a form of optimism about the possible future of the human race on this earth; but it is by no means dependent on such optimism, and indeed in the greater thinkers it is accompanied by very ambivalent feelings about ordinary human nature. It rarely, however, takes the form of resignation: the Age of Reason is a fighting age. When in perhaps his most quoted phrase Voltaire has the much-tried characters of *Candide* settle down and decide *"il faut cultiver notre jardin"* (we must cultivate our garden), he is surely cultivating his own favorite irony; at any rate, the gardens of his estate at Ferney turned out to be almost impossibly extensive, world wide, in fact.

It is tempting in our psycho-sociological times to assert that the enjoyment of life displayed by the writers and artists of the Age of Reason is in part an enjoyment of status. From a twentieth-century vantage point, the Age of Reason looks to be the last in which the artist, the writer, the "intellectual" if you like, could feel he was understanded of the many, appreciated by the many, looked up to by the many. It was a kind of honeymoon of the intellectual with the masses. The intellectual could still draw comfort from his old family connections with noble patrons and with endowed learning, and yet enjoy his new part as advocate for the non-literate middle classes. The French Revolution, which really did end a good deal, ended this honeymoon. The romantics were soon organizing *Davidsbunde* against the philistines, damning the middle classes, beginning that characteristic alienation of the intellectual from the rest of humanity which has gone so far today in the West.

In part because they were trying very hard to be understood by a wide audience, the writers and artists of this age achieved a kind of clarity, simplicity, and universality, which is the final generalization we shall make about their "style." There were of course the erudite, the cultivators of arcana, the writers for a topical present that, become the past, necessarily now requires footnoting. But the romantic De Quincey was quite wrong in asserting that a "rude mind" would find it easier to comprehend Milton and Shakespeare than Pope. Exposed to a random sampling of all three, it looks now as though the rude mind would be about equally helpless with all three, with Shakespeare's Renaissance conceits, Milton's classical allusions, Pope's topical allusions. But in Pope the possessor of the rude mind would be bound to run into passage after passage like

> For forms of government let fools contest
> Whate'er is best administered is best,

which would be wholly clear to him. There is indeed in the Enlightenment a vein of heaviness, a fondness for rhetoric and the periodic style, especially clear in English prose of the later eighteenth century. But at its best the Age of Reason should be given credit for living up to its standards and speaking clearly and with dignity. The political credos of the age, which are still ours in the United States—the American Declaration of Independence, the English, American, and French Bills of Rights—have clarity with dignity; compared with them, the Communist Manifesto sounds shrill indeed—in fact, romantic.

II

The Founding Fathers, repudiate them as some of us may, as all of us do at times, are still our fathers. The Age of Reason is one we should try to understand, for we have to work immediately with what it has left us. If we go to the past solely to find the best that has been thought and done—surely a legitimate search— then it can be argued that all the previous "period" *Readers* in this series, save perhaps for the *Roman Reader,* have a range and depth in the achievement of the Beautiful and the Good not reached by the Age of Reason. We need not here quarrel with the verdict of the nineteenth century; the peaks are higher in the great age of Greece, in the Renaissance, and in many phases of art, thought, and letters in the Middle Ages. And the climbing of these peaks is an essential part of a liberal education.

But it is not all. There is something in the position

taken by so many of the taught in the United States —annoying though this position may be to many of their teachers—that the more recent past is more important for us than the more remote past. Surely we live in part on the heritage of the Greeks, the ancient Hebrews, the Middle Ages, the Renaissance. But most of us live much more intimately with what the Age of Reason has bequeathed us. For the seventeenth and eighteenth centuries set in many ways the pattern of our own times.

They set it most obviously and most inescapably in this: they marked the first time in the history of the world that reading ceased to be a monopoly of the very few. By the end of the eighteenth century we have, to use our own jargon, in the printed word a mass medium other than the pulpit, oral tradition, and the like. Printing, without which this could hardly have happened, took several centuries to get beyond an elite almost as confined as the elite that read the hand copies of old. Its first venture into the hands of the many was in sectarian religious quarrels. By the Age of Reason, however, costs had been reduced so that the pamphlet and the broadside, the nascent newspaper, helped by the new meeting places of the many, the coffee house and the social club, were available to thousands. Of course there was not yet universal literacy, not even in Scotland, Holland, or New England, where Calvinism first paved the way for it, but the really big step had been taken. The many in counting house and shop, the bourgeoisie, the skilled artisans, even a few farmers, had begun the habit of reading.

They had also begun to believe in a doctrine for which one can find only the faintest foreshadowings before the Age of Reason. They had begun to believe in progress---a word that before 1700 meant in both French and English no more than a physical moving, as when a royal personage made a progress through the realm. They could note already, if they lived a good span of years, that what we now call technology had made appreciable progress during their own lives. They could note that stagecoaches, for instance, moved faster and on better springs over better roads than in the old days. Gradually they and their intellectual leaders began to sketch the notions of moral, artistic, and intellectual progress, which reached their height in the doctrine of the perfectibility of man in Condorcet.

The new faith broke with the past, with the past of Renaissance humanism as well as that of medieval Christianity, in several ways. First of all, it insisted that all men may really hope and strive to be happy here on this earth; and by happiness was meant what ordinary unheroic common sense had long meant by happiness, enough good food and drink, comfortable lodging, agreeable sex life, a pleasant family life, and so on; in short, a life in which men have what they want. And they were beginning to want quite a lot. Second, they were beginning to listen to the rationalists who told them that the universe was the Newtonian world-machine, and not the universe of traditional Christianity. They were beginning to think of the universe as behaving in quite regular ways which left no room for the miraculous, the supernatural. The rationalist temperament was certainly not new in the seventeenth century; it is patent among the Greeks, especially among the Greeks of the Hellenistic Age. But the Age of Reason was the first time rationalism really made extensive converts among the many. It looks today as if the great aid to such conversion was the prestige and success of natural science, which in the Age of Reason for the first time offered ordinary men a substitute for the Christian cosmology. That is why the seventeenth, and not the fifteenth, century is the real turning point of history, the real beginnings of our own times.

Christianity was not destroyed—far from it. But it was—and is—forced by what the Age of Reason brought with it into the hardest struggle of its two thousand years, a struggle not against heresy or schism, but against a very different view of the place of man in the universe. With the Age of Reason, such basic Christian positions as Original Sin, the miraculous structure of the universe (using the word miraculous literally, not just figuratively and sloppily), the goodness of, the need for, suffering in this life to merit salvation in the next, the whole structure of Christian earthly social inequalities: all this was—and is—very hard to maintain in all Western hearts and heads at all times. Most Christian groups have in fact compromised with the Enlightenment; they have accepted modern democracy.

This modern democracy, and its major heresy, communism, are directly out of the eighteenth century. We are today living with a faith, an aspiration, that, rooted though it is in several thousand years of Western history, is still, in the forms we must live with, the child of the Age of Reason. Perhaps Americans in particular are not really quite aware of how new their faith is. But to few before the eighteenth century would universal rights to life, liberty, and the pursuit of happiness have seemed in any real sense rights at all —especially if they are understood, as one suspects Jefferson himself really meant them to be, as rights to a *good* life, to an *enjoyable* liberty, and to the *successful* pursuit of happiness. The democrat, chastened

though he may be by all that has happened since
1789, must still share something of the hopes of
Condorcet, or he is surely no democrat. He must
believe that evil, human suffering, human frustration,
are at least in part attributable to those institutions,
to that "environment," which the men of the Age of
Reason attacked with so much courage, gusto, and
unreason.

III

The way of the anthologist is hard. His little nosegay,
even if it is in fact a rather large bouquet, will never
quite satisfy anyone else, and will not even satisfy
him. It is certain that even the compiler of a collection
of the best of Tocharian—that easternmost of Indo-
European tongues, of which there survive only the
scrappiest of desert-preserved bits—would feel quite
honestly obliged to begin by apologizing for having
had to make such a meager selection from so abundant
a source. But the relentless pressure of space . . . It
would be hard enough to choose what seems sub-
jectively to the chooser the best or most interesting from nearly two centuries of Western art and
letters. An editor of one of these *Readers,* however,
must keep the choice of the best subordinate to the
choice of the characteristic, the representative, must
make no mere anthology but rather a sampling of the
variety and range of human culture at a given time.
Under these conditions any choice from among the
millions—indeed, taking into account the newspaper
and periodical press, official documents and the like,
the billions—of words printed in the Age of Reason
and still surviving, for their rag paper was very good,
must need apology indeed.

Above all, this need to have range and variety

consonant with the reality of the age, this need to show as much of the whole spectrum as possible, has meant that no one thinker can be fairly represented with a long work. The excerpts have to be short, or fairly short, have indeed to be edited. Again, the main currents of the Age of Reason could be made clear from perhaps half a dozen of the greater men—say, Descartes, Locke, Voltaire, Diderot, Rousseau, Hume. But how many fascinating eddies, how many fertile branches, how much in short of the age *as it really was* would thus be omitted!

Finally, the bulk of any representative collection of writings of the Age of Reason must come from work done in the English and French languages. The Germans belong, and are here represented, but by no means to the extent they must be for a *Romantic Reader*. Italy is here presented by Beccaria, whose *On Crimes and Punishments* is central to the Enlightenment, and by Casanova, a cosmopolitan if there ever was one. In the smaller countries, Holland, Denmark, Sweden, even to a certain extent in the Iberian peninsula, the Enlightenment did indeed flourish. But a surprising amount of writing on the Continent was done in French, which in this period became a *lingua franca* for diplomacy and almost, but not quite, became what Latin had been, a *lingua franca* for the full range of the art and science of the written word. Russia's literate culture, Western style, is still in these years quite literally borrowed, and no Russian has to be included in a collection of this sort.

Men born and brought up in what is now the United States must, however, be so included. Indeed, if you are looking for a "representative man," in the Emersonian sense, for the Age of Reason, you could do much worse than pick Jefferson. Just how "American" these men are, even though some of them helped make the American Revolution, is legitimately debatable. They lack the cultural self-consciousness of nationality the succeeding generation in this country had, and especially they lack its touchy sense of cultural inferiority. They have for the most part the characteristic gusto, the willingness to face the facts of life without excessive moral indignation, and, above all, the feeling of belonging, of being a normal part of the American whole—at least until the 1790s—which American intellectuals have never since quite recaptured. Let us say that they are Americans in the sense that Hume and Adam Smith are Scots—but no more so. They all belong to the community of the Enlightenment, a community broken certainly by very bitter wars of interest and ambition, but not yet by wars of romantic nationalism. The roots of this romantic nationalism are indeed in this period; but what grew out of these roots must be shown in a later *Reader*.

An *Age of Reason Reader* and a *Romantic Reader* must of course overlap in time. The editor leaves much to his successor: he leaves the "portents of the coming storm," the Gothic novel, the tale of horror, "Sturm und Drang," the depths and mysteries of the Celts; he leaves the Rousseau of the *Confessions* and the *Nouvelle Héloise* and the writings of the last years of obvious madness; above all, he leaves Edmund Burke, whom he would like to claim for the Age of Reason but dares not.

This *Reader* owes much to the kindness of the staffs of the libraries of Harvard University and of Dartmouth College. Malcolm Cowley has helped throughout and to him is due a translation from La Bruyère and the suggestion that this *Reader* begin with Descartes'

"I think, therefore I am" and end with the festival of Reason in the *ci-devant* cathedral of Notre-Dame de Paris (neither Mr. Cowley nor the editor meaning by this arrangement to be any more ironical than history itself). Professor Frank Manuel of Brandeis University has provided so many admirable suggestions that he deserves mention as an assistant editor. Dr. L. S. Greenbaum of the University of Massachusetts has helped greatly with translations. Mr. Christiaan Lievestro of Harvard University has enlightened me on the Dutch Enlightenment. Professors Arthur M. Wilson of Dartmouth College, Leo Gershoy of New York University, W. T. Jones of Pomona College, and Dr. O. H. Taylor of Harvard University have all been helpful in various ways. Professor F. L. Baumer of Yale, Professor John H. Stewart of Western Reserve, Richard Wilbur, and Marianne Moore have been very generous in permitting the use of their translations from the French. Miss Elizabeth F. Hoxie has labored effectively through stacks of books and manuscripts. To all these the editor wishes to extend his thanks.

SUGGESTIONS
FOR FURTHER READING

Readers who wish a detailed account of the history of the seventeenth and eighteenth centuries, including cultural and intellectual history as well as the political and military narrative, will find it in the following volumes of the *Rise of Modern Europe*, edited by W. L. Langer and published by Harper & Brothers, New York, 1934—:

Friedrich, C. J. *The Age of the Baroque, 1610-1660* (1952).

Nussbaum, F. L. *The Triumph of Science and Reason, 1660-1685* (1953).

Wolf, J. B. *The Emergence of the Great Powers, 1685-1715* (1951).

Roberts, Penfield. *The Quest for Security, 1715-1740* (1947).

Dorn, W. L. *Competition for Empire, 1740-1763* (1940).

Gershoy, Leo. *From Despotism to Revolution, 1763-1789* (1944).

Brinton, Crane. *A Decade of Revolution, 1789-1799* (1934).

Bruun, Geoffrey. *Europe and the French Imperium, 1799-1814* (1938).

Each of these volumes has a long bibliographical essay, with brief critical remarks about each important work listed. From these lists the advanced student can launch himself into almost any problem in the history of the Age of Reason.

The following list of suggested readings, therefore, has the limited aim of suggesting to the general reader books that will extend and deepen his appreciation of what the men and women of the Age of Reason were like. They should, as should this *Reader*, lead him directly to the works of these men and women themselves, to what historians still call the "sources."

I. GENERAL WORKS

A. On the general history of ideas

Becker, C. L. *Heavenly City of the Eighteenth-Century Philosophers*. New Haven: Yale University Press, 1932.

Cassirer, Ernst. *The Philosophy of the Enlightenment*. Princeton: Princeton University Press, 1951.

Clark, G. N. *The Seventeenth Century*. 2nd ed. New York: Oxford University Press, 1947.

Dieckmann, Herbert. "An Interpretation of the Eighteenth Century," *Modern Language Quarterly*. December 1954. A review of the Cassirer book above, but invaluable in its own right.

Hazard, Paul. *The European Mind, 1680-1715*. New Haven: Yale University Press, 1953.

————. *European Thought in the Eighteenth Century*. New Haven: Yale University Press, 1954.

Lovejoy, A. O. *Essays in the History of Ideas*. 2nd ed. Baltimore: Johns Hopkins University Press, 1952.

Manuel, F. E. *The Age of Reason*. Ithaca: Cornell University Press, 1951.

Mowat, R. B. *The Age of Reason*. Boston: Houghton, Mifflin & Co., 1934.

Smith, Preserved. *The History of Modern Culture*. Vol. I. The Great Instauration. Vol. II. The Enlightenment. New York: Henry Holt & Co., 1934.

Taine, H. A. *The Ancient Regime*. Book III. The Spirit and the Doctrine. New York: Henry Holt & Co., 1885.

Willey, Basil. *The Seventeenth-Century Background.* New York: Columbia University Press, 1942. (Also by Anchor Books.)

———. *The Eighteenth-Century Background.* New York: Columbia University Press, 1941.

B. On particular disciplines or phases

PHILOSOPHY AND METHOD

Höffding, Harald. *History of Modern Philosophy.* 2 vols. New York: Dover Publications, 1955.

Lange, F. A. *History of Materialism.* New York: Humanities Press, 1950.

Lecky, W. E. H. *History of the Rise and Influence of the Spirit of Rationalism in Europe.* 2 vols. Rev. ed. New York: Appleton, 1914.

Robertson, J. M. *A Short History of Free Thought, Ancient and Modern.* 2nd ed. London: Watts, 1906.

SCIENCE

Herbert Butterfield. *The Origins of Modern Science.* New York: The Macmillan Co., 1951.

Clark, G. N. *Science and Social Welfare in the Age of Newton.* 2nd ed. New York: Oxford University Press, 1942.

White, H. D. *A History of the Warfare of Science with Theology.* 2 vols. New York: George Braziller, 1955.

Whitehead, A. N. *Science and the Modern World.* New York: The Macmillan Co., 1948. (Also by Mentor Books, New American Library.)

Wolf, Abraham. *A History of Science, Technology, and Philosophy in the Sixteenth and Seventeenth Centuries.* 2nd ed. New York: The Macmillan Co., 1950.

———. *A History of Science, Technology, and Philosophy in the Eighteenth Century.* 2nd ed. New York: The Macmillan Co., 1952.

POLITICAL AND SOCIAL THOUGHT

Black, J. B. *The Art of History.* New York: Crofts, 1926. Deals with Gibbon, Hume, Robertson, Voltaire.

Bury, J. B. *A History of Freedom of Thought.* 2nd ed. New York: Oxford University Press, 1952.

————. *The Idea of Progress.* New ed. New York: Dover Publications, 1955.

Butts, R. F. *A Cultural History of Education.* New York: McGraw-Hill Book Co., 1947.

Fairchild, H. N. *The Noble Savage: a Study in Romantic Nationalism.* New York: Columbia University Press, 1928.

Laski, H. J. *The Rise of European Liberalism.* London: George Allen & Unwin, 1947.

Sabine, G. H. *A History of Political Theory.* Rev. ed. New York: Henry Holt & Co., 1950.

Schumpeter, Joseph. *History of Economic Analysis.* New York: Oxford University Press, 1954.

Teggart, F. J., ed. *The Idea of Progress.* Berkeley: University of California Press, 1925.

Tinker, C. B. *Nature's Simple Plan.* Princeton: Princeton University Press, 1922.

THE ARTS

Hauser, Arnold. *The Social History of Art.* New York: Alfred A. Knopf, Inc., 1951.

Leichentrett, Hugo. *Music, History, and Ideas.* Cambridge: Harvard University Press, 1938.

Sypher, Wylie. *Four Stages of Renaissance Style: Transformations in Art and Literature, 1400-1700.* New York: Doubleday & Co., 1955. (An Anchor Book.)

II. BY COUNTRIES

A. France

Cobban, Alfred. *Rousseau and the Modern State.* London: George Allen & Unwin, 1934.

Green, F. C. *Minuet: A Critical Survey of French and British Literary Ideas in the Eighteenth Century.* New York: E. P. Dutton & Co., 1935.

———. *Rousseau and the Idea of Progress.* New York: Oxford University Press, 1950.

Guérard, A. L. *Life and Death of an Ideal: France in the Classical Age.* New York: Charles Scribner's Sons, 1928.

Hearnshaw, F. J. C., ed. *The Social and Political Ideas of Some Great French Thinkers of the Age of Reason.* New York: Barnes & Noble, Inc., 1950.

Higgs, Henry. *The Physiocrats.* New York: The Macmillan Co., 1897.

Josephson, Matthew. *J.-J. Rousseau.* New York: Harcourt, Brace & Co., 1931.

Martin, Kingsley. *The Rise of French Liberal Thought.* Rev. ed. New York: New York University Press, 1954.

Morley, John. *Voltaire.* New York: The Macmillan Co., 1923.

———. *Rousseau.* 2 vols. New York: The Macmillan Co., 1923.

———. *Diderot.* 2 vols. New York: The Macmillan Co., 1905.

Noyes, Alfred. *Voltaire.* New York: Sheed & Ward, 1936.

Schapiro, J. S. *Condorcet and the Rise of Liberalism.* New York: Harcourt, Brace & Co., 1934.

Torrey, N. L. *The Spirit of Voltaire.* New York: Columbia University Press, 1938.

Wickwar, W. H. *Baron d'Holbach, a Prelude to the French Revolution.* New York: Burt Franklin, 1935.

B. Great Britain

Gooch, G. P. *English Democratic Ideas in the Seventeenth Century.* 2nd ed. Cambridge, England: Cambridge University Press, 1927.

Greig, J. Y. T. *Hume.* London: J. Cape, 1931.

Grierson, H. J. C. *Cross-Currents in English Literature of the Seventeenth Century.* London: Chatto & Windus, 1929.

Hearnshaw, F. J. C., ed. *The Social and Political Ideas of Some English Thinkers of the Augustan Age.* New York: Barnes & Noble, Inc., 1950.

Kronenberger, Louis. *Kings and Desperate Men: Life in Eighteenth-Century England.* New York: Alfred A. Knopf, Inc., 1942.

Lamprecht, S. P. *The Moral and Political Philosophy of John Locke.* New York: Columbia University Press, 1918.

Laski, H. J. *English Political Thought from Locke to Bentham.* New York: Henry Holt & Co., 1920.

Quintana, R. B. *The Mind and Art of Swift.* New ed. New York: Oxford University Press, 1953.

Sitwell, Edith. *Alexander Pope.* London: Faber & Faber, 1930. (Also in Penguin series.)

Stephen, Leslie. *English Thought in the Eighteenth Century.* 2 vols. New York: Peter Smith, 1949.

———. *English Literature and Society in the Eighteenth Century.* London: Duckworth, 1947.

———. *The English Utilitarians.* Vol. I. Bentham. 3 vols. in 1. New York: Peter Smith, 1950.

C. Germany

Aris, Reinhold, *Political Thought in Germany, 1789-1815.* London: George Allen & Unwin, 1936.

Bruford, W. H. *Germany in the Eighteenth Century: the Social Background of the Literary Revival.* New ed. Cambridge, England: Cambridge University Press, 1952.

Cassirer, Ernst. *Rousseau, Kant, Goethe: Two Essays.* Princeton: Princeton University Press, 1947.

Ergang, R. R. *Herder and the Foundations of German Nationalism.* New York: Columbia University Press, 1931.

Francke, Kuno. *History of German Literature as Determined by Social Forces.* 12th impression. New York: Henry Holt & Co., 1927.

Garland, H. B. *Lessing.* Cambridge, England: Cambridge University Press, 1937.

Lindsay, A. D. *Philosophy of Immanuel Kant.* London: T. C. and E. C. Jack, 1919.

Robertson, J. G. *History of German Literature*. Rev. ed. New York: G. P. Putnam's Sons, 1931.

D. Italy

Croce, Benedetto. *The Philosophy of G.-B. Vico*. London: Latimer, 1913.

Phillipson, Coleman. *Three Criminal Reformers: Beccaria, Bentham, Romilly* New York: E. P. Dutton & Co., 1923.

E. United States

Chinard, Gilbert. *Thomas Jefferson: Apostle of Americanism*. Boston: Little, Brown & Co., 1929.

Faÿ, Bernard. *The Revolutionary Spirit in France and in America*. New York: Harcourt, Brace & Co., 1927.

Gabriel, R. H. *Course of American Democratic Thought*. New York: Ronald Press, 1940.

Kraus, Michael. *The Atlantic Civilization: Eighteenth-Century Origins*. Ithaca: Cornell University Press, 1949.

Miller, Perry. *The New England Mind: The Seventeenth Century*. New ed. Cambridge: Harvard University Press, 1954.

————. *The New England Mind: From Colony to Province*. Cambridge: Harvard University Press, 1953.

Parrington, V. L. *Main Currents in American Thought*. Vol. I, The Colonial Mind, in 1 vol. ed. New York: Harcourt, Brace & Co., 1939.

Savelle, Max. *Seeds of Liberty: the Genesis of the American Mind*. New York: Alfred A. Knopf, Inc., 1948.

Tyler, M. C. *History of American Literature, 1607-1765*. New ed. Ithaca: Cornell University Press, 1949.

Van Doren, Carl. *Benjamin Franklin*. New York: The Viking Press, 1938.

SOURCES

From Bacon and Locke to Bentham and Jefferson, the best-known works of the Age of Reason are available in many formats, from library editions of *Works* down to inexpensive paper-covered editions. Of current series of standard works, the following are readily available: Everyman's Library (E. P. Dutton), World's Classics (Oxford University Press), Modern Library (Random House), Classics Club (W. J. Black), University Classics (Packard & Co.), the Viking Portable Library (Viking Press), Library of Liberal Arts (Liberal Arts Press), Mentor (New American Library), Pocket Books, and, indeed, many others. An older, out-of-print series, the Bohn Classics, is still abundant in second-hand bookshops. A recent development in American publishing is the relatively inexpensive paperback reprints of contemporary critical and expository writing. Many of the books listed on pp. 27-32 are, or will be, available in such series as Vintage (Knopf), Anchor (Doubleday), Anvil (Van Nostrand), Mentor (New American Library), Pocket Books, Contemporary Affairs Series (Beacon), English paperbacks (Penguin and Pelican).

The excerpts in this *Reader* have necessarily to be parts of wholes, and must fail to do full justice to the work of the thinkers who set their stamp on the age. For the reader who wants a supplementary approach through the longer works of the most influential thinkers, the following specific list of relatively inexpensive books is suggested.

Locke, John. *On Politics and Education.* Classics Club College Edition. New York: D. Van Nostrand Co., 1947.
————. *Essay Concerning Human Understanding* (abridged). Everyman's Library.

Hume, David. *Enquiry Concerning Human Understanding.* Liberal Arts Press.

———. *Moral and Political Philosophy,* ed. by H. D. Aiken. Hafner Library of Classics.

Voltaire. *The Portable Voltaire,* ed. by Ben Ray Redman. New York: The Viking Press, 1949.

Rousseau. *The Social Contract & Discourses,* tr. by G. D. H. Cole. Everyman's Library.

———. *Confessions.* Everyman's Library.

———. *Emile.* Everyman's Library.

Diderot. *Rameau's Nephew and Other Works.* New York: Anchor Books, 1956.

———. *Selected Philosophical Writings.* Cambridge University Press, 1953.

———. *Diderot: Interpreter of Nature,* ed. by Jonathan Kemp. New York: International Publishers, 1943.

[There are many duplications in these three selections.]

Jefferson. *The Complete Jefferson,* ed. by S. K. Padover. New York: Duell, Sloan & Pearce, 1943.

BIOGRAPHICAL LIST
OF AUTHORS

Adams, John (1735-1826). American statesman and political philosopher: Second President of the United States. A conservative, but still a good child of the Enlightenment.

Addison, Joseph (1672-1719). English essayist, Whig man of letters, the embodiment of English Augustan taste. He is the "Atticus" of Pope's famous satire.

Alembert, Jean Le Rond d' (1717-1783). French mathematician and *philosophe*, whose long introduction to *La Grande Encyclopédie* is a splendid summary of the point of view of the Enlightenment.

Bacon, Francis, Baron Verulam, Viscount St. Albans (1561-1626). English philosopher of science, essayist, statesman. First modern publicist of natural science as a formal discipline.

Bayle, Pierre (1647-1706). French scholar and critic, whose *Dictionary* (1697) anticipates much of the eighteenth-century Enlightenment.

Beaumarchais, Pierre Augustin Caron de (1732-1799). French man of affairs and playwright, whose famous valet Figaro is one of the real precursors of the French Revolution. Beaumarchais' career has more than a touch of the adventurer. Among other activities, he helped run munitions of war to the rebelling American colonies after 1775.

Beccaria, Cesare Bonesana, Marchese di (1735-1794). Italian economist, best known for his pioneering work in penology, *On Crimes and Punishments*.

Bentham, Jeremy (1748-1833). English philosopher and

jurist, founder of the influential group of English Utilitarians. The English writer perhaps nearest the center
of the Age of Reason.

Boswell, James (1740-1795). The famous Scottish biogra-
pher of Samuel Johnson. The Boswell papers now being published are making him even better known for
himself.

Buffon, Georges Louis Leclerc, Comte de (1707-1788).
French naturalist, the best known of the old "natural
historians," author of a famous essay on style, delivered
as an address on his entrance to the French Academy.

Casanova de Seingalt, Giovanni Jacopo (1725-1798). Italian adventurer and writer of memoirs, one of the fabulous characters of an Age of Reason which somehow had
place for adventurers—indeed, for charlatans.

Chamfort, Sébastien Roch Nicolas (1741-1794). French
journalist and wit, last of a long line of aphorists, guil-
lotined during the Reign of Terror.

Chénier, André Marie de (1762-1794). French poet, victim
of the guillotine during the Terror.

Chesterfield, Philip Dormer Stanhope, 4th Earl of (1694-
1773). English statesman, author of *Letters to His Son*,
which have long had a reputation for Machiavellian
realism.

Condorcet, Marie Jean Antoine Nicolas de Caritat, Marquis de (1743-1794), French *philosophe*, Girondist
deputy in the Convention, outlawed and killed by the
triumphant Jacobins; he wrote in hiding under out-
lawry one of the most extreme statements of the doctrine
of human progress and perfectibility.

Congreve, William (1670-1729). English wit and dramatist,
chronologically later than the Restoration, but a superior
writer of "Restoration comedy."

Cotes, Roger (1682-1716). English astronomer and mathematician, who wrote the preface to the second edition of
Sir Isaac Newton's *Principia*.

Day, Thomas (1748-1789). English philanthropist, writer,

and eccentric. His *Sandford and Merton,* long a famous book for boys, is a fine piece of "philosophic" piety.

Defoe, Daniel (1661-1731). English writer, prolific anticipator of modern journalism and "realism," author of *Robinson Crusoe.*

Descartes, René (1596-1650). French mathematician and philosopher, one of the great founders of modern rationalism.

Diderot, Denis (1713-1784). French *philosophe,* chief factor in making *La Grande Encyclopédie,* a subtle mind, now recognized as a major figure in the Age of Reason, in some ways most "modern" of them all.

Dryden, John (1631-1700). English poet, dramatist, and political satirist; a writer who helped greatly in establishing modern literary English.

Dumarsais, César Chesneau (1676-1756). French grammarian and philosopher, contributor to *La Grande Encyclopédie.*

Edwards, Jonathan (1703-1758). American divine, whose clear and well-trained eighteenth-century mind was devoted to the defense of revealed religion.

Fénelon, François de Salignac de La Mothe (1651-1715). Archbishop of Cambrai, French divine and man of letters, whose Utopian romance *Telemachus* was long a family book.

Fielding, Henry (1707-1754). English novelist, whose *Tom Jones* (1749) remains a by no means unread classic.

Fontenelle, Bernard Le Bovier de (1657-1757). French writer, one of the earliest popularizers of the new science. Died a centenarian.

Franklin, Benjamin (1706-1790). American philosopher, scientist, and statesman, a Yankee son of the Enlightenment, a self-made polymath.

Frederick II, King of Prussia (1712-1786). Always known as Frederick the Great, this Hohenzollern sport (biologically speaking) was a very typical eighteenth-century enlightened intellectual. He wrote in French.

Gay, John (1685-1732). English dramatist and poet, whose *Beggar's Opera* (1728) was one of the hits of the century.

Gibbon, Edward (1737-1794). English historian of the *Decline and Fall of the Roman Empire*, and also the author of a revealing *Autobiography*.

Goldsmith, Oliver (1728-1774). English man of letters, on the sentimental side of the Age of Reason.

Harvey, William (1578-1657). English anatomist, who first established the circulation of the blood.

Helvétius, Claude Adrien (1715-1771). Parisian-born *philosophe*, whose studies *De l'homme et de l'esprit* are typical of the shallower rationalism of the Enlightenment.

Hervey, John, Baron Hervey of Ickworth (1696-1743). English lord, nicknamed "Lord Fanny," the "Sporus" of Pope's satire; he left admirable memoirs of the reign of George II.

Hobbes, Thomas (1588-1679). English philosopher, author of a major work in political theory, the *Leviathan*, and a forerunner of eighteenth-century "materialism."

Hume, David (1711-1776). Scottish philosopher and historian, one of the few great skeptics in an age of faith in reason.

Jefferson, Thomas (1743-1826). American statesman and *philosophe*, third President of the United States. In his old age, he conducted a fascinating—and very eighteenth-century—correspondence with his old rival John Adams.

Kant, Immanuel (1724-1804). German metaphysician and moralist, a good child of the Age of Reason whose reputation actually increased in the Romantic Age.

La Bruyère, Jean de (1645-1696). French moralist, author of the *Characters*, sketches after the fashion set by Theophrastus in ancient Greece.

Laclos, Pierre Ambroise François Choderlos de (1741-1803). French novelist, one of the earliest in a long line of French novelists preoccupied with the psychology of love.

La Fontaine, Jean de (1621-1695). French poet, the most famous of modern fabulists.

La Rochefoucauld, François, Duc de (1613-1680). French great noble, one of the most famous—and in some eyes most cynical—of aphorists.

Leibnitz, Gottfried Wilhelm, Freiherr von (1646-1716). German philosopher and mathematician, a wide-ranging cosmopolitan man of letters.

Lessing, Gotthold Ephraim (1729-1781). German dramatist and critic, a characteristic figure of the German *Aufklärung* (Enlightenment).

Locke, John (1632-1704). English philosopher, the great "empiricist" who with the great "rationalist" Descartes formed the philosophic background of the Enlightenment.

Madison, James (1751-1836). American statesman, fourth President of the United States; in his contributions to the *Federalist*, a major political thinker.

Mandeville, Bernard (1670?-1733). English moralist, Dutch by birth, whose *Fable of the Bees* was the scandal of his age.

Mercier, Louis Sébastien (1740-1814). French journalist and man of letters, a skilled reporter of Paris life before and after the Revolution.

Milton, John (1608-1674). English poet and Puritan moralist, whose *Areopagitica* is a classic defense of one of the cardinal beliefs of the Age of Reason, freedom of the press.

Molière. Real name Jean Baptiste Poquelin (1622-1673). French actor and playwright, one of the world's greatest writers of comedy.

Montesquieu, Charles de Secondat, Baron de la Brède et de (1689-1755). French *philosophe*, author of the *Spirit of the Laws* (1748), a pioneering attempt at a sociological study of the law, and one of the dominant figures of the first generation of the Enlightenment.

Pascal, Blaise (1623-1662). French scientist and man of letters, ardent Christian of Jansenist sympathies, whose great unfinished defense of Christianity we know as the *Pensées.*

Pepys, Samuel (1633-1703). English civil servant (secretary to the Admiralty) and frank and full diarist.

Pope, Alexander (1688-1744). English poet, author of the *Essay on Man,* in which he puts elegantly the beliefs of "natural" religion.

Quesnay, François (1694-1774). French physician and economist, one of the leaders of the physiocratic school, from which the famous phrase *laissez-faire, laissez-passer.*

Racine, Jean (1639-1699). French dramatic poet, master of the forms of French classical poetry, and a subtle analyst of human passions.

Restif (or Rétif), Nicolas Edme, known as Restif de La Bretonne (1734-1806). French novelist. Printer by trade, he published many of his own works. A "realist," he wrote about the seamier side of Parisian life, but his *Vie de mon père* (1779) is an idyl of peasant life.

Retz, Jean François Paul de Gondi, Cardinal de (1614-1679). French prelate and statesman, active in the civil war known as the *Fronde,* a distinguished writer of memoirs.

Rousseau, Jean Jacques (1712-1778). French man of letters, Genevan-born, enigmatic child of the Age of Reason, and father of the Romantic Age.

Saint-Pierre, Jacques Henri Bernardin de (1737-1814). French writer whose *Paul and Virginia* (1788) is one of the more extreme statements of "nature's simple plan."

Saint-Simon, Louis de Rouvroy, Duc de (1675-1755). French great lord and writer of memoirs, a Proustian character in the Age of Reason.

Sévigné, Marie, Marquise de (1626-1696). French lady of the Court, perhaps the most famous of letter writers.

Shaftesbury, Anthony Ashley Cooper, 3rd Earl of (1671-1713). English man of letters and philanthropist; in his writings a gentle and hopeful free thinker, much indebted to Spinoza.

Smith, Adam (1723-1790). Scottish economist and moralist, whose *Wealth of Nations* is a landmark in the development of classical economics.

Swift, Jonathan (1667-1745). Irish-born English man of letters, satirist, and pamphleteer; a sensible Augustan doubled with a darkly pessimistic man of feeling.

Thiers, Louis Adolphe (1797-1877). French statesman and historian, whose many-volumed *History of the French Revolution* is well and soberly documented.

Turgot, Anne Robert Jacques, Baron de l'Aulne (1727-1781). French statesman, economist, and political writer; a *philosophe* too active in affairs to write a great deal.

Vauvenargues, Luc de Clapiers, Marquis de (1715-1747). French moralist, a rebel and a man of ambition, whose early death cut short a striking career.

Voltaire, François Marie Arouet de (1694-1778). French man of letters and culture-hero of the whole Enlightenment. Voltaire is a pen name; he was born Arouet, son of a Parisian notary.

Walpole, Horace, 4th Earl of Orford (1717-1797). Son of Sir Robert Walpole, the Augustan prime minister; author of the *Castle of Otranto* (1765), an early "Gothic" novel, and a letter writer of genius.

Wesley, John (1703-1791). English divine, founder of Methodism, indefatigable worker in the cause of his faith.

White, Gilbert (1720-1793). English divine and natural historian, whose *Natural History of Selborne* was a pioneer in a genre, "nature-writing," perhaps more literary than scientific in its later developments.

CHRONOLOGICAL TABLE, 1600–1800

DATES	WAR AND POLITICS	SCIENCE, PHILOSOPHY, EXPLORATION	ART AND LETTERS	DATES
1603		Champlain's first explorations in New France		1603
1605		Francis Bacon: Advancement of Learning		1605
1607		English settlement of Jamestown in Virginia		1607
1610		Galileo: Discovery, with aid of telescope, of satellites of Jupiter	Rubens: "Raising of the Cross"	1610
1616			Death of Shakespeare	1616
1618-48	Thirty Years' War, mostly in Germany. Beginning of French preponderance. Last of religious wars.			1618-48
1628	Petition of Right in England attempts to limit royal power	Harvey: Circulation of the blood		1628
1630			Poussin: "Triumph of Flora"	1630
1632			Rembrandt: "Anatomy Lesson"	1632
1635			French Academy founded	1635
1637		Descartes: Discourse on Method	Corneille: The Cid	1637
1639-49	Civil War in British Isles			1639-49
1640-80	Frederick William, the Great Elector, in Prussia			1640-80

1648	Independence of Netherlands and Switzerland recognized	
1649	Execution of Charles I of England	
1649-53 1656	Civil Wars of the Fronde in France	Bernini: Colonnade of St. Peter's, Rome
1660	Restoration of monarchy in England (Charles II).	Royal Society (scientific academy) founded in England (c. 1660)
1660-1661 1715	Personal rule of Louis XIV in France	Beginnings of Palace of Versailles
1666		Academy of Sciences (French)
1667		Milton: Paradise Lost
1668		La Fontaine: Fables
1669		Molière: Tartuffe
1673		Wycherley: The Country Wife
1675		Wren: St. Paul's Cathedral, London
1677		Racine: Phèdre
1681		Dryden: Absalom and Achitophel
1682	La Salle's voyage down the Mississippi	
1684	Leibnitz publishes his version of calculus dispute with Newton over priority	

DATES	WAR AND POLITICS	SCIENCE, PHILOSOPHY, EXPLORATION	ART AND LETTERS	DATES
1686		Newton: First book of the *Principia*		1686
1688	"Glorious Revolution" in England. James II dethroned, William III of Orange brought in. Limitation of monarchy and beginnings of parliamentary supremacy.		Perrault: *Parallel of the Ancients and Moderns*	1688
1688-97	War of the League of Augsburg			1688-97
1690		Locke: *Essay Concerning Human Understanding*		1690
1697		Bayle: *Dictionary*		1697
1701-14	War of the Spanish Succession. Defeat of France, loss of part of her colonies, and the beginning of British preponderance. (See Seven Years' War, 1756-63)			1701-14
1704			Swift: *Battle of the Books*	1704
1705			Vanbrugh: Blenheim Palace	1705
1706			Mansart: Dome of the Invalides, Paris	1706
1711		Shaftesbury: *Characteristics*	Poppelmann: Zwinger Palace, Dresden	1711
1714	House of Hanover in England (George I)			1714
1715			Pope: *The Iliad.* Vol. I	1715

Year	Political	Intellectual	Arts
1715-74	Louis XV King of France— "After us the deluge"		
1717			Watteau: "Embarcation for Cythera"
1722			Bach: Well-tempered Clavichord, Part I
1726-29		Voltaire in England	
1739		Hume: Treatise of Human Nature	
1740-48	War of the Austrian Succession		
1740-80	Maria Theresa, by Pragmatic Sanction, Empress		
1740-86	Frederick II, the Great, King of Prussia		
1742			Handel: Messiah
1745			Palace of Sans-Souci, Potsdam
1748		Montesquieu: Spirit of the Laws	
1751-80		La Grande Encyclopédie, 35 vols.	La Grande Encyclopédie, 35 vols.
1752		Franklin's experiments with electricity by use of kite	
1756-63	Seven Years' War. See War of the Spanish Succession, 1701-14. These two world wars complete the loss to Britain of France's colonial empire and mark the rise of Prussia to the status of a great power.		

DATES	WAR AND POLITICS	SCIENCE, PHILOSOPHY, EXPLORATION	ART AND LETTERS	DATES
1757			Diderot: *The Natural Son*; Voltaire: *Candide*	1757
1760-1820	George III King of England			1760-1820
1762		Rousseau: *Social Contract*		1762
1766			Lessing: *Laocoön*	1766
1767-69		Bougainville in the Pacific		1767-69
1768-71		Cook's first Pacific explorations		1768-71
c. 1770		Watt's steam engine "Industrial revolution" begins in Britain		c. 1770
1773			Haydn: "Maria Theresa Symphony"	1773
1774		Priestley: dephlogisticated air (oxygen)		1774
1774-93	Louis XVI last King of France of the old regime			1774-93
1775			Beaumarchais: *Barber of Seville*	1775
1775-83	War of the American Revolution			1775-83
1776		Adam Smith: *Wealth of Nations*		1776
1776-88			Gibbon: *Decline and Fall of the Roman Empire*	1776-88
1777			Sheridan: *School for Scandal*	1777
1780-90		Lavoisier completes Priestley's work to found modern chemistry		1780-90

Year			
1781		Kant: *Critique of Pure Reason*	Gainsborough: Portrait of the Duchess of Devonshire
1783			
1785-1815		Hutton, William Smith, Lamarck found earth sciences	
1787	American Constitutional Convention in Philadelphia		Mozart: *Don Giovanni*
1787-88		The *Federalist Papers*	
1789	Beginning of the French Revolution	French Declaration of the Rights of Man and the Citizen; Bentham: *Principles of Morals and Legislation*	
1791			Boswell: *Life of Johnson*
1792-1815	Wars of the French Revolution and Napoleon, really one world war		
1793	Execution of Louis XVI of France		
1793-94	Reign of Terror		David: "Rape of the Sabines"
1795			
1799	Napoleon seizes power by coup d'état		

Prologue

THE BIRTH OF
REASON

"I Think, Therefore I Am"

[FROM *A Discourse on Method*]

RENÉ DESCARTES

1637

Like a man who walks alone and in darkness, I
resolved to go so slowly, and to use so much circum-
spection in everything, that if I did not advance
speedily, at least I should keep from falling. I would
not even have desired to begin by entirely rejecting
any of the opinions which had formerly been able to
slip into my belief without being introduced there by
reason, had I not first spent much time in projecting the
work which I was to undertake, and in seeking the true
method of arriving at a knowledge of everything of
which my understanding should be capable.

When I was younger, I had devoted a little study to logic, among philosophical matters, and to geometrical analysis and to algebra, among mathematical matters—three arts or sciences which, it seemed, ought to be able to contribute something to my design. But on examining them I noticed that the syllogisms of logic and the greater part of the rest of its teachings serve rather for explaining to other people the things we already know, or even, like the art of Lully, for speaking without judgment of things we know not, than for instructing us of them. And although they indeed contain many very true and very good precepts, there are always so many others mingled therewith that it is almost as difficult to separate them as to extract a Diana or a Minerva from a block of marble not yet rough hewn. Then, as to the analysis of the ancients and the algebra of the moderns, besides that they extend only to extremely abstract matters and appear to have no other use, the first is always so restricted to the consideration of figures that it cannot exercise the understanding without greatly fatiguing the imagination, and in the other one is so bound down to certain rules and ciphers that it has been made a confused and obscure art which embarrasses the mind, instead of a science which cultivates it. This made me think that some other method must be sought, which, while combining the advantages of these three, should be free from their defects. And as a multitude of laws often furnishes excuses for vice, so that a state is much better governed when it has but few, and those few strictly observed, so in place of the great number of precepts of which logic is composed, I believed that I should find the following four sufficient, provided that I made a firm and constant resolve not once to omit to observe them.

The first was, never to accept anything as true when I did not recognize it clearly to be so, that is to say, to carefully avoid precipitation and prejudice, and to include in my opinions nothing beyond that which should present itself so clearly and so distinctly to my mind that I might have no occasion to doubt it.

The second was, to divide each of the difficulties which I should examine into as many portions as were possible, and as should be required for its better solution.

The third was, to conduct my thoughts in order, by beginning with the simplest objects, and those most easy to know, so as to mount little by little, as if by steps, to the most complex knowledge, and even assuming an order among those which do not naturally precede one another.

And the last was, to make everywhere enumerations so complete, and surveys so wide, that I should be sure of omitting nothing.

The long chains of perfectly simple and easy reasons, which geometers are accustomed to employ in order to arrive at their most difficult demonstrations, had given me reason to believe that all things which can fall under the knowledge of man succeed each other in the same way, and that provided only we abstain from receiving as true any opinions which are not true, and always observe the necessary order in deducing one from the other, there can be none so remote that they may not be reached, or so hidden that they may not be discovered. And I was not put to much trouble to find out which it was necessary to begin with, for I knew already that it was with the simplest and most easily known; and considering that of all those who have heretofore sought truth in the sciences it is the mathematicians alone who have been able to find demonstrations, that is to say, clear and certain reasons, I did not doubt that I must start with the same things that they have considered, although I hoped for no other profit from them than that they would accustom my mind to feed on truths and not to content itself with false reasons. But I did not therefore design to try to learn all those particular sciences which bear the general name of mathematics: and seeing that although their objects were different they nevertheless all agree, in that they consider only the various relations or proportions found therein, I thought it would be better worth while if I merely examined these proportions in general, supposing them only in subjects which would serve to render the knowledge of them more easy to me, and even, also, without in any wise restricting them thereto, in order to be the better able to apply them subsequently to every other subject to which they should be suitable. Then, having remarked that in order to know them I should sometimes need to consider each separately, I had to suppose them in lines, because I found nothing more simple, or which I could more distinctly represent to my imagination and to my senses; but to retain them, or to comprehend many of them together, it was necessary that I should express them by certain ciphers as short as possible, and in this way I should borrow all the best in geometrical analysis, and in algebra, and correct all the faults of the one by means of the other.

I do not know whether I ought to discuss with you the earlier of my meditations, for they are so metaphysical and so out of the common that perhaps they would not be to everyone's taste; and yet, in order that it may be judged whether the bases I have taken are sufficiently firm, I am in some measure constrained to

speak of them. I had remarked for long that, in conduct, it is sometimes necessary to follow opinions
known to be very uncertain, just as if they were indubitable, as has been said above; but then, because I
desired to devote myself only to the research of truth,
I thought it necessary to do exactly the contrary, and
reject as absolutely false all in which I could conceive
the least doubt, in order to see if afterwards there did
not remain in my belief something which was entirely
indubitable. Thus, because our senses sometimes deceive us, I wanted to suppose that nothing is such as
they make us imagine it; and because some men err in
reasoning, even touching the simplest matters of geometry, and make paralogisms, and judging that I was as
liable to fail as any other, I rejected as false all the
reasons which I had formerly accepted as demonstrations; and finally, considering that all the thoughts
which we have when awake can come to us also when
we sleep, without any of them then being true, I
resolved to feign that everything which had ever entered into my mind was no more true than the illusions
of my dreams. But immediately afterwards I observed
that while I thus desired everything to be false, I,
who thought, must of necessity be something; and remarking that this truth, *I think, therefore I am,* was so
firm and so assured that all the most extravagant sup-
positions of the sceptics were unable to shake it, I
judged that I could unhesitatingly accept it as the first
principle of the philosophy I was seeking.

Then, examining attentively what I was, and seeing
that I could feign that I had no body, and that there
was no world or any place where I was, but that nevertheless I could not feign that I did not exist, and that,
on the contrary, from the fact that I thought to doubt
of the truth of other things, it followed very evidently

that I was; while if I had only ceased to think, although all else which I had previously imagined had been true I had no reason to believe that I might have been, therefore I knew that I was a substance whose essence or nature is only to think, and which, in order to be, has no need of any place, and depends on no material thing; so that this I, that is to say, the soul by which I am what I am, is entirely distinct from the body, and even easier to know than the body, and although the body were not, the soul would not cease to be all that it is.

After that I considered generally what is requisite to make a proposition true and certain; for since I had just found one which I knew to be so, I thought that I ought also to know in what this certainty consisted. And having remarked that there is nothing at all in this, *I think, therefore I am,* which assures me that I speak the truth, except that I see very clearly that in order to think it is necessary to exist, I judged that I might take it as a general rule that the things which we conceive very clearly and very distinctly are all true, and that there is difficulty only in seeing plainly which things they are that we conceive distinctly.

After this, and reflecting upon the fact that I doubted, and that in consequence my being was not quite perfect (for I saw clearly that to know was a greater perfection than to doubt), I bethought myself to find out from whence I had learned to think of something more perfect than I; and I knew for certain that it must be from some nature which was in reality more perfect. For as regards the thoughts I had of many other things outside myself, as of the sky, the earth, light, heat, and a thousand more, I was not so much at a loss to know whence they came, because, remarking nothing in them which seemed to make them superior to me, I could believe that if they were true they were dependencies of my nature, inasmuch as it had some perfection, and if they were not true that I derived them from nothing—that is to say, that they were in me because I had some defect. But it could not be the same with the idea of a Being more perfect than my own, for to derive it from nothing was manifestly impossible; and since it is no less repugnant to me that the more perfect should follow and depend on the less perfect than that out of nothing should proceed something, I could not derive it from myself; so that it remained that it had been put in me by a nature truly more perfect than I, which had in itself all perfections of which I could have any idea; that is, to explain myself in one word, God.

Trans. G. B. Rawlings (London: Walter Scott, 1901).

I. *Proper Studies:*

MANNERS, MORALS, POLITICS

"The Proper Study..."

[FROM *An Essay on Man,* EPISTLE II]

ALEXANDER POPE

1733.

Know then thyself, presume not God to scan,
The proper study of mankind is Man.
Placed on this isthmus of a middle state,
A being darkly wise and rudely great:
With too much knowledge for the Sceptic side,
With too much weakness for the Stoic's pride,
He hangs between, in doubt to act or rest;
In doubt to deem himself a God or Beast;
In doubt his mind or body to prefer;
Born but to die, and reas'ning but to err;
Alike in ignorance, his reason such,

Whether he thinks too little or too much;
Chaos of thought and passion, all confused;
Still by himself abused or disabused;
Created half to rise, and half to fall;
Great lord of all things, yet a prey to all;
Sole judge of truth, in endless error hurl'd;
The glory, jest, and riddle of the world!

   Go, wondrous creature! mount where Science guides;
Go, measure earth, weigh air, and state the tides;
Instruct the planets in what orbs to run,
Correct old Time, and regulate the sun;
Go, soar with Plato to th' empyreal sphere,
To the first good, first perfect, and first fair;
Or tread the mazy round his followers trod,
And quitting sense call imitating God;
As eastern priests in giddy circles run,
And turn their heads to imitate the sun.
Go, teach Eternal Wisdom how to rule—
Then drop into thyself, and be a fool!

   Superior beings, when of late they saw
A mortal man unfold all Nature's law,
Admired such wisdom in an earthly shape,
And show'd a NEWTON as we show an ape.
Could he, whose rules the rapid comet bind,
Describe or fix one movement of his mind?
Who saw its fires here rise, and there descend,
Explain his own beginning or his end?
Alas! what wonder! Man's superior part
Uncheck'd may rise, and climb from art to art;
But when his own great work is but begun,
What Reason weaves, by Passion is undone.

   Trace Science then, with modesty thy guide;
First strip off all her equipage of pride;
Deduct what is but vanity or dress,
Or learning's luxury, or idleness,

is on his right side, his stockings have fallen over his heels, and his shirt is hanging outside his breeches. . . . He enters the king's apartment and walks under a chandelier, which catches his periwig and leaves it hanging in the air: all the courtiers look at it and laugh. Ménalque looks too and laughs louder than the rest; he peers at everyone in the assembly, trying to see who is showing his ears and who has lost his periwig. If he goes walking in the city, after a short time he thinks he is lost, he becomes upset, he asks passers-by the name of the street; it is precisely the one where he lives. Thereupon he goes into his house and comes rushing out again, thinking he has made a mistake. After a visit to the Palais de Justice, he finds a coach waiting at the foot of the grand stairway and gets into it, convinced that it is his own. . . .

Another day he goes calling on a lady; soon persuading himself that he is the host, he settles back in an armchair without any thought of leaving it. He begins to suspect that the lady doesn't know when to go; he keeps waiting for her to rise and let him attend to his own affairs; then late in the evening, getting bored with the conversation and feeling hungry, he invites her to supper; she laughs, and so loudly that he comes to himself. . . . He plays cards and loses the money in his purse. Wishing to continue the game, he goes to his private chamber, opens a wardrobe, and takes out a casket, from which he dips a handful of coins. He thinks he has put the casket back again, but then he hears barking in the wardrobe that has just been closed. Astonished at this phenomenon, he opens it a second time and bursts out laughing when he sees his dog, which he has locked up instead of the casket.

He is playing backgammon, he calls for a glass of water, which a servant brings just when it is his turn to play. He holds the dice box in one hand and the glass in the other; then, as he is quite thirsty, he swallows the dice and almost swallows the box, while he throws the glass of water on the board and drenches the other player. At a levee that he is privileged to attend, he spits on the bed and throws his hat on the floor, thinking that he has done the contrary.[1] He is with a boating party and asks the time; someone offers him a watch; hardly has he glanced at it when, forgetting the hour and the watch, he tosses the latter into the river, as he might do with any worthless object in his hand. He writes a long letter, scatters powder over it several times, and each time empties the powder into the inkwell. Nor is that all: he writes a second letter and, after sealing both of them, puts down the wrong addresses. A duke and peer receives one of the two letters and, having opened it, reads these words: *Master Oliver, do not fail to send my supply of hay immediately.* . . . His tenant farmer receives the other letter, opens it, and has it read to him; it begins: *Monseigneur, I have received with blind submissiveness the orders that Your Highness deigned to send me.* . . .

From *Les Caractères*, eighth edition (Paris: 1694), trans. Malcolm Cowley.

---

[1] It would have been quite proper, at the time, for Ménalque to have thrown his hat on the bed and to have spit on the floor. [Trans. note.]

❖ ❖ ❖

Concerning Virtue or Merit

[FROM *Characteristics of Men, Manners,
Opinions, Times,* etc.]

ANTHONY ASHLEY COOPER,
EARL OF SHAFTESBURY

1699

Thus have we endeavoured to prove what was proposed in the beginning. And since in the common and
known sense of vice and illness, no one can be vicious
or ill except either—

1. By the deficiency or weakness of natural affections;

Or, 2. By the violence of the selfish;

Or, 3. By such as are plainly unnatural:

it must follow that, if each of these are pernicious and
destructive to the creature, insomuch that his com-
pletest state of misery is made from hence, to be
wicked or vicious is to be miserable and unhappy.

And since every vicious action must in proportion,
more or less, help towards this mischief and self-ill, it
must follow that every vicious action must be self-
injurious and ill.

On the other side, the happiness and good of virtue
has been proved from the contrary effect of other affections, such as are according to Nature and the economy
of the species or kind. We have cast up all those particulars from whence (as by way of addition and sub-
traction) the main sum or general account of happiness

is either augmented or diminished. And if there be no article exceptionable in this scheme of moral arithmetic, the subject treated may be said to have an evidence as great as that which is found in numbers or mathematics. For let us carry scepticism ever so far, let us doubt, if we can, of everything about us, we cannot doubt of what passes within ourselves. Our passions and affections are known to us. They are certain, whatever the objects may be on which they are employed. Nor is it of any concern to our argument how these exterior objects stand: whether they are realities or mere illusions; whether we wake or dream. For ill dreams will be equally disturbing; and a good dream (if life be nothing else) will be easily and happily passed. In this dream of life, therefore, our demonstrations have the same force; our balance and economy hold good, and our obligation to virtue is in every respect the same.

Upon the whole there is not, I presume, the least degree of certainty wanting in what has been said concerning the preferableness of the mental pleasures to the sensual; and even of the sensual, accompanied with good affection, and under a temperate and right use, to those which are no ways restrained, nor supported by anything social or affectionate.

Nor is there less evidence in what has been said of the united structure and fabric of the mind, and of those passions which constitute the temper or soul, and on which its happiness or misery so immediately depend. It has been shown that in this constitution the impairing of any one part must instantly tend to the disorder and ruin of other parts, and of the whole itself, through the necessary connection and balance of the affections; that those very passions through which men are vicious are of themselves a torment and disease; and that whatsoever is done which is knowingly ill must be of ill consciousness; and in proportion as the act is ill must impair and corrupt social enjoyment, and destroy both the capacity of kind affection and the consciousness of meriting any such. So that neither can we participate thus in joy or happiness with others, nor receive satisfaction from the mutual kindness or imagined love of others, on which, however, the greatest of all our pleasures are founded.

If this be the case of moral delinquency, and if the state which is consequent to this defection from Nature be of all other the most horrid, oppressive, and miserable, 'twill appear "that to yield or consent to anything ill or immoral is a breach of interest, and leads to the greatest ills"; and "that on the other side, everything which is an improvement of virtue, or an establishment of right affection and integrity, is an advancement of interest, and leads to the greatest and most solid happiness and enjoyment."

Thus the wisdom of what rules, and is first and chief in Nature, has made it to be according to the private interest and good of everyone to work towards the general good, which if a creature ceases to promote, he is actually so far wanting to himself, and ceases to promote his own happiness and welfare. He is on this account directly his own enemy, nor can he any otherwise be good or useful to himself than as he continues good to society, and to that whole of which he is himself a part. So that virtue, which of all excellences and beauties is the chief and most amiable; that which is the prop and ornament of human affairs; which upholds communities, maintains union, friendship, and correspondence amongst men; that by which countries, as well as private families, flourish and are happy, and for want of which everything comely, conspicuous, great, used to join with the Church were reconciled at this time with the admitting the Dissenters to preach to them, so the Dissenters, who with an uncommon prejudice had broken off from the communion of the Church of England, were now content to come to their parish churches, and to conform to the worship which they did not approve of before; but as the terror of the infection abated, those things all returned again to their less desirable channel, and to the course they were in before.

I mention this but historically. I have no mind to enter into arguments to move either or both sides to a more charitable compliance one with another. I do not see that it is probable such a discourse would be either suitable or successful; the breaches seem rather to widen, and tend to a widening further, than to closing, and who am I that I should think myself able to influence either one side or other? But this I may repeat again, that 'tis evident death will reconcile us all; on the other side the grave we shall be all brethren again. In heaven, whither I hope we may come from all parties and persuasions, we shall find neither prejudice or scruple; there we shall be of one principle and of one opinion. Why we cannot be content to go hand in hand to the place where we shall join heart and hand without the least hesitation, and with the most complete harmony and affection—I say, why we cannot do so here I can say nothing to, neither shall I say anything more of it but that it remains to be lamented.

I could dwell a great while upon the calamities of this dreadful time, and go on to describe the objects that appeared among us every day, the dreadful extravagancies which the distraction of sick people drove them into; how the streets began now to be fuller of frightful objects, and families to be made even a terror to themselves. But after I have told you, as I have above, that one man, being tied in his bed, and finding no other way to deliver himself, set the bed on fire with his candle, which unhappily stood within his reach, and burnt himself in his bed; and how another, by the insufferable torment he bore, danced and sung naked in the streets, not knowing one ecstasy from another; I say, after I have mentioned these things, what can be added more? What can be said to represent the misery of these times more lively to the reader, or to give him a more perfect idea of a complicated distress?

I must acknowledge that this time was terrible, that I was sometimes at the end of all my resolutions, and that I had not the courage that I had at the beginning. As the extremity brought other people abroad, it drove me home, and except having made my voyage down to Blackwall and Greenwich, as I have related, which was an excursion, I kept afterwards very much within doors, as I had for about a fortnight before. I have said already that I repented several times that I had ventured to stay in town, and had not gone away with my brother and his family, but it was too late for that now; and after I had retreated and stayed within doors a good while before my impatience led me abroad, then they called me, as I have said, to an ugly and dangerous office, which brought me out again; but as that was expired while the height of the distemper lasted, I retired again, and continued close ten or twelve days more, during which many dismal spectacles represented themselves in my view, out of my own windows and in our own street, as that particularly from Harrow Alley, of the poor outrageous creature which danced and sung in his agony; and many others there were. Scarce a day or night passed over but some dismal thing or other happened at the end of that Harrow Alley, which was a place full of poor people, most of them belonging to the butchers, or to employments depending upon the butchery.

Sometimes heaps and throngs of people would burst out of the alley, most of them women, making a dreadful clamour, mixed or compounded of screeches, cryings, and calling one another, that we could not conceive what to make of it. Almost all the dead part of the night the dead-cart stood at the end of that alley, for if it went in it could not well turn again, and could go in but a little way. There, I say, it stood to receive dead bodies, and as the churchyard was but a little way off, if it went away full it would soon be back again. It is impossible to describe the most horrible cries and noise the poor people would make at their bringing the dead bodies of their children and friends out of the cart, and by the number one would have thought there had been none left behind, or that there were people enough for a small city living in those places. Several times they cried "Murder," sometimes "Fire"; but it was easy to perceive it was all distraction, and the complaints of distressed and distempered people.

I believe it was everywhere thus at that time, for the plague raged for six or seven weeks beyond all that I have expressed, and came even to such a height that, in the extremity, they began to break into that excellent order of which I have spoken so much in behalf of the magistrates, namely, that no dead bodies were seen in the streets or burials in the daytime, for there was a necessity in this extremity to bear with its being otherwise for a little while.

One thing I cannot omit here, and indeed I thought it was extraordinary, at least it seemed a remarkable will want much advice to divert you from falling into many errours, fopperies, and follies, to which your sex is subject. I have always borne an entire friendship to your father and mother; and the person they have chosen for your husband, has been for some years past, my particular favourite; I have long wished you might come together, because I hoped that from the goodness of your disposition, and by following the counsel of wise friends, you might in time make yourself worthy of him. Your parents were so far in the right, that they did not produce you much into the world, whereby you avoided many wrong steps, which others have taken, and have fewer ill impressions to be removed; but they failed, as it is generally the case, in too much neglecting to cultivate your mind; without which, it is impossible to acquire or preserve the friendship and esteem of a wise man, who soon grows weary of acting the lover, and treating his wife like a mistress, but wants a reasonable companion, and a true friend through every stage of his life. It must be therefore your business to qualify yourself for those offices; wherein I will not fail to be your director, as long as I shall think you deserve it, by letting you know how you are to act, and what you ought to avoid.

And beware of despising or neglecting my instructions, whereon will depend not only your making a good figure in the world, but your own real happiness, as well as that of the person, who ought to be dearest to you.

I must therefore desire you, in the first place, to be very slow in changing the modest behaviour of a virgin: it is usual in young wives, before they have been many weeks married, to assume a bold forward look and manner of talking; as if they intended to signify in all companies that they were no longer girls, and consequently that their whole demeanour, before they got a husband, was all but a countenance and constraint upon their nature: whereas, I suppose, if the votes of wise men were gathered, a very great majority would be in favour of those ladies, who, after they were entered into that state, rather chose to double their portion of modesty and reservedness.

I must likewise warn you strictly against the least degree of fondness to your husband before any witness whatsoever, even before your nearest relations, or the very maids of your chamber. This proceeding is so exceeding odious and disgustful to all, who have either good breeding or good sense, that they assign two very unamiable reasons for it; the one is gross hypocrisy, and the other has too bad a name to mention. If there is any difference to be made, your husband is the lowest person in company either at home or abroad, and every gentleman present has a better claim to all marks of civility and distinction from you. Conceal your esteem and love in your own breast, and reserve your kind looks and language for private hours, which are so many in the four and twenty, that they will afford time to employ a passion as exalted as any that was ever described in a French romance.

Upon this head I should likewise advise you to differ in practice from those ladies, who affect abundance of uneasiness, while their husbands are abroad; start with every knock at the door, and ring the bell incessantly for the servants to let in their master; will not eat a bit at dinner or supper, if the husband happens to stay out; and receive him at his return with such a medley of chiding and kindness, and catechising him where he has been, that a shrew from Billingsgate would be a more easy and eligible companion.

Of the same leaven are those wives, who, when

their husbands are gone a journey, must have a letter every post, upon pain of fits and hystericks; and a day must be fixed for their return home, without the least allowance for business, or sickness, or accidents, or weather: upon which I can only say, that, in my observation, those ladies, who are apt to make the greatest clutter on such occasions, would liberally have paid a messenger for bringing them news, that their husbands had broken their necks on the road.

You will perhaps be offended, when I advise you to abate a little of that violent passion for fine clothes, so predominant in your sex. It is a little hard, that ours, for whose sake you wear them, are not admitted to be of your council. I may venture to assure you, that we will make an abatement at any time of four pounds a yard in a brocade, if the ladies will but allow a suitable addition of care in the cleanliness and sweetness of their persons. For the satirical part of mankind will needs believe, that it is not impossible to be very fine and very filthy; and that the capacities of a lady are sometimes apt to fall short, in cultivating cleanliness and finery together. I shall only add, upon so tender a subject, what a pleasant gentleman said concerning a silly woman of quality; that nothing could make her supportable but cutting off her head; for his ears were offended by her tongue, and his nose by her hair and teeth.

I am wholly at a loss how to advise you in the choice of company, which however is a point of as great importance as any in your life. If your general acquaintance be among ladies, who are your equals or superiors, provided they have nothing of what is commonly called an ill reputation, you think you are safe; and this, in the style of the world, will pass for good company. Whereas, I am afraid it will be hard for you to pick out one female acquaintance in this town, from whom you will not be in manifest danger of contracting some foppery, affectation, vanity, folly, or vice. Your only safe way of conversing with them is, by a firm resolution to proceed in your practice and behaviour directly contrary to whatever they shall say or do: and this I take to be a good general rule, with very few exceptions. For instance, in the doctrines they usually deliver to young married women for managing their husbands; their several accounts of their own conduct in that particular, to recommend it to your imitation; the reflections they make upon others of their sex for acting differently; their directions how to come off with victory upon any dispute or quarrel you may have with your husband; the arts, by which you may discover and practise upon his weak side; when to work by flattery and insinuation, when to melt him with tears, and when to engage him with a high hand: in these, and a thousand other cases, it will be prudent to retain as many of their lectures in your memory as you can, and then determine to act in full opposition to them all.

I hope, your husband will interpose his authority to limit you in the trade of visiting: half a dozen fools are, in all conscience, as many as you should require; and it will be sufficient for you to see them twice a year; for I think the fashion does not exact, that visits should be paid to friends.

I advise, that your company at home should consist of men, rather than women. To say the truth, I never yet knew a tolerable woman to be fond of her own sex. I confess when both are mixed and well chosen, and put their best qualities forward, there may be an intercourse of civility and good will; which, with the addition of some degree of sense, can make conversation or any amusement agreeable. But a knot of ladies, got together by themselves, is a very school of impertinence and detraction, and it is well if those be the worst.

Let your men acquaintance be of your husband's choice, and not recommended to you by any she companions; because they will certainly fix a coxcomb upon you, and it will cost you some time and pains, before you can arrive at the knowledge of distinguishing such a one from a man of sense. . . .

If you are in company with men of learning, though they happen to discourse of arts and sciences out of your compass, yet you will gather more advantage by listening to them, than from all the nonsense and frippery of your own sex; but if they be men of breeding, as well as learning, they will seldom engage in any conversation where you ought not to be a hearer, and in time have your part. If they talk of the manners and customs of the several kingdoms of Europe, of travels into remoter nations, of the state of your own country, or of the great men and actions of Greece and Rome; if they give their judgment upon English and French writers either in verse or prose, or of the nature and limits of virtue and vice; it is a shame for an English lady not to relish such discourses, not to improve by them, and endeavour by reading and information to have her share in those entertainments, rather than turn aside, as it is the usual custom, and consult with the woman who sits next her about a new cargo of fans.

It is a little hard, that not one gentleman's daughter in a thousand should be brought to read or understand her own natural tongue, or to be judge of the easiest books that are written in it; as any one may find, who can have the patience to hear them, when they are disposed to mangle a play or a novel, where the least word out of the common road is sure to disconcert them; and it is no wonder, when they are not so much as taught to spell in their childhood, nor can ever attain to it in their whole lives. I advise you therefore to read aloud, more or less, every day to your husband, if he will permit you, or to any other friend (but not a female one) who is able to set you right; and as for spelling, you may compass it in time by making collections from the books you read.

I know very well, that those who are commonly called learned women, have lost all manner of credit by their impertinent talkativeness and conceit of themselves; but there is an easy remedy for this, if you once consider, that after all the pains you may be at, you never can arrive in point of learning to the perfection of a schoolboy. The reading I would advise you to, is only for improvement of your own good sense, which will never fail of being mended by discretion. It is a wrong method, and ill choice of books, that makes those learned ladies just so much the worse for what they have read; and therefore it shall be my care to direct you better, a task for which I take myself to be not ill qualified; because I have spent more time, and have had more opportunities than many others, to observe and discover, from what source the various follies of women are derived. . . .

From *The Works of the Rev. Jonathan Swift, D.D.*, Vol. VI. ed. John Nichols (Edinburgh and Perth, London, J. Johnson *et al.*, 1808).

❖ ❖ ❖

Private Vices Are Public Virtues

[FROM *The Fable of the Bees*]

BERNARD MANDEVILLE

1714

The prodigality I call a noble sin is not that which has avarice for its companion and makes men unreasonably profuse to some of what they unjustly extort from others, but that agreeable good-natured vice that makes the chimney smoke, and all the tradesmen smile. I mean the unmixed prodigality of heedless and voluptuous men, that being educated in plenty, abhor the vile thoughts of lucre, and lavish away only what others took pains to scrape together; such as indulge their inclinations at their own expense, that have the continual satisfaction of bartering old gold for new pleasures, and from the excessive largeness of a diffusive soul, are made guilty of despising too much what most people over-value.

When I speak thus honourably of this vice, and treat it with so much tenderness and good manners as I do, I have the same thing at heart that made me give so many ill names to the reverse of it, viz., the interest of the public; for as the avaricious does no good to himself, and is injurious to all the world besides, except his heir, so the prodigal is a blessing to the whole society, and injures nobody but himself. It is true, that as most of the first are knaves, so the latter are all fools;

yet they are delicious morsels for the public to feast on, and may, with as much justice as the French call the monks the partridges of the women, be styled the Woodcocks of the society. Was it not for prodigality, nothing could make us amends for the rapine and extortion of avarice in power. When a covetous statesman is gone, who spent his whole life in fattening himself with the spoils of the nation, and had by pinching and plundering heaped up an immense treasure, it ought to fill every good member of the society with joy, to behold the uncommon profuseness of his son. This is refunding to the public what was robbed from it. Resuming of grants is a barbarous way of stripping, and it is ignoble to ruin a man faster than he does it himself, when he sets about it in such good earnest. Does he not feed an infinite number of dogs of all sorts and sizes, though he never hunts; keep more horses than any nobleman in the kingdom, though he never rides them, and give as large an allowance to an ill-favoured whore as would keep a duchess, though he never lies with her? Is he not still more extravagant in those things he makes use of? Therefore let 'im alone or praise him, call him public-spirited lord, nobly bountiful and magnificently generous, and in a few years he will suffer himself to be stripped his own way. As long as the nation has its own back again, we ought not to quarrel with the manner in which the plunder is repaid.

Abundance of moderate men I know that are enemies to extremes will tell me that frugality might happily supply the place of the two vices I speak of, that, if men had not so many profuse ways of spending wealth, they would not be tempted to so many evil practices to scrape it together, and consequently that the same number of men by equally avoiding both extremes, might render themselves more happy, and be less vicious without than they could with them. Whoever argues thus shows himself a better man than he is a politician. Frugality is like honesty, a mean, starving virtue, that is only fit for small societies of good, peaceable men, who are contented to be poor so they may be easy; but in a large, stirring nation you may have soon enough of it. It is an idle dreaming virtue that employs no hands, and therefore very useless in a trading country, where there are vast numbers that one way or other must be all set to work. Prodigality has a thousand inventions to keep people from sitting still, that frugality would never think of; and as this must consume a prodigious wealth, so avarice again knows innumerable tricks to rake it together, which frugality would scorn to make use of.

Authors are always allowed to compare small things to great ones, especially if they ask leave first. *Si licet exemplis,* etc., but to compare great things to mean, trivial ones is insufferable, unless it be in burlesque; otherwise I would compare the body politic (I confess the simile is very low) to a bowl of punch. Avarice should be the souring, and prodigality the sweetening of it. The water I would call the ignorance, folly and credulity of the floating insipid multitude; whilst wisdom, honour, fortitude, and the rest of the sublime qualities of men, which, separated by art from the dregs of nature, the fire of glory has exalted and refined into a spiritual essence, should be an equivalent to brandy. I don't doubt but a Westphalian, Laplander, or any other dull stranger that is unacquainted with the wholesome composition, if he was to taste the several ingredients apart, would think it impossible they should make any tolerable liquor. The lemons would be too sour, the sugar too luscious, the brandy he will say is too strong ever to be drank in any quan-

good opinion which he is anxious to entertain concerning his own performances. Experience and success may in time give him a little more confidence in his own judgment. He is at all times, however, liable to be most severely mortified by the unfavourable judgments of the public. Racine was so disgusted by the indifferent success of his *Phædra*, the finest tragedy, perhaps, that is extant in any language, that, though in the vigour of his life, and at the height of his abilities, he resolved to write no more for the stage. That great poet used frequently to tell his son that the most paltry and impertinent criticism had always given him more pain than the highest and justest eulogy had ever given him pleasure. The extreme sensibility of Voltaire to the slightest censure of the same kind is well known to everybody. The *Dunciad* of Mr. Pope is an everlasting monument of how much the most correct, as well as the most elegant and harmonious of all the English poets, had been hurt by the criticisms of the lowest and most contemptible authors. Gray (who joins to the sublimity of Milton the elegance and harmony of Pope, and to whom nothing is wanting to render him, perhaps, the first poet in the English language, but to have written a little more) is said to have been so much hurt, by a foolish and impertinent parody of two of his finest odes, that he never afterwards attempted any considerable work. Those men of letters who value themselves upon what is called fine writing in prose approach somewhat to the sensibility of poets.

Mathematicians, on the contrary, who may have the most perfect assurance, both of the truth and of the importance of their discoveries, are frequently very indifferent about the reception which they may meet with from the public. The two greatest mathematicians that I ever have had the honour to be known to, and,

I believe, the two greatest that have lived in my time,
Dr. Robert Simpson of Glasgow, and Dr. Matthew
Stewart of Edinburgh, never seemed to feel even the
slightest uneasiness from the neglect with which the
ignorance of the public received some of their most
valuable works. The great work of Sir Isaac Newton,
his *Mathematical Principles of Natural Philosophy*, I
have been told, was for several years neglected by the
public. The tranquillity of that great man, it is probable never suffered upon that account, the interruption
of a single quarter of an hour. Natural philosophers, in
their independency upon the public opinion, approach
nearly to mathematicians, and, in their judgments concerning the merit of their own discoveries and observations, enjoy some degree of the same security and tranquillity.

The morals of those different classes of men of letters
are, perhaps, sometimes somewhat affected by this very
great difference in their situation with regard to the
public.

Mathematicians and natural philosophers, from their
independency upon the public opinion, have little
temptation to form themselves into factions and cabals,
either for the support of their own reputation, or for the
depression of that of their rivals. They are almost always men of the most amiable simplicity of manners,
who live in good harmony with one another, are the
friends of one another's reputation, enter into no intrigue in order to secure the public applause, but are
pleased when their works are approved of, without being either much vexed or very angry when they are
neglected.

It is not always the same case with poets, or with
those who value themselves upon what is called fine
writing. They are very apt to divide themselves into a

sort of literary factions; each cabal being often avow-
edly, and almost always secretly, the mortal enemy of
the reputation of every other, and employing all the
mean arts of intrigue and solicitation to preoccupy the
public opinion in favour of the works of its own members, and against those of its enemies and rivals. In
France, Despreaux and Racine did not think it below
them to set themselves at the head of a literary cabal,
in order to depress the reputation, first of Quinault and
Perrault, and afterwards of Fontenelle and La Motte,
and even to treat the good La Fontaine with a species
of most disrespectful kindness. In England, the amiable
Mr. Addison did not think it unworthy of his gentle
and modest character to set himself at the head of a
little cabal of the same kind, in order to keep down the
rising reputation of Mr. Pope. Mr. Fontenelle, in writing the lives and characters of the members of the
Academy of Sciences, a society of mathematicians and
natural philosophers, has frequent opportunities of cele-
brating the amiable simplicity of their manners; a
quality which, he observes, was so universal among
them as to be characteristical, rather of that whole
class of men of letters, than of any individual. Mr.
d'Alembert, in writing the lives and characters of the
members of the French Academy, a society of poets
and fine writers, or of those who are supposed to be
such, seems not to have had such frequent opportunities of making any remark of this kind, and nowhere
pretends to represent this amiable quality as characteristical of that class of men of letters whom he cele-
brates.

(Philadelphia: Anthony Finley, 1817.)

❖ ❖ ❖

Reflections on Manners, Morals and the Stage

[FROM "An Epistle to Mr. d'Alembert"]

JEAN JACQUES ROUSSEAU

1758

The state of man hath its pleasures, which are derived from his nature, and arise from his occupations, his connections and his necessities; and as these pleasures are most agreeable to uncorrupted, innocent minds, they render all others in a manner useless. A father, a son, a husband, a citizen, lie under obligations of so pleasing and interesting a nature, that they can want no amusement more agreeable than the discharge of them. The proper employment of our time encreases its value; while the better it is employed, the less have we still to spare. Thus we find that the habit of labour renders idleness tiresome, and that a good conscience deprives us of all taste for frivolous pleasures. But it is the being dissatisfied with ourselves; it is the weight of indolence; it is the loss of taste for simple and natural pleasures, that give occasion to the expediency of artificial entertainments. I do not like to see the heart set upon theatrical amusements, as if it was uneasy or unhappy within itself. The answer of the barbarian to a person who had been extolling the magnificence of the circus, and the games instituted at Rome, was

dictated by nature itself. Have the Romans, said that
honest creature, no wives nor children? The barbarian
was in the right. People imagine themselves to be in
company at the theatre, but it is there that everybody
is alone. We repair thither to forget our relations, our
friends, our neighbours; to interest ourselves in fabulous representations, to mourn over the imaginary misfortunes of the dead, or to laugh at the expence of the
living. But I should have perceived that this is not the
language of the present age. Let us endeavour, therefore, to assume one that will be better understood.

To enquire whether public amusements are good or
bad in themselves is a question too vague and indeterminate: it would be to examine into a relation before
we had fixed the terms of it. They are made for the
people, and it is only from their effects on the people,
that we are to determine their real good or bad qualities. There may be an almost infinite variety of such
entertainments; and there is a like variety in the manners, constitutions and characters of different people.
I allow that man is every where the same; but when he
is variously modified by religion, government, laws,
customs, prepossessions, and climates, he becomes so
different from himself that the question no longer is
what is proper for mankind in general, but what is
proper for him in such a particular age and country.
Hence it is that the dramatic pieces of Menander, calculated for the Athenian stage, were ill-suited for that
of Rome. Hence the combats of the gladiators, which,
under the republican government, animated the people
with courage, and a love of glory, only served, under
the emperours, to render the populace brutal, blood-
thirsty, and cruel. The very same objects, exhibited under different circumstances, taught the people at one

time to despise their own lives, and at another to sport with the lives of others. . . .

Let us not ascribe to the theatre . . . the power of changing sentiments and manners, when it can only pursue and embellish them. A dramatic writer who should oppose the general taste of the public, would soon be left to write only for himself. When Molière corrected the comic drama, he attacked only ridiculous modes and characters; but in doing this, he indulged the public taste,* as did also Corneille. It was the old French stage that began to displease this taste: because, while the nation improved in politeness, the stage still retained its primitive barbarism.

It is for the same reason that, as the general taste is so greatly altered since their times, the very best pieces of these two authors, if now first brought on the stage, would infallibly be damned. The connoisseurs may admire them as much as they please; the public admire them rather because they are ashamed to do otherwise, than from any real beauties they discover in them. It is said, indeed, that a good piece can never miscarry; truly I believe it; but this is because a really good piece is never disgusting to the manners of the times. There cannot be the least doubt that the very best tragedy of Sophocles would be totally damned in our theatres. It is impossible for us to put ourselves in the place of people, to whom we bear no sort of resemblance. . . .

* Had even Molière lived earlier, he would have found it difficult to keep his ground; the most perfect of all his writings being damned in its first appearance, because he brought it out too early; the age not being enlightened enough to receive *The Misanthrope*. [Rousseau's note.]

I should be glad to see it clearly and concisely demonstrated, how the drama can produce sentiments in us that we had not before in our minds, and cause us to judge of moral entities otherwise than we judge of them within ourselves. Believe me, these mighty pretensions, if examined into, will be all found to be insignificant and puerile. If the beauty of virtue were the work of art, it would have been long since defaced! As to myself, let me be treated as a bad man for saying that mankind were born good, I care not, as I think I have fully proved it. The source of our love for virtue, and our hatred to vice, is seated within ourselves, and is not to be found in the play. No art can produce it, although it may take advantage of it. The love of the beautiful* is a sentiment as natural to the human heart as that of self-love. It does not spring from any arrangement or disposition of the scenes: the writer doth not carry it to the theatre, he finds it there; and it is by flattering this purity of sentiment he is enabled to draw forth those tears which sometimes flow from the audience. . . .

Of all Molière's comedies, this [*The Misanthrope*] is that which affords us the clearest insight into the nature of his design in writing for the stage, and enables us best to judge of the real effects of his dramatic performances. As the first object was to please the public, he consulted the general taste of the people; on which he formed his plan, and according to this, drew a contrast between contrary failings; thence forming his characters, and interspersing them throughout his

* I mean here what is *morally* beautiful: for let philosophers say what they please, this love is implanted in human nature, as an innate principle of conscience. [Rousseau's note.]

plays. His design was not to draw a man of probity, but a man of the world: so that it is plain he did not want to correct vice, but folly; to which end, as I have already observed, he found vice to be a very proper instrument. Being determined, therefore, to expose to ridicule the several defects opposed to the qualifications of an agreeable and social character; and having exhausted his subjects, there remained for him only one species of the ridiculous on which to exercise his talent; this was the extravagance of virtue, an extravagance which is looked upon by the world as the most ridiculous of all; and this is what he has done in his *Misanthrope*.

You cannot deny me two things; the one is that Alcestes in this play is described on the whole as an upright, sincere, ingenuous, and worthy man: the other is that the author has endeavoured to make his character appear ridiculous. This is sufficient, in my opinion, to render Molière inexcusable. It may be objected, indeed, that the object of the poet's ridicule is not the virtue of Alcestes, but a real defect, his hatred of mankind. But it is not true that Alcestes entertains any such hatred: let not the reader be imposed on by the mere name of misanthrope, as if the character which bears it were an enemy to humankind. Such an enmity would not be merely a defect, but a depravation of nature, and the greatest of all vices: for all the social virtues being reducible to benevolence, nothing can be more directly contrary to them than inhumanity. Could a real misanthrope exist, he would indeed be a monster, that would be so far from exciting our laughter, that he would fill us with horrour. . . .

A certain proof that Alcestes is not a misanthrope in the literal sense of the word is that with all his grumbling he does not fail to interest and please us. None of the audience indeed would probably chuse to resemble him, because such rigid integrity is very troublesome: but not one of them all would be averse to the having connections with a man of his character, which would never be the case were he a declared enemy to mankind. In all the other pieces of Molière, the ridiculous personage is rendered odious or despicable: but in this, notwithstanding Alcestes has real foibles which we may laugh at very innocently, we yet feel such a respect for him in our hearts, as it is not in our power to suppress. On this occasion it is that the force of virtue prevails over the art of the poet, and does honour to his character. Molière, although he wrote some plays that are very exceptionable, was himself an honest man, and never could the pencil of an honest man be brought entirely to disguise in odious colours the features of sincerity and probity. To this it may be added that Molière hath put into the mouth of Alcestes so many of his own maxims that many persons have thought he intended to draw it for his own character. This appeared from the concern evidently shewn by the pit, on the first night of representation, on account of their not being of the misanthrope's opinion with regard to the sonnet; as it was very plain that it was the real opinion of the author.

This virtuous character, however, is exhibited as ridiculous; it is true, indeed, that in some respects he is so, and what sufficiently shews the poet's design to make him appear so, is the contrast which he hath made between the character of Alcestes and that of his friend Philintes. This Philintes is the sensible man of the play; one of those honest men in high life whose maxims greatly resemble those of knaves; one of those moderate men who think things always go well, because they

are interested in their not going better; who are satisfied with everybody, because they care for nobody; who
maintain, round a plentiful table, that it is impossible
the poor should be starving; and having their own
pockets well lined, are very averse to hear any advocate
for poverty: one of those who, if their own house were
secure, would not give themselves any trouble, though
all the rest of the world was ransacked and plundered,
massacred and destroyed; God Almighty having blessed
them with an admirable share of patience to support
the misfortunes of other people.

From "An Epistle from J. J. Rousseau, to Mr. d'Alembert" in
The Miscellaneous Works of Mr. J. J. Rousseau (London: T.
Becket and P. A. De Hondt, 1767).

On Men of Letters

[FROM "Reflections on the Present State
of the Republic of Letters"]

JEAN LE ROND D'ALEMBERT

1760

Moral philosophers are fond of asking how men
lived in what is called a state of *pure nature,* before
there were organized societies and laws, and whether
such a state was one of peace or war. They have
written on this question endlessly, as on all questions
where the pros or the cons can be maintained at will,
without danger of being contradicted by actual experience. From all these dissertations one can learn

what one can usually learn from metaphysical discussions—that is, nothing.

Yet there is, it seems to me, a shorter way to decide the question; that is, to examine the way in which men of letters have behaved throughout the centuries. For the man of letters is in relation to other men of letters almost in that state of pure nature about which we talk so much without really knowing what we are talking about. They struggle for renown much as, it is maintained, men without laws and government struggled, or would have struggled, for their food acorns. But in society no one has the right to live to the complete detriment of his fellows; therefore the laws regulate, at least roughly, the distribution of acorns— that is, the bare necessities of life—among men. On the contrary, in the best regulated society it is possible to live without renown, and often, indeed, to live more happily without it. Those who made the laws, therefore, have left this phantom to be disputed over by those who prize it.

Literary renown is then the reward of the first to take it: the sceptre belongs to him who seizes it, or who has the skill to have it offered him. Passed endlessly from hand to hand, it is the prize of the strongest or the cleverest. Usually the cleverest enjoys it but briefly, for it comes back to the strongest and stays in his possession.

To gain this sceptre, or at least to snatch off a few ornaments from it, men of letters write and intrigue, praise or tear to pieces. Some of them indeed protest that they scorn renown, all the while desiring it very much. But no one is the dupe of their protests, which do not prevent their getting renown if they deserve it, and which make them ridiculous only if they disdain it without deserving it.

Among men of letters there is one group against which the arbiters of taste, the important people, the rich people, are united: this is the pernicious, the damnable group of *philosophes,* who hold that it is possible to be a good Frenchman without courting those in power, a good citizen without flattering national prejudices, a good Christian without persecuting anybody. These *philosophes* believe it right to make more of an honest if little-known writer than of a well-known writer without enlightenment and without principles, to hold that foreigners are not inferior to us in every respect, and to prefer, for example, a government under which the people are not slaves to one under which they are.

This way of thinking is for many people an unpardonable crime. What shocks them most of all, they say, is the tone the *philosophes* use, the tone of dogmatism, the tone of the master who knows. I admit that those of the *philosophes* who do indeed deserve this reproach would have done well to avoid deserving it. When it is necessary to hurt with what is said, it is wrong to hurt still more by the tone in which it is said. The writer is always master of his tone, his way of saying things. Truth can hardly be too modest. Truth indeed, just by being truth, runs always a sufficiently great risk of being rejected. But after all, this truth, so feared, so hated, so insulted, is so rare and precious, it seems to me, that those who tell it may be pardoned a little excess of fervour. The writer who wants to write more than ephemerally has got to be right. Form is in itself of little importance—it is something for the moment, for the passing generation, but nothing for the next one, still less for distant posterity. If a dogmatic tone, one that tells the truth crudely, shocks our delicate judges, they will do well never to open geometry books; they won't find more insolent ones.

The *philosophes*, they say, are enemies of authority. This is a more serious reproach and deserves a serious reply. The *philosophes* respect authority in the monarch, to whom it belongs, and whose love of truth and justice they recognize. They would respect power in the hands of those to whom he confided it, even though it were abused. What would they gain by attacking such power? Who would guarantee them against oppression? Who would take their part? A thousand voices would be raised to overwhelm them, and not one to defend them. What resolution can they take, save to obey and keep silent? What prerogative have they to claim to be dispensed from obedience? If they were persecuted, they would at most defend themselves. To protest is not to revolt. No, no, if legitimate authority has in these days been weakened under attack, it has not been from attacks by men of letters or *philosophes*, but rather by those who most openly declare themselves the enemies of the *philosophes*.

Let us speak without disguise or constraint. If those men we call *philosophes* haunted more often the antechambers of ministers, courted ladies of well-known piety, put themselves forward as advocates of persecution and intolerance, they would not be the targets for all the insults that are hurled at them. But they honour the great and flee them; they revere true piety and detest persecuting zeal; they believe the first of Christian duties is charity; and finally, as has been said elsewhere (for there are truths good to repeat for certain

ears), they respect that which they ought to, and prize
that which they can. This is their real crime.

From "Réflexions sur l'état présent de la republique des lettres,"
Œuvres et correspondences inédites de d'Alembert (Paris: Perrin,
1887); trans. C. B.

❖ ❖ ❖

The Principle of Utility

[FROM *An Introduction to the Principles
of Morals and Legislation*]

JEREMY BENTHAM

1789

1. Nature has placed mankind under the governance
of two sovereign masters, *pain* and *pleasure*. It is for
them alone to point out what we ought to do, as well
as to determine what we shall do. On the one hand
the standard of right and wrong, on the other the chain
of causes and effects, are fastened to their throne. They
govern us in all we do, in all we say, in all we think:
every effort we can make to throw off our subjection,
will serve but to demonstrate and confirm it. In words
a man may pretend to abjure their empire: but in
reality he will remain subject to it all the while. The
principle of utility recognizes this subjection, and assumes it for the foundation of that system, the object
of which is to rear the fabric of felicity by the hands
of reason and of law. Systems which attempt to question it deal in sounds instead of sense, in caprice instead
of reason, in darkness instead of light.

But enough of metaphor and declamation: it is not by such means that moral science is to be improved.

II. The principle of utility is the foundation of the present work: it will be proper therefore at the outset to give an explicit and determinate account of what is meant by it. By the principle of utility is meant that principle which approves or disapproves of every action whatsoever, according to the tendency which it appears to have to augment or diminish the happiness of the party whose interest is in question: or, what is the same thing in other words, to promote or to oppose that happiness. I say of every action whatsoever; and therefore not only of every action of a private individual, but of every measure of government.

III. By utility is meant that property in any object, whereby it tends to produce benefit, advantage, pleasure, good, or happiness, (all this in the present case comes to the same thing) or (what comes again to the same thing) to prevent the happening of mischief, pain, evil, or unhappiness to the party whose interest is considered: if that party be the community in general, then the happiness of the community: if a particular individual, then the happiness of that individual.

IV. The interest of the community is one of the most general expressions that can occur in the phraseology of morals: no wonder that the meaning of it is often lost. When it has a meaning it is this. The community is a fictitious *body*, composed of the individual persons who are considered as constituting as it were its *members*. The interest of the community then is, what?—the sum of the interests of the several members who compose it.

V. It is in vain to talk of the interest of the community, without understanding what is the interest of the individual. A thing is said to promote the interest, or to be *for* the interest, of an individual, when it tends to add to the sum total of his pleasures: or, what comes to the same thing, to diminish the sum total of his pains.

VI. An action then may be said to be conformable to the principle of utility, or, for shortness' sake, to utility, (meaning with respect to the community at large) when the tendency it has to augment the happiness of the community is greater than any it has to diminish it.

VII. A measure of government (which is but a particular kind of action, performed by a particular person or persons) may be said to be conformable to or dictated by the principle of utility, when in like manner the tendency which it has to augment the happiness of the community is greater than any which it has to diminish it.

VIII. When an action, or in particular a measure of government, is supposed by a man to be conformable to the principle of utility, it may be convenient, for the purposes of discourse, to imagine a kind of law or dictate, called a law or dictate of utility: and to speak of the action in question, as being conformable to such law or dictate.

IX. A man may be said to be a partisan of the principle of utility, when the approbation or disapprobation he annexes to any action, or to any measure, is determined by and proportioned to the tendency which he conceives it to have to augment or to diminish the happiness of the community: or in other words, to its conformity or unconformity to the laws or dictates of utility.

X. Of an action that is conformable to the principle of utility one may always say either that it is one that ought to be done, or at least that it is not one that

ought not to be done. One may say also, that it is
right it should be done; at least that it is not wrong
it should be done: that it is a right action; at least
that it is not a wrong action. When thus interpreted,
the words *ought,* and *right* and *wrong,* and others of
that stamp, have a meaning: when otherwise, they have
none.

XI. Has the rectitude of this principle been ever
formally contested? It should seem that it had, by
those who have not known what they have been meaning. Is it susceptible of any direct proof? it should seem
not: for that which is used to prove everything else,
cannot itself be proved: a chain of proofs must have
their commencement somewhere. To give such proof
is as impossible as it is needless.

XII. Not that there is or ever has been that human
creature breathing however stupid or perverse, who
has not on many, perhaps on most occasions of his
life, deferred to it. By the natural constitution of the
human frame, on most occasions of their lives men in
general embrace this principle, without thinking of it:
if not for the ordering of their own actions, yet for
the trying of their own actions, as well as of those of
other men. There have been, at the same time, not
many, perhaps, even of the most intelligent, who have
been disposed to embrace it purely and without reserve. There are even few who have not taken some
occasion or other to quarrel with it, either on account of
their not understanding always how to apply it, or on
account of some prejudice or other which they were
afraid to examine into, or could not bear to part with.
For such is the stuff that man is made of: in principle
and in practice, in a right track and in a wrong one,
the rarest of all human qualities is consistency.

XIII. When a man attempts to combat the principle

of utility, it is with reasons drawn, without his being aware of it, from that very principle itself. His arguments, if they prove anything, prove not that the principle is *wrong*, but that, according to the applications he supposes to be made of it, it is *misapplied*. Is it possible for a man to move the earth? Yes; but he must first find out another earth to stand upon.

(Oxford: Clarendon Press, 1879.)

Coming of Age in Tahiti

[FROM *Supplement to the Voyage of Bougainville*]

DENIS DIDEROT

1772

In the sharing of Bougainville's crew among the Tahitians, the almoner was allotted to Orou; they were about the same age, thirty-five to thirty-six. Orou had then only his wife and three daughters, called Asto, Palli, and Thia. They undressed the almoner, bathed his face, hands, and feet, and served him a wholesome and frugal meal. When he was about to go to bed, Orou, who had been absent with his family, reappeared, and presenting to him his wife and three daughters, all naked, said: "You have eaten, you are young and in good health; if you sleep alone you will sleep badly, for man needs a companion beside him at night. There is my wife, there are my daughters; choose the one who pleases you best. But if you wish to oblige me you will give preference to the youngest of my daughters, who has not yet had any children." The mother added: "Alas! But it's no good complaining about it; poor Thia! it is not her fault."

The almoner answered that his religion, his office, good morals and decency would not allow him to accept these offers.

Orou replied: "I do not know what this thing is that you call 'religion'; but I can only think ill of it, since it prevents you from tasting an innocent pleasure to which nature, the sovereign mistress, invites us all; prevents you from giving existence to one of your own kind, from doing a service which a father, mother and children all ask of you, from doing something for a host who has received you well, and from enriching a nation, by giving it one more citizen. I do not know what this thing is which you call your 'office,' but your first duty is to be a man and to be grateful. I do not suggest that you should introduce into your country the ways of Orou, but Orou, your host and friend, begs you to lend yourself to the ways of Tahiti. Whether the ways of Tahiti are better or worse than yours is an easy question to decide. Has the land of your birth more people than it can feed? If so, your ways are neither worse nor better than ours. But can it feed more than it has? Our ways are better than yours. As to the sense of decency which you offer as objection, I understand you; I agree that I was wrong, and I ask your pardon. I do not want you to injure your health; if you are tired, you must have rest; but I hope that you will not continue to sadden us. See the care you have made appear on all these faces; they fear lest you should have found blemishes on them which merit your disdain. But when it is only the pleasure of doing honour to one of my daughters, amidst her companions and sisters, and of doing a good action, won't that suffice you? Be generous!"

The Almoner: It's not that: they are all equally beautiful; but my religion! my office!

Orou: They are mine and I offer them to you; they are their own and they give themselves to you. Whatever may be the purity of conscience which the thing "religion" and the thing "office" prescribe, you can accept them without scruple. I am not abusing my authority at all; be sure that I know and respect the rights of the individual.

Here the truthful almoner agrees that Providence had never exposed him to such violent temptation. He was young, he became agitated and tormented; he turned his eyes away from the lovely suppliants, and then regarded them again; he raised his hands and eyes to the sky. Thia, the youngest, clasped his knees and said: "Stranger, do not distress my father and mother, do not afflict me. Honour me in the hut, among my own people; raise me to the rank of my sisters, who mock me. Asto, the eldest, already has three children; the second, Palli, has two; but Thia has none at all. Stranger, honest stranger, do not repulse me; make me a mother, make me a child that I can one day lead by the hand, by my side, here in Tahiti; who may be seen held at my breast in nine months' time; one of whom I shall be so proud and who will be part of my dowry when I go from my parents' hut to another's. I shall perhaps be more lucky with you than with our young Tahitians. If you will grant me this favour I shall never forget you; I shall bless you all my life. I shall write your name on my arm and on your son's; we shall pronounce it always with joy. And when you leave these shores, my good wishes will go with you on the seas till you reach your own land."

The candid almoner said that she clasped his knees, and gazed into his eyes so expressively and so touchingly; that she wept; that her father, mother and sisters withdrew; that he remained alone with her, and that, still saying "my religion, my office," he found himself the next morning lying beside the young girl, who overwhelmed him with caresses, and who invited her parents and sisters, when they came to their bed in the morning, to join their gratitude to hers. Asto and Palli, who had withdrawn, returned bringing food, fruits and drink. They kissed their sister and made vows over her. They all ate together.

Then Orou, left alone with the almoner, said to him: "I see that my daughter is well satisfied with you and I thank you. But would you teach me what is meant by this word 'religion' which you have repeated so many times and so sorrowfully?"

The almoner, after having mused a moment, answered: "Who made your hut and the things which furnish it?"

Orou: I did.

The Almoner: Well then, we believe that this world and all that it contains is the work of a maker.

Orou: Has he feet, hands, and a head then?

The Almoner: No.

Orou: Where is his dwelling place?

The Almoner: Everywhere.

Orou: Here too?

The Almoner: Here.

Orou: We have never seen him.

The Almoner: One doesn't see him.

Orou: That's an indifferent father then! He must be old, for he will at least be as old as his work.

The Almoner: He does not age. He spoke to our ancestors, gave them laws, prescribed the manner in which he wished to be honoured; he ordered a certain behaviour as being good, and he forbade them certain other actions as being wicked.

Orou: I follow you; and one of the actions he forbade them, as wicked, was to lie with a woman or a girl? Why, then, did he make two sexes?

The Almoner: That they might unite; but with certain requisite conditions, after certain preliminary ceremonies in consequence of which the man belongs to the woman and only to her; and the woman belongs to the man, and only to him.

Orou: For their whole lives?

The Almoner: For the whole of their lives.

Orou: So that if it happened that a woman should lie with a man other than her husband, or a husband with another woman . . . but that couldn't happen. Since the maker is there and this displeases him, he will know how to prevent them doing it.

The Almoner: No; he lets them do it, and they sin against the law of God (for it is thus we call the great maker), against the law of the country; and they commit a crime.

Orou: I should be sorry to offend you by what I say, but if you would permit me, I would give you my opinion.

The Almoner: Speak.

Orou: I find these singular precepts opposed to nature and contrary to reason, made to multiply crimes and to plague at every moment this old maker, who has made everything, without help of hands, or head, or tools, who is everywhere and is not seen anywhere, who exists today and tomorrow and yet is not a day older, who commands and is not obeyed, who can prevent and yet does not do so. Contrary to nature because these precepts suppose that a free, thinking and sentient being can be the property of a being like himself. On what is this law founded? Don't you see that in your country they have confused the thing which has neither consciousness nor thought, nor desire, nor will; which one picks up, puts down, keeps or exchanges, without injury to it, or without its complaining, have confused this with the thing which cannot be exchanged or acquired, which has liberty, will, desire, which can give or refuse itself for a moment or forever, which laments and suffers, and which cannot become an article of commerce, without its character being forgotten and violence done to its nature, contrary to the general law of existence? In fact, nothing could appear to you more senseless than a precept which refuses to admit that change which is a part of us, which commands a constancy which cannot be found there, and which violates the liberty of the male and female by chaining them forever to each other; more senseless than a fidelity which limits the most capricious of enjoyments to one individual; than an oath of the immutability of two beings made of flesh; and all that in the face of a sky which never for a moment remains the same, in caverns which threaten destruction, below a rock which falls to powder, at the foot of a tree which cracks, on a stone which rocks? Believe me, you have made the condition of man worse than that of animals. I do not know what your great maker may be; but I rejoice that he has never spoken to our forefathers, and I wish that he may never speak to our children; for he might tell them the same foolishness, and they commit the folly of believing it. Yesterday, at supper, you mentioned "magistrates" and "priests," whose authority regulates your conduct; but, tell me, are they the masters of good and evil? Can they make what is just to be unjust, and unjust, just? Does it rest with them to attribute good to harmful actions, and evil to innocent or useful actions? You could not think it, for, at that rate, there would be neither true nor false, good nor bad, beautiful nor ugly; or at any rate only what pleased your great maker, your magistrates, and your priests to pronounce so. And from one moment to another you would be obliged to change your ideas and your conduct. One day someone would tell you, on behalf of one of your three masters, to kill, and you would be obliged by your conscience to kill; another day, "steal," and you would have to steal; or "do not eat this fruit," and you would not dare to eat it; "I forbid you this vegetable or animal," and you would take care not to touch them. There is no good thing that could not be forbidden you, and no wickedness that you could not be ordered to do. And what would you be reduced to, if your three masters, disagreeing among themselves, should at once permit, enjoin, and forbid you the same thing, as I believe must often happen. Then, to please the priest you must become embroiled with the magistrate; to satisfy the magistrate you must displease the great maker; and to make yourself agreeable to the great maker you must renounce nature. And do you know what will happen then? You will neglect all of them, and you will be neither man, nor citizen, nor pious; you will be nothing; you will be out of favour with all the kinds of authorities, at odds even with yourself, tormented by your heart, persecuted by your enraged masters; and wretched as I saw you yesterday evening when I offered my wife and daughters to you, and you cried out, "But my religion, my office!"

Do you want to know what is good and what is bad in all times and in all places? Hold fast to the nature of things and of actions; to your relations with your fellows; to the influence of your conduct on your individual usefulness and the general good. You are mad if you believe that there is anything, high or low in the universe, which can add to or subtract from the laws of nature. Her eternal will is that good should be preferred to evil, and the general good to the individual good. You may ordain the opposite but you will not be obeyed. You will multiply the number of malefactors and the wretched by fear, punishment, and remorse. You will deprave consciences; you will corrupt minds. They will not know what to do or what to avoid. Disturbed in their state of innocence, at ease with crime, they will have lost their guiding star. Answer me sincerely; in spite of the express orders of your three lawgivers, does a young man, in your country, never lie with a young girl without their permission?

The Almoner: I should deceive you if I asserted it.

Orou: Does a woman who has sworn to belong only to her husband never give herself to another man?

The Almoner: Nothing is more common.

Orou: Your lawgivers either punish or do not punish; if they punish they are ferocious beasts who fight against nature; if they do not punish, they are imbeciles who have exposed their authority to contempt by an empty prohibition.

The Almoner: The culprits who escape the severity of the law are punished by popular condemnation.

Orou: That is to say, justice is exercised through the lack of common sense of the whole nation, and the foolishness of opinion does duty for laws.

The Almoner: A girl who has been dishonoured will not find a husband.

Orou: Dishonoured! Why?

The Almoner: An unfaithful wife is more or less despised.

Orou: Despised! But why?

The Almoner: The young man is called a cowardly seducer.

Orou: A coward, a seducer! But why?

The Almoner: The father and mother and child are desolated. The unfaithful husband is a libertine; the betrayed husband shares his wife's shame.

Orou: What a monstrous tissue of extravagances you've just revealed to me! And yet you don't say everything; for as soon as one allows oneself to dispose at pleasure of the ideas of justice and ownership, to take away or to give an arbitrary character to things, to attribute or deny good or evil to certain actions, capriciously, then one can be censorious, vindictive, suspicious, tyrannical, envious, jealous, deceitful. There is spying, quarrelling, cheating, and lying; daughters deceive their parents, wives their husbands. Girls, yes, I don't doubt it, will strangle their infants, suspicious fathers will hate and neglect theirs, mothers will leave them and abandon them to their fates. And crime and debauchery will show themselves in all their forms. I know all that as if I had lived among you. It is so, because it must be so; and your society, of which your leader boasts because of its good regulations, will only be a swarm of hypocrites who secretly trample all laws under foot; or of unfortunates who are themselves the instruments of their own suffering in submitting; or of imbeciles in whom prejudices have quite stifled the voice of nature; or of abnormal monsters in whom nature does not protest her rights.

The Almoner: So it would seem. But don't you marry then?

Orou: Yes, we marry.

The Almoner: But what does it consist in?

Orou: A mutual consent to live in the same hut and to lie in the same bed for as long as we find it good to do so.

The Almoner: And when you find it no longer good?

Orou: We separate.

The Almoner: What becomes of the children?

Orou: Oh, stranger! Your last question finally reveals to me the profound misery of your country. You must understand, my friend, that here the birth of a child is always a good fortune, and its death a subject for regret and tears. A child is precious because he ought to become a man; therefore we have a care for it, quite other than for our animals and plants. A child born causes both domestic and public joy. It is an increase of fortune for the hut and of strength for the nation. It means more hands and arms in Tahiti. We see in him a farmer, fisher, hunter, soldier, husband and father. When she returns from her husband's cabin to that of her parents, a woman takes with her the children which she had taken as dowry; those born during their companionship are shared; and as nearly as can be, males and females are divided, so that each one retains an equal number of boys and girls.

From *Diderot, Interpreter of Nature,* trans. Jean Stewart and Jonathan Kemp (London: Lawrence & Wishart, 1937).

people who have at any time been most industrious after wisdom; so that language is but the instrument conveying to us things useful to be known. And though a linguist should pride himself to have all the tongues that Babel cleft the world into, yet if he have not studied the solid things in them as well as the words and lexicons, he were nothing so much to be esteemed a learned man as any yeoman or tradesman competently wise in his mother dialect only.

Hence appear the many mistakes which have made learning generally so unpleasing and so unsuccessful. First, we do amiss to spend seven or eight years merely in scraping together so much miserable Latin and Greek as might be learned otherwise easily and delightfully in one year. And that which casts our proficiency therein so much behind, is our time lost partly in too oft idle vacancies given both to schools and universities; partly in a preposterous exaction, forcing the empty wits of children to compose themes, verses, and orations, which are the acts of ripest judgment, and the final work of a head filled, by long reading and observing, with elegant maxims and copious invention. These are not matters to be wrung from poor striplings, like blood out of the nose, or the plucking of untimely fruit; besides the ill habit which they get of wretched barbarizing against the Latin and Greek idiom with their untutored Anglicisms, odious to be read, yet not to be avoided without a well-continued and judicious conversing among pure authors digested, which they scarce taste. Whereas, if after some preparatory grounds of speech by their certain forms got into memory, they were led to the praxis thereof in some chosen short book lessoned thoroughly to them, they might then forthwith proceed to learn the substance of good things, and arts in due order, which would bring the whole language quickly into their power. This I take to be the most rational and most profitable way of learning languages, and whereby we may best hope to give account to God of our youth spent herein.

And for the usual method of teaching arts, I deem it to be an old error of universities not yet well recovered from the scholastic grossness of barbarous ages, that instead of beginning with arts most easy (and those be such as are most obvious to the sense), they present their young unmatriculated novices, at first coming, with the most intellective abstractions of logic and metaphysics; so that they, having but newly left those grammatic flats and shallows where they stuck unreasonably to learn a few words with lamentable construction, and now on the sudden transported under another climate to be tossed and turmoiled with their unballasted wits in fathomless and unquiet deeps of controversy, do for the most part grow into hatred and contempt of learning, mocked and deluded all this while with ragged notions and babblements, while they expected worthy and delightful knowledge; till poverty or youthful years call them importunately their several ways, and hasten them, with the sway of friends, either to an ambitious and mercenary or ignorantly zealous divinity: some allured to the trade of law, grounding their purposes, not on the prudent and heavenly contemplation of justice and equity, which was never taught them, but on the promising and pleasing thoughts of litigious terms, fat contentions, and flowing fees; others betake them to state affairs, with souls so unprincipled in virtue and true generous breeding that flattery and court-shifts and tyrannous aphorisms appear to them the highest points of wisdom, instilling their barren hearts with a conscientious slavery, if, as I rather think, it be not feigned. Others, lastly, of a more delicious and airy spirit, retire themselves—knowing no better—to the enjoyments of ease and luxury, living out their days in feast and jollity; which indeed is the wisest and the safest course of all these, unless they were with more integrity undertaken. And these are the errors, and these are the fruits, of misspending our prime youth at the schools and universities as we do, either in learning mere words, or such things chiefly as were better unlearnt.

I shall detain you now no longer in the demonstration of what we should not do, but straight conduct ye to a hillside where I will point ye out the right path of a virtuous and noble education; laborious indeed at the first ascent, but else so smooth, so green, so full of goodly prospect and melodious sounds on every side, that the harp of Orpheus was not more charming. I doubt not but ye shall have more ado to drive our dullest and laziest youth, our stocks and stubs, from the infinite desire of such a happy nurture, than we have now to hale and drag our choicest and hopefullest wits to that asinine feast of sow-thistles and brambles which is commonly set before them as all the food and entertainment of their tenderest and most docible age. I call therefore a complete and generous education that which fits a man to perform justly, skilfully, and magnanimously all the offices, both private and public, of peace and war. And how all this may be done between twelve and one and twenty, less time than is now bestowed in pure trifling at grammar and sophistry, is to be thus ordered.

First, to find out a spacious house and ground about it fit for an academy, and big enough to lodge a hundred and fifty persons, whereof twenty or thereabout may be attendants, all under the government of one, who shall be thought of desert sufficient, and ability either to do all or wisely to direct and oversee it done. This place should be at once both school and university, not needing a remove to any other house of scholarship, except it be some peculiar college of law or physic, where they mean to be practitioners; but as for those general studies which take up all our time from Lily to the commencing, as they term it, Master of Art, it should be absolute. After this pattern, as many edifices may be converted to this use as shall be needful in every city throughout this land, which would tend much to the increase of learning and civility everywhere. This number, less or more thus collected, to the convenience of a foot company, or interchangeably two troops of cavalry, should divide their day's work into three parts as it lies orderly: their studies, their exercise, and their diet.

For their studies: first, they should begin with the chief and necessary rules of some good grammar, either that now used or any better; and while this is doing, their speech is to be fashioned to a distinct and clear pronunciation, as near as may be to the Italian, especially in the vowels. For we Englishmen, being far northerly, do not open our mouths in the cold air wide enough to grace a southern tongue, but are observed by all other nations to speak exceeding close and inward, so that to smatter Latin with an English mouth is as ill a hearing as law French. Next, to make them expert in the usefullest points of grammar, and withal to season them and win them early to the love of virtue and true labour, ere any flattering seducement or vain principle seize them wandering, some easy and delightful book of education would be read to them, whereof the Greeks have store, as Cebes, Plutarch, and other

Socratic discourses. But in Latin we have none of classic authority extant, except the two or three first books of Quintilian and some select pieces elsewhere.

But here the main skill and groundwork will be to temper them such lectures and explanations, upon every opportunity, as may lead and draw them in willing obedience, inflamed with the study of learning and the admiration of virtue, stirred up with high hopes of living to be brave men and worthy patriots, dear to God and famous to all ages; that they may despise and scorn all their childish and ill-taught qualities to delight in manly and liberal exercises, which he who hath the art and proper eloquence to catch them with, what with mild and effectual persuasions and what with the intimation of some fear, if need be, but chiefly by his own example, might in a short space gain them to an incredible diligence and courage, infusing into their young breasts such an ingenuous and noble ardour as would not fail to make many of them renowned and matchless men. At the same time, some other hour of the day, might be taught them the rules of arithmetic; and soon after the elements of geometry, even playing, as the old manner was. After evening repast, till bedtime, their thoughts will be best taken up in the easy grounds of religion and the story of Scripture. . . .

The course of study hitherto briefly described is, what I can guess by reading, likest to those ancient and famous schools of Pythagoras, Plato, Isocrates, Aristotle, and such others, out of which were bred up such a number of renowned philosophers, orators, historians, poets, and princes all over Greece, Italy, and Asia, besides the flourishing studies of Cyrene and Alexandria. But herein it shall exceed them and supply a defect as great as that which Plato noted in the commonwealth of Sparta; whereas that city trained up and the early corruption of youth is now become so general a complaint that he cannot be thought wholly impertinent who brings the consideration of this matter on the stage, and offers something, if it be but to excite others, or afford matter of correction: for errors in education should be less indulged than any. These, like faults in the first concoction, that are never mended in the second or third, carry their afterwards incorrigible taint with them through all the parts and stations of life.

I imagine the minds of children as easily turned this or that way as water itself: and though this be the principal part, and our main care should be about the inside, yet the clay cottage is not to be neglected. I shall therefore begin with the case, and consider first the health of the body, as that which perhaps you may rather expect from that study I have been thought more peculiarly to have applied myself to; and that also which will be soonest dispatched, as lying, if I guess not amiss, in a very little compass.

One thing the mention of the girls brings into my mind, which must not be forgot; and that is, that your son's clothes be never made strait, especially about the breast. Let nature have scope to fashion the body as she thinks best. She works herself a great deal better and exacter than we can direct her. And if women were themselves to frame the bodies of their children in their wombs, as they often endeavour to mend their shapes when they are out, we should as certainly have no perfect children born, as we have few well-shaped that are strait-laced, or much tampered with. This consideration should, methinks, keep busy people (I will not say ignorant nurses and bodice-makers) from meddling in a matter they understand not; and they should be afraid to put nature out of her way in fashioning the parts, when they know not how the least and meanest is made. And yet I have seen so many instances of children receiving great harm from strait-lacing, that I cannot but conclude there are other creatures as well as monkeys, who, little wiser than they, destroy their young ones by senseless fondness, and too much embracing.

Narrow breasts, short and stinking breath, ill lungs, and crookedness, are natural and almost constant effects of hard bodice, and clothes that pinch. That way of making slender waists and fine shapes serves but the more effectually to spoil them. Nor can there indeed but be disproportion in the parts, when the nourishment prepared in the several offices of the body cannot be distributed as nature designs. And therefore what wonder is it, if, it being laid where it can, on some part not so braced, it often makes a shoulder or hip higher or bigger than its just proportion? 'Tis generally known that the women of China (imagining I know not what kind of beauty in it) by bracing and binding them hard from their infancy, have very little feet. I saw lately a pair of China shoes, which I was told were for a grown woman: they were so exceedingly disproportioned to the feet of one of the same age among us, that they would scarce have been big enough for one of our little girls. Besides this, 'tis observed that their women are also very little and short-lived; whereas the men are of the ordinary stature of other men, and live to a proportionable age. These defects in the female sex in that country are by some imputed to the unreasonable binding of their feet, whereby the free circulation of the blood is hindered, and the growth and health of the whole body suffers. And how often do we see that some small part of the foot being injured by a wrench or a blow, the whole leg or thigh thereby lose their strength and nourishment, and dwindle away? How much greater inconveniences may we expect, when the thorax, wherein is placed the heart and seat of life, is unnaturally compressed, and hindered from its due expansion?

That which every gentleman (that takes any care of his education) desires for his son, besides the estate he leaves him, is contained, I suppose, in these four things, *virtue, wisdom, breeding* and *learning*. I will not trouble myself whether these names do not some of them sometimes stand for the same thing, or really include one another. It serves my turn here to follow the popular use of these words, which, I presume, is clear enough to make me be understood, and I hope there will be no difficulty to comprehend my meaning.

I place *virtue* as the first and most necessary of those endowments that belong to a man or a gentleman; as absolutely requisite to make him valued and beloved by others, acceptable or tolerable to himself. Without that, I think, he will be happy neither in this nor the other world.

As the foundation of this, there ought very early to be imprinted on his mind a true notion of God, as of the independent Supreme Being, Author and Maker of all things, from Whom we receive all our good, Who loves us, and gives us all things. And consequent to this, instill into him a love and reverence of this Supreme Being. This is enough to begin with, without going to explain this matter any farther; for fear lest by talking too early to him of spirits, and being unseasonably forward to make him understand the incomprehensible nature of that Infinite Being, his head be either filled with false or perplexed with unintelligible notions of Him. Let him only be told upon occasion, that God made and governs all things, hears and sees everything, and does all manner of good to those that love and obey Him; you will find, that being told of such a God, other thoughts will be apt to rise up fast enough in his mind about Him; which, as you observe them to have any mistakes, you must set right. . . .

Having laid the foundations of virtue in a true notion of a God, such as the creed wisely teaches, as far as his age is capable, and by accustoming him to pray to Him, the next thing to be taken care of is to keep him exactly to speaking of truth, and by all the ways imaginable inclining him to be good-natured. Let him know that twenty faults are sooner to be forgiven than the straining of truth to cover anyone by an excuse. And to teach him betimes to love and be good-natured to others is to lay early the true foundation of an honest man; all injustice generally springing from too great love of ourselves and too little of others.

This is all I shall say of this matter in general, and is enough for laying the first foundations of virtue in a child. As he grows up, the tendency of his natural inclination must be observed; which, as it inclines him more than is convenient on one or t'other side from the right path of virtue, ought to have proper remedies applied. For few of Adam's children are so happy, as not to be born with some bias in their natural temper, which it is the business of education either to take off or counterbalance. But to enter into particulars of this would be beyond the design of this short treatise of education. I intend not a discourse of all the virtues and vices, how each virtue is to be attained, and every particular vice by its peculiar remedies cured, though I have mentioned some of the most ordinary faults, and the ways to be used in correcting them.

Wisdom I take in the popular acceptation, for a man's managing his business ably and with foresight in this world. This is the product of a good natural temper, application of mind, and experience together, and so above the reach of children. The greatest thing that in them can be done towards it is to hinder them, as much as may be, from being cunning; which, being the ape of wisdom, is the most distant from it that can be: and as an ape for the likeness it has to a man, wanting what really should make him so, is by so much the uglier; cunning is only the want of understanding, which, because it cannot compass its ends by direct ways, would do it by a trick and circumvention; and the mischief of it is, a cunning trick helps but once, but hinders ever after. No cover was ever made so big or so fine as to hide itself: nobody was ever so cunning as to conceal their being so; and when they are once discovered, everybody is shy, everybody distrustful of crafty men; and all the world forwardly join to oppose and defeat them; whilst the open, fair, wise man has everybody to make way for him, and goes directly to his business. To accustom a child to have true notions of things, and not to be satisfied till he has them, to raise his mind to great and worthy thoughts, and to keep him at a distance from falsehood and cunning, which has always a broad mixture of falsehood in it, is the fittest preparation of a child for wisdom. The rest, which is to be learned from time, experience, and observation, and an acquaintance with men, their tempers, and designs, is not to be expected in the ignorance and inadvertency of childhood, or the inconsiderate heat and unweariness of youth. All that can be done towards it, during this unripe age, is, as I have said, to accustom them to truth and sincerity, to a submission to reason, and as much as may be to reflection on their own actions.

The next good quality belonging to a gentleman is *good breeding*. There are two sorts of ill breeding: the one a sheepish bashfulness, and the other a misbecoming negligence and disrespect in our carriage; both which are avoided by duly observing this one rule, *not to think meanly of ourselves, and not to think meanly of others*.

Keep them from vice and vicious dispositions, and such a kind of behaviour in general will come with every degree of their age, as is suitable to that age and the company they ordinarily converse with; and as they grow in years, they will grow in attention and application. But that your words may always carry weight and authority with them, if it shall happen upon any occasion that you bid him leave off the doing of any even childish things, you must be sure to carry the point, and not let him have the mastery. But yet, I say, I would have the father seldom interpose his authority and command in these cases, or in any other, but such as have a tendency to vicious habits. I think there are better ways of prevailing with them: and a gentle persuasion in reasoning, when the first point of submission to your will is got, will most times do much better.

It will perhaps be wondered that I mention *reasoning* with children; and yet I cannot but think that the true way of dealing with them. They understand it as early as they do language; and, if I misobserve not, they love to be treated as rational creatures sooner than is imagined. 'Tis a pride should be cherished in them, and, as much as can be, made the greatest instrument to turn them by.

But when I talk of reasoning, I do not intend any other but such as is suited to the child's capacity and apprehension. Nobody can think a boy of three or seven years old should be argued with as a grown man. Long discourses and philosophical reasonings, at best, amaze and confound but do not instruct children. When I say, therefore, that they must be *treated as rational creatures,* I mean that you should make them sensible, by the mildness of your carriage, and the composure even in your correction of them, that what you do is reasonable in you, and useful and necessary for them; and that it is not out of *caprichio,* passion, or fancy that you command or forbid them anything. This they are capable of understanding; and there is no virtue they should be excited to nor fault they should be kept from which I do not think they may be convinced of; but it must be by such reasons as their age and understandings are capable of, and those proposed always in very few and plain words.

You will wonder, perhaps, that I put *learning* last, especially if I tell you I think it the least part. This may seem strange in the mouth of a bookish man; and this making usually the chief, if not only bustle and stir about children, this being almost that alone which is thought on, when people talk of education, makes it the greater paradox. When I consider what ado is made about a little Latin and Greek, how many years are spent in it, and what a noise and business it makes to no purpose, I can hardly forbear thinking that the parents of children still live in fear of the schoolmaster's rod, which they look on as the only instrument of education; as a language or two to be its whole business. How else is it possible that a child should be chained to the oar seven, eight, or ten of the best years of his life, to get a language or two, which, I think, might be had at a great deal cheaper rate of pains and time, and be learned almost in playing?

Seventh ed. (London, 1712).

On Reasoning with Children

[FROM *Emile*]

JEAN JACQUES ROUSSEAU

1762

Reasoning should not begin too soon—Locke's great maxim was that we ought to reason with children, and just now this maxim is much in fashion. I think, however, that its success does not warrant its reputation, and I find nothing more stupid than children who have been so much reasoned with. Reason, apparently a compound of all other faculties, the one latest developed, and with most difficulty, is the one proposed as agent in unfolding the faculties earliest used! The noblest work of education is to make a reasoning man, and we expect to train a young child by making him reason! This is beginning at the end; this is making an instrument of a result. If children understood how to reason they would not need to be educated. But by addressing them from their tenderest years in a language they cannot understand, you accustom them to be satisfied with words, to find fault with whatever is said to them, to think themselves as wise as their teachers, to wrangle and rebel. And what we mean they shall do from reasonable motives we are forced to obtain from them by adding the motive of avarice, or of fear, or of vanity.

Nature intends that children shall be children before they are men. If we insist on reversing this order we shall have fruit early indeed, but unripe and tasteless, and liable to early decay; we shall have young savants and old children. Childhood has its own methods of seeing, thinking, and feeling. Nothing shows less sense than to try to substitute our own methods for these. I would rather require a child ten years old to be five feet tall than to be judicious. Indeed, what use would he have at that age for the power to reason? It is a check upon physical strength, and the child needs none.

In attempting to persuade your pupils to obedience you add to this alleged persuasion force and threats, or worse still, flattery and promises. Bought over in this way by interest, or constrained by force, they pretend to be convinced by reason. They see plainly that as soon as you discover obedience or disobedience in their conduct, the former is an advantage and the latter a disadvantage to them. But you ask of them only what is distasteful to them; it is always irksome to carry out the wishes of another, so by stealth they carry out their own. They are sure that if their disobedience is not known they are doing well; but they are ready, for fear of greater evils, to acknowledge, if found out, that they are doing wrong. As the reason for the duty required is beyond their capacity, no one can make them really understand it. But the fear of punishment, the hope of forgiveness, your importunity, their difficulty in answering you, extort from them the confession required of them. You think you have convinced them, when you have only wearied them out or intimidated them.

What results from this? First of all that, by imposing upon them a duty they do not feel as such, you set them against your tyranny, and dissuade them from loving you; you teach them to be dissemblers, deceitful, wilfully untrue, for the sake of extorting rewards or of escaping punishments. Finally, by habituating them to cover a secret motive by an apparent motive, you give them the means of constantly misleading you, of concealing their true character from you, and of satisfying yourself and others with empty words when their occasion demands. You may say that the law, although binding on the conscience, uses constraint in dealing with grown men. I grant it; but what are these men but children spoiled by their education? This is precisely what ought to be prevented. With children use force, with men reason; such is the natural order of things. The wise man requires no laws.

Trans. Eleanor Worthington (Boston: Ginn, Heath & Co., 1883).

POLITICS AND ECONOMICS

❖ ❖ ❖

To Make the Punishment Fit

[FROM *On Crimes and Punishments*]

CESARE BONESANA,
MARCHESE DI BECCARIA

1764

TO THE READER

Some remnants of the laws of an ancient conquering people, which a prince who reigned in Constantinople some twelve hundred years ago caused to be compiled, mixed up afterwards with Lombard rites and packed in the miscellaneous volumes of private and obscure commentators—these are what form that set of traditional opinions which from a great part of Europe receive nevertheless the name of laws; and to this day it is a fact, as disastrous as it is common, that some opinion of Carpzovius, some old custom pointed out by Clarus, or some form of torture suggested in terms of complacent ferocity by Farinaccius, constitute the laws, so carelessly followed by those, who in all trembling ought to exercise their government over the lives and fortunes of men. These laws, the dregs of the most barbarous ages, are examined in this book in so far as regards criminal jurisprudence, and I have dared to expose their faults to the directors of the public happiness in a style which may keep at a distance the unenlightened and intolerant multitude. . . .

There are three sources of the moral and political principles which govern mankind, namely, revelation, natural law, and social conventions. With regard to their principal object there is no comparison between the first and the other two, but they all resemble one another in this, that they all three conduce to the happiness of this present mortal life. To consider the different relations of social conventions is not to exclude those of revelation and natural law; rather it is the thousandfold changes which revelation and natural law, divine and immutable though they be, have undergone in the depraved mind of man, by his own fault, owing to false religions and arbitrary notions of virtue and vice, that make it appear necessary to examine, apart from all other considerations, the result of purely human conventions, expressed or implied, for the public need and welfare: this being an idea in which every sect and every moral system must necessarily agree; and it will always be a laudable endeavour, which seeks to constrain the headstrong and unbelieving to conform to the principles that induce men to live together in society.

There are, then, three distinct kinds of virtue and vice—the religious, the natural, and the political. These three kinds ought never to conflict, although all the consequences and duties that flow from any one of them do not necessarily flow from the others. The natural law does not require all that revelation re-

quires, nor does the purely social law require all that
natural law requires; but it is most important to distinguish the consequences of the conventional law—
that is, of the express or tacit agreements among men—
from the consequences of the natural law or of revelation, because therein lies the limit of that power, which
can rightly be exercised between man and man without a special mandate from the Supreme Being. Consequently the idea of political virtue may, without any
slur upon it, be said to be variable; that of natural
virtue would be always clear and manifest, were it not
obscured by the stupidity or the passions of men;
whilst the idea of religious virtue remains ever one and
the same, because revealed directly from God and by
Him preserved.

It would, therefore, be a mistake to ascribe to one
who only discusses social conventions and their consequences, principles contrary either to natural law or to
revelation, for the reason that he does not discuss them.
It would be a mistake, when he speaks of a state of war
as anterior to a state of society, to understand it in the
sense of Hobbes, as meaning that no obligation nor
duty is prior to the existence of society, instead of understanding it as a fact due to the corruption of human nature and the want of any expressed sanction. It
would be a mistake to impute it as a fault to a writer
who is considering the results of the social compact that
he does not admit them as pre-existent to the formation
of the compact itself.

Divine justice and natural justice are in their essence
immutable and constant, because the relation between
similar things is always the same; but human or political justice, being nothing more than a relation between
a given action and a given state of society, may vary

according as such action becomes necessary or useful to society; nor is such justice easily discernible, save by one who analyzes the complex and very changeable relations of civil combinations. When once these principles, essentially distinct, become confused, there is no more hope of sound reasoning about public matters. It appertains to the theologian to fix the boundaries between the just and the unjust, insofar as regards the intrinsic goodness or wickedness of an act; to fix the relations between the politically just and unjust appertains to the publicist; nor can the one object cause any detriment to the other, when it is obvious how the virtue that is purely political ought to give place to that immutable virtue which emanates from God. . . .

CRIMES AND PENALTIES

The knowledge of the true relations between a sovereign and his subjects, and of those between different nations; the revival of commerce by the light of philosophical truths, diffused by printing; and the silent international war of industry, the most humane and the most worthy of rational men—these are the fruits which we owe to the enlightenment of this century. But how few have examined and combated the cruelty of punishments, and the irregularities of criminal procedures, a part of legislation so elementary and yet so neglected in almost the whole of Europe; and how few have sought, by a return to first principles, to dissipate the mistakes accumulated by many centuries, or to mitigate, with at least that force which belongs only to ascertained truths, the excessive caprice of ill-directed power, which has presented up to this time but one long example of lawful and cold-blooded atrocity! And yet the groans of the weak, sacrificed to the cruelty of the ignorant or to the indolence of the rich; the barbarous tortures, multiplied with a severity as useless as it is prodigal, for crimes either not proved or quite chimerical; the disgusting horrors of a prison, enhanced by that which is the cruelest executioner of the miserable—namely, uncertainty—these ought to startle those rulers whose function it is to guide the opinion of men's minds.

The immortal President, Montesquieu, has treated cursorily of this matter; and truth, which is indivisible, has forced me to follow the luminous footsteps of this great man; but thinking men, for whom I write, will be able to distinguish my steps from his. Happy shall I esteem myself if, like him, I shall succeed in obtaining the secret gratitude of the unknown and peaceable followers of reason, and if I shall inspire them with that pleasing thrill of emotion with which sensitive minds respond to the advocate of the interests of humanity.

To examine and distinguish all the different sorts of crimes and the manner of punishing them would now be our natural task, were it not that their nature, which varies with the different circumstances of times and places, would compel us to enter upon too vast and wearisome a mass of detail. But it will suffice to indicate the most general principles and the most pernicious and common errors, in order to undeceive no less those who, from a mistaken love of liberty, would introduce anarchy, than those who would be glad to reduce their fellow men to the uniform regularity of a convent.

What will be the penalty suitable for such and such crimes?

Is death a penalty really *useful and necessary* for the security and good order of society?

Are torture and torments *just,* and do they attain the *end* which the law aims at?

What is the best way of preventing crimes?

Are the same penalties equally useful in all times?

What influence have they on customs?

These problems deserve to be solved with such geometrical precision as shall suffice to prevail over the clouds of sophistication, over seductive eloquence, or timid doubt. Had I no other merit than that of having been the first to make clearer to Italy that which other nations have dared to write and are beginning to practise, I should deem myself fortunate; but if, in maintaining the rights of men and of invincible truth, I should contribute to rescue from the spasms and agonies of death any unfortunate victim of tyranny or ignorance, both so equally fatal, the blessings and tears of a single innocent man in the transports of his joy would console me for the contempt of mankind.

OATHS

A contradiction between the laws and the natural feelings of mankind arises from the oaths which are required of an accused, to the effect that he will be a truthful man when it is his greatest interest to be false; as if a man could really swear to contribute to his own destruction, or as if religion would not be silent with most men when their interest spoke on the other side. The experience of all ages has shown that men have abused religion more than any other of the precious gifts of heaven; and for what reason should criminals respect it, when men esteemed as the wisest have often violated it? Too weak, because too far removed from the senses, are for the mass of people the motives which religion opposes to the tumult of fear and the love of life. The affairs of heaven are conducted by laws absolutely different from those which govern human affairs; so why compromise those by these? Why place men in the terrible dilemma of either sinning against God or concurring in their own ruin? The law, in fact, which enforces such an oath commands a man either to be a bad Christian or to be a martyr. The oath becomes gradually a mere formality, thus destroying the force of religious feelings, which for the majority of men are the only pledge of their honesty. How useless oaths are has been shown by experience, for every judge will bear me out when I say that no oath has ever yet made any criminal speak the truth; and the same thing is shown by reason, which declares all laws to be useless, and consequently injurious, which are opposed to the natural sentiments of man. Such laws incur the same fate as dams placed directly in the main stream of a river: either they are immediately thrown down and overwhelmed, or a whirlpool formed by themselves corrodes and undermines them imperceptibly.

TORTURE

A cruelty consecrated among most nations by custom is the torture of the accused during his trial, on the pretext of compelling him to confess his crime, of clearing up contradictions in his statements, of discovering his accomplices, of purging him in some metaphysical and incomprehensible way from infamy, or finally of finding out other crimes of which he may possibly be guilty, but of which he is not accused.

A man cannot be called *guilty* before sentence has been passed on him by a judge, nor can society deprive him of its protection till it has been decided that he has broken the condition on which it was granted. What, then, is that right but one of mere might by which a judge is empowered to inflict a punishment on a citizen whilst his guilt or innocence are still undetermined? The following dilemma is no new one: either the crime is certain or uncertan; if certain, no other punishment is suitable for it than that affixed to it by law; and torture is useless, for the same reason that the criminal's confession is useless. If it is uncertain, it is wrong to torture an innocent person, such as the law adjudges him to be, whose crimes are not yet proved.

What is the political object of punishments? The intimidation of other men. But what shall we say of the secret and private tortures which the tyranny of custom exercises alike upon the guilty and the innocent? It is important, indeed, that no open crime shall pass unpunished; but the public exposure of a criminal whose crime was hidden in darkness is utterly useless. An evil that has been done and cannot be undone can only be punished by civil society insofar as it may affect others with the hope of impunity. If it be true that there are a greater number of men who either from fear or virtue respect the laws than of those who transgress them, the risk of torturing an innocent man should be estimated according to the probability that any man will have been more likely, other things being equal, to have respected than to have despised the laws.

But I say in addition: it is to seek to confound all the relations of things to require a man to be at the same time accuser and accused, to make pain the crucible of truth, as if the test of it lay in the muscles and sinews of an unfortunate wretch. The law which ordains the use of torture is a law which says to men: "Resist pain; and if Nature has created in you an inextinguishable self-love, if she has given you an inalienable right of self-defence, I create in you a totally contrary affection, namely, an heroic self-hatred, and I command you to accuse yourselves, and to speak the truth between the laceration of your muscles and the dislocation of your bones."

This infamous crucible of truth is a still-existing monument of that primitive and savage legal system which called trials by fire and boiling water, or the accidental decisions of combat, *judgments of God,* as if the rings of the eternal chain in the control of the First Cause must at every moment be disarranged and put out for the petty institutions of mankind. The only difference between torture and the trial by fire and water is, that the result of the former seems to depend on the will of the accused, and that of the other two on a fact which is purely physical and extrinsic to the sufferer; but the difference is only apparent, not real. The avowal of truth under tortures and agonies is as little free as was in those times the prevention without fraud of the usual effects of fire and boiling water. Every act of our will is ever proportioned to the force of the sensible impression which causes it, and the sensibility of every man is limited. Hence the impression produced by pain may be so intense as to occupy a man's entire sensibility and leave him no other liberty than the choice of the shortest way of escape, for the present moment, from his penalty. Under such circumstances the answer of the accused is as inevitable as the impressions produced by fire and water; and the innocent man who is sensitive will declare himself guilty, when by so doing he hopes to bring his agonies

to an end. All the difference between guilt and innocence is lost by virtue of the very means which they
profess to employ for its discovery.

Torture is a certain method for the acquittal of robust villains and for the condemnation of innocent but
feeble men. See the fatal drawbacks of this pretended
test of truth—a test, indeed, that is worthy of canni-
bals; a test which the Romans, barbarous as they too
were in many respects, reserved for slaves alone, the
victims of their fierce and too highly lauded virtue.
Of two men, equally innocent or equally guilty, the
robust and courageous will be acquitted, the weak and
the timid will be condemned, by virtue of the following exact train of reasoning on the part of the judge:
"I as judge had to find you guilty of such and such a
crime; you, A B, have by your physical strength been
able to resist pain, and therefore I acquit you; you,
C D, in your weakness have yielded to it; therefore I
condemn you. I feel that a confession extorted amid
torments can have no force, but I will torture you
afresh unless you corroborate what you have now confessed."

The result, then, of torture is a matter of temperament, of calculation, which varies with each man
according to his strength and sensibility; so that by
this method a mathematician might solve better than a
judge this problem: "Given the muscular force and
the nervous sensibility of an innocent man, to find the
degree of pain which will cause him to plead guilty
to a given crime."

From *Tratto dei Delitti è delle Pene*, newly trans. in James A.
Farrar, *Crimes and Punishments* (London: Chatto & Windus,
1880).

❖ ❖ ❖

On the Freedom of the Press

[FROM *Areopagitica*]

JOHN MILTON

1644

I deny not but that it is of greatest concernment in the church and commonwealth to have a vigilant eye how books demean themselves, as well as men, and thereafter to confine, imprison, and do sharpest justice on them as malefactors. For books are not absolutely dead things, but do contain a potency of life in them to be as active as that soul was whose progeny they are; nay, they do preserve as in a vial the purest efficacy and extraction of that living intellect that bred them. I know they are as lively, and as vigorously produc-tive, as those fabulous dragon's teeth; and being sown up and down, may chance to spring up armed men. And yet, on the other hand, unless wariness be used, as good almost kill a man as kill a good book: who kills a man kills a reasonable creature, God's image; but he who destroys a good book, kills reason itself, kills the image of God, as it were, in the eye. Many a man lives a burden to the earth; but a good book is the precious life-blood of a master spirit, embalmed and treasured up on purpose to a life beyond life. 'Tis true, no age can restore a life, whereof, perhaps, there is no great loss; and revolutions of ages do not oft recover the loss of a rejected truth, for the want of which whole nations fare the worse. We should be wary, therefore, what persecution we raise against the living labours of public men, how we spill that seasoned life of man preserved and stored up in books; since we see a kind of homicide may be thus committed, sometimes a martyrdom; and if it extend to the whole impression, a kind of massacre, whereof the execution ends not in the slaying of an elemental life, but strikes at that ethereal and fifth essence, the breath of reason itself, slays an immortality rather than a life. . . .

And again, if it be true that a wise man, like a good refiner, can gather gold out of the drossiest volume, and that a fool will be a fool with the best book, yea, or without book, there is no reason that we should deprive a wise man of any advantage to his wisdom, while we seek to restrain from a fool that which, being restrained, will be no hindrance to his folly. For if there should be so much exactness always used to keep that from him which is unfit for his reading, we should, in the judgment of Aristotle not only, but of Solomon and of our Saviour, not vouchsafe him good precepts, and by consequence not willingly admit him to good books; as being certain that a wise man will make better use of an idle pamphlet than a fool will do of sacred Scripture.

'Tis next alleged we must not expose ourselves to temptations without necessity, and next to that, not employ our time in vain things. To both these objections one answer will serve, out of the grounds already laid, that to all men such books are not temptations nor vanities, but useful drugs and materials wherewith to temper and compose effective and strong medicines, which man's life cannot want. The rest, as children and childish men, who have not the art to qualify and prepare these working minerals, well may be exhorted to forbear, but hindered forcibly they cannot be by all the licensing that sainted Inquisition could ever yet contrive. . . .

And lest some should persuade ye, Lords and Commons, that these arguments of learned men's discouragement at this your order are mere flourishes and not real, I could recount what I have seen and heard in other countries where this kind of inquisition tyrannizes, when I have sat among their learned men (for that honour I had), and been counted happy to be born in such a place of philosophic freedom as they supposed England was, while themselves did nothing but bemoan the servile condition into which learning amongst them was brought; that this was it which had damped the glory of Italian wits; that nothing had been there written now these many years but flattery and fustian. There it was that I found and visited the famous Galileo, grown old, a prisoner to the Inquisition, for thinking in astronomy otherwise than the Franciscan and Dominican licensers thought. And though I knew that England then was groaning loudest under the prelatical yoke, nevertheless I took it as a pledge of future happiness that other nations were so persuaded of her liberty.

From *Prose Works* (London: Wm. Ball, 1838).

❖ ❖ ❖

A Tough-Minded View of Power and Nature

[FROM *Leviathan*]

THOMAS HOBBES

1651

Natural power is the eminence of the faculties of body, or mind: as extraordinary strength, form, prudence, arts, eloquence, liberality, nobility. *Instrumental* are those powers which, acquired by these, or by fortune, are means and instruments to acquire more: as riches, reputation, friends, and the secret working of God, which men call good luck. For the nature of power is in this point, like to fame, increasing as it proceeds; or like the motion of heavy bodies, which the further they go, make still the more haste.

The greatest of human powers is that which is compounded of the powers of most men, united by consent, in one person, natural, or civil, that has the use of all their powers depending on his will, such as is the power of a commonwealth: or depending on the wills of each particular; such as is the power of a faction or of divers factions leagued. Therefore to have servants is power; to have friends is power: for they are strengths united.

Also riches joined with liberality is power; because it procureth friends, and servants: without liberality, not so; because in this case they defend not; but expose men to envy, as a prey.

Reputation of power is power; because it draweth with it the adherence of those that need protection.

So is reputation of love of a man's country, called popularity, for the same reason.

Also, what quality soever maketh a man beloved, or feared of many; or the reputation of such quality, is power; because it is a means to have the assistance, and service of many.

Good success is power; because it maketh reputation of wisdom, or good fortune; which makes men either fear him, or rely on him.

Affability of men already in power, is increase of power; because it gaineth love.

Reputation of prudence in the conduct of peace or war is power; because to prudent men we commit the government of ourselves more willingly than to others.

Nobility is power, not in all places, but only in those commonwealths where it has privileges: for in such privileges consisteth their power.

Eloquence is power, because it is seeming prudence.

Form is power; because being a promise of good, it recommendeth men to the favour of women and strangers.

The sciences are small power; because not eminent· and therefore, not acknowledged in any man; nor are at all, but in a few, and in them, but of a few things. For science is of that nature, as none can understand it to be, but such as in a good measure have attained it.

Arts of public use, as fortification, making of engines, and other instruments of war; because they confer to defence, and victory, are power: and though the true mother of them be science, namely the mathematics; yet, because they are brought into the light, by the hand of the artificer, they be esteemed, the midwife passing with the vulgar for the mother, as his issue.

The *value*, or WORTH of a man, is, as of all other things, his price; that is to say, so much as would be given for the use of his power: and therefore is not absolute; but a thing dependent on the need and judgment of another. An able conductor of soldiers is of great price in time of war present, or imminent; but in peace not so. A learned and uncorrupt judge is much worth in time of peace; but not so much in war. And as in other things, so in men, not the seller, but the buyer, determines the price. For let a man, as most men do, rate themselves at the highest value they can; yet their true value is no more than it is esteemed by others.

Nature hath made men so equal, in the faculties of the body, and mind; as that though there be found one man sometimes manifestly stronger in body, or of quicker mind than another; yet when all is reckoned together, the difference between man, and man, is not so considerable, as that one man can thereupon claim to himself any benefit, to which another may not pretend, as well as he. For as to the strength of body, the weakest has strength enough to kill the strongest, either by secret machination, or by confederacy with others, that are in the same danger with himself.

And as to the faculties of the mind, setting aside the arts grounded upon words, and especially that skill of proceeding upon general and infallible rules, called science; which very few have, and but in few things; as being not a native faculty, born with us; nor attained, as prudence, while we look after somewhat else; I find yet a greater equality amongst men than that of strength. For prudence is but experience, which equal time equally bestows on all men, in those things they equally apply themselves unto. That which may perhaps make such equality incredible is but a vain conceit of one's own wisdom, which almost all men think they have in a greater degree than the vulgar; that is, than all men but themselves, and a few others, whom by fame, or for concurring with themselves, they approve. For such is the nature of men that howsoever they may acknowledge many others to be more witty, or more eloquent, or more learned; yet they will hardly believe there be many so wise as themselves; for they see their own wit at hand, and other men's at a distance. But this proveth rather that men are in that point equal, than unequal. For there is not ordinarily a greater sign of the equal distribution of anything, than that every man is contented with his share.

From this equality of ability ariseth equality of hope in the attaining of our ends. And therefore if any two men desire the same thing, which nevertheless they cannot both enjoy, they become enemies; and in the way to their end, which is principally their own conservation, and sometimes their delectation only, endeavour to destroy, or subdue one another. And from hence it comes to pass that where an invader hath no more to fear than another man's single power; if one plant, sow, build, or possess a convenient seat, others may probably be expected to come prepared with forces united, to dispossess, and deprive him, not only of the fruit of his labour, but also of his life, or liberty. And the invader again is in the like danger of another. . . .

Hereby it is manifest that during the time men live

without a common power to keep them all in awe, they are in that condition which is called war; and such a war, as is of every man, against every man. For WAR consisteth not in battle only, or the act of fighting; but in a tract of time, wherein the will to contend by battle is sufficiently known: and therefore the notion of *time* is to be considered in the nature of war; as it is in the nature of weather. For as the nature of foul weather lieth not in a shower or two of rain, but in an inclination thereto of many days together: so the nature of war consisteth not in actual fighting, but in the known disposition thereto, during all the time there is no assurance to the contrary. All other time is PEACE.

Whatsoever therefore is consequent to a time of war, where every man is enemy to every man; the same is consequent to the time, wherein men live without other security than what their own strength, and their own invention shall furnish them withal. In such condition, there is no place for industry; because the fruit thereof is uncertain: and consequently no culture of the earth; no navigation, nor use of the commodities that may be imported by sea; no commodious building; no instruments of moving, and removing, such things as require much force; no knowledge of the face of the earth; no account of time; no arts; no letters; no society; and which is worst of all, continual fear, and danger of violent death; and the life of man, solitary, poor, nasty, brutish, and short.

(Oxford: J. Thornton, 1881.)

❖ ❖ ❖

Property and Society

[FROM *Two Treatises on Government*]

JOHN LOCKE

1690

Whether we consider natural reason, which tells us that men, being once born, have a right to their preservation, and consequently to meat and drink and such other things as Nature affords for their subsistence, or "revelation," which gives us an account of those grants God made of the world to Adam, and to Noah and his sons, it is very clear that God, as King David says (Psalm cxv: 16), "has given the earth to the children of men," given it to mankind in common. But, this being supposed, it seems to some a very great difficulty how anyone should ever come to have a property in anything. I will not content myself to answer, that, if it be difficult to make out "property" upon a supposition that God gave the world to Adam and his posterity in common, it is impossible that any man but one universal monarch should have any "property" upon a supposition that God gave the world to Adam and his heirs in succession, exclusive of all the rest of his posterity; but I shall endeavour to show how men might come to have a property in several parts of that which God gave to mankind in common, and that without any express compact of all the commoners.

God, who hath given the world to men in common,

hath also given them reason to make use of it to the best advantage of life and convenience. The earth and all that is therein is given to men for the support and comfort of their being. And though all the fruits it naturally produces, and beasts it feeds, belong to mankind in common, as they are produced by the spontaneous hand of Nature, and nobody has originally a private dominion exclusive of the rest of mankind in any of them, as they are thus in their natural state, yet being given for the use of men, there must of necessity be a means to appropriate them some way or other before they can be of any use, or at all beneficial, to any particular men. The fruit or venison which nourishes the wild Indian, who knows no enclosure, and is still a tenant in common, must be his, and so his—i.e., a part of him, that another can no longer have any right to it before it can do him any good for the support of his life.

Though the earth and all inferior creatures be common to all men, yet every man has a "property" in his own "person." This nobody has any right to but himself. The "labour" of his body and the "work" of his hands, we may say, are properly his. Whatsoever, then, he removes out of the state that Nature hath provided and left it in, he hath mixed his labour with it, and joined to it something that is his own, and thereby makes it his property. It being by him removed from the common state Nature placed it in, it hath by this labour something annexed to it that excludes the common right of other men. For this "labour" being the unquestionable property of the labourer, no man but he can have a right to what that is once joined to, at least where there is enough, and as good left in common for others.

He that is nourished by the acorns he picked up

under an oak, or the apples he gathered from the trees
in the wood, has certainly appropriated them to himself. Nobody can deny but the nourishment is his. I
ask, then, when did they begin to be his? when he
digested? or when he ate? or when he boiled? or when
he brought them home? or when he picked them up?
And it is plain, if the first gathering made them not
his, nothing else could. That labour put a distinction
between them and common. That added something to
them more than Nature, the common mother of all,
had done, and so they became his private right. And
will anyone say he had no right to those acorns or
apples he thus appropriated because he had not the
consent of all mankind to make them his? Was it a
robbery thus to assume to himself what belonged to
all in common? If such a consent as that was necessary,
man had starved, notwithstanding the plenty God had
given him. We see in commons, which remain so by
compact, that it is the taking any part of what is common, and removing it out of the state Nature leaves it
in, which begins the property, without which the common is of no use. And the taking of this or that part
does not depend on the express consent of all the commoners. Thus, the grass my horse has bit, the turfs my
servant has cut, and the ore I have digged in any place,
where I have a right to them in common with others,
become my property without the assignation or consent
of anybody. The labour that was mine, removing them
out of that common state they were in, hath fixed my
property in them.

By making an explicit consent of every commoner
necessary to anyone's appropriating to himself any part
of what is given in common, children or servants could
not cut the meat which their father or master had provided for them in common without assigning to every-

one his peculiar part. Though the water running in the
fountain be everyone's, yet who can doubt but that in
the pitcher is his only who drew it out? His labour
hath taken it out of the hands of Nature where it was
common, and belonged equally to all her children, and
hath thereby appropriated it to himself.

Thus this law of reason makes the deer that Indian's who hath killed it; it is allowed to be his goods
who hath bestowed his labour upon it, though, before,
it was the common right of everyone. And amongst
those who are counted the civilized part of mankind,
who have made and multiplied positive laws to determine property, this original law of Nature for the beginning of property, in what was before common, still
takes place, and by virtue thereof, what fish anyone
catches in the ocean, that great and still remaining
common of mankind; or what ambergris anyone takes
up here is by the labour that removes it out of that
common state Nature left it in, made his property who
takes that pains about it. And even amongst us, the
hare that anyone is hunting is thought his who pursues
her during the chase. For being a beast that is still
looked upon as common, and no man's private possession, whoever has employed so much labour about any
of that kind as to find and pursue her has thereby removed her from the state of Nature wherein she was
common, and hath begun a property.

It will, perhaps, be objected to this, that if gathering
the acorns or other fruits of the earth, etc., makes a
right to them, then anyone may engross as much as
he will. To which I answer, Not so. The same law of
Nature that does by this means give us property, does
also bound that property too. "God has given us all
things richly." Is the voice of reason confirmed by
inspiration? But how far has He given it us "to enjoy"?

As much as anyone can make use of to any advantage of life before it spoils, so much he may by his labour fix a property in. Whatever is beyond this is more than his share, and belongs to others. Nothing was made by God for man to spoil or destroy. And thus considering the plenty of natural provisions there was a long time in the world, and the few spenders, and to how small a part of that provision the industry of one man could extend itself and engross it to the prejudice of others, especially keeping within the bounds set by reason of what might serve for his use, there could be then little room for quarrels or contentions about property so established.

But the chief matter of property being now not the fruits of the earth and the beasts that subsist on it, but the earth itself, as that which takes in and carries with it all the rest, I think it is plain that property in that too is acquired as the former. As much land as a man tills, plants, improves, cultivates, and can use the product of, so much is his property. He by his labour does, as it were, enclose it from the common. Nor will it invalidate his right to say everybody else has an equal title to it, and therefore he cannot appropriate, he cannot enclose, without the consent of all his fellow commoners, all mankind. God, when He gave the world in common to all mankind, commanded man also to labour, and the penury of his condition required it of him. God and his reason commanded him to subdue the earth—i.e., improve it for the benefit of life and therein lay out something upon it that was his own, his labour. He that, in obedience to this command of God, subdued, tilled, and sowed any part of it, thereby annexed to it something that was his property, which another had no title to, nor could without injury take from him.

Nor was this appropriation of any parcel of land, by

improving it, any prejudice to any other man, since there was still enough and as good left, and more than the yet unprovided could use. So that, in effect, there was never the less left for others because of his enclosure for himself. For he that leaves as much as another can make use of does as good as take nothing at all. Nobody could think himself injured by the drinking of another man, though he took a good draught, who had a whole river of the same water left him to quench his thirst. And the case of land and water, where there is enough of both, is perfectly the same.

God gave the world to men in common, but since He gave it them for their benefit and the greatest conveniencies of life they were capable to draw from it, it cannot be supposed He meant it should always remain common and uncultivated. He gave it to the use of the industrious and rational (and labour was to be his title to it); not to the fancy or covetousness of the quarrelsome and contentious. He that had as good left for his improvement as was already taken up needed not to complain, ought not to meddle with what was already improved by another's labour; if he did it is plain he desired the benefit of another's pains, which he had no right to, and not the ground which God had given him, in common with others, to labour on, and whereof there was as good left as that already possessed, and more than he knew what to do with, or his industry could reach to.

It is true, in land that is common in England or any other country, where there are plenty of people under government who have money and commerce, no one can enclose or appropriate any part without the consent of all his fellow commoners; because this is left common by compact—i.e., by the law of the land, which is not to be violated. And, though it be common in respect of some men, it is not so to all mankind, but is the joint propriety of this country, or this parish. Besides, the remainder, after such enclosure, would not be as good to the rest of the commoners as the whole was, when they could all make use of the whole; whereas in the beginning and first peopling of the great common of the world it was quite otherwise. The law man was under was rather for appropriating. God commanded, and his wants forced him to labour. That was his property, which could not be taken from him wherever he had fixed it. And hence subduing or cultivating the earth and having dominion, we see, are joined together. The one gave title to the other. So that God, by commanding to subdue, gave authority so far to appropriate. And the condition of human life, which requires labour and materials to work on, necessarily introduces private possessions.

The measure of property Nature well set, by the extent of men's labour and the conveniency of life. No man's labour could subdue or appropriate all, nor could his enjoyment consume more than a small part; so that it was impossible for any man, this way, to entrench upon the right of another or acquire to himself a property to the prejudice of his neighbour, who would still have room for as good and as large a possession (after the other had taken out his) as before it was appropriated. Which measure did confine every man's possession to a very moderate proportion, and such as he might appropriate to himself without injury to anybody in the first ages of the world, when men were more in danger to be lost, by wandering from their company, in the then vast wilderness of the earth, than to be straitened for want of room to plant in.

The same measure may be allowed still, without

prejudice to anybody, full as the world seems. For, supposing a man or family, in the state they were at first, peopling of the world by the children of Adam or Noah, let him plant in some inland vacant places of America. We shall find that the possessions he could make himself, upon the measures we have given, would not be very large, nor, even to this day, prejudice the rest of mankind or give them reason to complain or think themselves injured by this man's encroachment, though the race of men have now spread themselves to all the corners of the world, and do infinitely exceed the small number at the beginning. Nay, the extent of ground is of so little value without labour that I have heard it affirmed that in Spain itself a man may be permitted to plough, sow, and reap, without being disturbed, upon land he has no other title to, but only his making use of it. But, on the contrary, the inhabitants think themselves beholden to him who, by his industry on neglected, and consequently waste land, has increased the stock of corn, which they wanted. But be this as it will, which I lay no stress on, this I dare boldly affirm, that the same rule of propriety—viz., that every man should have as much as he could make use of, would hold still in the world, without straitening anybody, since there is land enough in the world to suffice double the inhabitants, had not the invention of money, and the tacit agreement of men to put a value on it, introduced (by consent) larger possessions and a right to them; which, how it has done, I shall by and by show more at large.

This is certain, that in the beginning, before the desire of having more than men needed had altered the intrinsic value of things, which depends only on their usefulness to the life of man, or had agreed that a little piece of yellow metal, which would keep without wasting or decay, should be worth a great piece of flesh or a whole heap of corn, though men had a right to appropriate by their labour, each one to himself, as much of the things of Nature as he could use, yet this could not be much, nor to the prejudice of others, where the same plenty was still left, to those who would use the same industry.

Before the appropriation of land, he who gathered as much of the wild fruit, killed, caught, or tamed as many of the beasts as he could—he that so employed his pains about any of the spontaneous products of Nature as any way to alter them from the state Nature put them in, by placing any of his labour on them, did thereby acquire a propriety in them; but if they perished in his possession without their due use—if the fruits rotted or the venison putrefied before he could spend it, he offended against the common law of Nature, and was liable to be punished: he invaded his neighbour's share, for he had no right farther than his use called for any of them, and they might serve to afford him conveniencies of life.

The same measures governed the possession of land, too. Whatsoever he tilled and reaped, laid up and made use of before it spoiled, that was his peculiar right; whatsoever he enclosed, and could feed and make use of, the cattle and product was also his. But if either the grass of his enclosure rotted on the ground, or the fruit of his planting perished without gathering and laying up, this part of the earth, notwithstanding his enclosure, was still to be looked on as waste, and might be the possession of any other. Thus, at the beginning, Cain might take as much ground as he could till and make it his own land, and yet leave enough to Abel's sheep to feed on: a few acres would serve for both their possessions. But as families increased and industry enlarged their stocks, their possessions enlarged with the need of them; but yet it was commonly without any fixed property in the ground they made use of till they incorporated, settled themselves together, and built cities, and then, by consent, they came in time to set out the bounds of their distinct territories and agree on limits between them and their neighbors, and by laws within themselves settled the properties of those of the same society. . . .

The greatest part of things really useful to the life of man, and such as the necessity of subsisting made the first commoners of the world look after—as it doth the Americans now—are generally things of short duration, such as—if they are not consumed by use—will decay and perish of themselves. Gold, silver, and diamonds are things that fancy or agreement hath put the value on, more than real use and the necessary support of life. Now of those good things which Nature hath provided in common, everyone has a right (as has been said) to as much as he could use, and had a property in all he could effect with his labour; all that his industry could extend to, to alter from the state Nature had put it in, was his. He that gathered a hundred bushels of acorns or apples had thereby a property in them; they were his goods as soon as gathered. He was only to look that he used them before they spoiled, else he took more than his share, and robbed others. And, indeed, it was a foolish thing, as well as dishonest, to hoard up more than he could make use of. If he gave away a part to anybody else, so that it perished not uselessly in his possession, these he also made use of. And if he also bartered away plums that would have rotted in a week, for nuts that would last good for his eating a whole year, he did no injury; he wasted not the common stock; destroyed no part of the portion of goods that belonged to others, so long as nothing perished uselessly in his hands. Again, if he would give his nuts for a piece of metal, pleased with its colour, or exchange his sheep for shells, or wool for a sparkling pebble or a diamond, and keep those by him all his life, he invaded not the right of others; he might heap up as much of these durable things as he pleased; the exceeding of the bounds of his just property not lying in the largeness of his possession, but the perishing of anything uselessly in it.

And thus came in the use of money; some lasting thing that men might keep without spoiling, and that, by mutual consent, men would take in exchange for the truly useful but perishable supports of life.

And as different degrees of industry were apt to give men possessions in different proportions, so this invention of money gave them the opportunity to continue and enlarge them. For supposing an island, separate from all possible commerce with the rest of the world, wherein there were but a hundred families, but there were sheep, horses, and cows, with other useful animals, wholesome fruits, and land enough for corn for a hundred thousand times as many, but nothing in the island, either because of its commonness or perishableness, fit to supply the place of money: what reason could anyone have there to enlarge his possessions beyond the use of his family, and a plentiful supply to its consumption, either in what their own industry produced, or they could barter for like perishable, useful commodities with others? Where there is not something both lasting and scarce, and so valuable to be hoarded up, there men will not be apt to enlarge their possessions of land, were it never so rich, never so free for them to take. For I ask, what would a man value ten thousand or a hundred thousand acres of excellent land, ready cultivated and well stocked, too, with cattle, in the middle of the inland parts of America, where he had no hopes of commerce with other parts of the world, to draw money to him by the sale of the product? It would not be worth the enclosing, and we should see him give up again to the wild common of Nature whatever was more than would supply the conveniencies of life, to be had there for him and his family.

Thus, in the beginning, all the world was America, and more so than that is now; for no such thing as money was anywhere known. Find out something that hath the use and value of money amongst his neighbours, you shall see the same man will begin presently to enlarge his possessions.

But since gold and silver, being little useful to the life of man, in proportion to food, raiment, and carriage, has its value only from the consent of men—whereof labour yet makes in great part the measure—it is plain that the consent of men have agreed to a disproportionate and unequal possession of the earth —I mean out of the bounds of society and compact; for in governments the laws regulate it; they having, by consent, found out and agreed in a way how a man may, rightfully and without injury, possess more than he himself can make use of by receiving gold and silver, which may continue long in a man's possession without decaying for the overplus, and agreeing those metals should have a value.

And thus, I think, it is very easy to conceive, without any difficulty, how labour could at first begin a title of property in the common things of Nature, and how the spending it upon our uses bounded it; so that there could then be no reason of quarrelling about title, nor any doubt about the largeness of possession it gave.

Right and conveniency went together. For as a man had a right to all he could employ his labour upon, so he had no temptation to labour for more than he could make use of. This left no room for controversy about the title, nor for encroachment on the right of others. What portion a man carved to himself was easily seen; and it was useless, as well as dishonest, to carve himself too much, or take more than he needed. . . .

Man being born, as has been proved, with a title to perfect freedom and an uncontrolled enjoyment of all the rights and privileges of the law of Nature, equally with any other man, or number of men in the world, has by nature a power not only to preserve his property —that is, his life, liberty, and estate, against the injuries and attempts of other men, but to judge of and punish the breaches of that law in others, as he is persuaded the offence deserves, even with death itself, in crimes where the heinousness of the fact, in his opinion, requires it. But because no political society can be, nor subsist, without having in itself the power to preserve the property, and in order thereunto punish the offences of all those of that society, there, and there only, is political society where every one of the members has quitted this natural power, resigned it up into the hands of the community in all cases that exclude him not from appealing for protection to the law established by it. And thus all private judgment of every particular member being excluded, the community comes to be umpire, and by understanding indifferent rules and men authorized by the community for their execution, decides all the differences that may happen between any members of that society concerning any matter of right, and punishes those offences which any member hath committed against the society with such penalties as the law has established; whereby it is easy to discern who are, and are not, in political society together. Those who are united into one body, and have a common established law and judicature to appeal to, with authority to decide controversies between them and punish offenders, are in civil society one with another; but those who have no such common appeal, I mean on earth, are still in the state of Nature, each being, where there is no other, judge for himself and executioner; which is, as I have before showed it, the perfect state of Nature.

And thus the commonwealth comes by a power to set down what punishment shall belong to the several transgressions they think worthy of it, committed amongst the members of that society (which is the power of making laws), as well as it has the power to punish any injury done unto any of its members by anyone that is not of it (which is the power of war and peace); and all this for the preservation of the property of all the members of that society, as far as is possible. But though every man entered into society has quitted his power to punish offences against the law of Nature in prosecution of his own private judgment, yet with the judgment of offences which he has given up to the legislative, in all cases where he can appeal to the magistrate, he has given up a right to the commonwealth to employ his force for the execution of the judgments of the commonwealth whenever he shall be called to it, which, indeed, are his own judgments, they being made by himself or his representative. And herein we have the original of the legislative and executive power of civil society, which is to judge by standing laws how far offences are to be punished when committed within the commonwealth; and also by occasional judgments founded on the present circumstances of the fact, how far injuries from without are to be vindicated, and in both these to employ all the force of all the members when there shall be need.

Wherever, therefore, any number of men so unite into one society as to quit every one his executive power of the law of Nature, and to resign it to the public, there and there only is a political or civil society. And this is done wherever any number of men, in the state of Nature, enter into society to make one people one body politic under one supreme government: or else when anyone joins himself to, and incorporates with any government already made. For hereby he authorizes the society, or which is all one, the legislative thereof, to make laws for him as the public good of the society shall require, to the execution whereof his own assistance (as to his own decrees) is due. And this puts men out of a state of Nature into that of a commonwealth, by setting up a judge on earth with authority to determine all the controversies and redress the injuries that may happen to any member of the commonwealth, which judge is the legislative or magistrates appointed by it. And wherever there are any number of men, however associated, that have no such decisive power to appeal to, there they are still in the state of Nature.

And hence it is evident that absolute monarchy, which by some men is counted for the only government in the world, is indeed inconsistent with civil society, and so can be no form of civil government at all. For the end of civil society being to avoid and remedy those inconveniencies of the state of Nature which necessarily follow from every man's being judge in his own case, by setting up a known authority to which every one of that society may appeal upon any injury received, or controversy that may arise, and which every one of

the society ought to obey. Wherever any persons are
who have not such an authority to appeal to, and decide any difference between them there, those persons
are still in the state of Nature. And so is every absolute
prince in respect of those who are under his dominion.

For he being supposed to have all, both legislative
and executive, power in himself alone, there is no
judge to be found, no appeal lies open to anyone, who
may fairly and indifferently, and with authority decide,
and from whence relief and redress may be expected
of any injury or inconveniency that may be suffered
from him, or by his order. So that such a man, however entitled, Czar, or Grand Signior, or how you
please, is as much in the state of Nature, with all under
his dominion, as he is with the rest of mankind. For
wherever any two men are, who have no standing rule
and common judge to appeal to on earth, for the determination of controversies of right betwixt them, there
they are still in the state of Nature, and under all the
inconveniencies of it, with only this woeful difference
to the subject, or rather slave of an absolute prince.
That whereas, in the ordinary state of Nature, he has a
liberty to judge of his right, according to the best of
his power to maintain it; but whenever his property is
invaded by the will and order of his monarch, he has
not only no appeal, as those in society ought to have,
but, as if he were degraded from the common state
of rational creatures, is denied a liberty to judge of,
or defend his right, and so is exposed to all the misery
and inconveniencies that a man can fear from one,
who being in the unrestrained state of Nature, is yet
corrupted with flattery and armed with power.

For he that thinks absolute power purifies men's
blood, and corrects the baseness of human nature, need
read but the history of this, or any other age, to be

convinced to the contrary. He that would have been insolent and injurious in the woods of America would not probably be much better on a throne, where perhaps learning and religion shall be found out to justify all that he shall do to his subjects, and the sword presently silence all those that dare question it. For what the protection of absolute monarchy is, what kind of fathers of their countries it makes princes to be, and to what a degree of happiness and security it carries civil society, where this sort of government is grown to perfection, he that will look into the late relation of Ceylon may easily see.

(London: R. Butler, 1821.)

❖ ❖ ❖

The State of Nature

[FROM "A Dissertation on the Origin and Foundation of the Inequality of Mankind"]

JEAN JACQUES ROUSSEAU

1754

I don't think I have any contradiction to fear, in allowing man to be possessed of the only natural virtue, which could not be denied him by the most violent declaimer against human virtues. I mean that of compassion; a disposition suitable to creatures so weak, and subject to so many evils as we certainly are: a virtue by so much the more universal and useful to mankind, as it takes place of all manner of reflection; and at the same time so natural, that the very brutes themselves give sometimes evident proofs of it. Not to mention the tenderness of mothers for their offspring; and of the perils they will themselves encounter to save their young from danger: it is well known that horses show a reluctance to trample on living bodies; that one animal never passes by the dead carcass of another of the same species without being sensibly affected: nay, there are even some who give their fellow brutes a kind of burial; while the mournful lowings of the cattle when they enter the slaughter house, sufficiently publish the impressions made on them by the horrid spectacle with which they are struck. We find, with pleasure, the author of the *Fable of the Bees* obliged to own that man is a compassionate and sensible being; and to lay aside his phlegm and subtlety of style, in the example he gives us, to present us with the pathetic description of a man who, from a place of confinement, is compelled to behold a wild beast tear a child from the arms of its mother, grinding its tender limbs with its murdering teeth, and dragging out its palpitating entrails with its claws. What horrid agitations must not the eye-witness of so shocking a scene experience, although not personally concerned! What anxiety must he not suffer at not being able to give any assistance to the fainting mother and expiring infant!

Such is the pure emotion of nature prior to all kinds of reflection! Such the force of natural compassion, which the greatest depravity of manners hath as yet hardly been able to destroy! for we daily find at our theatrical exhibitions, that those very men are affected and sympathize with the unfortunate, nay shed tears at their sufferings, who, if in the tyrant's place, would probably add to the torments of their enemies. Mandeville well knew that, in spite of all our morality, men would have never been otherwise than monsters, had not nature bestowed on them a sense of compassion, in aid of their reason: but he did not see that from this quality alone flowed all those social virtues, of which he disputed man's being in possession. In fact, what is generosity, clemency or humanity, but compassion applied to the weak, to the guilty, or to mankind in general? Nay, even benevolence and friendship, if we judge rightly, will appear to be only the effects of compassion, constantly exerted towards a particular object: for to wish that another person may not suffer pain and uneasiness, what is it less than to wish him happy? Were it even true, as is pretended by some, that pity is no more than a sentiment, which puts us in the place of the suffering object; a sentiment obscure though lively in a savage, developed though feeble in civilized man; this truth would have no other effect than to confirm my argument. Our compassion must, in fact, be so much the more strong, the more intimately the animal, beholding any kind of distress, takes part, or identifies himself with the animal that suffers. Now, it is plain that such identification must have been much more perfect in a state of nature than it is in a state of reason. It is reason that engenders self-love, and it is reflection that cultivates and confirms it: it is that which makes man shrink into himself; it is that which makes him keep at a distance from everything that may disturb or afflict him. It is philosophy that detaches him from the rest of the world; that bids him exultingly say to himself, at sight of the misfortunes of others, You may perish if you will, I am secure.

The first person, who, having inclosed a piece of ground, bethought himself of saying *This is mine,* and found people simple enough to believe him, was the real founder of civil society. From how many crimes, battles and murders, from how many horrors and misfortunes would not that man have saved mankind, who should have pulled up the stakes, or filled up the ditch, crying out to his fellows, "Beware of listening to this impostor; you are undone if you once forget that the fruits of the earth belong to us all, and that the earth itself belongs to nobody." But there is great probability that things were arrived to such a pitch, that they could no longer continue in the same state: for this idea of property depends so much on prior ideas, which could only be successively acquired, that it could not be suggested all at once to the human mind. Mankind must have made a very considerable progress, they must have amassed a great stock of knowledge and industry; which they must also have transmitted and increased from age to age, before they arrived at this last term of a state of nature.

Thus have I endeavoured to trace the origin and display the progress of the inequality of mankind; with the institution and abuse of political societies, as far as these things are capable of being deduced from the nature of man merely by the light of reason, and independent of those sacred tenets which give the sanction of divine right to sovereign authority. The inferences which may be drawn from a view of this exhibition, are, *first*, that as there is hardly any inequality among men in a state of nature, all the inequality which now prevails, owes its strength and growth to the development of our faculties and the improvement of our understanding; becoming at length permanent and lawful by the establishment of property and the institution of laws. *Secondly*, it follows that a moral inequality, authorized by any right merely arbitrary, clashes with natural right, as often as it does not combine in the same proportion as physical inequality; a distinction which determines sufficiently what we ought to think of that species of inequality which prevails in all civilized countries; since it is plainly contrary to the law of nature that infants should command old men, fools conduct philosophers, and that the privileged few should gorge themselves with superfluities, while the starving multitude are in want of the common necessaries of life.

From *The Miscellaneous Works of Mr. J. J. Rousseau* (London: T. Becket and P. A. De Hondt, 1767).

❖ ❖ ❖

Forcing a Man to Be Free

[FROM *The Social Contract*]

JEAN JACQUES ROUSSEAU

1762

We will suppose that men in a state of nature are arrived at that crisis, when the strength of each individual is insufficient to defend him from the attacks he is subject to. This primitive state can therefore subsist no longer; and the human race must perish, unless they change their manner of life.

As men cannot create for themselves new forces, but merely unite and direct those which already exist, the only means they can employ for their preservation is to form by aggregation an assemblage of forces that may be able to resist all assaults, be put in motion as one body, and act in concert upon all occasions.

This assemblage of forces must be produced by the concurrence of many: and as the force and the liberty of a man are the chief instruments of his preservation, how can he engage them without danger, and without neglecting the care which is due to himself? This doubt, which leads directly to my subject, may be expressed in these words:

"Where shall we find a form of association which will defend and protect with the whole aggregate force the person and the property of each individual; and by which every person, while united with ALL, shall obey only HIMSELF, and remain as free as before the union?" Such is the fundamental problem, of which the *Social Contract* gives the solution.

The articles of this contract are so unalterably fixed by the nature of the act, that the least modification renders them vain and of no effect. They are the same everywhere, and are everywhere understood and admitted, even though they may never have been formally announced: so that, when once the social pact is violated in any instance, all the obligations it created cease; and each individual is restored to his original rights, and resumes his native liberty, as the consequence of losing that conventional liberty for which he exchanged them.

All the articles of the social contract will, when clearly understood, be found reducible to this single point—*the total alienation of each associate, and all his rights, to the whole community.* For every individual gives himself up entirely—the condition of every person is alike; and being so, it would not be the interest of any one to render himself offensive to others.

Nay, more than this—the alienation is made without any reserve; the union is as complete as it can be, and no associate has a claim to anything: for if any individual was to retain rights not enjoyed in general by all, as there would be no common superior to decide between him and the public, each person being in some points his own proper judge, would soon pretend to be so in everything; and thus would the state of nature be revived, and the association become tyrannical or be annihilated.

In fine, each person gives himself to ALL, but not to any INDIVIDUAL: and as there is no one associate over whom the same right is not acquired which is ceded to him by others, each gains an equivalent for what he loses, and finds his force increased for preserving that which he possesses.

If, therefore, we exclude from the social compact all that is not essentially necessary, we shall find it reduced to the following terms:

"We each of us place, in common, his person, and all his power, under the supreme direction of the general will; and we receive into the body each member as an indivisible part of the whole."

From that moment, instead of so many separate persons as there are contractors, this act of association produces a moral collective body, composed of as many members as there are voices in the assembly; which from this act receives its unity, its common self, its life, and its will. This public person, which is thus formed by the union of all the private persons, took formerly the name of *city*,* and now takes that of

---

* The true sense of this word is almost entirely lost amongst the moderns. The name of *city* is now generally used to signify a corporate town, and that of *citizen* applied to a burgess of such a corporation. Men do not seem to

republic or *body politic*. It is called by its members *state* when it is passive, and *sovereign* when in activity: and whenever it is spoken of with other bodies of a similar kind, it is denominated *power*. The associates take collectively the name of *people*, and separately that of *citizens*, as participating in the sovereign authority; they are also styled *subjects*, because they are subjected to the laws. But these terms are frequently confounded, and used one for the other; and a man must understand them well to distinguish when they are properly employed.

It is necessary to observe here, that the will of the public, expressed by a majority of votes, which can enforce obedience from the subjects to the sovereign power, in consequence of the double character under

---

know that *houses* make a *town*, and *citizens* a *city*. The Carthaginians once paid dear for a mistake of this kind.

I have never seen it mentioned that the title of *civis* was ever given to the subjects of any prince; not even to the Macedonians formerly, or to the English at present, although their government approaches nearer to a free one than that of any other people. The French alone use the name of *citizen* familiarly to all, because they have no true idea of it, as appears by their dictionaries: and without knowing its meaning they are in danger of falling into the crime of lese majesty, by usurping the title which they have no pretension to. The word *citizen* with them means a power, and not a right: and Bodin made a very gross mistake, when, in speaking of *citizens* and *burgesses*, he mistook the one for the other. M. d'Alembert was better acquainted with the meaning of these terms, and under the article *Geneve* he has very properly marked the difference between the four orders of men (indeed I may say five, by including the foreigners) which are found there; and of which, two orders only compose the republic. No other French author that I know of has comprehended the true sense of the word *citizen*. [Rousseau's note.]

which the members of that body appear, cannot bind the sovereign power to itself; and that it is against the nature of the body politic for the sovereign power to impose any one law which it cannot alter. Were they to consider themselves as acting under one character only, they would be in the situation of individuals forming each a contract with himself: but this is not the case; and therefore there can be no fundamental obligatory law established for the body of the people, not even the social contract. But this is of little moment, as that body could not very well engage itself to others in any manner which would not derogate from the contract. With respect to foreigners, it becomes a single being, an individual only.

The sovereign power being formed only of the individuals which compose it, neither has, or can have, any interest contrary to theirs; consequently the sovereign power requires no guarantee towards its subjects, because it is impossible that the body should seek to injure all its members: and we shall see presently that it can do no injury to any individual. The sovereign power, by its nature, must, while it exists, be everything it ought to be: but it is not so with subjects towards the sovereign power; to which, notwithstanding the common interest subsisting between them, there is nothing to answer for the performance of their engagements, if some means is not found of ensuring their fidelity.

In fact, each individual may, as a man, have a private will, dissimilar or contrary to the general will which he has as a citizen. His own particular interest may dictate to him very differently from the common interest; his mind, naturally and absolutely independent, may regard what he owes to the common cause as a gratuitous contribution, the omission of which would be less injurious to others than the payment would be burthensome to himself; and considering the moral person which constitutes the state as a creature of the imagination, because it is not a man, he may wish to enjoy the rights of a citizen, without being disposed to fulfil the duties of a subject: an injustice which would in its progress cause the ruin of the body politic.

In order therefore to prevent the social compact from becoming a vain form, it tacitly comprehends this engagement, which alone can give effect to the others —that whoever refuses to obey the general will, shall be compelled to it by the whole body, which is in fact only forcing him to be free; for this is the condition which guarantees his absolute personal independence to every citizen of the country: a condition which gives motion and effect to the political machine; which alone renders all civil engagements legal; and without which they would be absurd, tyrannical, and subject to the most enormous abuses.

From *An Inquiry into the Nature of the Social Contract*, trans. from the French of John James Rousseau (London: Robinson, 1791).

❖ ❖ ❖

A Realistic View
of Clashing Interests

[*The Federalist No.* 10]

JAMES MADISON

1787

Among the numerous advantages promised by a well-constructed Union, none deserves to be more accurately developed than its tendency to break and control the violence of faction. The friend of popular governments never finds himself so much alarmed for their character and fate, as when he contemplates their propensity to this dangerous vice. He will not fail, therefore, to set a due value on any plan which, without violating the principles to which he is attached, provides a proper cure for it. The instability, injustice, and confusion introduced into the public councils, have, in truth, been the mortal diseases under which popular governments have everywhere perished; as they continue to be the favourite and fruitful topics from which the adversaries to liberty derive their most specious declamations. The valuable improvements made by the American constitutions on the popular models, both ancient and modern, cannot certainly be too much admired; but it would be an unwarrantable partiality, to contend that they have as effectually obviated the danger on this side, as was wished and expected. Complaints are everywhere heard from our most considerate and virtuous citizens, equally the friends of public and private faith, and of public and personal liberty, that our governments are too unstable, that the public good is disregarded in the conflicts of rival parties, and that measures are too often decided, not according to the rules of justice and the rights of the minor party, but by the superior force of an interested and overbearing majority. However anxiously we may wish that these complaints had no foundation, the evidence of known facts will not permit us to deny that they are in some degree true. It will be found, indeed, on a candid review of our situation, that some of the distresses under which we labour have been erroneously charged on the operation of our governments; but it will be found, at the same time, that other causes will not alone account for many of our heaviest misfortunes; and, particularly, for that prevailing and increasing distrust of public engagements, and alarm for private rights, which are echoed from one end of the continent to the other. These must be chiefly, if not wholly, effects of the unsteadiness and injustice with which a factious spirit has tainted our public administrations.

By a faction, I understand a number of citizens, whether amounting to a majority or minority of the whole, who are united and actuated by some common impulse of passion, or of interest, adverse to the rights of other citizens, or to the permanent and aggregate interests of the community.

There are two methods of curing the mischiefs of faction: the one, by removing its causes; the other, by controlling its effects.

There are again two methods of removing the causes of faction: the one, by destroying the liberty which is essential to its existence; the other, by giving to every citizen the same opinions, the same passions, and the same interests.

It could never be more truly said than of the first remedy, that it was worse than the disease. Liberty is to faction what air is to fire, an aliment without which it instantly expires. But it could not be less folly to abolish liberty, which is essential to political life, because it nourishes faction, than it would be to wish the annihilation of air, which is essential to animal life, because it imparts to fire its destructive agency.

The second expedient is as impracticable as the first would be unwise. As long as the reason of man continues fallible, and he is at liberty to exercise it, different opinions will be formed. As long as the connection subsists between his reason and his self-love, his opinions and his passions will have a reciprocal influence on each other; and the former will be objects to which the latter will attach themselves. The diversity in the faculties of men, from which the rights of property originate, is not less an insuperable obstacle to a uniformity of interests. The protection of these faculties is the first object of government. From the protection of different and unequal faculties of acquiring property, the possession of different degrees and kinds of property immediately results; and from the influence of these on the sentiments and views of the respective proprietors, ensues a division of the society into different interests and parties.

The latent causes of faction are thus sown in the nature of man; and we see them everywhere brought into different degrees of activity, according to the different circumstances of civil society. A zeal for different opinions concerning religion, concerning government, and many other points, as well of speculation as of practice; an attachment to different leaders ambitiously contending for pre-eminence and power; or to persons of other descriptions whose fortunes have been interesting to the human passions, have, in turn, divided mankind into parties, inflamed them with mutual animosity, and rendered them much more disposed to vex and oppress each other than to co-operate for their common good. So strong is this propensity of mankind to fall into mutual animosities, that where no substantial occasion presents itself, the most frivolous and fanciful distinctions have been sufficient to kindle their unfriendly passions and excite their most violent conflicts. But the most common and durable source of factions has been the various and unequal distribution of property. Those who hold and those who are without property have ever formed distinct interests in society. Those who are creditors, and those who are debtors, fall under a like discrimination. A landed interest, a manufacturing interest, a mercantile interest, a moneyed interest, with many lesser interests, grow up of necessity in civilized nations, and divide them into different classes, actuated by different sentiments and views. The regulation of these various and interfering interests forms the principal task of modern legislation, and involves the spirit of party and faction in the necessary and ordinary operations of the government.

No man is allowed to be a judge in his own cause, because his interest would certainly bias his judgment, and, not improbably, corrupt his integrity. With equal, nay with greater reason, a body of men are unfit to be both judges and parties at the same time; yet what are many of the most important acts of legislation, but so many judicial determinations, not indeed concerning the rights of single persons, but concerning the rights of large bodies of citizens? And what are the different classes of legislators but advocates and parties to the causes which they determine? Is a law proposed concerning private debts? It is a question to which the creditors are parties on one side and the debtors on the other. Justice ought to hold the balance between them. Yet the parties are, and must be, themselves the judges; and the most numerous party, or, in other words, the most powerful faction must be expected to prevail. Shall domestic manufactures be encouraged, and in what degree, by restrictions on foreign manufactures? are questions which would be differently decided by the landed and the manufacturing classes, and probably by neither with a sole regard to justice and the public good. The apportionment of taxes on the various descriptions of property is an act which seems to require the most exact impartiality; yet there is, perhaps, no legislative act in which greater opportunity and temptation are given to a predominant party to trample on the rules of justice. Every shilling with which they overburden the inferior number, is a shilling saved to their own pockets.

It is in vain to say that enlightened statesmen will be able to adjust these clashing interests, and render them all subservient to the public good. Enlightened statesmen will not always be at the helm. Nor, in many cases, can such an adjustment be made at all without taking into view indirect and remote considerations, which will rarely prevail over the immediate interest which one party may find in disregarding the rights of another or the good of the whole.

The inference to which we are brought is, that the *causes* of faction cannot be removed, and that relief is only to be sought in the means of controlling its *effects*.

If a faction consists of less than a majority, relief is supplied by the republican principle, which enables the majority to defeat its sinister views by regular vote.

It may clog the administration, it may convulse the society; but it will be unable to execute and mask its violence under the forms of the Constitution. When a majority is included in a faction, the form of popular government, on the other hand, enables it to sacrifice to its ruling passion or interest both the public good and the rights of other citizens. To secure the public good and private rights against the danger of such a faction, and at the same time to preserve the spirit and the form of popular government, is then the great object to which our inquiries are directed. Let me add that it is the great desideratum by which this form of government can be rescued from the opprobrium under which it has so long laboured, and be recommended to the esteem and adoption of mankind.

By what means is this object attainable? Evidently by one of two only. Either the existence of the same passion or interest in a majority at the same time must be prevented, or the majority, having such co-existent passion or interest, must be rendered, by their number and local situation, unable to concert and carry into effect schemes of oppression. If the impulse and the opportunity be suffered to coincide, we well know that neither moral nor religious motives can be relied on as an adequate control. They are not found to be such on the injustice and violence of individuals, and lose their efficacy in proportion to the number combined together, that is, in proportion as their efficacy becomes needful.

From this view of the subject it may be concluded that a pure democracy, by which I mean a society consisting of a small number of citizens, who assemble and administer the government in person, can admit of no cure for the mischiefs of faction. A common passion or interest will, in almost every case, be felt by a majority of the whole; a communication and concert result from the form of government itself; and there is nothing to check the inducements to sacrifice the weaker party or an obnoxious individual. Hence it is that such democracies have ever been spectacles of turbulence and contention; have ever been found incompatible with personal security or the rights of property; and have in general been as short in their lives as they have been violent in their deaths. Theoretic politicians, who have patronized this species of government, have erroneously supposed that by reducing mankind to a perfect equality in their political rights, they would, at the same time, be perfectly equalized and assimilated in their possessions, their opinions, and their passions.

A republic, by which I mean a government in which the scheme of representation takes place, opens a different prospect, and promises the cure for which we are seeking. Let us examine the points in which it varies from pure democracy, and we shall comprehend both the nature of the cure and the efficacy which it must derive from the Union.

The two great points of difference between a democracy and a republic are: first, the delegation of the government, in the latter, to a small number of citizens elected by the rest; secondly, the greater number of citizens, and greater sphere of country, over which the latter may be extended.

The effect of the first difference is, on the one hand, to refine and enlarge the public views, by passing them through the medium of a chosen body of citizens, whose wisdom may best discern the true interest of their country, and whose patriotism and love of justice will be least likely to sacrifice it to temporary or partial considerations. Under such a regulation, it may well happen that the public voice, pronounced by the repre-

sentatives of the people, will be more consonant to the
public good than if pronounced by the people themselves, convened for the purpose. On the other hand,
the effect may be inverted. Men of factious tempers,
of local prejudices, or of sinister designs, may, by intrigue, by corruption, or by other means, first obtain
the suffrages, and then betray the interests, of the
people. The question resulting is, whether small or
extensive republics are more favourable to the election
of proper guardians of the public weal; and it is clearly
decided in favour of the latter by two obvious considerations:

In the first place, it is to be remarked that, however
small the republic may be, the representatives must be
raised to a certain number, in order to guard against
the cabals of a few; and that, however large it may be,
they must be limited to a certain number, in order to
guard against the confusion of a multitude. Hence, the
number of representatives in the two cases not being
in proportion to that of the two constituents, and being
proportionally greater in the small republic, it follows
that, if the proportion of fit characters be not less in
the large than in the small republic, the former will
present a greater option, and consequently a greater
probability of a fit choice.

In the next place, as each representative will be
chosen by a greater number of citizens in the large
than in the small republic, it will be more difficult for
unworthy candidates to practise with success the vicious
arts by which elections are too often carried; and the
suffrages of the people being more free, will be more
likely to centre in men who possess the most attractive
merit and the most diffusive and established characters.

It must be confessed that in this, as in most other
cases, there is a mean, on both sides of which incon-

veniences will be found to lie. By enlarging too much the number of electors, you render the representatives too little acquainted with all their local circumstances and lesser interests; as by reducing it too much, you render him unduly attached to these, and too little fit to comprehend and pursue great and national objects. The federal Constitution forms a happy combination in this respect; the great and aggregate interests being referred to the national, the local and particular to the State legislatures.

The other point of difference is, the greater number of citizens and extent of territory which may be brought within the compass of republican than of democratic government; and it is this circumstance principally which renders factious combinations less to be dreaded in the former than in the latter. The smaller the society, the fewer probably will be the distinct parties and interests composing it; the fewer the distinct parties and interests, the more frequently will a majority be found of the same party; and the smaller the number of individuals composing a majority, and the smaller the compass within which they are placed, the more easily will they concert and execute their plans of oppression. Extend the sphere, and you take in a greater variety of parties and interests; you make it less probable that a majority of the whole will have a common motive to invade the rights of other citizens; or if such a common motive exists, it will be more difficult for all who feel it to discover their own strength, and to act in unison with each other. Besides other impediments, it may be remarked that, where there is a consciousness of unjust or dishonourable purposes, communication is always checked by distrust in proportion to the number whose concurrence is necessary.

Hence, it clearly appears, that the same advantage

which a republic has over a democracy, in controlling the effects of faction, is enjoyed by a large over a small republic—is enjoyed by the Union over the States composing it. Does the advantage consist in the substitution of representatives whose enlightened views and virtuous sentiments render them superior to local prejudices and to schemes of injustice? It will not be denied that the representation of the Union will be most likely to possess these requisite endowments. Does it consist in the greater security afforded by a greater variety of parties, against the event of any one party being able to outnumber and oppress the rest? In an equal degree does the increased variety of parties comprised within the Union, increase this security. Does it, in fine, consist in the greater obstacles opposed to the concert and accomplishment of the secret wishes of an unjust and interested majority? Here, again, the extent of the Union gives it the most palpable advantage.

The influence of factious leaders may kindle a flame within their particular States, but will be unable to spread a general conflagration through the other States. A religious sect may degenerate into a political faction in a part of the Confederacy; but the variety of sects dispersed over the entire face of it must secure the national councils against any danger from that source. A rage for paper money, for an abolition of debts, for an equal division of property, or for any other improper or wicked project, will be less apt to pervade the whole body of the Union than a particular member of it; in the same proportion as such a malady is more likely to taint a particular country or district, than an entire State.

In the extent and proper structure of the Union therefore, we behold a republican remedy for the dis eases most incident to republican government. And according to the degree of pleasure and pride we feel in being republicans, ought to be our zeal in cherishing the spirit and supporting the character of Federalists.

PUBLIUS

From *Selections from THE FEDERALIST*, ed. Henry S. Commager (New York: Appleton-Century-Crofts, 1949; a Crofts Classic).

❖ ❖ ❖

The Physiocratic Formula

[*General Rules for the Economic Government of an Agricultural Kingdom*]

FRANÇOIS QUESNAY

1758

1. Sovereign authority should be exercised by one; it should be superior to all members of society and above the unjust aspirations of private interests, for the object of rulership and of obedience is the security and the protection of the legitimate interests of all. The principle of the separation of power through a system of checks and balances is a sinister idea which can only lead to discord among the great and to the oppression of the small. The division of society into different groups of citizens in such a way that one group exercises sovereign authority over the others is in opposition to the national interest, and tends to give rise to conflicts between the private interests of different classes of

citizens: such division would invert the system of government of an agricultural kingdom which has to unite all interests in a supreme end—namely, the prosperity of agriculture, which is the source of all wealth of the nation as well as that of all citizens.

II. The nation should be instructed in the general laws of the natural order, which for obvious reasons constitutes the most perfect order. The study of human jurisprudence is not at all sufficient to produce capable statesmen; those who devote themselves to public administration must be instructed also in the principles of the natural order, which is most advantageous to men organized in society. Moreover, it is necessary that the sum total of the practical and enlightened knowledge which the nation acquires through experience and reflection be added to the general science of government, so that sovereign authority, always guided by .evidence, may decree the best possible laws and see to it that they are observed in the interest of the security of all and in order to achieve the greatest possible prosperity of society.

III. Let the sovereign and the nation never forget that the land is the only source of wealth and that it is agriculture which multiplies it. For the increase of wealth assures the increase of population. Men and wealth make agriculture prosperous, expand trade, stimulate industry, and increase and perpetuate riches. Upon this rich source depends the success of all parts of the administration of the kingdom.

IV. The property rights in land and personal wealth should be guaranteed to their legitimate owners; for the safety of property is the real basis of the economic order of society. Without this safety of property, the land would remain uncultivated. There would be neither proprietors nor peasants to make the necessary investments required in agriculture if they had not the guarantee that their land and the products thereof belonged to them. It is this feeling of security and the guarantee of permanent ownership which gives people the incentive to work and to employ their wealth in the improvement and cultivation of the land as well as in trade and industry. Only the sovereign power is capable of guaranteeing the safety of property of the subjects who have an original right (*droit primitif*) to the division of the fruits of the land, which is the sole source of wealth.

v. Taxes should not be destructive or out of proportion to the sum total of the national revenue. Any increase of taxes should be dependent upon the increase of this revenue. Moreover, taxes should be levied directly and without delay on the net product of land and not on wages or on the price of foodstuffs, in which case they would not only be expensive to administer but would also be detrimental to trade and would destroy annually part of the national revenues. Nor should taxes be levied on the cultivators of the soil, for the advances in agriculture should be considered as a capital fund which must be preserved in the most careful manner in order to provide the money required for the government as well as the income and the subsistence for all classes of citizens: otherwise, taxes degenerate into a system of spoliation causing a general decline which must promptly ruin the state.

vi. The advances of the cultivators of the soil must be adequate to make possible, with the aid of annual expenses, the greatest possible product; for if the advances are not adequate, annual expenditures will increase in proportion and will yield a smaller net product.

vii. The entire annual revenue ought to find its

way back into the circulation of wealth and should pass through this process to the fullest extent; there should not be created pecuniary fortunes, or at least the magnitude of such fortunes should not exceed the amount of pecuniary fortunes re-entering into circulation. For, otherwise these fortunes are bound to interfere with the distribution of one part of the annual national revenue; the owners of these fortunes would intercept for their own use part of the national capital —thereby interfering with the return into circulation of the advances in agriculture, the wages of artisans, and the expenses on consumption which have to be made by the various classes of persons engaged in remunerative professions. This interception of national capital would have the effect of diminishing the reproduction of the national revenue and of the fund available for taxes.

VIII. The economic government should concern itself only with the encouragement of productive outlays and trade in raw produce, and should not intervene at all in matters pertaining to the sterile expenditures.

IX. A nation with a substantial area of agricultural land and capable of carrying on an extensive trade in raw produce should not encourage too much the use of money and the employment of men in the manufacturing and trade of luxuries at the expense of work and outlays in agriculture. For, above all, the kingdom ought to be well populated with well-to-do cultivators of the soil.

X. Never should a part of the annual revenue leave the country without compensation in money or in merchandise.

XI. Emigration of inhabitants who take their wealth with them should be avoided.

XII. The children of rich, independent peasants

should stay in the rural areas in order to perpetuate the labour force. For if some discontent causes them to leave rural areas and to move to the cities, they will carry with them the riches of their fathers which were used in the cultivation of the soil. It is not so much human beings but riches which ought to be attracted into the rural areas; for the greater the amount of capital employed in the cultivation of the soil, the fewer the number of men required in agriculture and the greater its prosperity and its revenue. This is true, for example, with reference to the large-scale and efficient production of grain (*grande culture*) by well-to-do peasant farmers, in contrast to the small-scale production (*petite culture*) of poor and dependent peasants (*metayers*) who work with oxen or cows.

XIII. Everybody ought to be free to raise on his land such products as his interests, his abilities, and the nature of the soil seem to suggest as the most profitable crops. Monopoly should not be encouraged in agriculture, since it is likely to reduce the net social revenue. The prejudice which tends to promote an abundance of necessities in preference to other products and to the detriment of the price of both is based upon a short-run point of view which fails to take into account the effects of foreign trade . . . which determines the price of the foodstuffs that each nation is able to raise with the greatest advantage. Apart from the funds designed for the cultivation of the soil, it is primarily the revenue and the tax fund which are riches of the greatest importance, in view of the fact that they permit the protection of the subjects against famine and foreign enemies, as well as the maintenance of the glory and the power of the monarch and the prosperity of the nation.

XIV. The increase of livestock should be encouraged,

for it is these animals which provide the manure which renders possible rich harvests.

xv. The lands used for the production of grains should be combined, as far as possible, into large holdings administered by well-to-do farmers; for costs of maintenance and repair of structures are smaller in the case of large farm enterprises, which operate with proportionately lower costs and yield a much higher net product than small farms. The existence of a great number of small peasants is not in harmony with the national interest. The most independent part of the population, which is also most easily available for the various occupations and the different kinds of work which separate men into different classes, is the part maintained by the net product. Each economically worth-while measure of economy in the performance of work which can be carried out with the aid of animals, machines, water power, etc., is advantageous for the nation and the state, because a greater net product secures a higher income available for other services and other works.

xvi. International trade in raw produce should not be prohibited, for the rate of reproduction is determined by the extent of the market.

xvii. It is important to create outlets for, and to facilitate the shipment of, agricultural and manufactured products by keeping roads in good condition and by improving ocean shipping and navigation on inland waterways. For the greater the reduction of the costs of trade, the greater the addition to the national revenue.

xviii. The price of foodstuffs and finished articles in the kingdom should not be reduced; for the mutual exchange of commodities with foreign countries becomes disadvantageous for a nation under these circumstances. Upon the price depends the return. Abundance with cheapness is not wealth; scarcity and dearness are misery; abundance and dearness are opulence.

XIX. It should not be assumed that cheapness of foodstuffs is beneficial for the common people. The low price of foodstuffs tends to reduce the wages of the common men, lowers their standard of living, leaves them with fewer work and employment opportunities, and diminishes the national revenue.

XX. The standard of living of the poorer classes of citizens should not be lowered, for these classes would then be unable to contribute their share to the consumption of consumers' goods which can be consumed only within the country. Such a reduction of consumption would have the effect of curtailing the reproduction of wealth, and thus lower the national revenue.

XXI. The proprietors and members of the professional groups should not engage in hoarding (*épargnes stériles*), which would have the effect of withdrawing from circulation and distribution part of their revenues or gains.

XXII. Luxury of a purely decorative kind (*luxe de décoration*) should under no circumstances be encouraged at the expense of outlays which might otherwise be devoted to agriculture, to its improvement, or to the consumption of essential commodities. Such expenditures tend to maintain the low price and sale abroad of raw produce and guarantee the reproduction of national wealth.

XXIII. The nation should not suffer any loss in its reciprocal foreign trade even if such trade were profitable for merchants who would gain by the sale of goods abroad at the expense of their compatriots. For the increase of the fortunes of these merchants would cause a contraction in the circulation of wealth, which would have negative effects on the process of distribution and the reproduction of the national revenue.

XXIV. One should not be deceived by an apparent advantage resulting from international trade by simply taking into account the balance of monetary payments without considering the greater or smaller profit yielded by the goods sold and bought. For frequently the nation which receives a surplus of money is the loser, and this loss affects negatively the distribution and reproduction of national revenue.

XXV. Complete liberty of trade should be maintained. For complete freedom of competition is the safest, the most exacting, and, from the point of view of the nation and the state, the most profitable method of control of domestic and external trade.

XXVI. It is less important to increase population than to increase revenue. For a higher standard of living rendered possible by greater revenue is to be preferred to an urgent need of necessities which would result from an excess of population over revenues; moreover, a higher standard of living makes available more funds for the requirements of the state as well as additional means to make agriculture prosper.

XXVII. The government should be less concerned with economies than with measures necessary for the prosperity of the kingdom. For very great expenditures may cease to be excessive if they lead to an increase of wealth. However, simple expenditures must not be confused with abuses. For abuses could completely absorb the wealth of the nation as well as that of the sovereign.

XXVIII. The administration of government finances either with respect to public revenues or public expenditures should not give rise to pecuniary fortunes which withdraw one part of the revenues from circulation, distribution, and reproduction.

XXIX. The means required to finance extraordinary public expenditures should be obtained from funds available in times of prosperity and should not be borrowed from financiers. For financial fortunes are secret wealth which knows neither king nor fatherland.

XXX. The state should avoid loans giving rise to financial incomes (*rentes financières*); such loans burden the state with debts which are not only all-consuming, but also, through the intermediary of negotiable papers, give rise to financial transactions where discounts add more and more to sterile pecuniary fortunes. These fortunes tend to separate finance from agriculture and deprive the rural areas of funds required for the improvement and cultivation of the land.

From *Readings in Economics*, ed. K. William Kapp and Lore L. Kapp (New York: Barnes & Noble, Inc., 1949; College Outline Series).

❖ ❖ ❖

Classical Economics

[FROM *The Wealth of Nations*]

ADAM SMITH

1776

ON PINMAKING

To take an example, therefore, from a very trifling manufacture, but one in which the division of labour has been very often taken notice of, the trade of the pinmaker; a workman not educated to this business (which the division of labour has rendered a distinct trade), nor acquainted with the use of the machinery employed in it (to the invention of which the same division of labour has probably given occasion), could scarce, perhaps, with his utmost industry, make one pin in a day, and certainly could not make twenty. But in the way in which this business is now carried on, not only the whole work is a peculiar trade, but it is divided into a number of branches, of which the greater part are likewise peculiar trades. One man draws out the wire, another straights it, a third cuts it, a fourth points it, a fifth grinds it at the top for receiving the head; to make the head requires two or three distinct operations; to put it on is a peculiar business, to whiten the pins is another; it is even a trade by itself to put them into the paper; and the important business of making a pin is, in this manner, divided into about eighteen distinct operations, which in some manufactories are all performed by distinct hands, though in others the same man will sometimes perform two or three of them. I have seen a small manufactory of this kind where ten men only were employed, and where some of them consequently performed two or three distinct operations. But though they were very poor, and therefore but indifferently accommodated with the necessary machinery, they could when they exerted themselves make among them about twelve pounds of pins in a day. There are in a pound upwards of four thousand pins of a middling size. Those ten persons, therefore, could make among them upwards of forty-eight thousand pins in a day. Each person, therefore, making a tenth part of forty-eight thousand pins, might be considered as making four thousand eight hundred pins in a day. But if they had all wrought separately and independently, and without any of them having been educated to this peculiar business, they certainly could not each of them have made twenty, perhaps not one in a day; that is, certainly, not the two hundred and fortieth, perhaps not the four thousand eight hundredth part of what they are at present capable of performing, in consequence of a proper division and combination of their different operations.

ON FREEDOM OF TRADE

The unproductive class, that of merchants, artificers, and manufacturers, is maintained and employed altogether at the expense of the two other classes—of that of proprietors, and of that of cultivators. They furnish it both with the materials of its work and with the fund of its subsistence, with the corn and cattle which it consumes while it is employed about that work. The proprietors and cultivators finally pay both the wages of all the workmen of the unproductive class, and the profits of all their employers. Those workmen and their employers are properly the servants of the proprietors and cultivators. They are only servants who work without doors, as menial servants work within. Both the one and the other, however, are equally maintained at the expense of the same masters. The labour of both is equally unproductive. It adds nothing to the value of the sum total of the rude produce of the land. Instead of increasing the value of that sum total, it is a charge and expense which must be paid out of it.

The unproductive class, however, is not only useful, but greatly useful to the other two classes. By means of the industry of merchants, artificers, and manufacturers, the proprietors and cultivators can purchase both the foreign goods and the manufactured produce of their own country which they have occasion for, with the produce of a much smaller quantity of their own labour than what they would be obliged to employ if they were to attempt, in an awkward and unskilful manner, either to import the one or to make the other for their own use. By means of the unproductive class, the cultivators are delivered from many cares which would otherwise distract their attention from the cultivation of land. The superiority of produce, which, in consequence of this undivided attention, they are enabled to raise, is fully sufficient to pay the whole expense which the maintenance and employment of the unproductive class costs either the proprietors or themselves. The industry of merchants, artificers, and manufacturers, though in its own nature altogether unproductive, yet contributes in this manner indirectly to increase the produce of the land. It increases the productive powers of productive labour, by leaving it at liberty to confine itself to its proper employment, the cultivation of land; and the plough goes frequently the easier and the better by means of the labour of the man whose business is most remote from the plough.

It can never be the interest of the proprietors and cultivators to restrain or to discourage in any respect the industry of merchants, artificers, and manufacturers. The greater the liberty which this unproductive class enjoys, the greater will be the competition in all the different trades which compose it, and the cheaper will the other two classes be supplied, both with foreign goods and with the manufactured produce of their own country.

It can never be the interest of the unproductive class

to oppress the other two classes. It is the surplus produce of the land, or what remains after deducting the
maintenance, first, of the cultivators, and afterwards
of the proprietors, that maintains and employs the
unproductive class. The greater this surplus, the
greater must likewise be the maintenance and employment of that class. The establishment of perfect justice, of liberty, and of perfect equality, is the
very simple secret which most effectually secures the
highest degree of prosperity to all the three classes.

The merchants, artificers, and manufacturers of those
mercantile states which, like Holland and Hamburg,
consist chiefly of this unproductive class, are in the
same manner maintained and employed altogether at
the expense of the proprietors and cultivators of land.
The only difference is, that those proprietors and cultivators are, the greater part of them, placed at a most
inconvenient distance from the merchants, artificers,
and manufacturers whom they supply with the materials of their work and the fund of their subsistence, are
the inhabitants of other countries, and the subjects of
other governments.

Such mercantile states, however, are not only useful,
but greatly useful to the inhabitants of those other
countries. They fill up, in some measure, a very important void, and supply the place of the merchants,
artificers, and manufacturers whom the inhabitants of
those countries ought to find at home, but whom, from
some defect in their policy, they do not find at home.

It can never be the interest of those landed nations,
if I may call them so, to discourage or distress the
industry of such mercantile states, by imposing high
duties upon their trade, or upon the commodities
which they furnish. Such duties, by rendering those
commodities dearer, could serve only to sink the real

value of the surplus produce of their own land, with which, or, what comes to the same thing, with the price of which those commodities are purchased. Such duties could serve only to discourage the increase of that surplus produce, and consequently the improvement and cultivation of their own land. The most effectual expedient, on the contrary, for raising the value of that surplus produce, for encouraging its increase, and consequently the improvement and cultivation of their own land, would be to allow the most perfect freedom to the trade of all such mercantile nations.

This perfect freedom of trade would even be the most effectual expedient for supplying them, in due time, with all the artificers, manufacturers, and merchants whom they wanted at home, and for filling up in the properest and most advantageous manner that very important void which they felt there.

The continual increase of the surplus produce of their land would, in due time, create a greater capital than what could be employed with the ordinary rate of profit in the improvement and cultivation of land; and the surplus part of it would naturally turn itself to the employment of artificers and manufacturers at home. But those artificers and manufacturers, finding at home both the materials of their work and the fund of their subsistence, might immediately, even with much less art and skill, be able to work as cheap as the like artificers and manufacturers of such mercantile states, who had both to bring from a great distance. Even though, from want of art and skill, they might not for some time be able to work as cheap, yet, finding a market at home, they might be able to sell their work there as cheap as that of the artificers and manufacturers of such mercantile states, which could not be brought to that market but from so great a distance; and as their art and skill improved, they would soon be able to sell it cheaper. The artificers and manufacturers of such mercantile states, therefore, would immediately be rivalled in the market of those landed nations, and soon after undersold and justled out of it altogether. The cheapness of the manufactures of those landed nations, in consequence of the gradual improvements of art and skill, would, in due time, extend their sale beyond the home market, and carry them to many foreign markets, from which they would in the same manner gradually justle out many of the manufactures of such mercantile nations.

This continual increase both of the rude and manufactured produce of those landed nations would in due time create a greater capital than could, with the ordinary rate of profit, be employed either in agriculture or in manufactures. The surplus of this capital would naturally turn itself to foreign trade, and be employed in exporting to foreign countries such parts of the rude and manufactured produce of its own country as exceeded the demand of the home market. In the exportation of the produce of their own country, the merchants of a landed nation would have an advantage of the same kind over those of mercantile nations, which its artificers and manufacturers had over the artificers and manufacturers of such nations: the advantage of finding at home that cargo, and those stores and provisions, which the others were obliged to seek for at a distance. With inferior art and skill in navigation, therefore, they would be able to sell that cargo as cheap in foreign markets as the merchants of such mercantile nations; and with equal art and skill they would be able to sell it cheaper. They would soon, therefore, rival those mercantile nations in this branch of foreign trade, and in due time would justle them out of it altogther.

According to this liberal and generous system, therefore, the most advantageous method in which a landed nation can raise up artificers, manufacturers, and merchants of its own, is to grant the most perfect freedom of trade to the artificers, manufacturers, and merchants of all other nations. It thereby raises the value of the surplus produce of its own land, of which the continual increase gradually establishes a fund which in due time necessarily raises up all the artificers, manufacturers, and merchants whom it has occasion for.

When a landed nation, on the contrary, oppresses either by high duties or by prohibitions the trade of foreign nations, it necessarily hurts its own interest in two different ways. First, by raising the price of all foreign goods and of all sorts of manufactures, it necessarily sinks the real value of the surplus produce of its own land, with which, or, what comes to the same thing, with the price of which, it purchases those foreign goods and manufactures. Secondly, by giving a sort of monopoly of the home market to its own merchants, artificers, and manufacturers, it raises the rate of mercantile and manufacturing profit in proportion to that of agricultural profit, and consequently either draws from agriculture a part of the capital which had before been employed in it, or hinders from going to it a part of what would otherwise have gone to it. This policy, therefore, discourages agriculture in two different ways: first, by sinking the real value of its produce, and thereby lowering the rate of its profit; and, secondly, by raising the rate of profit in all other employments. Agriculture is rendered less advantageous, and trade and manufactures more advantageous than they otherwise would be; and every man is tempted by his own interest to turn, as much as he can, both his capital and his industry from the former to the latter employments.

From *An Inquiry into the Nature and Causes of the Wealth of Nations*, ed. J. E. T. Rogers (Oxford: Clarendon Press, 1880).

THE PRINCIPLES
OF 1776 AND 1789

❖ ❖ ❖

The American
Declaration of Independence

[*Passed by the Continental Congress, July 4, 1776.*]

When in the Course of human Events, it be- comes necessary for one People to dissolve the Political Bands which have connected them with another, and to assume among the Powers of the Earth, the separate and equal Station to which the Laws of Nature and of Nature's God entitle them, a decent Respect to the Opinions of Mankind requires that they should declare the causes which impel them to the Separation.

We hold these Truths to be self-evident, that all Men are created equal, that they are endowed by their Creator with certain unalienable Rights, that among these are Life, Liberty, and the Pursuit of Happiness— That to secure these Rights, Governments are instituted among Men, deriving their just Powers from the Consent of the Governed, that whenever any Form of Government becomes destructive of these Ends, it is the Right of the People to alter or to abolish it, and to institute new Government, laying its Foundation on such Principles, and organizing its Powers in such Form, as to them shall seem most likely to effect their Safety and Happiness. Prudence, indeed, will dictate that Governments long established should not be changed for light and transient Causes; and accordingly all Experience hath shewn, that Mankind are more disposed to suffer, while Evils are sufferable, than to right themselves by abolishing the Forms to which they are accustomed. But when a long Train of Abuses and Usurpations, pursuing invariably the same Object, evinces a Design to reduce them under absolute Despotism, it is their Right, it is their Duty, to throw off such Government, and to provide new Guards for their future Security. Such has been the patient Sufferance of these Colonies; and such is now the Necessity which constrains them to alter their former Systems of Government. The History of the present King of Great-Britain is a History of repeated Injuries and Usurpations, all having in direct Object the Establishment of an absolute Tyranny over these States. To prove this, let Facts be submitted to a candid World.

He has refused his Assent to Laws, the most wholesome and necessary for the public Good.

He has forbidden his Governors to pass Laws of immediate and pressing Importance, unless suspended in their Operation till his Assent should be obtained; and when so suspended, he has utterly neglected to attend to them.

He has refused to pass other Laws for the Accommodation of large Districts of People, unless those People would relinquish the Right of Representation in the Legislature, a Right inestimable to them, and formidable to Tyrants only.

He has called together Legislative Bodies at Places unusual, uncomfortable, and distant from the Depository of their public Records, for the sole Purpose of fatiguing them into Compliance with his Measures.

He has dissolved Representative Houses repeatedly, for opposing with manly Firmness his Invasions on the Rights of the People.

He has refused for a long Time, after such Dissolutions, to cause others to be elected; whereby the Legislative Powers, incapable of Annihilation, have returned to the People at large for their exercise; the State remaining in the mean time exposed to all the Dangers of Invasion from without, and Convulsions within.

He has endeavoured to prevent the Population of these States; for that Purpose obstructing the Laws for Naturalization of Foreigners; refusing to pass others to encourage their Migrations hither, and raising the Conditions of new Appropriations of Lands.

He has obstructed the Administration of Justice, by refusing his Assent to Laws for establishing Judiciary Powers.

He has made Judges dependent on his Will alone, for the Tenure of their Offices, and the Amount and Payment of their Salaries.

He has erected a Multitude of new Offices, and sent

hither Swarms of Officers to harass our People, and eat out their Substance.

He has kept among us, in Times of Peace, Standing Armies, without the consent of our Legislatures.

He has affected to render the Military independent of and superior to the Civil Power.

He has combined with others to subject us to a Jurisdiction foreign to our Constitution, and unacknowledged by our Laws; giving his Assent to their Acts of pretended Legislation:

For quartering large Bodies of Armed Troops among us:

For protecting them, by a mock Trial, from Punishment for any Murders which they should commit on the Inhabitants of these States:

For cutting off our Trade with all Parts of the World:

For imposing Taxes on us without our Consent:

For depriving us, in many Cases, of the Benefits of Trial by Jury:

For transporting us beyond Seas to be tried for pretended Offences:

For abolishing the free System of English Laws in a neighbouring Province, establishing therein an arbitrary Government, and enlarging its Boundaries, so as to render it at once an Example and fit Instrument for introducing the same absolute Rule into these Colonies:

For taking away our Charters, abolishing our most valuable Laws, and altering fundamentally the Forms of our Governments:

For suspending our own Legislatures, and declaring themselves invested with Power to legislate for us in all Cases whatsoever.

He has abdicated Government here, by declaring us out of his Protection and waging War against us.

He has plundered our Seas, ravaged our Coasts, burnt our Towns, and destroyed the Lives of our People.

He is, at this Time, transporting large Armies of foreign Mercenaries to compleat the Works of Death, Desolation, and Tyranny, already begun with circumstances of Cruelty and Perfidy, scarcely paralleled in the most barbarous Ages, and totally unworthy the Head of a civilized Nation.

He has constrained our fellow Citizens taken Captive on the high Seas to bear Arms against their Country, to become the Executioners of their Friends and Brethren, or to fall themselves by their Hands.

He has excited domestic Insurrections amongst us, and has endeavoured to bring on the Inhabitants of our Frontiers, the merciless Indian Savages, whose known Rule of Warfare, is an undistinguished Destruction, of all Ages, Sexes and Conditions.

In every stage of these Oppressions we have Petitioned for Redress in the most humble Terms: Our repeated Petitions have been answered only by repeated Injury. A Prince, whose Character is thus marked by every act which may define a Tyrant, is unfit to be the Ruler of a free People.

Nor have we been wanting in Attentions to our British Brethren. We have warned them from Time to Time of Attempts by their Legislature to extend an unwarrantable Jurisdiction over us. We have reminded them of the Circumstances of our Emigration and Settlement here. We have appealed to their native Justice and Magnanimity, and we have conjured them by the Ties of our common Kindred to disavow these Usurpations, which, would inevitably interrupt our Connections and Correspondence. They too have been deaf to the Voice of Justice and of Consanguinity. We must, therefore, acquiesce in the Necessity, which denounces our Separation, and hold them, as we hold the rest of Mankind, Enemies in War, in Peace, Friends.

We, therefore, the Representatives of the UNITED STATES OF AMERICA, in General Congress, Assembled, appealing to the Supreme Judge of the World for the Rectitude of our Intentions, do, in the Name, and by Authority of the good People of these Colonies, solemnly Publish and Declare, That these United Colonies are, and of Right ought to be, Free and Independent States; that they are absolved from all Allegiance to the British Crown, and that all political Connection between them and the State of Great-Britain, is and ought to be totally dissolved; and that as Free and Independent States, they have full Power to levy War, conclude Peace, contract Alliances, establish Commerce, and to do all other Acts and Things which Independent States may of right do. And for the support of this Declaration, with a firm Reliance on the Protection of divine Providence, we mutually pledge to each other our Lives, our Fortunes, and our sacred Honor.

❖ ❖ ❖

The Declaration of the
Rights of Man and the Citizen

*[Passed by the French National Assembly,
27 August 1789]*

The representatives of the French people, organized in National Assembly, considering that ignorance, forgetfulness, or contempt of the rights of man are the sole causes of public misfortunes and of the corruption of governments, have resolved to set forth in a solemn declaration the natural, inalienable, and sacred rights of man, in order that such declaration, continually before all members of the social body, may be a perpetual reminder of their rights and duties; in order that the acts of the legislative power and those of the executive power may constantly be compared with the aim of every political institution and may accordingly be more respected; in order that the demands of the citizens, founded henceforth upon simple and incontestable principles, may always be directed towards the maintenance of the Constitution and the welfare of all.

Accordingly, the National Assembly recognizes and proclaims, in the presence and under the auspices of the Supreme Being, the following rights of man and citizen.

1. Men are born and remain free and equal in

rights; social distinctions may be based only upon general usefulness.

2. The aim of every political association is the preservation of the natural and inalienable rights of man; these rights are liberty, property, security, and resistance to oppression.

3. The source of all sovereignty resides essentially in the nation; no group, no individual, may exercise authority not emanating expressly therefrom.

4. Liberty consists of the power to do whatever is not injurious to others; thus the enjoyment of the natural rights of every man has for its limits only those that assure other members of society the enjoyment of those same rights; such limits may be determined only by law.

5. The law has the right to forbid only actions that are injurious to society. Whatever is not forbidden by law may not be prevented, and no one may be constrained to do what it does not prescribe.

6. Law is the expression of the general will; all citizens have the right to concur personally, or through their representatives, in its formation; it must be the same for all, whether it protects or punishes. All citizens, being equal before it, are equally admissible to all public offices, positions, and employments, according to their capacity, and without other distinction than that of virtues and talents.

7. No man may be accused, arrested, or detained except in the cases determined by law, and according to the forms prescribed thereby. Whoever solicit, expedite, or execute arbitrary orders, or have them executed, must be punished; but every citizen summoned or apprehended in pursuance of the law must obey immediately; he renders himself culpable by resistance.

8. The law is to establish only penalties that are

absolutely and obviously necessary; and no one may be punished except by virtue of a law established and promulgated prior to the offence and legally applied.

9. Since every man is presumed innocent until declared guilty, if arrest be deemed indispensable, all unnecessary severity for securing the person of the accused must be severely repressed by law.

10. No one is to be disquieted because of his opinions, even religious, provided their manifestation does not disturb the public order established by law.

11. Free communication of ideas and opinions is one of the most precious of the rights of man. Consequently, every citizen may speak, write, and print freely, subject to responsibility for the abuse of such liberty in the cases determined by law.

12. The guarantee of the rights of man and citizen necessitates a public force; such a force, therefore, is instituted for the advantage of all and not for the particular benefit of those to whom it is entrusted.

13. For the maintenance of the public force and for the expenses of administration a common tax is indispensable; it must be assessed equally on all citizens in proportion to their means.

14. Citizens have the right to ascertain, by themselves or through their representatives, the necessity of the public tax, to consent to it freely, to supervise its use, and to determine its quota, assessment, payment, and duration.

15. Society has the right to require of every public agent an accounting of his administration.

16. Every society in which the guarantee of rights is not assured or the separation of powers not determined has no constitution at all.

17. Since property is a sacred and inviolable right,

no one may be deprived thereof unless a legally established public necessity obviously requires it, and upon condition of a just and previous indemnity.

Trans. J. H. Stewart, in *A Documentary Survey of the French Revolution* (New York: The Macmillan Co., 1951).

❖❖❖❖❖❖❖❖❖❖❖❖❖❖❖❖❖❖❖❖❖❖❖❖❖❖❖❖❖❖❖❖❖❖

The Heavenly City

❖ ❖ ❖

A Classical Utopia

[FROM *Adventures of Telemachus*]

François de Salignac de La Mothe
FÉNELON

1699

"But what shall I do," said Idomeneus, "if the people that I scatter over this fertile country should neglect to cultivate it?"

"You must do," said Mentor, "just contrary to what is commonly done; rapacious and inconsiderate princes think only of taxing those who are most industrious to improve their land; because, upon these, they suppose a tax will be more easily levied; and they spare those, whom idleness has made indigent. Reverse this mistaken and injurious conduct, which oppresses virtue, rewards vice, and encourages a supineness, that is equally fatal to the king and to the state. Let your taxes be heavy upon those who neglect the cultivation of their lands; and add, to your taxes, fines and other penalties if it is necessary; punish the negligent and the idle, as you would the soldier who should desert his post. On the contrary, distinguish those, who, in proportion as their families multiply, cultivate their lands with the greater diligence, by special privileges and immunities; every family will then become numerous; and every one will be animated to labour, not by the desire of gain only, but of honour; the state of husbandry being no longer wretched, will no longer be contemptible; the plough, once more held in honour, will be guided by the victorious hands that have defended the country; and it will not be less glorious to cultivate a paternal inheritance in the security of peace, than to draw the sword in its defence, when it is endangered by war. The whole country will bloom around you: the golden ears of ripe corn will again crown the temples of Ceres; Bacchus will tread the grapes in rich clusters under his feet; and wine, more delicious than nectar, will flow from the hills like a river: the vallies will resound to the song of the shepherds, who, dispersed along the banks of a transparent stream, shall join their voices with the pipe; while their flocks shall frolic round them, and feast upon the flowery pasture without fear of the wolf.

"O Idomeneus! will it not make you supremely happy, to be the source of such prosperity: to stretch your protection, like the shadow of a rock, over so many people, who will repose under it in security and peace? Will you not, in the consciousness of this, enjoy a noble elevation of mind, a calm sense of superior glory; such as can never touch the bosom of the tyrant, who lives only to desolate the earth, and who diffuses, not less through his own dominions, than those which he conquers from others, carnage and tumult, horror and anguish, consternation, famine, and despair? Happy, indeed, is the prince, whom his own greatness of soul, and the distinguishing favour of the gods, shall render thus the delight of his people, and the example of succeeding ages! The world, instead of taking up arms to oppose his power, will be found prostrate at his feet, and suing to be subject to his dominion."

"But," said Idomeneus, "when the people shall be thus blessed with plenty and peace, will not their happiness corrupt their manners; will they not turn against me, the very strength I have given them?"

"There is no reason to fear that," said Mentor; "the sycophants of prodigal princes have suggested it as a pretence for oppression; but it may easily be prevented. The laws which we have established with respect to agriculture will render life laborious; and the people, notwithstanding their plenty, will abound only in what is necessary, for we have prohibited the arts that furnish superfluities; and the plenty even of necessaries will be restrained within due bounds, by the facility of marriage, and the multiplication of families. In proportion as a family becomes numerous, their portion of land being still the same in extent, a more diligent cultivation will become necessary; and this will require incessant labour. Luxury and idleness only render people insolent and rebellious; they will have bread, indeed, and they will have bread enough; but they will have nothing more, except what they can gain, from their own ground, by the sweat of their brow.

"That your people may continue in this state of mediocrity, it will be necessary that you should now limit the extent of ground that each family is to possess. We have, you know, divided your people into seven classes, according to their different conditions; and each family, in each class, must be permitted to possess only such an extent of ground, as is absolutely necessary to subsist it. This regulation being inviolably observed, the nobles can never get possession of the lands of the poor; everyone will have land; but so much only, as will make a diligent cultivation necessary. If, in a long course of years, the people should be so much increased, that land cannot be found for them at home, they may be sent to form colonies abroad; which will be a new advantage to the mother country.

"I am of opinion that care should be taken, even to prevent wine from being too common in your kingdom: if you find that too many vines are planted, you should cause them to be grubbed up. Some of the most dreadful mischiefs that afflict mankind, proceed from wine; it is the cause of disease, quarrels, sedition, idleness, aversion to labour, and every species of domestic disorder. Let wine then be considered as a kind of medicine; or as a scarce liquor, to be used only at the sacrifices of the gods, or in seasons of public festivity. Do not, however, flatter yourself, that this regulation can ever take place without the sanction of your own example.

"The laws of Minos, with respect to the education of children, must also be inviolably preserved: public schools must be established, to teach them the fear of the gods; the love of their country; a reverence for the laws; and a preference of honour not only to pleasure, but to life. Magistrates must be appointed to superintend the conduct not of every family only, but every person; you must keep also your own eye upon them; for you are a king, only to be the shepherd of your people, and to watch over your flock night and day. By this unremitted vigilance, you will prevent many disorders and many crimes; such as you cannot prevent, you must immediately punish with severity; for, in this case, severity to the individual is clemency to the public: it stops those irregularities at their source, which would deluge the country with misery and guilt; the taking away of one life, upon a proper occasion, will be the preservation of many; and will make a prince sufficiently feared, without general or frequent severity. It is a detestable maxim, that the security of the prince depends only upon the oppression of the people. Should no care be taken to improve their knowledge or their morals? Instead of being taught to love him, whom they are born to obey; should they be driven by terror to despair; and reduced to the dreadful necessity of either throwing off the yoke of their tyrant, or perishing under its weight? Can this be the way to reign with tranquillity? can this be the path that leads to glory?

"Remember, that the sovereign who is most absolute, is always least powerful: he seizes upon all, and his grasp is ruin. He is, indeed, the sole proprietor of whatever his state contains; but, for that reason, his state contains nothing of value: the fields are uncultivated, and almost a desert; the towns lose some of their few inhabitants every day; and trade every day declines. The king, who must cease to be a king when he ceases to have subjects, and who is great only in virtue of his people, is himself insensibly losing his character and power, as the number of his people, from whom alone both are derived, insensibly diminishes; and his dominions are at length exhausted of money and of men: the loss of men, is the greatest, and the most irreparable he can sustain. Absolute power degrades every subject to a slave; the tyrant is flattered, even to an appearance of adoration; and everyone trembles at the glance of his eye: but, at the least revolt, this enormous power perishes by its own excess. It derived no strength from the love of the people; it wearied and provoked all that it could reach; and rendered every individual of the state impatient of its continuance. At the first stroke of opposition, the idol is overturned, broken to pieces, and trodden under foot: contempt, hatred, fear, resentment, distrust, and every other passion of the soul, unite against so hateful a despotism. The king, who, in his vain prosperity, found no man bold enough to tell him the truth; in his adversity, finds no man kind enough to excuse his faults, or to defend him against his enemies."

Idomeneus then hastened to distribute his uncultivated lands, to people them with useful artificers: and to carry all the counsels of Mentor into execution; reserving for the builders, such parts as had been allotted them, which they were not to cultivate, till they had finished the city.

Trans. Dr. J. Hawkesworth (London: Harrison, 1784).

❖ ❖ ❖

A Late-Eighteenth-Century
Utopia

[FROM *Memoirs of the Year Two Thousand
Five Hundred*]

LOUIS SÉBASTIEN MERCIER

1770

THE CARRIAGES

I observed that all who went took the right hand,
and all who came the left.* This simple method of
avoiding obstruction has been lately discovered; so
true it is that all useful inventions are produced by
time.† By this regulation all obstructions are avoided,
and every passage is left free. From the public festivals,
where the greatest concourse of people resort, to enjoy
an entertainment of which they are naturally fond, and
of which it would be unjust to deprive them, each
one returns to his home without detriment or danger. I
saw not there that ridiculous and turbulent sight of an
innumerable number of coaches entangled with each
other, and the whole body remain immoveable for

---

* A stranger can by no means conceive what it is that in
France occasions a perpetual movement among the people,
who, from morning to evening, are absent from their houses,
frequently without any business, though in an incomprehensible agitation. [All notes are Mercier's.]

† This method, I am informed, has been long used in the
imperial city of Vienna.

three hours together; while the gilded fop, the helpless wretch who suffers himself to be drawn along, forgetting that he has legs, cries out from the coach window, and laments that he is not able to advance.‡

The greatest quantity of people form a circulation that is free, easy, and perfectly regular. I met a hundred carriages loaded with provisions or moveables for one coach, and even in that there was only a man who appeared to be infirm. What are become, I said, of those carriages completely gilt, painted, and varnished, that in my time crowded the streets of Paris? Have you then no farmers of taxes, no courtesans,** no *petits maîtres*? Formerly those three despicable tribes insulted the public, and vied with each other in attracting the regard of the honest citizen, who fled with precipitation before them, lest he should be crushed by their chariot wheels. The nobility of my days regarded the streets of Paris as the lists of the Olympic games, and placed their glory in the havock they made with their horses; then it was, "Let him save himself that can."

"Those sort of courses," [my host] replied, "are no longer permitted. Just sumptuary laws have suppressed that barbarous luxury, which served only to propagate a race of lackies and horses.†† The favourites of for-

---

‡ This droll sight of a number of carriages intended for expedition, blocked up for a long time by each other, while the masters are fretting and the coachmen swearing, affords some satisfaction to the persecuted foot passenger.

** We have seen a superb carriage, drawn by six horses, sumptuously harnessed, through two rows of wondering artisans, who bare-headed saluted a—strumpet.

†† Those expensive sots, who parade with a crowd of valets, have been justly compared to certain insects, who, though they have many feet are remarkably slow in motion.

tune no longer indulge in that criminal luxury so injurious to the poor. The nobles of our day use their own legs, and therefore have more money and less of the gout.

"You see, however, some coaches; they belong to ancient magistrates, or to men distinguished by their services, and bending under the weight of years. It is permitted to them only to roll slowly over the pavement, where the lowest citizen is respected. Should one of these have the misfortune to lame any passenger, he would instantly descend from his coach, place the injured person in it, and at his own expence, provide him with a carriage for the remainder of his days. But this never happens; they who are permitted to have coaches are men of merit, who think it no disgrace to let their horses give place to a citizen.

"Our sovereign himself frequently goes on foot amongst us; sometimes he even honours our dwellings with his presence; and almost always, when tired with walking, rests himself in the shop of some artisan;‡‡ he loves to observe that natural equality which ought to reign among men; he meets in our eyes with nothing but love and gratitude; our acclamations proceed from the heart, and his heart receives them with complacency; he is a second Henry IV; he has the same dignity of soul, the same benevolence of temper, the same noble simplicity; but he is more fortunate: the public ways receive from his footsteps a sacred impression that everyone reveres; none dare breed riot; they are ashamed to cause the least disorder. 'If the king should come by,' they say; that sole reflection would, I believe, stop a civil war. How powerful is example, when it proceeds from the first person in the nation!

‡‡ This was a frequent practice of the late Stanislaus, king of Poland, in the latter part of his life.

how does it affect! what command it has over all men!
it becomes an inviolable law."

Trans. W. Hooper (Philadelphia: Thomas Dobson, 1795).

Towards a Society of Nations

[FROM "Idea of a Universal History"]

IMMANUEL KANT

1784

PROPOSITION: *The problem of the establishment of a
perfect constitution of society depends upon the
problem of a system of international relations adjusted to law; and, apart from this latter problem,
cannot be solved.*

To what purpose is labour bestowed upon a civil
constitution adjusted to law for individual men, i.e.,
upon the creation of a commonwealth? The same anti-
social impulses, which first drove men to such a creation, is again the cause, that every commonwealth in
its external relations, i.e., as a state in reference to
other states, occupies the same ground of lawless and
uncontrolled liberty; consequently each must anticipate
from the other the very same evils which compelled
individuals to enter the social state. Nature accordingly
avails herself of the spirit of enmity in man, as existing
even in the great national corporations of that animal,
for the purpose of attaining through the inevitable
antagonism of this spirit a state of rest and security;
i.e., by wars, by the immoderate exhaustion of inces-

sant preparations for war, and by the pressure of evil consequences which war at last entails upon any nation even through the midst of peace—she drives nations to all sorts of experiments and expedients; and finally, after infinite devastations, ruin, and universal exhaustion of energy, to one which reason should have suggested without the cost of so sad an experience; viz., to quit the barbarous condition of lawless power, and to enter into a federal league of nations, in which even the weakest member looks for its rights and for protection—not to its own power, or its own adjudication, but to this great confederation (*Fœdus Amphictyonum*), to the united power, and the adjudication of the collective will. Visionary as this idea may seem, and as such laughed at the Abbé de Saint-Pierre[1] and in Rousseau (possibly because they deemed it too near to its accomplishment)—it is notwithstanding the inevitable resource and mode of escape under that pressure of evil which nations reciprocally inflict; and, hard as it may be to realize such an idea, states must of necessity be driven at last to the very same resolution to which the savage man of nature was driven with equal reluctance—viz., to sacrifice brutal liberty, and to seek peace and security in a civil constitution founded upon law. All wars therefore are so many tentative essays (not in the intention of man, but in the intention of nature) to bring about new relations of states, and by revolutions and dismemberments to form new political bodies: these again, either from internal defects or external attacks, cannot support themselves, but must undergo similar revolutions; until

[1] Charles Irénée Castel, Abbé de Saint-Pierre, French moralist, author of a plan for universal peace; not to be confused with Bernardin de Saint-Pierre (p. 439). [C.B.'s note.]

at last, partly by the best possible arrangement of civil
government within, and partly by common concert and
legal compact without, a condition is attained which,
like a well-ordered commonwealth, can maintain itself
in the way of an automaton.

Now, whether (in the first place) it is to be antici-
pated from an epicurean concourse of efficient causes
that states, like atoms, by accidental shocking together,
should go through all sorts of new combinations to be
again dissolved by the fortuitous impulse of fresh
shocks, until at length by pure accident some combination emerges capable of supporting itself (a case of
luck that could hardly be looked for); or whether (in
the second place) we should rather assume that nature
is in this instance pursuing her regular course of raising
our species gradually from the lower steps of animal
existence to the very highest of a human existence, and
that not by any direct interposition in our favour, but
through man's own spontaneous and artificial efforts
(spontaneous, but yet extorted from him by his situation), and in this apparently wild arrangement of
things is developing with perfect regularity the original
tendencies she has implanted: or whether (in the third
place) it is more reasonable to believe that out of all
this action and reaction of the human species upon itself nothing in the shape of a wise result will ever issue;
that it will continue to be as it has been; and therefore
that it cannot be known beforehand, but that the discord, which is so natural to our species, will finally
prepare for us a hell of evils under the most moral
condition of society, such as may swallow up this very
moral condition itself and all previous advance in culture by a reflux of the original barbaric spirit of desolation (a fate, by the way, against which it is impossible
to be secured under the government of blind chance,

with which liberty uncontrolled by law is identical, unless by underlaying this chance with a secret nexus of wisdom)—to all this the answer turns upon the following question; whether it be reasonable to assume a final purpose of all natural processes and arrangements in the parts, and yet a want of purpose in the whole? What therefore the objectless condition of savage life effected in the end, viz., that it checked the development of the natural tendencies in the human species, but then, by the very evils it thus caused, drove man into a state where those tendencies could unfold and mature themselves, namely, the state of civilisation; that same service is performed for states by the barbaric freedom in which they are now existing, viz., that, by causing the dedication of all national energies and resources to war, by the desolations of war and still more by causing the necessity of standing continually in a state of preparation for war, it checks the full development of the natural tendencies in its progress; but on the other hand, by these very evils and their consequences, it compels our species at last to discover some law of counterbalance to the principle of antagonism between nations, and in order to give effect to this law to introduce a federation of states and consequently a cosmopolitical condition of security (or police)—corresponding to that municipal security which arises out of internal police. This federation will itself not be exempt from danger, else the powers of the human race would go to sleep; it will be sufficient that it contain a principle for restoring the equilibrium between its own action and reaction, and thus checking the two functions from destroying each other. Before this last step is taken, human nature—then about halfway advanced in its progress—is in the deepest abyss of evils under the deceitful semblance of external prosperity; and Rousseau was not so much in the wrong when he preferred the condition of the savage to that of the civilized man at the point where he has reached, but is hesitating to take the final step of his ascent. We are at this time in a high degree of *culture* as to arts and sciences. We are *civilized* to superfluity in what regards the graces and decorums of life. But to entitle us to consider ourselves *moralized* much is still wanting. Yet the idea of morality belongs even to that of *culture;* but the use of this idea, as it comes forward in mere *civilisation,* is restrained to its influence on manners, as seen in the principle of honour, in respectability of deportment, etc. Nothing indeed of a true moral influence can be expected so long as states direct all their energies to idle plans of aggrandizement by force, and thus incessantly check the slow motions by which the intellect of the species is unfolding and forming itself, to say nothing of their shrinking from all *positive* aid to those motions. But all good, that is not engrafted upon moral good, is mere show and hollow speciousness—the dust and ashes of mortality. And in this delusive condition will the human race linger, until it shall have toiled upwards in the way I have mentioned from its present chaotic abyss of political relations.

From "Idea of a Universal History on a Cosmo-Political Plan," trans. Thomas De Quincey, *Works,* Vol. XII (Edinburgh: Adam and Charles Black, 1862-1880).

❖ ❖ ❖

On Progress

[FROM "Discourse at the Sorbonne"]

ANNE ROBERT JACQUES TURGOT

1750

ON THE SUCCESSIVE ADVANCES OF THE HUMAN MIND

The phenomena of Nature, subjected to constant laws, are confined in a circle of ever the same revolutions. All perishes and all revives; in these successive generations, by which vegetables and animals reproduce themselves, time only gathers back in each case the image of what it had made disappear.

The succession of man, on the contrary, offers from age to age a spectacle ever varied. Reason, the passions, liberty, incessantly produce new events. All the ages are linked together by a sequence of causes and effects which connect the existing state of the world with all that has preceded it. The multiform signs of language and of writing, by giving to men the means of insuring the possession of their ideas and of communicating them to others, have made of all the individual funds of knowledge a common treasure, which one generation transmits to the next, along with an inheritance always increased by the discoveries of each age; thus the human race seen from its origin appears to the eye of a philosopher as one vast whole, which itself, like each individual composing it, has had its infancy and its development.

We see societies establishing themselves, nations forming themselves, which in turn dominate over other nations or become subject to them. Empires rise and fall; laws, forms of government, one succeeding another; the arts, the sciences, are discovered and are cultivated; sometimes retarded and sometimes accelerated in their progress, they pass from one region to another. Self-interest, ambition, vainglory, perpetually change the scene of the world, inundate the earth with blood. Yet in the midst of their ravages manners are gradually softened, the human mind takes enlightenment, separate nations draw nearer to each other, commerce and policy connect at last all parts of the globe, and the total mass of the human race, by the alternations of calm and agitation, of good conditions and of bad, marches always, although slowly, towards still higher perfection. . . .

An art suddenly rises by which are spread, in all directions, the thoughts and the glory of the great men of the past. Until now how slow, in every sense, progress has been! For two thousand years back medals have presented to all eyes characters impressed on bronze, and, after so many ages, it occurs for the first time to some obscure man that characters might be impressed on paper! As soon as the treasures of antiquity, drawn from the dust, pass into all hands, penetrate into all places, enlightenment is brought to the minds that were losing themselves in ignorance, and then genius is called forth from the depth of its retreat. The time has come.

Emerge, Europe, from the darkness that covered you! Immortal names of the Medicis, of Leo X, of Francis I, may you be consecrated forever, may the patrons of the arts share the glory of those who cultivated them! I salute you, Italy, happy land, for the second time the country of letters and of taste, the source whence their waters are shed to fertilize our regions. Our France, as yet, views your progress, but from a distance. Her language is still infected with some remnant of barbarism. . . .

And now that multiplicity of facts, of experiences, of instruments, of ingenious operations, which the practice of the arts had accumulated during so many ages, has been drawn from obscurity by the work of the printing press, the productions of the two worlds, brought together by an immense commerce, have become the foundation of a natural history and philosophy hitherto unknown, and freed at last from grotesque speculations. On all sides attentive eyes are fixed on Nature. Slight chances turned to profit bring forth discoveries. The son of an artisan in Zeeland, while amusing himself, brings together two convex glasses in a tube, and the limits of our senses are removed. In Italy the eyes of Galileo have discovered a new celestial world. Now Kepler, while seeking in the stars the numbers of Pythagoras, has found the two famous laws of the course of the planets which will become one day, in the hands of Newton, the key to the universe. Bacon had already traced for posterity the road she had to follow. . . . Great Descartes! if to find truth has not been always given to you, you have at least destroyed tyranny and error [that obscured it]. . . . At last all the clouds are dissipated. What a glorious light is cast on all sides! What a crowd of great men on all paths of knowledge! What perfection of human reason! One man, Newton, has submitted the infinite to the calculus; has unveiled the nature and properties of light, which, while revealing to us everything else, had concealed itself; he has placed in his balance the stars, the earth, and all the forces of Nature.

Amidst these vicissitudes of sciences, of arts, of all that is human, rejoice, gentlemen, in the satisfaction of seeing that the Religion to which you have consecrated your hearts and your talents, always herself, always pure, always entire, stands perpetuated in the Church, preserving all the characters of the seal which the Divinity has stamped upon it. You will be her ministers and you will be worthy of her. The Faculty expects from you her glory, the Church of France her enlightenment, Religion her defenders; genius, learning, piety, unite to give foundation for their hopes.

From *The Life and Writings of Turgot*, ed. W. Walker Stephens (London: Longmans, Green & Co., 1895).

The Perfectibility of Man

[FROM *Sketch for a Historical Picture of the Human Mind* [1]]

ANTOINE NICOLAS DE CARITAT, MARQUIS DE CONDORCET

1794

THE TENTH STAGE

THE FUTURE PROGRESS OF THE HUMAN MIND

If man can, with almost complete assurance, predict phenomena when he knows their laws, and if, even when he does not, he can still, with great expectation

[1] Condorcet in 1793-1794 wrote this book, which can be regarded as a testament of the Age of Reason, under out-

of success, forecast the future on the basis of his experience of the past, why, then, should it be regarded as a fantastic undertaking to sketch, with some pretence to truth, the future destiny of man on the basis of his history? The sole foundation for belief in the natural sciences is this idea, that the general laws directing the phenomena of the universe, known or unknown, are necessary and constant. Why should this principle be any less true for the development of the intellectual and moral faculties of man than for the other operations of nature? Since beliefs founded on past experience of like conditions provide the only rule of conduct for the wisest of men, why should the philosopher be forbidden to base his conjectures on these same foundations, so long as he does not attribute to them a certainty superior to that warranted by the number,

---

lawry and in hiding at the home of an old friend, Mme. Vernet, in the rue Servandoni at Paris. Identified with the moderate or Girondin faction in the Convention, he was proscribed along with them by the victorious Jacobin Montagnards after their *coup d'état* of June 2, 1793. He used his leisure in the rue Servandoni to write, certainly without any of the normal library materials of scholarship, a long-planned survey of human history as it seemed to his *philosophe*'s eye, a kind of continuation and *mise au point* of the work of two of his masters, Turgot and d'Alembert. The death that threatened him every moment he worked on this book —a threat that no reader could possibly suspect from this serene and confident text—overtook him when in March 1794 rumors of a search of Mme. Vernet's home drove him to inadequately prepared flight on foot. Arrested and jailed in a Paris suburb, he was found dead, almost certainly from exhaustion and not from suicide, the next morning. This book was put together from manuscripts left with Mme. Vernet. Some of the earlier nine epochs or stages of the human mind are incomplete, or assembled from notes, but this tenth *époque*, Condorcet's Utopia, must be essentially what he meant it to be. [C.B.'s note.]

the constancy, and the accuracy of his observations?

Our hopes for the future condition of the human race can be subsumed under three important heads: the abolition of inequality between nations, the progress of equality within each nation, and the true perfection of mankind. Will all nations one day attain that state of civilization which the most enlightened, the freest and the least burdened by prejudices, such as the French and the Anglo-Americans, have attained already? Will the vast gulf that separates these peoples from the slavery of nations under the rule of monarchs, from the barbarism of African tribes, from the ignorance of savages, little by little disappear?

Is there on the face of the earth a nation whose inhabitants have been debarred by nature herself from the enjoyment of freedom and the exercise of reason?

Are those differences which have hitherto been seen in every civilized country in respect of the enlightenment, the resources, and the wealth enjoyed by the different classes into which it is divided, is that inequality between men which was aggravated or perhaps produced by the earliest progress of society, are these part of civilization itself, or are they due to the present imperfections of the social art? Will they necessarily decrease and ultimately make way for a real equality, the final end of the social art, in which even the effects of the natural differences between men will be mitigated and the only kind of inequality to persist will be that which is in the interests of all and which favours the progress of civilization, of education, and of industry, without entailing either poverty, humiliation, or dependence? In other words, will men approach a condition in which everyone will have the knowledge necessary to conduct himself in the ordinary affairs of life, according to the light of his own reason, to preserve his mind free from prejudice, to understand his rights and to exercise them in accordance with his conscience and his creed; in which everyone will become able, through the development of his faculties, to find the means of providing for his needs; and in which at last misery and folly will be the exception, and no longer the habitual lot of a section of society?

Is the human race to better itself, either by discoveries in the sciences and the arts, and so in the means to individual welfare and general prosperity; or by progress in the principles of conduct or practical morality; or by a true perfection of the intellectual, moral, or physical faculties of man, an improvement which may result from a perfection either of the instruments used to heighten the intensity of these faculties and to direct their use or of the natural constitution of man?

In answering these three questions we shall find in the experience of the past, in the observation of the progress that the sciences and civilization have already made, in the analysis of the progress of the human mind and of the development of its faculties, the strongest reasons for believing that nature has set no limit to the realization of our hopes.

If we glance at the state of the world today we see first of all that in Europe the principles of the French Constitution are already those of all enlightened men. We see them too widely propagated, too seriously professed, for priests and despots to prevent their gradual penetration even into the hovels of their slaves; there they will soon awaken in these slaves the remnants of their common sense and inspire them with that smouldering indignation which not even constant humiliation and fear can smother in the soul of the oppressed.

As we move from nation to nation, we can see in each what special obstacles impede this revolution and what attitudes of mind favour it. We can distinguish the nations where we may expect it to be introduced gently by the perhaps belated wisdom of their governments, and those nations where its violence intensified by their resistance must involve all alike in a swift and terrible convulsion.

Can we doubt that either common sense or the senseless discords of European nations will add to the effects of the slow but inexorable progress of their colonies, and will soon bring about the independence of the New World? And then will not the European population in these colonies, spreading rapidly over that enormous land, either civilize or peacefully remove the savage nations who still inhabit vast tracts of its land?

Survey the history of our settlements and commercial undertakings in Africa or in Asia, and you will see how our trade monopolies, our treachery, our murderous contempt for men of another colour or creed, the insolence of our usurpations, the intrigues or the exaggerated proselytic zeal of our priests, have destroyed the respect and goodwill that the superiority of our knowledge and the benefits of our commerce at first won for us in the eyes of the inhabitants. But doubtless the moment approaches when, no longer presenting ourselves as always either tyrants or corrupters, we shall become for them the beneficent instruments of their freedom.

The sugar industry, establishing itself throughout the immense continent of Africa, will destroy the shameful exploitation which has corrupted and depopulated that continent for the last two centuries.

Already in Great Britain, friends of humanity have set us an example; and if the Machiavellian government of that country has been restrained by public opinion from offering any opposition, what may we not expect of this same spirit, once the reform of a servile and venal constitution has led to a government worthy of a humane and generous nation? Will not France hasten to imitate such undertakings dictated by philanthropy and the true self-interest of Europe alike? Trading stations have been set up in the French islands, in Guiana and in some English possessions, and soon we shall see the downfall of the monopoly that the Dutch have sustained with so much treachery, persecution and crime. The nations of Europe will finally learn that monopolistic companies are nothing more than a tax imposed upon them in order to provide their governments with a new instrument of tyranny.

So the peoples of Europe, confining themselves to free trade, understanding their own rights too well to show contempt for those of other peoples, will respect this independence, which until now they have so insolently violated. Their settlements, no longer filled with government hirelings hastening, under the cloak of place or privilege, to amass treasure by brigandry and deceit, so as to be able to return to Europe and purchase titles and honour, will now be peopled with men of industrious habit, seeking in these propitious climates the wealth that eluded them at home. The love of freedom will retain them there, ambition will no longer recall them, and what have been no better than the counting houses of brigands will become colonies of citizens propagating throughout Africa and Asia the principles and the practice of liberty, knowledge and reason, that they have brought from Europe. We shall see the monks who brought only shameful superstition to these peoples, and aroused their antagonism by the threat of yet another tyranny, replaced by men occupied in propagating amongst them the truths that will promote their happiness and in teaching them about their interests and their rights. Zeal for the truth is also one of the passions, and it will turn its efforts to distant lands, once there are no longer at home any crass prejudices to combat, any shameful errors to dissipate. . . .

The progress of these peoples is likely to be more rapid and certain than our own because they can receive from us everything that we have had to find out for ourselves, and in order to understand those simple truths and infallible methods which we have acquired only after long error, all that they need to do is to follow the expositions and proofs that appear in our speeches and writings. If the progress of the Greeks was lost to later nations, this was because of the absence of any form of communication between the different peoples, and for this we must blame the tyrannical domination of the Romans. But when mutual needs have brought all men together, and the great powers have established equality among societies as well as among individuals and have raised respect for the independence of weak states and sympathy for ignorance and misery to the rank of political principles, when maxims that favour action and energy have ousted those which would compress the province of human faculties, will it then be possible to fear that there are still places in the world inaccessible to enlightenment, or that despotism in its pride can raise barriers against truth that are insurmountable for long?

The time will therefore come when the sun will shine only on free men who know no other master but their reason; when tyrants and slaves, priests and their stupid or hypocritical instruments, will exist only in works of history and on the stage; and when we shall think of them only to pity their victims and their dupes; to maintain ourselves in a state of vigilance by thinking on their excesses; and to learn how to recognize and so to destroy, by force of reason, the first seeds of tyranny and superstition, should they ever dare to reappear amongst us.

In looking at the history of societies we shall have had occasion to observe that there is often a great difference between the rights that the law allows its citizens and the rights that they actually enjoy, and, again, between the equality established by political codes and that which in fact exists amongst individuals: and we shall have noticed that these differences were one of the principal causes of the destruction of freedom in the ancient republics, of the storms that troubled them, and of the weakness that delivered them over to foreign tyrants.

These differences have three main causes: inequality in wealth; inequality in status between the man whose means of subsistence are hereditary and the man whose means are dependent on the length of his life, or, rather, on that part of his life in which he is capable of work; and, finally, inequality in education.

We therefore need to show that these three sorts of real inequality must constantly diminish without, however, disappearing altogether: for they are the result of natural and necessary causes, which it would be foolish and dangerous to wish to eradicate; and one could not even attempt to bring about the entire disappearance of their effects without introducing even more fecund sources of inequality, without striking more direct and more fatal blows at the rights of man.

It is easy to prove that wealth has a natural tendency to equality, and that any excessive disproportion could not exist, or at least would rapidly disappear, if civil laws did not provide artificial ways of perpetuating and uniting fortunes; if free trade and industry were allowed to remove the advantages that accrued wealth derives from any restrictive law or fiscal privilege; if taxes on covenants, the restrictions placed on their free employment, their subjection to tiresome formalities, and the uncertainty and inevitable expense involved in implementing them did not hamper the activity of the poor man and swallow up his meagre capital; if the administration of the country did not afford some men ways of making their fortune that were closed to other citizens; if prejudice and avarice, so common in old age, did not preside over the making of marriages; and if, in a society enjoying simpler manners and more sensible institutions, wealth ceased to be a means of satisfying vanity and ambition, and if the equally misguided notions of austerity, which condemn spending money in the cultivation of the more delicate pleasures, no longer insisted on the hoarding of all one's earnings.

Let us turn to the enlightened nations of Europe, and observe the size of their present populations in relation to the size of their territories. Let us consider, in agriculture and industry, the proportion that holds between labour and the means of subsistence, and we shall see that it would be impossible for those means to be kept at their present level, and consequently for the population to be kept at its present size, if a great number of individuals were not almost entirely dependent for the maintenance of themselves and their family either on their own labour or on the interest from capital invested so as to make their labour more productive. Now both these sources of income depend on the life and even on the health of the head of the family. They provide what is rather like a life annuity, save that it is more dependent on chance; and in consequence there is a very real difference between people living like this and those whose resources are not at all subject to the same risks, who live either on revenue from land, or on the interest on capital, which is almost independent of their own labour.

Here then is a necessary cause of inequality, of dependence and even of misery, which ceaselessly threatens the most numerous and most active class in our society.

We shall point out how it can be in great part eradicated by guaranteeing people in old age a means of livelihood produced partly by their own savings and partly by the savings of others who make the same outlay, but who die before they need to reap the reward; or, again, on the same principle of compensation, by securing for widows and orphans an income which is the same and costs the same for those families which suffer an early loss and for those which suffer it later; or again by providing all children with the capital necessary for the full use of their labour, available at the age when they start work and found a family, a capital which increases at the expense of those whom premature death prevents from reaching this age. It is to the application of the calculus to the probabilities of life and the investment of money that we owe the idea of these methods which have already been successful, although they have not been applied in a sufficiently comprehensive and exhaustive fashion to render them really useful, not merely to a few individuals, but to society as a whole, by making it possible to prevent those periodic disasters which strike at so many families and which are such a recurrent source of misery and suffering.

We shall point out that schemes of this nature, which

can be organized in the name of the social authority and become one of its greatest benefits, can also be the work of private associations, which will be formed without any real risk, once the principles for the proper working of these schemes have been widely diffused and the mistakes which have been the undoing of a large number of these associations no longer hold terrors for us. . . .

So we might say that a well-directed system of education rectifies natural inequality in ability instead of strengthening it, just as good laws remedy natural inequality in the means of subsistence, and just as in societies where laws have brought about this same equality, liberty, though subject to a regular constitution, will be more widespread, more complete, than in the total independence of savage life. Then the social art will have fulfilled its aim, that of assuring and extending to all men enjoyment of the common rights to which they are called by nature.

The real advantages that should result from this progress, of which we can entertain a hope that is almost a certainty, can have no other term than that of the absolute perfection of the human race; since, as the various kinds of equality come to work in its favour by producing ampler sources of supply, more extensive education, more complete liberty, so equality will be more real and will embrace everything which is really of importance for the happiness of human beings.

It is therefore only by examining the progress and the laws of this perfection that we shall be able to understand the extent or the limits of our hopes.

No one has ever believed that the mind can gain knowledge of all the facts of nature or attain the ultimate means of precision in the measurement, or in the analysis of the facts of nature, the relations between objects and all the possible combinations of ideas. Even the relations between magnitudes, the mere notion of quantity or extension, taken in its fullest comprehension, gives rise to a system so vast that it will never be mastered by the human mind in its entirety, that there will always be a part of it, always indeed the larger part of it, that will remain forever unknown. People have believed that man can never know more than a part of the objects that the nature of his intelligence allows him to understand, and that he must in the end arrive at a point where the number and complexity of the objects that he already knows have absorbed all his strength so that any further progress must be completely impossible.

But since, as the number of known facts increases, the human mind learns how to classify them and to subsume them under more general facts, and, at the same time, the instruments and methods employed in their observation and their exact measurement acquire a new precision; since, as more relations between various objects become known, man is able to reduce them to more general relations, to express them more simply, and to present them in such a way that it is possible to grasp a greater number of them with the same degree of intellectual ability and the same amount of application; since, as the mind learns to understand more complicated combinations of ideas, simpler formulae soon reduce their complexity; so truths that were discovered only by great effort, that could at first only be understood by men capable of profound thought, are soon developed and proved by methods that are not beyond the reach of common intelligence. If the methods which have led to these new combinations of ideas are ever exhausted, if their application to hitherto unsolved questions should demand exertions greater than either the time or the capacity of the learned would permit, some method of a greater generality or simplicity will be found so that genius can continue undisturbed on its path. The strength and the limits of man's intelligence may remain unaltered; and yet the instruments that he uses will increase and improve, the language that fixes and determines his ideas will acquire greater breadth and precision, and, unlike mechanics, where an increase of force means a decrease of speed, the methods that lead genius to the discovery of truth increase at once the force and the speed of its operations.

Therefore, since these developments are themselves the necessary consequences of progress in detailed knowledge, and since the need for new methods in fact only arises in circumstances that give rise to new methods, it is evident that, within the body of the sciences of observation, calculation and experiment, the actual number of truths may always increase, and that every part of this body may develop, and yet man's faculties be of the same strength, activity and extent.

If we apply these general reflections to the various sciences, we can find in each of them examples of progressive improvement that will remove any doubts about what we may expect for the future. We shall point out in particular the progress that is both likely and imminent in those sciences which prejudice regards as all but exhausted. We shall give examples of the manner and extent of the precision and unity which could accrue to the whole system of human knowledge as the result of a more general and philosophical application of the sciences of calculation to the various branches of knowledge. We shall show how favourable to our hopes would be a more universal system of education by giving a greater number of people the elementary knowledge which could awaken their interest in a particular branch of study, and by providing conditions favourable to their progress in it; and how these hopes would be further raised if more men possessed the means to devote themselves to these studies, for at present even in the most enlightened countries scarcely one in fifty of the people who have natural talents receives the necessary education to develop them; and how, if this were done, there would be a proportionate increase in the number of men destined by their discoveries to extend the boundaries of science.

We shall show how this equality in education and the equality which will come about among the different nations would accelerate the advance of these sciences whose progress depends on repeated observations over a large area; what benefits would thereby accrue to mineralogy, botany, zoology and meteorology; and what a vast disproportion holds in all these sciences between the poverty of existing methods, which have nevertheless led to useful and important new truths, and the wealth of those methods which man would then be able to employ.

We shall show how even the sciences in which discovery is the fruit of solitary meditation would benefit from being studied by a greater number of people, in the matter of those improvements in detail which do not demand the intellectual energy of an inventor but suggest themselves to mere reflection.

If we turn now to the arts, whose theory depends on these same sciences, we shall find that their progress, depending as it does on that of theory, can have no other limits; that the procedures of the different arts can be perfected and simplified in the same way as the methods of the sciences; new instruments, machines and looms can add to man's strength and can improve at once the quality and the accuracy of his productions, and can diminish the time and labour that has to be expended on them. The obstacles still in the way of this progress will disappear, accidents will be foreseen and prevented, the insanitary conditions that are due either to the work itself or to the climate will be eliminated.

A very small amount of ground will be able to produce a great quantity of supplies of greater utility or higher quality; more goods will be obtained for a smaller outlay; the manufacture of articles will be achieved with less wastage in raw materials and will make better use of them. Every type of soil will produce those things which satisfy the greatest number of needs; of several alternative ways of satisfying needs of the same order, that will be chosen which satisfies the greatest number of people and which requires least labour and least expenditure. So, without the need for sacrifice, methods of preservation and economy in expenditure will improve in the wake of progress in the arts of producing and preparing supplies and making articles from them.

So not only will the same amount of ground support more people, but everyone will have less work to do, will produce more, and satisfy his wants more fully.

With all this progress in industry and welfare, which establishes a happier proportion between men's talents and their needs, each successive generation will have larger possessions, either as a result of this progress or through the preservation of the products of industry; and so, as a consequence of the physical constitution of the human race, the number of people will increase. Might there not then come a moment when these necessary laws begin to work in a contrary direction; when, the number of people in the world finally exceeding the means of subsistence, there will in consequence ensue a continual diminution of happiness and population, a true retrogression, or at best an oscillation between good and bad? In societies that have reached this stage, will not this oscillation be a perennial source of more or less periodic disaster? Will it not show that a point has been attained beyond which all further improvement is impossible, that the perfectibility of the human race has after long years arrived at a term beyond which it may never go?

There is doubtless no one who does not think that such a time is still very far from us; but will it ever arrive? It is impossible to pronounce about the likelihood of an event that will occur only when the human species will have necessarily acquired a degree of knowledge of which we can have no inkling. And who would take it upon himself to predict the condition to which the art of converting the elements to the use of man may in time be brought?

But even if we agree that the limit will one day arrive, nothing follows from it that is in the least alarming as far as either the happiness of the human race or its indefinite perfectibility is concerned. If we consider that, before all this comes to pass, the progress of reason will have kept pace with that of the sciences, and that the absurd prejudices of superstition will have ceased to corrupt and degrade the moral code by its harsh doctrines instead of purifying and elevating it, we can assume that by then men will know that, if they have a duty towards those who are not yet born, that duty is not to give them existence but to give them happiness; their aim should be to promote the general welfare of the human race or of the society in which they live or of the family to which they belong, rather than foolishly to encumber the world with useless and wretched beings. It is, then, possible that there should be a limit to the amount of food that can be produced, and, consequently, to the size of the population of the world, without this involving that untimely destruction of some of those creatures who have been given life, which is so contrary to nature and to social prosperity. . . .

Organic perfectibility or deterioration amongst the various strains in the vegetable and animal kingdom can be regarded as one of the general laws of nature. This law also applies to the human race. No one can doubt that, as preventive medicine improves and food and housing become healthier, as a way of life is established that develops our physical powers by exercise without ruining them by excess, as the two most virulent causes of deterioration, misery and excessive wealth, are eliminated, the average length of human life will be increased and a better health and a stronger physical constitution will be ensured. The improvement of medical practice, which will become more efficacious with the progress of reason and of the social order, will mean the end of infectious and hereditary diseases and illnesses brought on by climate, food, or working conditions. It is reasonable to hope that all other diseases may likewise disappear as their distant causes are discovered. Would it be absurd, then, to suppose that this perfection of the human species might be capable of indefinite progress; that the day will come when death will be due only to extraordinary accidents or to the decay of the vital forces, and that ultimately the average span between birth and decay will have no assignable value? Certainly man will not become immortal, but will not the interval between the first breath that he draws and the time when in the natural course of events, without disease or accident, he expires, increase indefinitely? Since we are now speaking of a progress that can be represented with some accuracy in figures or on a graph, we shall take this opportunity of explaining the two meanings that can be attached to the word *indefinite*.

In truth, this average span of life, which we suppose will increase indefinitely as time passes, may grow in conformity either with a law such that it continually approaches a limitless length but without ever reaching it, or with a law such that through the centuries it reaches a length greater than any determinate quantity that we may assign to it as its limit. In the latter case such an increase is truly indefinite in the strictest sense of the word, since there is no term on this side of which it must of necessity stop. In the former case it is equally indefinite in relation to us if we cannot fix the limit it always approaches without ever reaching, and particularly if, knowing only that it will never stop, we are ignorant in which of the two senses the term *indefinite* can be applied to it. Such is the present condition of our knowledge as far as the perfectibility of the human race is concerned; such is the sense in which we may call it indefinite.

So, in the example under consideration, we are bound to believe that the average length of human life will forever increase unless this is prevented by physical revolutions; we do not know what the limit is which it can never exceed. We cannot tell even whether the general laws of nature have determined such a limit or not.

But are not our physical faculties and the strength, dexterity and acuteness of our senses, to be numbered among the qualities whose perfection in the individual may be transmitted? Observation of the various breeds of domestic animals inclines us to believe that they are, and we can confirm this by direct observation of the human race.

Finally may we not extend such hopes to the intellectual and moral faculties? May not our parents, who transmit to us the benefits or disadvantages of their constitution, and from whom we receive our shape and features, as well as our tendencies to certain physical affections, hand on to us also that part of the physical organization which determines the intellect, the power of the brain, the ardour of the soul or the moral sensibility? Is it not probable that education, in perfecting these qualities, will at the same time influence, modify and perfect the organization itself? Analogy, investigation of the human faculties and the study of certain facts, all seem to give substance to such conjectures, which would further push back the boundaries of our hopes.

These are the questions with which we shall conclude this final stage. How consoling for the philosopher, who laments the errors, the crimes, the injustices which still pollute the earth, and of which he is often the victim, is this view of the human race, emancipated from its shackles, released from the empire of fate and from that of the enemies of its progress, advancing with a firm and sure step along the path of truth, virtue and happiness! It is the contemplation of this prospect that rewards him for all his efforts to assist the progress of reason and the defence of liberty. He dares to regard these strivings as part of the eternal chain of human destiny; and in this persuasion he is filled with the true delight of virtue and the pleasure of having done some lasting good, which fate can never destroy by a sinister stroke of revenge, by calling back the reign of slavery and prejudice. Such contemplation is for him an asylum, in which the memory of his persecutors cannot pursue him; there he lives in thought with man restored to his natural rights and dignity, forgets man tormented and corrupted by greed, fear, or envy; there he lives with his peers in an Elysium created by reason and graced by the purest pleasures known to the love of mankind.

Trans. June Barraclough (London: George Weidenfeld and Nicolson, 1955).

II. *The Ways of Reason:*

PHILOSOPHY AND NATURAL SCIENCE

The New Science: Aphorisms on Method

[FROM *Novum Organun*]

FRANCIS BACON,
BARON VERULAM, VISCOUNT ST. ALBANS

1620

Man, being the servant and interpreter of Nature, can do and understand so much and so much only as he has observed in fact or in thought of the course of nature: beyond this he neither knows anything nor can do anything.

Neither the naked hand nor the understanding left to itself can effect much. It is by instruments and helps that the work is done, which are as much wanted for the understanding as for the hand. And as the instruments of the hand either give motion or guide it, so the instruments of the mind supply either suggestions for the understanding or cautions.

Human knowledge and human power meet in one; for where the cause is not known the effect cannot be produced. Nature to be commanded must be obeyed; and that which in contemplation is as the cause is in operation as the rule.

The subtlety of nature is greater many times over than the subtlety of the senses and understanding; so that all those specious meditations, speculations, and glosses in which men indulge are quite from the purpose, only there is no one by to observe it.

The logic now in use serves rather to fix and give stability to the errors which have their foundation in commonly received notions than to help the search after truth. So it does more harm than good.

The syllogism is not applied to the first principles of sciences, and is applied in vain to intermediate axioms; being no match for the subtlety of nature. It commands assent therefore to the proposition, but does not take hold of the thing.

The syllogism consists of propositions, propositions consist of words, words are symbols of notions. Therefore if the notions themselves (which is the root of the matter) are confused and overhastily abstracted from the facts, there can be no firmness in the superstructure. Our only hope therefore lies in a true induction.

There is no soundness in our notions whether logical or physical. Substance, Qu 'ty, Action, Passion, Essence itself, are not sound notions: much less are Heavy, Light, Dense, Rare, Moist, Dry, Generation, Corruption, Attraction, Repulsion, Element, Matter, Form, and the like; but all are fantastical and ill defined.

The conclusions of human reason as ordinarily applied in matter of nature, I call for the sake of distinction *Anticipations of Nature* (as a thing rash or premature). That reason which is elicited from facts by a just and methodical process, I call *Interpretation of Nature*.

Anticipations are a ground sufficiently firm for consent; for even if men went mad all after the same fashion, they might agree one with another well enough.

For the winning of assent, indeed, anticipations are far more powerful than interpretations; because being collected from a few instances, and those for the most part of familiar occurrence, they straightway touch the understanding and fill the imagination; whereas interpretations on the other hand, being gathered here and there from very various and widely dispersed facts, cannot suddenly strike the understanding; and therefore they must needs, in respect of the opinions of the time, seem harsh and out of tune; much as the mysteries of faith do.

In sciences founded on opinions and dogmas, the use of anticipations and logic is good; for in them the object is to command assent to the proposition, not to master the thing.

Though all the wits of all the ages should meet together and combine and transmit their labours, yet will no great progress ever be made in science by means of anticipations; because radical errors in the first concoction of the mind are not to be cured by the excellence of functions and remedies subsequent.

It is idle to expect any great advancement in science from the superinducing and engrafting of new things upon old. We must begin anew from the very foundations, unless we would revolve forever in a circle with mean and contemptible progress.

The honour of the ancient authors, and indeed of all, remains untouched; since the comparison I challenge is not of wits or faculties, but of ways and methods, and the part I take upon myself is not that of a judge, but of a guide.

This must be plainly avowed: no judgment can be rightly formed either of my method or of the discoveries to which it leads, by means of anticipations (that is to say, of the reasoning which is now in use); since I cannot be called on to abide by the sentence of a tribunal which is itself on its trial.

The doctrine of those who have denied that certainty could be attained at all, has some agreement with my way of proceeding at the first setting out; but they end in being infinitely separated and opposed. For the holders of that doctrine assert simply that nothing can be known; I also assert that not much can be known in nature by the way which is now in use. But then they go on to destroy the authority of the senses and understanding; whereas I proceed to devise and supply helps for the same.

The idols and false notions which are now in possession of the human understanding, and have taken deep root therein, not only so beset men's minds that truth can hardly find entrance, but even after entrance obtained, they will again in the very instauration of the sciences meet and trouble us, unless men being forewarned of the danger fortify themselves as far as may be against their assaults.

There are four classes of Idols which beset men's minds. To these for distinction's sake I have assigned names—calling the first class *Idols of the Tribe;* the second, *Idols of the Cave;* the third, *Idols of the Market Place;* the fourth, *Idols of the Theatre.*

The formation of ideas and axioms by true induction is no doubt the proper remedy to be applied for the keeping off and clearing away of idols. To point them out, however, is of great use; for the doctrine of Idols is to the Interpretation of Nature what the doctrine of the refutation of Sophisms is to common Logic.

The Idols of the Tribe have their foundation in human nature itself, and in the tribe or race of men. For it is a false assertion that the sense of man is the measure of things. On the contrary, all perceptions as well of the sense as of the mind are according to the measure of the individual and not according to the measure of the universe. And the human understanding is like a false mirror, which, receiving rays irregularly, distorts and discolours the nature of things by mingling its own nature with it.

The Idols of the Cave are the idols of the individual man. For everyone (besides the errors common to human nature in general) has a cave or den of his own, which refracts and discolours the light of nature; owing either to his own proper and peculiar nature; or to his education and conversation with others; or to the reading of books, and the authority of those whom he esteems and admires, or to the differences of impressions, accordingly as they take place in a mind preoccupied and predisposed or in a mind indifferent and settled; or the like. So that the spirit of man (according as it is meted out to different individuals) is in fact a thing variable and full of perturbation, and governed as it were by chance. Whence it was well observed by Heraclitus that men look for sciences in their own lesser worlds, and not in the greater or common world.

There are also Idols formed by the intercourse and association of men with each other, which I call Idols of the Market Place, on account of the commerce and consort of men there. For it is by discourse that men associate; and words are imposed according to the apprehension of the vulgar. And therefore the ill and unfit choice of words wonderfully obstructs the understanding. Nor do the definitions or explanations wherewith in some things learned men are wont to guard and defend themselves, by any means set the matter right. But words plainly force and overrule the understanding, and throw all into confusion, and lead men away into numberless empty controversies and idle fancies.

Lastly, there are Idols which have immigrated into men's minds from the various dogmas of philosophies, and also from wrong laws of demonstration. These I call Idols of the Theatre; because in my judgment all the received systems are but so many stage plays, representing worlds of their own creation after an unreal and scenic fashion. Nor is it only of the systems now in vogue, or only of the ancient sects and philosophies, that I speak; for many more plays of the same kind may yet be composed and in like artificial manner set forth; seeing that errors the most widely different have nevertheless causes for the most part alike. Neither again do I mean this only of entire systems, but also of many principles and axioms in science, which by tradition, credulity, and negligence have come to be received.

From *The New Organon*, ed. James Spedding, R. L. Ellis, and D. D. Heath, in *Works*, Vol. IV (London: Longmans & Co., 1870).

❖ ❖ ❖

There Are No Innate Ideas

[FROM *An Essay Concerning Human Understanding*]

JOHN LOCKE

1690

1. *Idea is the object of thinking.*—Every man being conscious to himself that he thinks, and that which his mind is applied about whilst thinking being the ideas that are there, it is past doubt that men have in their minds several ideas, such as are those expressed by the words, "whiteness, hardness, sweetness, thinking, motion, man, elephant, army, drunkenness," and others. It is in the first place then to be enquired, How he comes by them? I know it is a received doctrine, that men have native ideas and original characters stamped upon their minds in their very first being. This opinion I have at large examined already; and, I suppose, what I have said in the foregoing Book will be much more

easily admitted, when I have shown whence the understanding may get all the ideas it has, and by what
ways and degrees they may come into the mind; for
which I shall appeal to everyone's own observation
and experience.

2. *All ideas come from sensation or reflection.*
—Let us then suppose the mind to be, as we say, white
paper, void of all characters, without any ideas; how
comes it to be furnished? Whence comes it by that
vast store, which the busy and boundless fancy of man
has painted on it with an almost endless variety?
Whence has it all the materials of reason and knowledge? To this I answer, in one word, from EXPERI-
ENCE; in that all our knowledge is founded, and
from that it ultimately derives itself. Our observation,
employed either about external sensible objects, or
about the internal operations of our minds, perceived
and reflected on by ourselves, is that which supplies
our understandings with all the materials of thinking.
These two are the fountains of knowledge, from whence
all the ideas we have, or can naturally have, do spring.

3. *The objects of sensation one source of ideas.*
—First, our senses, conversant about particular sensible
objects, do convey into the mind several distinct perceptions of things, according to those various ways
wherein those objects do affect them; and thus we come
by those *ideas* we have of yellow, white, heat, cold,
soft, hard, bitter, sweet, and all those which we call
sensible qualities; which when I say the senses convey
into the mind, I mean, they from external objects convey into the mind what produces there those perceptions. This great source of most of the ideas we have,
depending wholly upon our senses, and derived by
them to the understanding, I call, SENSATION.

4. *The operations of our minds the other source of*

them. —Secondly, the other fountain, from which experience furnisheth the understanding with ideas, is the perception of the operations of our own minds within us, as it is employed about the ideas it has got; which operations, when the soul comes to reflect on and consider, do furnish the understanding with another set of ideas which could not be had from things without: and such are perception, thinking, doubting, believing, reasoning, knowing, willing, and all the different actings of our own minds; which we being conscious of, and observing in ourselves, do from these receive into our understanding as distinct ideas, as we do from bodies affecting our senses. This source of ideas every man has wholly in himself: and though it be not sense, as having nothing to do with external objects, yet it is very like it, and might properly enough be called internal sense. But as I call the other Sensation, so I call this REFLECTION, the ideas it affords being such only as the mind gets by reflecting on its own operations within itself. By Reflection, then, in the following part of this discourse, I would be understood to mean that notice which the mind takes of its own operations, and the manner of them, by reason whereof there come to be ideas of these operations in the understanding. These two, I say, viz., external material things as the objects of Sensation, and the operations of our own minds within as the objects of Reflection, are, to me, the only originals from whence all our ideas take their beginnings. The term *operations* here, I use in a large sense, as comprehending not barely the actions of the mind about its ideas, but some sort of passions arising sometimes from them, such as is the satisfaction or uneasiness arising from any thought.

5. *All our ideas are of the one or the other of these.* —The understanding seems to me not to have the least

glimmering of any ideas which it doth not receive from one of these two. *External objects* furnish the mind with the ideas of sensible qualities, which are all those different perceptions they produce in us; and *the mind* furnishes the understanding with ideas of its own operations. These, when we have taken a full survey of them, and their several modes, combinations, and relations, we shall find to contain all our whole stock of ideas; and that we have nothing in our minds which did not come in one of these two ways. Let anyone examine his own thoughts, and thoroughly search into his understanding, and then let him tell me, whether all the original ideas he has there, are any other than of the objects of his senses, or of the operations of his mind considered as objects of his reflection; and how great a mass of knowledge soever he imagines to be lodged there, he will, upon taking a strict view, see that he has not any idea in his mind but what one of these two have imprinted, though perhaps with infinite variety compounded and enlarged by the understanding, as we shall see hereafter.

Ed. A. S. Pringle-Pattison (Oxford: Clarendon Press, 1924).

❖ ❖ ❖

FROM "On Locke's Essay on Human Understanding"

GOTTFRIED WILHELM LEIBNITZ

1696

I find so many marks of unusual penetration in what Mr. Locke has given us on the Human Understanding and on Education, and I consider the matter so important, that I have thought I should not employ the time to no purpose which I should give to such profitable reading; so much the more as I have myself meditated·deeply upon the subject of the foundations of our knowledge. This is my reason for putting upon this sheet some of the reflections which have occurred to me while reading his Essay on the Understanding.

Of all researches, there is none of greater importance. since it is the key to all others. The first book considers chiefly the principles said to be born with us. Mr. Locke does not admit them, any more than he admits innate ideas. He has doubtless had good reasons for opposing himself on this point to ordinary prejudices, for the name of ideas and principles is greatly abused. Common philosophers manufacture for themselves principles according to their fancy; and the Cartesians, who profess greater accuracy, do not cease to intrench themselves behind so-called ideas of extension, of matter, and of the soul, desiring to avoid thereby the necessity of proving what they advance, on the pretext that those who will meditate on these ideas will discover in them the same thing as they; that is to say, that those who will accustom themselves to their jargon and mode of thought will have the same prepossessions, which is very true.

My view, then, is that nothing should be taken as first principles but experiences and the axiom of identity or (what is the same thing) contradiction, which is primitive, since otherwise there would be no difference between truth and falsehood; and all investigation would cease at once, if to say yes or no were a matter of indifference. We cannot, then, prevent ourselves from assuming this principle as soon as we wish to reason. All other truths are demonstrable, and I value very highly the method of Euclid, who, without stopping at what would be supposed to be sufficiently proved by the so-called ideas, has demonstrated (for instance) that in a triangle one side is always less than the sum of the other two. Yet Euclid was right in taking some axioms for granted, not as if they were truly primitive and indemonstrable, but because he would have come to a standstill if he had wished to reach his conclusions only after an exact discussion of principles. Thus he judged it proper to content himself with having pushed the proofs up to this small number of propositions, so that it may be said that if they are true, all that he says is also true. He has left to others the task of demonstrating further these principles themselves, which besides are already justified by experience; but with this we are not satisfied in these matters. This is why Apollonius, Proclus, and others have taken the pains to demonstrate some of Euclid's axioms. Philosophers should imitate this method of procedure in order finally to attain some fixed principles, even though they be only provisional, after the way I have just mentioned.

As for ideas, I have given some explanation of them in a brief essay printed in the *Actes des Sçavans* of Leipzig for November, 1684 (p. 537), which is entitled "Meditationes de Cognitione, Veritate, et Ideis"; and I could have wished that Mr. Locke had seen and examined it; for I am one of the most docile of men, and nothing is better suited to advance our thought than the considerations and remarks of clever persons, when they are made with attention and sincerity. I shall only say here, that true or real ideas are those whose execution we are assured is possible; the others are doubtful, or (in case of proved impossibility) chimerical. Now the possibility of ideas is proved as much *a priori* by demonstrations, by making use of the possibility of other more simple ideas, as *a posteriori* by experience; for what exists cannot fail to be possible. But primitive ideas are those whose possibility is indemonstrable, and which are in truth nothing else than the attributes of God.

I do not find it absolutely essential for the beginning or for the practice of the art of thinking to decide the question whether there are ideas and truths born with us; whether they all come to us from without or from ourselves; we will reason correctly provided we observe what I have said above, and proceed in an orderly way and without prejudice. The question of the origin of our ideas and of our maxims is not preliminary in Philosophy, and we must have made great progress in order to solve it successfully. I think, however, that I can say that our ideas, even those of sensible things, come from within our own soul, of which view you can the better judge by what I have published upon the nature and connection of substances and what is called the union of the soul with the body. For I have found that these things had not been well understood. I am nowise in favor of Aristotle's *tabula rasa;* and there is something substantial in what Plato called *reminiscence*. There is even something more; for we not only have a reminiscence of all our past thoughts, but also a presentiment of all our future thoughts. It is true that this is confused, and fails to distinguish them, in much the same way as when I hear the noise of the sea I hear that of all the particular waves which make up the noise as a whole, though without discerning one wave from another. Thus it is true in a certain sense, as I have explained, that not only our ideas, but also our sensations, spring from within our own soul, and that the soul is more independent than is thought, although it is always true that nothing takes place in it which is not determined, and nothing is found in creatures that God does not continually create. . . .

From *New Essays Concerning Human Understanding,* trans. A. G. Langley (New York: The Macmillan Co., 1896).

❖ ❖ ❖

Definition of a *Philosophe*

[FROM *La Grande Encyclopédie*]

Attributed to
CÉSAR CHESNEAU DUMARSAIS

1778

Reason is to the philosopher what grace is to the Christian.

Grace causes the Christian to act, reason the philosopher.

Other men are carried away by their passions, their actions not being preceded by reflection: these are the men who walk in darkness. On the other hand, the philosopher, even in his passions, acts only after reflection; he walks in the dark, but by a torch.

The philosopher forms his principles from an infinity of particular observations. Most people adopt principles without thinking of the observations that have produced them: they believe that maxims exist, so to speak, by themselves. But the philosopher takes maxims from their source; he examines their origin; he knows their proper value, and he makes use of them only in so far as they suit him.

Truth is not for the philosopher a mistress who corrupts his imagination and whom he believes is to be found everywhere; he contents himself with being able to unravel it where he can perceive it. He does not confound it with probability; he takes for true what is true, for false what is false, for doubtful what is doubtful, and for probable what is only probable. He does more, and here you have a great perfection of the philosopher: when he has no reason by which to judge, he knows how to live in suspension of judgment. . . .

The philosophic spirit is, then, a spirit of observation and exactness, which relates everything to true principles; but the philosopher does not cultivate the mind alone, he carries his attention and needs further. . . .

Our philosopher does not believe in exiling himself from this world, he does not believe that he is in enemy country; he wishes to enjoy with wise economy the goods which nature offers him; he wishes to find pleasure with others, and in order to find it, he must make it: thus he tries to be agreeable to those with whom chance and his choice have thrown him, and at the same time he finds what is agreeable to him. He is an honest man who wishes to please and to make himself useful.

The majority of the great, whose dissipations do not leave enough time to meditate, are savage towards those whom they do not believe to be their equals. The ordinary philosophers who meditate too much, or rather who meditate badly, are savage towards everybody; they flee men, and men avoid them. But our philosopher who knows how to strike a balance between retreat from and commerce with men, is full of humanity. He is Terence's Chrémès who feels that he is a man, and that humanity alone is interested in the good and bad fortune of his neighbour. *Homo sum, humani a me nihil alienum puto.*

It would be useless to remark here how jealous the philosopher is of everything calling itself honour and probity. Civil society is, so to speak, a divinity for him on earth; he burns incense to it, he honours it by probity, by an exact attention to his duties, and by a sincere desire not to be a useless or embarrassing member of it. The sentiments of probity enter as much into the mechanical constitution of the philosopher as the illumination of the mind. The more you find reason in a man, the more you find in him probity. On the other hand, where fanaticism and superstition reign, there reign the passions and anger. The temperament of the philosopher is to act according to the spirit of order or reason; as he loves society extremely, it is more important to him than to other men to bend every effort to produce only effects conformable to the idea of the honest man. . . .

This love of society, so essential to the philosopher, makes us see how very true was the remark of Marcus Aurelius: "How happy will the people be when kings are philosophers or philosophers are kings!"

"The Encyclopedia," in *Main Currents of Western Thought,* ed. Franklin Le Van Baumer (New York: Alfred A. Knopf, Inc., 1952).

Men Are Reasonable

[FROM *A Treatise on Man*]

CLAUDE ADRIEN HELVETIUS

1773

. . . I have examined,

11. "If all men, commonly well organized, have not an equal aptitude to understanding?"

I agree in the first place, that as all our ideas come

to us by the senses, we ought to regard the mind or understanding either as the mere effect of the greater or less degree of perfection in the five senses; or of an occult and indeterminable cause, to which has been vaguely given the name of organization.

To prove the falsity of this opinion, we must have recourse to experience, form a clear idea of the word Mind or Understanding and distinguish it from the soul. This distinction made, we must observe,

On what objects the mind acts.

How it acts.

If all its operations are not reducible to the observing of the resemblances and differences, the agreements and disagreements that different objects have among themselves and with us; and if, in consequence, all judgments formed on corporeal objects are not mere sensations.

If it be not the same with judgments formed on ideas to which are given the names of abstract, collective, etc.

If in every case to judge and compare can be anything else than *alternate inspection*, that is to say, *sensation*.

If we can feel the impression of objects without comparing them with each other.

If such comparison does not suppose an interest to compare them.

If that interest be not the sole and unknown cause of all our ideas, our actions, our pains, our pleasures, and, in short, our sociability.

From whence I observe, that as this interest, in its last analysis, takes its source in corporeal sensibility; that this sensibility is consequently the sole principle of human ideas and actions.

That there is no rational motive for rejecting this opinion.

That this opinion, once demonstrated and acknowledged for true, we must necessarily regard the inequality of understandings as the effect,

Either of the unequal extent of the memory;

Or of the greater or less perfection of the five senses.

That in fact, it is neither the extent of the memory, nor the extreme fineness of the senses, that produces, and ought to produce the extent of the understanding.

That with regard to the fineness of the senses, men commonly well organized differ only in the degrees of their sensations.

That this small difference does not change the relation of their sensations to each other, and consequently has no influence over the understanding, which is not, and cannot be anything else than a knowledge of the true relations objects have to each other.

The cause of the different opinions of men.

That this difference is the effect of the uncertain signification of words; such as

Good,

Interest, and

Virtue.

That if words were precisely defined, and their definitions ranged in a dictionary, all the propositions of morality, politics, and metaphysics would become as susceptible of demonstration as the truths of geometry.

That from the moment the same ideas are annexed to the same words, all minds adopting the same principles, would draw from them the same conclusions.

That it is impossible, as all objects appear to all men to have the same relations, that by comparing objects with each other, men (either in the material world, as is proved by geometry, or in the intellectual world, which is proved by metaphysics), should not form the same conclusions.

That the truth of this proposition is proved by the resemblance of the fairy tales, philosophic tales, and religious tales of all countries, and by the uniformity of impositions, employed everywhere by the ministers of false religions, to preserve and increase their authority over the people.

From all these facts it results, that as the greater or less fineness of the senses does not at all change the proportion in which objects strike us, all men, commonly well organized, have an equal aptitude to understanding.

To augment proofs of this important truth, I have added a demonstration of it in the same section, by another series of propositions. I have shown that the most sublime ideas, once simplified, are, by the consent of all philosophers, reducible to this clear proposition, *that white is white, and black is black.*

That every truth of this kind is comprehensible by all understandings; and that therefore there is not any truth, however great and general it may be, which clearly represented, and disengaged from the obscurity of words, cannot be equally conceived by all men commonly well organized. Now to be equally able to comprehend the highest truths, is to have an equal aptitude to understanding. Such is the conclusion of the second section.

III. The object of this section is an inquiry concerning the causes to which the inequality of understandings is to be attributed.

These causes are reducible to two.

The one is the unequal desire that men have to knowledge.

The other, the diversity of positions in which chance places them; a diversity from which results that of their instruction, and their ideas. To show that it is to these two causes only we ought to refer the difference and inequality of understandings, I have proved that most of our discoveries are the gifts of chance.

That these same gifts are not granted to all.

This distribution however is not so unequal as imagined.

That in this respect chance is less neglectful of us than we are, if I may use the expression, neglectful of chance.

That in fact all men commonly well organized have an equal power of understanding, but that power is dead in them, when not put in action by some passion, such as the love of esteem, glory, etc.

That men owe to such passions only the attention proper to fecundate the ideas offered to them by chance.

That without passions their minds might be, so to say, regarded as perfect machines, whose movement is suspended till the passions put them in action.

From whence I conclude, that the inequality of understandings in men is the produce of chance, and of the unequal vivacity of their passions; but whether those passions are the effects of the strength of temperament, is what I examine in the following section.

iv. I there demonstrate,

That men commonly well organized are susceptible of the same degree of passion.

That their unequal force is always the effect of the difference of situations in which chance has placed them.

That the original character of each man (as Pascal observes) is nothing more than the produce of his first habits: that man is born without ideas, without passions, and without other wants than those of hunger and thirst, and consequently without character: that he often changes it without any change in his organization: that those changes, independent of the greater or less fineness of his senses, operate according to the changes that happen in his situation and ideas.

That the diversity of characters depends solely on the different manners in which the sentiment of self-love is modified in men.

That this sentiment, the necessary effect of corporeal sensibility, is common to all, and produces in all the love of power.

That this desire produces envy, the love of wealth, of glory, importance, justice, virtue, intolerance, in short, all the factitious passions, whose several names mean nothing more than the different applications of the love of power.

This truth established, I show, by a short genealogy of the passions, that if the love of power be nothing more than the mere effect of corporeal sensibility, and if all men commonly well organized are sensible, all are consequently susceptible of the sort of passion proper to put in action the equal aptitude they have to understanding. . . .

Trans. W. Hooper (London: B. Law, 1777).

❖ ❖ ❖

Men Aren't Quite That Reasonable

[FROM "Refutation of Helvetius"]

DENIS DIDEROT

About 1774

Text of Helvetius, On Man: "I consider intelligence, genius, and virtue as the product of teaching."

Comment of Diderot: And of nothing but teaching?

Helvetius: "This idea seems to me to hold true always."

Diderot: It is a false idea and can therefore never be proved true.

Helvetius: "My critics have granted me that education has on genius, on the character of individuals and societies, more influence than has been usually believed."

Diderot: And that's all they can grant you.

Helvetius: "If the educational system makes us almost entirely what we are, why blame the teacher for the ignorance and stupidity of his pupils?"

Diderot: I know of no philosophy of education so consoling for parents and so encouraging for teachers. This is its advantage.

But I know of none more harmful for children thus considered capable of everything; I know of none more calculated to produce a society of mediocrities, and to damage the genius who can do but one thing—though that superbly; I know of none more dangerous in its encouragement of educational administrators who, after having tried in vain to mould a class of students to a discipline for which they have no natural bent, proceed to turn them out into a world where they are no longer good for anything.

Is man born good or bad?

If you call a man good who does good, a man bad who does evil, then surely man is born neither good nor bad. I should say the same thing were the question one of being born bright or stupid.

But is man born with a natural, an organic, *bent* towards saying stupid things—and doing them—towards harming himself and his fellows, towards listening to or disregarding parental advice, towards diligence or laziness, fair-mindedness or indignation, respect for law, or contempt for it? Only a person who has never actually seen two children in his life, who has never heard them cry in their cradles, can have doubts as to how to answer these questions. Man is born nothing, but every man is born with aptitudes towards a certain kind of living.

M. Helvetius, I take it you're a hunter?

Yes.

Do you see that puppy?

The one with bow legs, long, low-swung body, narrow muzzle, red-spotted paws and hide?

Yes. What is it?

He's a basset. This breed has good scent, ardour, courage; he will burrow into a fox's den at the risk of coming out with torn ears and sides.

And this other one?

He's a hound, a tireless animal. His tough hide lets him penetrate into the thorniest bushes. . . .

And this other one?

A setter. I can't tell you much about him from a look. Will he be gentle or not? Will he have a good nose or not? It's a question of breeding.

And this fourth puppy?

He looks as though he'd grow up into a fine bird dog.

These then are all dogs?

Yes.

Now, tell me. I have a fine kennel man. Can't I ask him to rear the basset so that he will be a hound, the hound so that he will be a racing greyhound, the greyhound a terrier, the terrier a poodle?

Don't try it!

Why not? They have just been born, they are nothing; fit for everything, education can make them whatever I want them to be.

You're making fun of me.

M. Helvetius, you are quite right. But what if among human beings there should be the same variety of individuals as among dogs, if each of us had his own gait, his own game?

From "Réfutation d'Helvétius," *Œuvres complètes*, Vol. II, ed. J. Assézat (Paris: Garnier, 1875); trans. C.B.

❖ ❖ ❖

The Philosophical Dictionary
of a *Philosophe*

[FROM *Philosophical Dictionary*]

FRANÇOIS MARIE AROUET DE
VOLTAIRE

1750

DEMOCRACY

As a rule there is no comparison between the crimes
of great men, who are always ambitious, and the crimes
of the people, who always want, and can only want,
liberty and equality. These two sentiments, Liberty and
Equality, do not lead straight to calumny, rapine, as-
sassination, poisoning, the devastation of one's neighbours' lands, etc. But ambitious might and the mania
for power plunge men into all these crimes, whatever
the time, whatever the place.

Popular government is in itself, therefore, less iniqui-
tous, less abominable than despotic power.

The great vice of democracy is certainly not tyranny
and cruelty. There have been mountain-dwelling republicans who were savage and ferocious; but it was not
the republican spirit that made them so, it was nature.

The real vice of a civilized republic is expressed in
the Turkish fable of the dragon with many heads and
the dragon with many tails. The many heads injured

one another, and the many tails obeyed a single head which sought to devour everything.

Democracy seems suitable only to a very little country, and one that is happily situated. However small it may be, it will make many mistakes, because it will be composed of men. Discord will reign there as in a monastery; but there will be no St. Bartholomew, no Irish massacres, no Sicilian vespers, no Inquisition, no condemnation to the galleys for having taken some water from the sea without paying for it—unless one assumes that this republic is composed of devils in a corner of hell.

Which is better—runs the endless question—a republic or a monarchy? The dispute always resolves itself into an agreement that it is a very difficult business to govern men. The Jews had God Himself for their master, and see what has happened to them as a result: nearly always have they been oppressed and enslaved and even today they do not appear to cut a very pretty figure.

EQUALITY

It is clear that men, in the enjoyment of their natural faculties, are equal: they are equal when they perform animal functions, and when they exercise their understanding. The King of China, the Great Mogul, the Padisha of Turkey, cannot say to the least of men: "I forbid you to digest, to go to the privy, or to think." All the animals of each species are equal among themselves. Animals, by nature, have over us the advantage of independence. If a bull which is wooing a heifer is driven away with the blows of the horns by a stronger bull, it goes in search of another mistress in another field, and lives free. A cock, beaten by a cock, consoles itself in another poultry house. It is not so with us. A little vizier exiles a bostangi to Lemnos: the vizier

Azem exiles the little vizier to Tenedos: the padisha exiles the vizier Azem to Rhodes: the Janissaries put the padisha in prison, and elect another who will exile good Mussulmans as he chooses; people will still be very obliged to him if he limits his sacred authority to this small exercise.

If this world were what it seems it should be, if man could find everywhere in it an easy subsistence, and a climate suitable to his nature, it is clear that it would be impossible for one man to enslave another. If this globe were covered with wholesome fruits; if the air, which should contribute to our life, gave us no diseases and no premature deaths; if man had no need of lodging and bed other than those of the buck and the deer; then the Gengis Khans and the Tamerlanes would have no servants other than their children, who would be decent enough to help them in their old age.

In the natural state enjoyed by all untamed quadrupeds, birds, and reptiles, man would be as happy as they. Domination would then be a chimera, an absurdity of which no one would think; for why seek servants when you have no need of their service?

If it came into the head of some individual of tyrannous mind and brawny arm to enslave a neighbour less strong than he, the thing would be impossible; the oppressed would be on the Danube before the oppressor had taken his measures on the Volga.

All men then would be necessarily equal, if they were without needs. It is the poverty connected with our species which subordinates one man to another. It is not the inequality which is the real misfortune, it is the dependence. It matters very little that So-and-so calls himself "His Highness," and So-and-so "His Holiness"; but to serve the one or the other is hard.

A big family has cultivated fruitful soil; two little families nearby have thankless and rebellious fields; the two poor families have to serve the opulent family, or slaughter it. There is no difficulty in that. But one of the two indigent families offers its arms to the rich family in exchange for bread, while the other attacks and is defeated. The subservient family is the origin of the servants and the workmen; the beaten family is the origin of the slaves.

In our unhappy world it is impossible for men living in society not to be divided into two classes, the one the rich who command, the other the poor who serve; and these two classes are subdivided into a thousand, and these thousand still have different gradations.

When the lots are drawn you come to us and say: "I am a man like you. I have two hands and two feet, as much pride as you, nay more, a mind as disordered, at least, as inconsequent, as contradictory as yours. I am a citizen of San Marino, or of Ragusa, or Vaugirard: give me my share of the land. In our known hemisphere there are about fifty thousand million arpents to cultivate, some passable, some sterile. We are only about a thousand million featherless bipeds in this continent; that makes fifty arpents apiece: be just; give me my fifty arpents."

"Go and take them in the land of the Kaffirs," we answer, "or the Hottentots, or the Samoyedes; come to an amicable arrangement with them; here all the shares are taken. If you want to eat, be clothed, lodged, and warmed among us, work for us as your father did; serve us or amuse us, and you will be paid; otherwise you will be obliged to ask charity, which would be too degrading to your sublime nature, and would stop your being really the equal of kings, and even of country parsons, according to the pretensions of your noble pride."

II. All the poor are not unhappy. The majority were born in that state, and continual work keeps them from feeling their position too keenly; but when they do feel it, then one sees wars, like that of the popular party against the senate party in Rome, like those of the peasants in Germany, England, and France. All these wars finish sooner or later with the subjection of the people, because the powerful have money, and money is master of everything in a state. I say in a state, for it is not the same between nations. The nation which makes the best use of the sword will always subjugate the nation which has more gold and less courage.

All men are born with a sufficiently violent liking for domination, wealth, and pleasure, and with a strong taste for idleness; consequently, all men covet the money, the wives, or the daughters of other men; they wish to be their master, to subject them to all their caprices, and to do nothing, or at least to do only very agreeable things. You see clearly that with these fine inclinations it is as impossible for men to be equal as it is impossible for two preachers or two professors of theology not to be jealous of each other.

The human race, such as it is, cannot subsist unless there is an infinity of useful men who possess nothing at all; for it is certain that a man who is well off will not leave his own land to come to till yours, and if you have need of a pair of shoes, it is not the Secretary to the Privy Council who will make them for you. Equality, therefore, is at once the most natural thing and the most fantastic.

As men go to excess in everything when they can, this inequality has been exaggerated. It has been maintained in many countries that it was not permissible for a citizen to leave the country where chance has caused him to be born. The sense of this law is obviously: "This land is so bad and so badly governed, that we forbid any individual to leave it, for fear that everyone will leave it." Do better: make all your subjects wish to live in your country, and foreigners wish to come to it.

All men have the right in the bottom of their hearts to think themselves entirely equal to other men. It does not follow from this that the cardinal's cook should order his master to prepare him his dinner, but the cook can say: "I am a man like my master; like him I was born crying; like me he will die with the same pangs and the same ceremonies. Both of us perform the same animal functions. If the Turks take possession of Rome, and if then I am cardinal and my master cook, I shall take him into my service." This discourse is reasonable and just, but while waiting for the Great Turk to take possession of Rome, the cook must do his duty, or else all human society is disordered.

As regards a man who is neither a cardinal's cook, nor endowed with any other employment in the state; as regards a private person who is connected with nothing, but who is vexed at being received everywhere with an air of being patronized or scorned, who sees quite clearly that many monseigneurs have no more knowledge, wit, or virtue than he, and who at times is bored at waiting in their antechambers, what should he decide to do? Why, to take himself off.

FATHERLAND

A young journeyman pastrycook who had been to college, and who still knew a few of Cicero's phrases, boasted one day of loving his fatherland. "What do you mean by your fatherland?" a neighbour asked him. "Is it your oven? Is it the village where you were born and which you have never seen since? Is it the street in which dwelt your father and mother, who have been ruined with the result that you are reduced to baking little pies for a living? Is it the town hall where you will never be the police superintendent's clerk? Is it the church of Our Lady where you have not been able to become a choirboy, while a stupid man is archbishop and duke with an income of twenty thousand golden louis?"

The journeyman pastrycook did not know what to answer. A philosopher, who was listening to this conversation, concluded that in a fatherland of any extent there must often be several million men who have no fatherland.

You, pleasure-loving Parisians, who have never travelled farther than Dieppe to eat fresh fish; who know nothing but your brilliant town house, your pretty country house, and your box at an Opera where the rest of Europe persists in being bored; who speak your own language well enough because you know no other— you love all these things, and you love the girls you keep, the champagne which comes to you from Reims, the dividends which the Hotel-de-Ville pays you every six months; and you say you love your fatherland!

Now, in all conscience, does a financier sincerely love his fatherland?

The officer and the soldier who pillage their winter quarters, if one lets them—have they a very warm love for the peasants they ruin?

Where was the fatherland of the scarred Duc de Guise, was it in Nancy, Paris, Madrid, Rome? What fatherland have you, Cardinals de La Balue, Duprat, Lorraine, Mazarin? Where was the fatherland of Attila, and of a hundred other heroes of his type? I would like someone to tell me which was Abraham's fatherland.

The first man to write that one's fatherland is wherever one feels comfortable was, I believe, Euripides in his *Phaeton*. But the first man who left his birthplace to seek his comfort elsewhere had said it before him.

What, then, is a fatherland? Is it not a good field, whose owner, lodged in a well-kept house, can say: "This field that I till, this house that I have built, are mine. I live here protected by laws which no tyrant can infringe. When those who own fields and houses, like myself, meet in their common interest, I have my voice in the assembly; I am a part of everything, a part of the community, a part of the dominion—there is my fatherland"?

Very well. But is it better for your fatherland to be a monarchy or a republic? For four thousand years has this question been debated. Ask the rich for an answer, they all prefer aristocracy; question the people, they want democracy: only kings prefer royalty. How then is it that nearly the whole world is governed by monarchs? Ask the rats who proposed to hang a bell round the cat's neck. But in truth, the real reason is, as has been said, that men are very rarely worthy of governing themselves.

It is sad that in order to be a good patriot one often has to be the enemy of the rest of mankind. Whenever old Cato, that excellent citizen, spoke before the Roman senate, he always used to say: "Such is my opinion, and Carthage must be destroyed." To be a good patriot is to wish that one's city may be enriched by trade, and be powerful by arms. It is clear that one country cannot gain without another's losing, and that one cannot conquer without bringing misery to another.

Such then is the human state, that to wish greatness for one's country is to wish harm to one's neighbours. He who wished that his fatherland might never be greater, smaller, richer, or poorer, would be a citizen of the world.

LIBERTY OF THE PRESS

What harm can the prediction of Jean-Jacques[1] do to Russia? None. He is free to explain it in a mystical, typical, allegorical sense, according to custom. The nations which will destroy the Russians will be belles-lettres, mathematics, wit, and social graces, which degrade man and pervert nature.

From five to six thousand pamphlets have been printed in Holland against Louis XIV, none of which helped to make him lose the battles of Blenheim, Turin, and Ramillies.

In general, we have as natural a right to make use of our pens as of our tongue, at our peril, risk, and hazard. I know many books which have bored their readers, but I know of none which has done real evil. Theologians, or pretended politicians, cry: "Religion is destroyed, the government is lost, if you print certain truths or certain paradoxes. Never dare to think, till you have asked permission from a monk or a clerk. It is against the public welfare for a man to think for himself. Homer, Plato, Cicero, Virgil, Pliny, Horace, never published anything but with the approbation of the doctors of the Sorbonne and of the holy Inquisition.

"See into what horrible decadence the liberty of the press has brought England and Holland. It is true that they possess the commerce of the whole world, and

[1] Rousseau had predicted the imminent destruction of the Russian empire; his chief reason being that Peter I had sought to disseminate the arts and sciences. [Trans. note.]

that England is victorious on sea and land; but it is merely a false greatness, a false opulence: they are hastening to their ruin. An enlightened people cannot exist."

No one could reason more justly, my friends; but let us see, if you please, what state has been ruined by a book. The most dangerous, the most pernicious book of all, is that of Spinoza. Not only in the character of a Jew does he attack the New Testament, but in the character of a scholar he ruins the Old. His system of atheism is a thousand times better constructed and reasoned than those of Straton and of Epicurus. It requires the most profound sagacity to answer to the arguments by which he endeavours to prove that one substance cannot form another.

Like yourself, I detest this book, which I perhaps understand better than you, and to which you have replied very badly. But have you discovered that it has changed the face of the world? Has any preacher lost a florin of his income by the publication of the works of Spinoza? Is there a bishop whose rents have diminished? On the contrary, their revenues have doubled since his time: all the ill is limited to a small number of peaceable readers, who have examined Spinoza's arguments in their studies, and who have written for or against them in works that are little known.

For ourselves, you have hardly been consistent in having printed, *ad usum Delphini*, the atheism of Lucretius—as you have already been reproached with doing. No trouble, no scandal, has ensued from it; so Spinoza might be left to live in peace in Holland, as was Lucretius in Rome.

But if there appears among you any new book, the ideas of which shock your own—supposing you have any—or of which the author may be of a party contrary to yours—or what is worse, of which the author may not be of any party at all—then you cry out "Fire!" and all is noise, scandal, and uproar in your small corner of the earth. There is an abominable man who has declared in print that if we had no hands we would not be able to make shoes nor stockings. The devout cry out, furred doctors assemble, alarms multiply from college to college, from house to house, whole communities are disturbed. And why? For five or six pages, about which no one will give a fig at the end of three months. Does a book displease you? Refute it. Does it bore you? Don't read it.

Oh! you say to me, the books of Luther and Calvin have destroyed the Roman Catholic religion in one-half of Europe? Why not say also, that the books of the patriarch Photius have destroyed this Roman religion in Asia, Africa, Greece, and Russia?

You deceive yourself grossly, when you think that you have been ruined by books. The empire of Russia is two thousand leagues in extent, and there are not six men who are aware of the points disputed by the Greek and Latin Church. If the monk Luther, John Calvin, and the vicar Zwingli had been content with writing, Rome would still hold in subjugation all the states that it has lost; but these people and their adherents ran from town to town, from house to house, exciting the women, and they were supported by princes. The fury which tormented Amata and which, according to Virgil, whipped her like a top, was not more turbulent. Be assured that one enthusiastic, factious, ignorant, supple, vehement Capuchin—the emissary of some ambitious monks—who goes about preaching, confessing, communicating, and caballing, will much sooner overthrow a province than a hundred authors can enlighten it. It was not the Koran which made

Mohammed succeed: it was Mohammed who caused the success of the Koran.

No! Rome has not been vanquished by books. It has been vanquished because it revolted Europe by its rapacity, by the public sale of indulgences, by insulting men and wishing to govern them like domestic animals, for having abused its power to such an extent that it is astonishing a single village remains to it. Henry VIII, Elizabeth, the duke of Saxony, the landgrave of Hesse, the princes of Orange, the Condés and Colignys, have done all, and books nothing. Trumpets have never gained battles, nor caused any walls to fall except those of Jericho.

You fear books, as certain small cantons fear violins. Let men read, and let men dance—these two amusements will never do any harm to the world.

REASON

At the time when all France was mad over the Mississippi Bubble, and John Law was controller-general, there came to him a man who was always right, who always had reason on his side. Said he to Law, in the presence of a large crowd:

"Sir, you are the biggest madman, the biggest fool, or the biggest rogue who has yet appeared among us, and that is saying a great deal. This is how I prove it. You have imagined that a state's wealth can be increased tenfold with paper, but as this paper can represent only the money that is representative of true wealth—the products of the land and industry—you should have begun by giving us ten times more corn, wine, cloth, canvas, etc. That is not enough, you must be sure of your market. But you make ten times as many notes as we have of silver and commodities, therefore you are ten times more extravagant, or more inept, or more of a rogue than all the comptrollers who have preceded you. Now this is how I prove the major term of my thesis."

But he had hardly started his major when he was led off to a lunatic asylum.

When he came out of the asylum, where he studied hard and strengthened his reason, he went to Rome, where he asked for a public audience with the Pope, on condition that he would not be interrupted in his harangue. And he spoke to the Pope in these terms: "Holy Father, you are an antichrist and this is how I prove it to Your Holiness. I call antichrist the man who does the contrary to what Christ did and commanded. Now Christ was poor, and you are very rich; he paid tribute, and you exact tribute; he submitted to   e powers that were, and you have become a power yourself; he walked on foot, and you go to Castel Gandolfo in a sumptuous equipage; he ate whatever anyone was good enough to give him, and you want us to eat fish on Friday and Saturday, when we live far from sea and river; he forbade Simon Barjona to use a sword, and you have swords in your service, etc., etc., etc. Therefore in this sense Your Holiness is antichrist. In every other sense I hold you in great veneration, and I ask you for an indulgence *in articulo mortis*."

My man was put in the Castello St. Angelo.

When he came out of the Castello St. Angelo, he rushed to Venice, and asked to speak to the doge.

"Your Serenity," he said, "must be a very extravagant person to marry the sea every year: for, in the first place, one only marries the same person once; secondly, your marriage resembles Harlequin's, which was half made, seeing that it lacked but the consent of the bride; thirdly, how do you know that other maritime powers will not one day declare you incapable of consummating the marriage?"

Having spoken, he was shut up in the Tower of St. Mark's.

When he came out of the Tower of St. Mark's, he went to Constantinople, where he had an audience with the mufti, and spoke to him in these terms: "Your religion, although it has some good points, such as worship of a supreme Being, and the rule of being just and charitable, is otherwise nothing but a rehash of Judaism and a tedious collection of fairy tales. If the archangel Gabriel had brought the leaves of the Koran to Mohammed from some planet, all Arabia would have seen Gabriel come down; but nobody saw him. Therefore Mohammed was a brazen impostor who deceived imbeciles."

Hardly had he pronounced these words than he was run through with a sword. Nevertheless he had always been right, and had always had reason on his side.

SECT

Every sect, of every kind, is a rallying point for doubt and error. Scotist, Thomist, Realist, Nominalist, Papist, Calvinist, Molinist, and Jansenist are only pseudonyms.

There are no sects in geometry. One does not speak of a Euclidean, an Archimedean. When the truth is evident, it is impossible for parties and factions to arise. There has never been a dispute as to whether there is daylight at noon. The branch of astronomy which determines the course of the stars and the return of eclipses being once known, there is no dispute among astronomers.

In England one does not say: "I am a Newtonian, a

Lockian, a Halleyan." Why? Those who have read cannot refuse their assent to the truths taught by these three great men. The more Newton is revered, the less do people style themselves Newtonians; this word supposes that there are anti-Newtonians in England. Maybe we still have a few Cartesians in France, but only because Descartes' system is a tissue of erroneous and ridiculous speculations.

It is the same with the small number of matters of fact which are well established. The records of the Tower of London having been authentically gathered by Rymer, there are no Rymerians, because it occurs to no one to assail this collection. In it one finds neither contradictions, absurdities, nor prodigies; nothing which revolts the reason, nothing, consequently, which sectarians strive to maintain or upset by absurd arguments. Everyone agrees, therefore, that Rymer's records are worthy of belief.

You are a Mohammedan; therefore there are people who are not; therefore you might well be wrong.

What would be the true religion if Christianity did not exist? The religion in which there were no sects, the religion in which all minds were necessarily in agreement.

Well, to what dogma do all minds agree? To the worship of a God, and to honesty. All the philosophers of the world who have had a religion have said in all ages: "There is a God, and one must be just." There, then, is the universal religion established in all ages and throughout mankind. The point in which they all agree is therefore true, and the systems through which they differ are therefore false.

"My sect is the best," says a Brahmin to me. But, my friend, if your sect is good, it is necessary; for if it were not absolutely necessary you would admit to me that it was useless. If it is absolutely necessary, it is for all men. How, then, can it be that all men have not what is absolutely necessary to them? How is it possible for the rest of the world to laugh at you and your Brahma?

When Zoroaster, Hermes, Orpheus, Minos, and all the great men say: "Let us worship God, and let us be just," nobody laughs. But everyone hisses the man who claims that one cannot please God unless one is holding a cow's tail when one dies; or the man who wants one to have the end of one's prepuce cut off; or the man who consecrates crocodiles and onions; or the man who attaches eternal salvation to dead men's bones carried under one's shirt, or to a plenary indulgence which may be bought at Rome for two and a half sous.

Whence comes this universal competition in hisses and derision from one end of the world to the other? It is clear that the things at which everyone sneers are not very evidently true. What would we say of one of Sejanus's secretaries who dedicated to Petronius a bombastic book entitled: "The Truths of the Sibylline Oracles, Proved by the Facts"?

This secretary proves to you, first, that it was necessary for God to send on earth several sibyls one after the other; for He had no other means of teaching mankind. It is demonstrated that God spoke to these sibyls, for the word sibyl signifies *God's counsel*. They had to live a long time, for persons to whom God speaks should have this privilege, at the very least. They were twelve in number, for this number is sacred. They had certainly predicted all the events in the world, for Tarquinius Superbus bought three of their books from an old woman for a hundred crowns. "What incredulous fellow," adds the secretary, "will dare deny all these obvious facts which happened in a corner in the sight of the whole world? Who can deny the fulfillment of their prophecies? Has not Virgil himself quoted the predictions of the sibyls? If we have no first editions of the Sibylline Books, written at a time when people did not know how to read or write, have we not authentic copies? Impiety must be silent before such proofs." Thus did Houttevillus[2] speak to Sejanus. He hoped to have a position as augur which would be worth an income of fifty thousand francs, and he had nothing.

"What my sect teaches is obscure, I admit it," says a fanatic; and it is because of this obscurity that it must be believed; for the sect itself says it is full of obscurities. My sect is extravagant, therefore it is divine; for how should what appears so mad have been embraced by so many peoples, if it were not divine?" It is precisely like the Koran, which the Sunnites say has an angel's face and an animal's snout. Be not scandalized by the animal's snout, and worship the angel's face. Thus speaks this mad fellow. But a fanatic of another sect answers: "It is you who are t animal, and I who am the angel."

Well, who shall judge the case? Who shall decide between these two fanatics? Why, the reasonable, impartial man who is learned in a knowledge that is not that of words; the man free from prejudice and the lover of truth and justice—in short, the man who is not the foolish animal, and who does not think he is the angel.

Sect and *error* are synonymous. You are a Peripatetic and I a Platonist; we are therefore both wrong; for

---

[2] Voltaire is deliberately anachronistic. The contemporary Abbé Houtteville had written a defense of Christianity. [C.B.'s note.]

you combat Plato only because his fantasies have revolted you, while I am alienated from Aristotle only
because it seems to me that he does not know what
he is talking about. If one or the other had demonstrated the truth, there would be a sect no longer. To
declare oneself for the opinion of one or the other is
to take sides in a civil war. There are no sects in mathematics, in experimental physics. A man who examines
the relations between a cone and a sphere is not of the
sect of Archimedes: he who sees that the square of the
hypotenuse of a right-angled triangle is equal to the
square of the two other sides is not of the sect of
Pythagoras.

When you say that the blood circulates, that the air
is heavy, that the sun's rays are pencils of seven re-
frangible rays, you are not either of the sect of Harvey,
or the sect of Torricelli, or the sect of Newton; you
merely agree with the truth as demonstrated by them,
and the entire world will always be of your opinion.

This is the character of truth: it is of all time, it is
for all men, it has only to show itself to be recognized,
and one cannot argue against it. A long dispute means
that *both parties are wrong.*

Trans. H. I. Woolf (London: Allen & Unwin, 1924).

❖ ❖ ❖

A Reasonable Skeptic

[FROM *Treatise of Human Nature*]

DAVID HUME

1739-40

I would willingly establish it as a general maxim in the science of human nature, *that when any impression becomes present to us, it not only transports the mind to such ideas as are related to it, but likewise communicates to them a share of its force and vivacity.* All the operations of the mind depend, in a great measure, on its disposition when it performs them; and according as the spirits are more or less elevated, and the attention more or less fixed, the action will always have more or less vigour and vivacity. When, therefore, any object is presented which elevates and enlivens the thought, every action, to which the mind applies itself, will be more strong and vivid, as long as that disposition continues. Now, it is evident the continuance of the disposition depends entirely on the objects about which the mind is employed; and that any new object naturally gives a new direction to the spirits, and changes the disposition; as on the contrary, when the mind fixes constantly on the same object, or passes easily and insensibly along related objects, the disposition has a much longer duration. Hence it happens that when the mind is once enlivened by a present impression, it proceeds to form a more lively idea of the related objects, by a natural transition of the disposition from the one to the other. The change of the objects is so easy that the mind is scarce sensible of it, but applies itself to the conception of the related idea with all the force and vivacity it acquired from the present impression.

If, in considering the nature of relation, and that facility of transition which is essential to it, we can satisfy ourselves concerning the reality of this phenomenon, it is well: but I must confess I place my chief confidence in experience to prove so material a principle. We may therefore observe, as the first experiment to our present purpose, that upon the appearance of the picture of an absent friend, our idea of him is evidently enlivened by the *resemblance,* and that every passion, which that idea occasions, whether of joy or sorrow, acquires new force and vigour. In producing this effect there concur both a relation and a present impression. Where the picture bears him no resemblance, or at least was not intended for him, it never so much as conveys our thought to him: and where it is absent as well as the person; though the mind may pass from the thought of the one to that of the other; it feels its idea to be rather weakened than enlivened by that transition. We take a pleasure in viewing the picture of a friend when it is set before us; but when it is removed, rather choose to consider him directly than by reflection in an image, which is equally distant and obscure.

The ceremonies of the Roman Catholic religion may be considered as experiments of the same nature. The devotees of that strange superstition usually plead in excuse of the mummeries with which they are upbraided, that they feel the good effect of those external motions, and postures, and actions, in enlivening their devotion, and quickening their fervour, which otherwise would decay away, if directed entirely to distant and immaterial objects. We shadow out the objects of our faith, say they, in sensible types and images, and render them more present to us by the immediate presence of these types, than it is possible for us to do merely by an intellectual view and contemplation. Sensible objects have always a greater influence on the fancy than any other; and this influence they readily convey to those ideas to which they are related, and which they resemble. I shall only infer from these practices, and this reasoning, that the effect of resemblance in enlivening the idea is very common; and as in every case a resemblance and a present impression must concur, we are abundantly supplied with experiments to prove the reality of the foregoing principle.

We may add force to these experiments by others of a different kind, in considering the effects of *contiguity*, as well as of *resemblance*. It is certain that distance diminishes the force of every idea; and that, upon our approach to any object, though it does not discover itself to our senses, it operates upon the mind with an influence that imitates an immediate impression. The thinking on any object readily transports the mind to what is contiguous; but it is only the actual presence of an object that transports it with a superior vivacity. When I am a few miles from home, whatever relates to it touches me more nearly than when I am two hundred leagues distant; though even at that distance the reflecting on any thing in the neighbourhood of my friends and family naturally produces an idea of them. But as in this latter case, both the objects of the mind are ideas; notwithstanding there is an easy transition betwixt them; that transition alone is not able to give a superior vivacity to any of the ideas, for want of some immediate impression.

No one can doubt but causation has the same influence as the other two relations of resemblance and contiguity. Superstitious people are fond of the relics of saints and holy men, for the same reason that they seek after types and images, in order to enliven their devotion, and give them a more intimate and strong conception of those exemplary lives, which they desire to imitate. Now, it is evident one of the best relics a devotee could procure would be the handiwork of a saint; and if his clothes and furniture are ever to be considered in this light, it is because they were once at his disposal, and were moved and affected by him; in which respect they are to be considered as imperfect effects, and as connected with him by a shorter chain of consequences than any of those from which we learn the reality of his existence. This phenomenon clearly proves that a present impression with a relation of causation may enliven any idea, and consequently produce belief or assent, according to the precedent definition of it.

But why need we seek for other arguments to prove that a present impression with a relation or transition of the fancy may enliven any idea, when this very instance of our reasonings from cause and effect will alone suffice to that purpose? It is certain we must have an idea of every matter of fact which we believe. It is certain that this idea arises only from a relation to a present impression. It is certain that the belief superadds nothing to the idea, but only changes our manner of conceiving it, and renders it more strong and lively. The present conclusion concerning the influence of relation is the immediate consequence of all these steps;

and every step appears to me sure and infallible. There enters nothing into this operation of the mind but a present impression, a lively idea, and a relation or association in the fancy betwixt the impression and idea; so that there can be no suspicion of mistake.

In order to put this whole affair in a fuller light, let us consider it as a question in natural philosophy, which we must determine by experience and observation. I suppose there is an object presented, from which I draw a certain conclusion, and form to myself ideas, which I am said to believe or assent to. Here it is evident that however that object, which is present to my senses, and that other, whose existence I infer by reasoning, may be thought to influence each other by their particular powers or qualities; yet as the phenomenon of belief, which we at present examine, is merely internal, these powers and qualities, being entirely unknown, can have no hand in producing it. It is the present impression which is to be considered as the true and real cause of the idea, and of the belief which attends it. We must therefore endeavour to discover, by experiments, the particular qualities by which it is enabled to produce so extraordinary an effect.

First, then, I observe that the present impression has not this effect by its own proper power and efficacy, and, when considered alone as a single perception, limited to the present moment. I find that an impression, from which, on its first appearance, I can draw no conclusion, may afterwards become the foundation of belief, when I have had experience of its usual consequences. We must in every case have observed the same impression in past instances, and have found it to be constantly conjoined with some other impression. This is confirmed by such a multitude of experiments that it admits not of the smallest doubt.

From a second observation I conclude that the belief which attends the present impression, and is produced by a number of past impressions and conjunctions; that this belief, I say, arises immediately, without any new operation of the reason or imagination. Of this I can be certain, because I never am conscious of any such operation, and find nothing in the subject on which it can be founded. Now, as we call everything *custom* which proceeds from a past repetition, without any new reasoning or conclusion, we may establish it as a certain truth that all the belief, which follows upon any present impression, is derived solely from that origin. When we are accustomed to see two impressions conjoined together, the appearance or idea of the one immediately carries us to the idea of the other.

Being fully satisfied on this head, I make a third set of experiments, in order to know whether anything be requisite, beside the customary transition, towards the production of this phenomenon of belief. I therefore change the first impression into an idea; and observe that though the customary transition to the correlative idea still remains, yet there is in reality no belief nor persuasion. A present impression, then, is absolutely requisite to this whole operation; and when after this I compare an impression with an idea, and find that their only difference consists in their different degrees of force and vivacity, I conclude upon the whole that belief is a more vivid and intense conception of an idea, proceeding from its relation to a present impression.

Thus, all probable reasoning is nothing but a species of sensation. It is not solely in poetry and music we must follow our taste and sentiment, but likewise in philosophy. When I am convinced of any principle, it is only an idea which strikes more strongly upon me. When I give the preference to one set of arguments above another, I do nothing but decide from my feeling concerning the superiority of their influence. Objects have no discoverable connection together; nor is it from any other principle but custom operating upon the imagination that we can draw any inference from the appearance of one to the existence of another.

It will here be worth our observation that the past experience, on which all our judgments concerning cause and effect depend, may operate on our mind in such an insensible manner as never to be taken notice of, and may even in some measure be unknown to us. A person who stops short in his journey upon meeting a river in his way foresees the consequences of his proceeding forward; and his knowledge of these consequences is conveyed to him by past experience, which informs him of such certain conjunctions of causes and effects. But can we think that on this occasion he reflects on any past experience, and calls to remembrance instances that he has seen or heard of, in order to discover the effects of water on animal bodies? No, surely; this is not the method in which he proceeds in his reasoning. The idea of sinking is so closely connected with that of water, and the idea of suffocating with that of sinking, that the mind makes the transition without the assistance of the memory. The custom operates before we have time for reflection. The objects seem so inseparable that we interpose not a moment's delay in passing from the one or the other. But as this transition proceeds from experience, and not from any primary connection betwixt the ideas, we must necessarily acknowledge that experience may produce a belief and a judgment of causes and effects by a separate operation, and without being once thought of. This removes all pretext, if there yet remains any, for asserting that the mind is convinced by reasoning of that principle *that instances of which we have no experience must necessarily resemble those of which we have.* For we here find that the understanding or imagination can draw inferences from past experience without reflecting on it; much more without forming any principle concerning it, or reasoning upon that principle.

In general we may observe that in all the most established and uniform conjunctions of causes and effects, such as those of gravity, impulse, solidity, etc., the mind never carries its view expressly to consider any past experience: though in other associations of objects, which are more rare and unusual, it may assist the custom and transition of ideas by this reflection. Nay, we find in some cases that the reflection produces the belief without the custom; or, more properly speaking, that the reflection produces the custom in an *oblique* and *artificial* manner. I explain myself. It is certain that not only in philosophy, but even in common life, we may attain the knowledge of a particular cause merely by one experiment, provided it be made with judgment, and after a careful removal of all foreign and superfluous circumstances. Now, as after one experiment of this kind, the mind, upon the appearance either of the cause or the effect, can draw an inference concerning the existence of its correlative, and as a habit can never be acquired merely by one instance, it may be thought that belief cannot in this case be esteemed the effect of custom. But this difficulty will vanish, if we consider that, though we are here supposed to have had only one experiment of a particular effect, yet we have many millions to convince us of this principle, *that like objects, placed in like circumstances, will always produce like effects;* and as this principle has established itself by a sufficient custom, it bestows an evidence and firmness on any opinion to which it can be applied. The connection of the ideas is not habitual after one experiment; but this connection is comprehended under another principle that is habitual; which brings us back to our hypothesis. In all cases we transfer our experience to instances of which we have no experience, either *expressly* or *tacitly,* either *directly* or *indirectly.*

I must not conclude this subject without observing that it is very difficult to talk of the operations of the mind with perfect propriety and exactness; because common language has seldom made any very nice distinctions among them, but has generally called by the same term all such as nearly resemble each other. And as this is a source almost inevitable of obscurity and confusion in the author, so it may frequently give rise to doubts and objections in the reader, which otherwise he would never have dreamed of. Thus, my general position, that an opinion or belief is *nothing but a strong and lively idea derived from a present impression related to it,* may be liable to the following objection, by reason of a little ambiguity in those words *strong* and *lively.* It may be said that not only an impression may give rise to reasoning, but that an idea may also have the same influence; especially upon my principle, *that all our ideas are derived from correspondent impressions.* For suppose I form at present an idea of which I have forgot the correspondent impression, I am able to conclude, from this idea, that such an impression did once exist; and as this conclusion is attended with belief, it may be asked, from whence are the qualities of force and vivacity derived which constitute this belief? And to this I answer very readily, *from the present idea.* For as this idea is not here considered as the representation of any absent object, but as a real perception in the mind, of which we are intimately conscious, it must be able to bestow, on whatever is related to it, the same quality, call it *firmness,* or *solidity,* or *force,* or *vivacity,* with which the mind reflects upon it, and is assured of its present existence. The idea here supplies the place of an impression, and is entirely the same, so far as regards our present purpose.

Upon the same principles we need not be surprised to hear of the remembrance of an idea; that is, of the idea of an idea, and of its force and vivacity superior to the loose conceptions of the imagination. In thinking of our past thoughts we not only delineate out the objects of which we are thinking, but also conceive the action of the mind in the meditation, that certain *je-ne-sais-quoi,* of which it is impossible to give any definition or description, but which everyone sufficiently understands. When the memory offers an idea of this, and represents it as past, it is easily conceived how that idea may have more vigour and firmness than when we think of a past thought of which we have no remembrance.

There is implanted in the human mind a perception of pain and pleasure as the chief spring and moving principle of all its actions. But pain and pleasure have two ways of making their appearance in the mind; of which the one has effects very different from the other. They may either appear an impression to the actual feeling, or only in idea, as at present when I mention them. It is evident the influence of these upon our actions is far from being equal. Impressions always actuate the soul, and that in the highest degree; but it is not every idea which has the same effect. Nature has proceeded with caution in this case, and seems to have carefully avoided the inconveniences of two extremes. Did impressions alone influence the will, we should every moment of our lives be subject to the greatest calamities; because, though we foresaw their approach, we should not be provided by nature with any principle of action, which might impel us to avoid them. On the other hand, did every idea influence our actions, our condition would not be much mended. For such is the unsteadiness and activity of thought, that the images of everything, especially of goods and evils, are always wandering in the mind; and were it moved by every idle conception of this kind, it would never enjoy a moment's peace and tranquillity.

Nature has therefore chosen a medium, and has neither bestowed on every idea of good and evil the power of actuating the will, nor yet has entirely excluded them from this influence. Though an idle fiction has no efficacy, yet we find by experience that the ideas of those objects which we believe either are or will be existent produce in a lesser degree the same effect with those impressions, which are immediately present to the senses and perception. The effect, then, of belief is to raise up a simple idea to an equality with our impressions, and bestow on it a like influence on the passions. This effect it can only have by making an idea approach an impression in force and vivacity. For as the different degrees of force make all the original difference betwixt an impression and an idea, they must of consequence be the source of all the differences in the effects of these perceptions, and their removal, in whole or in part, the cause of every new resemblance they acquire. Wherever we can make an idea approach the impressions in force and vivacity, it will likewise imitate them in its influence on the mind; and *vice versa,* where it imitates them in that influence, as in the present case, this must proceed from its approaching them in force and vivacity. Belief, therefore, since it causes an idea to imitate the effects of the impressions, must make it resemble them in these qualities, and is nothing but *a more vivid and intense conception of any idea.* This, then, may both serve as an additional argument for the present system, and may give us a notion after what manner our reasonings from causation are able to operate on the will and passions.

As belief is almost absolutely requisite to the exciting of our passions, so the passions, in their turn, are very favourable to belief; and not only such facts as convey agreeable emotions, but very often such as give pain, do upon that account become more readily the objects of faith and opinion. A coward, whose fears are easily awakened, readily assents to every account of danger he meets with; as a person of a sorrowful and melancholy disposition is very credulous of everything that nourishes his prevailing passion. When any affecting object is presented, it gives the alarm, and excites immediately a degree of its proper passion; especially in persons who are naturally inclined to that passion. This emotion passes by an easy transition to the imagination; and, diffusing itself over our idea of the affecting object, makes us form that idea with greater force and vivacity, and consequently assent to it, according to the precedent system. Admiration and surprise have the same effect as the other passions; and accordingly we may observe that among the vulgar, quacks and projectors meet with a more easy faith upon account of their magnificent pretensions than if they kept themselves within the bounds of moderation. The first astonishment, which naturally attends their miraculous relations, spreads itself over the whole soul, and so vivifies and enlivens the idea that it resembles the inferences we draw from experience. This is a mystery, with which we may be already a little acquainted, and which we shall have further occasion to be let into in the progress of this Treatise.

From *Philosophical* Works, Vol. I (Boston: Little, Brown & Co., 1854).

❖ ❖ ❖

Some Limits of Reason

[FROM *The Theory of Moral Sentiments*]

ADAM SMITH

1759

That virtue consists in conformity to reason, is true in some respects; and this faculty may very justly be considered as, in some sense, the source and principle of approbation and disapprobation, and of all solid judgments concerning right and wrong. It is by reason that we discover those general rules of justice by which we ought to regulate our actions; and it is by the same faculty that we form these more vague and indeterminate ideas of what is prudent, of what is decent, of what is generous or noble, which we carry constantly about with us, and according to which we endeavour, as well as we can, to model the tenor of our conduct. The general maxims of morality are formed, like all other general maxims, from experience and induction. We observe, in a great variety of particular cases, what pleases or displeases our moral faculties, what these approve or disapprove of, and, by induction from this experience, we establish those general rules. But induction is always regarded as one of the operations of reason. From reason, therefore, we are very properly said to derive all those general maxims and ideas. It is by these, however, that we regulate the greater part of our moral judgments, which would be extremely uncertain and precarious, if they depended altogether upon what is liable to so many variations as immediate sentiment and feeling, which the different states of health and humour are capable of altering so essentially. As our most solid judgments, therefore, with regard to right and wrong, are regulated by maxims and ideas derived from an induction of reason, virtue may very properly be said to consist in a conformity to reason; and so far this faculty may be considered as the source and principle of approbation and disapprobation.

But though reason is undoubtedly the source of the general rules of morality, and of all the moral judgments which we form by means of them, it is altogether absurd and unintelligible to suppose that the first perceptions of right and wrong can be derived from reason, even in those particular cases, upon the experience of which the general rules are formed. These first perceptions, as well as all other experiments upon which any general rules are founded, cannot be the object of reason, but of immediate sense and feeling. It is by finding, in a vast variety of instances, that one tenor of conduct constantly pleases in a certain manner, and that another as constantly displeases the mind, that we form the general rules of morality. But reason cannot render any particular object either agreeable or disagreeable to the mind for its own sake. Reason may show that this object is the means of obtaining some other which is naturally either pleasing or displeasing, and in this manner may render it either agreeable or disagreeable, for the sake of something else. But nothing can be agreeable or disagreeable for its own sake, which is not rendered such by immediate sense and feeling. If virtue, therefore, in every particular instance, necessarily pleases for its own sake, and if vice as certainly displeases the mind, it cannot be reason, but immediate sense and feeling, which, in this manner, reconciles us to the one, and alienates us from the other.

Pleasure and pain are the great objects of desire and aversion; but these are distinguished, not by reason, but by immediate sense and feeling. If virtue, therefore, be desirable for its own sake, and if vice be, in the same manner, the object of aversion, it cannot be reason which originally distinguishes those different qualities, but immediate sense and feeling.

(Philadelphia: Anthony Finley, 1817.)

What Is Enlightenment?

IMMANUEL KANT

1784

Enlightenment is man's release from his self-incurred tutelage. Tutelage is man's inability to make use of his understanding without direction from another. Self-incurred is this tutelage when its cause lies not in lack of reason but in lack of resolution and courage to use it without direction from another. *Sapere aude!* [1] "Have courage to use your own reason!"—that is the motto of enlightenment.

Laziness and cowardice are the reasons why so great a portion of mankind, after nature has long since discharged them from external direction (*naturaliter maiorennes*), nevertheless remains under lifelong tutelage, and why it is so easy for others to set themselves up as their guardians. It is so easy not to be of age. If I have a book which understands for me, a pastor who has a conscience for me, a physician who decides my diet, and so forth, I need not trouble myself. I need not think, if I can only pay—others will readily undertake the irksome work for me.

That the step to competence is held to be very dangerous by the far greater portion of mankind (and by the entire fair sex)—quite apart from its being arduous—is seen to by those guardians who have so kindly assumed superintendence over them. After the guardians have first made their domestic cattle dumb and have made sure that these placid creatures will not dare take a single step without the harness of the cart to which they are confined, the guardians then show them the danger which threatens if they try to go alone. Actually, however, this danger is not so great, for by falling a few times they would finally learn to walk alone. But an example of this failure makes them timid and ordinarily frightens them away from all further trials.

For any single individual to work himself out of the life under tutelage which has become almost his nature is very difficult. He has come to be fond of this state,

[1] "Dare to know!" (Horace, *Ars poetica*). [Numbered notes are the trans.]

and he is for the present really incapable of making use of his reason, for no one has ever let him try it out. Statutes and formulas, those mechanical tools of the rational employment or rather misemployment of his natural gifts, are the fetters of an everlasting tutelage. Whoever throws them off makes only an uncertain leap over the narrowest ditch because he is not accustomed to that kind of free motion. Therefore, there are only few who have succeeded by their own exercise of mind both in freeing themselves from incompetence and in achieving a steady pace.

But that the public should enlighten itself is more possible; indeed, if only freedom is granted, enlightenment is almost sure to follow. For there will always be some independent thinkers, even among the established guardians of the great masses, who, after throwing off the yoke of tutelage from their own shoulders, will disseminate the spirit of the rational appreciation of both their own worth and every man's vocation for thinking for himself. But be it noted that the public, which has first been brought under this yoke by their guardians, forces the guardians themselves to remain bound when it is incited to do so by some of the guardians who are themselves capable of some enlightenment—so harmful is it to implant prejudices, for they later take vengeance on their cultivators or on their descendants. Thus the public can only slowly attain enlightenment. Perhaps a fall of personal despotism or of avaricious or tyrannical oppression may be accomplished by revolution, but never a true reform in ways of thinking. Rather, new prejudices will serve as well as old ones to harness the great unthinking masses.

For this enlightenment, however, nothing is required but freedom, and indeed the most harmless among all the things to which this term can properly be applied.

It is the freedom to make public use of one's reason at every point.[2] But I hear on all sides, "Do not argue!" The officer says: "Do not argue but drill!" The tax collector: "Do not argue but pay!" The cleric: "Do not argue but believe!" Only one prince in the world says, "Argue as much as you will, and about what you will, but obey!" Everywhere there is restriction on freedom.

Which restriction is an obstacle to enlightenment, and which is not an obstacle but a promoter of it? I answer: The public use of one's reason must always be free, and it alone can bring about enlightenment among men. The private use of reason, on the other hand, may often be very narrowly restricted without particularly hindering the progress of enlightenment. By the public use of one's reason I understand the use which a person makes of it as a scholar before the reading public. Private use I call that which one may make of it in a particular civil post or office which is intrusted to him. Many affairs which are conducted in the interest of the community require a certain mechanism through which some members of the community must passively conduct themselves with an artificial unanimity, so that the government may direct them to public ends, or at least prevent them from destroying those ends. Here argument is certainly not allowed—one must obey. But so far as a part of the mechanism regards himself at the same time as a member of the whole community or of a society of world citizens, and thus in the role of a scholar who addresses the public (in the proper sense of the word) through his writings, he certainly can argue without hurting the affairs for which he is in part responsible as a passive member. Thus it would

[2] It is this freedom Kant claimed later in his conflict with the censor, deferring to the censor in the "private" use of reason, i.e., in his lectures.

be ruinous for an officer in service to debate about the
suitability or utility of a command given to him by his
superior; he must obey. But the right to make remarks
on errors in the military service and to lay them before
the public for judgment cannot equitably be refused
him as a scholar. The citizen cannot refuse to pay the
taxes imposed on him; indeed, an impudent complaint
at those levied on him can be punished as a scandal
(as it could occasion general refractoriness). But the
same person nevertheless does not act contrary to his
duty as a citizen when, as a scholar, he publicly expresses his thoughts on the inappropriateness or even
the injustice of these levies. Similarly a clergyman is
obligated to make his sermon to his pupils in catechism
and his congregation conform to the symbol of the
church which he serves, for he has been accepted on
this condition. But as a scholar he has complete freedom, even the calling, to communicate to the public all
his carefully tested and well-meaning thoughts on that
which is erroneous in the symbol and to make suggestions for the better organization of the religious body
and church. In doing this, there is nothing that could
be laid as a burden on his conscience. For what he
teaches as a consequence of his office as a representative
of the church, this he considers something about which
he has no freedom to teach according to his own lights;
it is something which he is appointed to propound at
the dictation of and in the name of another. He will
say, "Our church teaches this or that; those are the
proofs which it adduces." He thus extracts all practical
uses for his congregation from statutes to which he
himself would not subscribe with full conviction but
to the enunciation of which he can very well pledge
himself because it is not impossible that truth lies hid-

den in them, and, in any case, there is at least nothing
in them contradictory to inner religion. For if he believed he had found such in them, he could not con-
scientiously discharge the duties of his office; he would
have to give it up. The use, therefore, which an appointed teacher makes of his reason before his congregation is merely private, because this congregation is
only a domestic one (even if it be a large gathering);
with respect to it, as a priest, he is not free, nor can
he be free, because he carries out the orders of another.
But as a scholar, whose writings speak to his public,
the world, the clergyman in the public use of his reason
enjoys an unlimited freedom to use his own reason and
to speak in his own person. That the guardians of the
people (in spiritual things) should themselves be in-
competent is an absurdity which amounts to the eternal-
ization of absurdities.

But would not a society of clergymen, perhaps a
church conference or a venerable classis (as they call
themselves among the Dutch), be justified in obligating
itself by oath to a certain unchangeable symbol in order
to enjoy an unceasing guardianship over each of its
members and thereby over the people as a whole, and
even to make it eternal? I answer that this is altogether
impossible. Such a contract, made to shut off all further
enlightenment from the human race, is absolutely null
and void even if confirmed by the supreme power, by
parliaments, and by the most ceremonious of peace
treaties. An age cannot bind itself and ordain to put the
succeeding one into such a condition that it cannot extend its (at best very occasional) knowledge, purify
itself of errors, and progress in general enlightenment.
That would be a crime against human nature, the
proper destination of which lies precisely in this prog-

ress; and the descendants would be fully justified in rejecting those decrees as having been made in an unwarranted and malicious manner.

The touchstone of everything that can be concluded as a law for a people lies in the question whether the people could have imposed such a law on itself. Now such a religious compact might be possible for a short and definitely limited time, as it were, in expectation of a better. One might let every citizen, and especially the clergyman, in the role of scholar, make his comments freely and publicly, i.e., through writing, on the erroneous aspects of the present institution. The newly introduced order might last until insight into the nature of these things had become so general and widely approved that through uniting their voices (even if not unanimously) they could bring a proposal to the throne to take those congregations under protection which had united into a changed religious organization according to their better ideas, without, however, hindering others who wish to remain in the order. But to unite in a permanent religious institution which is not to be subject to doubt before the public even in the lifetime of one man, and thereby to make a period of time fruitless in the progress of mankind toward improvement, thus working to the disadvantage of posterity— that is absolutely forbidden. For himself (and only for a short time) a man can postpone enlightenment in what he ought to know, but to renounce it for himself, and even more to renounce it for posterity, is to injure and trample on the rights of mankind.

And what a people may not decree for itself can even less be decreed for them by a monarch, for his lawgiving authority rests on his uniting the general public will in his own. If he only sees to it that all true or alleged improvement stands together with civil order, he can leave it to his subjects to do what they find necessary for their spiritual welfare. This is not his concern, though it is incumbent on him to prevent one of them from violently hindering another in determining and promoting this welfare to the best of his ability. To meddle in these matters lowers his own majesty, since by the writings in which his subjects seek to present their views he may evaluate his own governance. He can do this when, with deepest understanding, he lays upon himself the reproach. *Caesar non est supra grammaticos.* Far more does he injure his own majesty when he degrades his supreme power by supporting the ecclesiastical despotism of some tyrants in his state over his other subjects.

If we are asked, "Do we now live in an *enlightened age?*" the answer is, "No," but we do live in an *age of enlightenment.*[3] As things now stand, much is lacking which prevents men from being, or easily becoming, capable of correctly using their own reason in religious matters with assurance and free from outside direction. But, on the other hand, we have clear indications that the field has now been opened wherein men may freely deal with these things and that the obstacles to general enlightenment or the release from self-imposed tutelage are gradually being reduced. In this respect, this is the age of enlightenment, or the century of Frederick.

A prince who does not find it unworthy of himself to say that he holds it to be his duty to prescribe nothing to men in religious matters but to give them complete freedom while renouncing the haughty name of *tolerance,* is himself enlightened and deserves to be esteemed by the grateful world and posterity as the first, at least

[3] "Our age is, in especial degree, the age of criticism, and to criticism everything must submit." (*Critique of Pure Reason,* Preface to first ed., Smith trans.)

from the side of government, who divested the human race of its tutelage and left each man free to make use of his reason in matters of conscience. Under him venerable ecclesiastics are allowed, in the role of scholars, and without infringing on their official duties, freely to submit for public testing their judgments and views which here and there diverge from the established symbol. And an even greater freedom is enjoyed by those who are restricted by no official duties. This spirit of freedom spreads beyond this land, even to those in which it must struggle with external obstacles erected by a government which misunderstands its own interest. For an example gives evidence to such a government that in freedom there is not the least cause for concern about public peace and the stability of the community. Men work themselves gradually out of barbarity if only intentional artifices are not made to hold them in it.

I have placed the main point of enlightenment—the escape of men from their self-incurred tutelage—chiefly in matters of religion because our rulers have no interest in playing the guardian with respect to the arts and sciences and also because religious incompetence is not only the most harmful but also the most degrading of all. But the manner of thinking of the head of a state who favors religious enlightenment goes further, and he sees that there is no danger to his lawgiving in allowing his subjects to make public use of their reason and to publish their thoughts on a better formulation of his legislation and even their open-minded criticisms of the laws already made. Of this we have a shining example wherein no monarch is superior to him whom we honour.

But only one who is himself enlightened, is not afraid of shadows, and has a numerous and well-disciplined army to assure public peace can say: "Argue as much

as you will, and about what you will, only obey!"
A republic could not dare say such a thing. Here is
shown a strange and unexpected trend in human affairs
in which almost everything, looked at in the large, is
paradoxical. A greater degree of civil freedom appears
advantageous to the freedom of mind of the people, and
yet it places inescapable limitations upon it; a lower
degree of civil freedom, on the contrary, provides the
mind with room for each man to extend himself to his
full capacity. As nature has uncovered from under this
hard shell the seed for which she most tenderly cares
—the propensity and vocation to free thinking—this
gradually works back upon the character of the people,
who thereby gradually become capable of managing
freedom; finally, it affects the principles of government,
which finds it to its advantage to treat men, who are
now more than machines, in accordance with their
dignity.*

Königsberg, Prussia, September 30, 1784.

From *Foundations of the Metaphysics of Morals, What Is
Enlightenment?*, and a passage from *The Metaphysics of Morals*,
trans. and ed. Lewis White Beck (Chicago: The University of
Chicago Press, 1950).

* Today I read in the *Büschingsche Wöchentliche
Nachrichten* for September 13 an announcement of the
Berlinische Monatsschrift for this month, which cites
the answer to the same question by Herr Mendelssohn.
But this issue has not yet come to me; if it had, I would
have held back the present essay, which is now put forth
only in order to see how much agreement in thought can
be brought about by chance. [Kant's note.]

(Mendelssohn's answer was that enlightenment lay in
intellectual cultivation, which he distinguished from the
practical. Kant, quite in line with his later essay on theory
and practice, refuses to make this distinction fundamental.
[Note is the trans.])

❖ ❖ ❖

Science for the Ladies

[FROM *Conversations on the Plurality of Worlds*]

BERNARD LE BOVIER DE FONTENELLE

1686

FIFTH EVENING

That the fixed stars are so many suns, each of which enlighten other worlds.

The Marchioness expressed great impatience to know what would become of the fixed stars. Shall they be inhabited as the planets are? said she. Or shall they not be inhabited? In short, what do you make of them?

You will guess, perhaps, if you have a great desire to know, answered I. The fixed stars cannot be less distant from the Earth than twenty-seven thousand six hundred and fifty times the distance from hence to the Sun, which is thirty-three millions of leagues, and if you displease an astronomer, he will place them yet farther off. The distance from the Sun to Saturn, which is the most remote planet, is only three hundred and thirty millions of leagues; this is not anything with relation to the distance from the Sun or from the Earth to the fixed stars, they take not the trouble to count it. Their light as we see is lively and bright enough. If they receive it from the Sun, they must receive it very weak, after passing so far; by reflection it must be much weaker, they are then to send it to us at this great distance. It is impossible that reflected light, and which hath twice passed so far, should have the force and vivacity that the light of the fixed stars has. They are therefore luminous of themselves, and all of them, in one word, so many suns.

If I am not deceived, said the Marchioness, I already see to what you are leading. You are going to say, The fixed stars are so many suns, our Sun is the centre of a vortex, which turns round him, for why therefore shall not each fixed star be also the centre of a vortex, which shall have a motion round it? Our Sun hath planets that he enlightens, for why therefore should not each fixed star have planets that he enlightens?

I have not anything to answer, said I to her, than that which Phædrus said to Enone, *It is thee who hath named it.*

But replied she, I see the universe so great that I am lost in it: I no longer know where I am: I no longer know anything. What, shall all be divided into vortexes thrown confusedly one amongst another? Shall each fixed star be the centre of a vortex, as great perhaps as that in which we are situated? Shall all this immense space, which comprehends our Sun and our planets, be only a little parcel of the universe? Shall there be as many such spaces as there are fixed stars? This confounds me, troubles me, frights me.

And as for me, answered I, I am very easy about it. When the heavens appeared to me as only a blue vault, where the stars were fixed like nails, the universe appeared little and confined within narrow bounds, I seemed oppressed: presently they give an infinite extent and profoundity to this blue vault, in dividing it into a thousand and a thousand vortexes, it now seems to me that I breathe with more liberty, that I am in a much greater extent of air, and that the universe is far more magnificent. Nature hath not spared any-thing in producing it, she hath everywhere shown a profusion of riches, wholly worthy of her. Not anything can be so fine as to represent to ourselves this pro-digious number of vortexes, the middle of each of which is occupied by a sun, which causes divers planets to turn round him. The inhabitants of a planet of one of these infinite number of vortexes sees on all sides the suns of these vortexes, with which they are surrounded, but they cannot see the planets, who have only a weak light, which they borrow from their re-spective suns, and which they cannot send beyond their own vortex.

You offer me, said she, a kind of perspective so long that the sight cannot discover the end: I see clearly the inhabitants of the Earth, then you show me those of the Moon, and of the other planets of our vortex clearly enough, indeed, but less so than those of the Earth; after them come the inhabitants of the planets of other vortexes. But I acknowledge they are thrown at so vast, so infinite a distance, that whatever effort I make for seeing them, I can scarce perceive them. And, in fact, are they not almost annihilated even by the expressions you have been obliged to make use of when speaking of them? You have been obliged to call them inhabi-tants of one of the planets of one of those vortexes, whose number is infinite. We ourselves, with whom the same expression agrees, acknowledge that we scarce know where we are in the midst of so many worlds. As to me, I begin to see the Earth so exces-sively small that I believe I shall not hereafter have a very great desire for anything. Certainly, if we have so much ardour for grandeur, if we form designs upon designs, if we give ourselves so much pain, it is because we know not these vortexes. I now hope that my laziness will profit from my new light, and when I am reproached with my indolence I shall answer, Ah! if you did but know what the fixed stars are!

It was not proper that Alexander should trace them, replied I, for a certain author, who was of opinion that the Moon was inhabited, says very seriously that it was not possible for Aristotle to deny an opinion so reasonable, or to be ignorant of it (for how should a truth like this escape Aristotle?) But that he would never say anything of it for fear Alexander should run mad with despair at the sight of a world which he was not able to conquer. The best reason that could be given for making a mystery of the vortexes of the fixed stars, if they were known in those times, was this: it would have been an ill-judged method of making their court to such a prince to speak to him of so many other worlds. As to me who know them, I am sorry I cannot draw any utility from the knowledge I have. The most that it can do, according to your reasoning, is to cure me of ambition and uneasiness, evils that I am not at present troubled with. I have a little weakness in loving that which is beautiful, see my malady, and I believe these vortexes will not cure me of it. The other worlds render ours small, but they cannot destroy fine eyes, or a beautiful mouth, the value of these will always be the same, in spite of every world that can possibly exist.

This love is a strange thing, replied she, laughing; it is always safe, there is not any system whatever can hurt it. But tell me freely, is your system entirely true? Do not disguise anything from me, I will engage to you to keep a secret. It seems to me to be only founded on a light probability. A fixed star is of itself luminous like the Sun, and therefore must consequently be a sun, the centre and soul of a universe or system of worlds, and that it hath a variety of planets, which turn round it. Is this a necessity so absolute?

Hear, Madam, answered I, because we are in the humour always to mix the little follies of gallantry with our most serious discourses; we reason in mathematics as we reason in love; you know that if you grant ever so little to a lover, you must soon after grant him much more, see in the end how far he goes; a great way. In the same manner, grant but the least principle to a mathematician, he will then proceed, and, drawing a consequence or conclusion from it, you must grant him that also, and from that he draws another; and notwithstanding all you can do, he will lead you so far that you can scarce believe the whole which he has proved and you assented to. The more you give to these two sorts of people, the more they always take. You agree that when two things are alike in all which appears to us, we may then also believe they are alike in those things that do not appear to us, unless there are sufficient reasons to the contrary. From hence I have drawn this conclusion, that the Moon is inhabited, because that it resembles the Earth, the other planets because they resemble the Moon. I find that the fixed stars resemble our Sun, I have attributed to them all that belongs to them. You are engaged too far to retract, you must now go on with a good grace.

But, said she, upon the foundation of this resemblance that you have put between the fixed stars and our Sun, it must necessarily happen that the people of another great vortex only see it as a little fixed star, which only discovers itself to them during their nights.

This is beyond all doubt, answered I. Our Sun is so near us in comparison of the suns of other vortexes that his light ought to have infinitely more force upon our eyes than the light of those suns. We see only him when he appears, he effaces all the others; but in another great vortex there is another sun that reigns, and he in his turn effaces ours, which can only appear during their nights with the rest of the other strange suns, i.e., fixed stars. He is fixed with them to this great arch of the heavens, and there makes a part of some sign or assemblage of stars. As to the planets, which turn round him, our Earth, for example as they cannot see it so far off, so they never think of it. Thus all the suns are suns of day for the vortexes where they are placed, and suns of night for the other vortexes: in their own worlds they are the only one of the kind, elsewhere they only serve to make up a number.

May it not happen, however, replied she, that these worlds, notwithstanding this equality, differ in a thousand things? For notwithstanding this resemblance, which may in general hold true, yet they may differ in an infinite number of particulars.

Trans. by "A Gentleman" (London: Thomas Caslon, 1767).

❖ ❖ ❖

The Heart Is a Pump:
The New Physiology

[FROM *Essay on the Motions of the Heart and the Blood*]

WILLIAM HARVEY

1628

Were not the work indeed presented through you, my learned friends, I should scarce hope that it could come out scatheless and complete; for you have in general been the faithful witnesses of almost all the instances from which I have either collected the truth or confuted error; you have seen my dissections, and at my demonstrations of all that I maintain to be objects of sense, you have been accustomed to stand by and bear me out with your testimony. And as this book alone declares the blood to course and revolve by a new route, very different from the ancient and beaten pathway trodden for so many ages, and illustrated by such a host of learned and distinguished men, I was greatly afraid lest I might be charged with presumption did I lay my work before the public at home, or send it beyond seas for impression, unless I had first proposed its subject to you, had confirmed its conclusions by ocular demonstrations in your presence, had replied to your doubts and objections, and secured the assent and support of our distinguished President. For I was most intimately persuaded, that if I could make good my proposition before you and our College,[1] illustrious by its numerous body of learned individuals, I had less to fear from others; I even ventured to hope that I should have the comfort of finding all that you had granted me in your sheer love of truth, conceded by others who were philosophers like yourselves. For true philosophers, who are only eager for truth and knowledge, never regard themselves as already so thoroughly informed, but that they welcome further information from whomsoever and from whencesoever it may come; nor are they so narrow-minded as to imagine any of the arts or sciences transmitted to us by the ancients, in such a state of forwardness or completeness, that nothing is left for the ingenuity and industry of others; very many, on the contrary, maintain that all we know is still infinitely less than all that still remains unknown; nor do philosophers pin their faith to others' precepts in such wise that they lose their liberty, and cease to give credence to the conclusions of their proper senses. Neither do they swear such fealty to their mistress Antiquity, that they openly, and in sight of all, deny and desert their friend Truth. . . .

My dear colleagues, I had no purpose to swell this treatise into a large volume by quoting the names and writings of anatomists, or to make a parade of the strength of my memory, the extent of my reading, and the amount of my pains; because I profess both to learn and to teach anatomy, not from books but from dissections; not from the positions of philosophers but from the fabric of nature. . . .

[1] This work was addressed to the Royal College of Physicians. [C.B.'s note.]

From these and other observations of the like kind, I am persuaded it will be found that the motion of the heart is as follows:

First of all, the auricle contracts, and in the course of its contraction throws the blood (which it contains in ample quantity as the head of the veins, the storehouse and cistern of the blood) into the ventricle, which, being filled, the heart raises itself straightway, makes all its fibres tense, contracts the ventricles, and performs a beat, by which beat it immediately sends the blood supplied to it by the auricle into the arteries; the right ventricle sending its charge into the lungs by the vessel which is called vena arteriosa, but which, in structure and function, and all things else, is an artery; the left ventricle sending its charge into the aorta, and through this by the arteries to the body at large.

These two motions, one of the ventricles, another of the auricles, take place consecutively, but in such a manner that there is a kind of harmony or rhythm preserved between them, the two concurring in such wise that but one motion is apparent, especially in the warmer-blooded animals, in which the movements in question are rapid. Nor is this for any other reason than it is in a piece of machinery, in which, though one wheel gives motion to another, yet all the wheels seem to move simultaneously; or in that mechanical contrivance which is adapted to firearms, where the trigger being touched, down comes the flint, strikes against the steel, elicits a spark, which falling among the powder, it is ignited, upon which the flame extends, enters the barrel, causes the explosion, propels the ball, and the mark is attained—all of which incidents, by reason of the celerity with which they happen, seem to take place in the twinkling of an eye.

Thus far I have spoken of the passage of the blood from the veins into the arteries, and of the manner in which it is transmitted and distributed by the action of the heart; points to which some, moved either by the authority of Galen or Columbus, or the reasonings of others, will give in their adhesion. But what remains to be said upon the quantity and source of the blood which thus passes is of so novel and unheard-of character that I not only fear injury to myself from the envy of a few, but I tremble lest I have mankind at large for my enemies, so much doth wont and custom, that become as another nature. and doctrine once sown and that hath struck deep root, and respect for antiquity influence all men: Still the die is cast, and my trust is in my love of truth, and the candour that inheres in cultivated minds. And sooth to say, when I surveyed my mass of evidence, whether derived from vivisections, and my various reflections on them, or from the ventricles of the heart and the vessels that enter into and issue from them, the symmetry and size of these conduits—for nature doing nothing in vain, would never have given them so large a relative size without a purpose—or from the arrangement and intimate structure of the valves in particular, and of the other parts of the heart in general, with many things besides, I frequently and seriously bethought me, and long revolved in my mind, what might be the quantity of blood which was transmitted, in how short a time its passage might be effected, and the like; and not finding it possible that this could be supplied by the juices of the ingested aliment without the veins on the one hand becoming drained, and the arteries on the other getting ruptured through the excessive charge of blood, unless the blood should somehow find its way from the arteries into the veins, and so return to the right side of the heart; I began to think whether there might not be *a motion, as it were, in a circle.* Now this I afterwards found to be true; and I finally saw that the blood, forced by the action of the left ventricle into the arteries, was distributed to the body at large, and its several parts, in the same manner as it is sent through the lungs, impelled by the right ventricle into the pulmonary artery, and that it then passed through the veins and along the vena cava, and so round to the left ventricle in the manner already indicated. . . .

The heart, consequently, is the beginning of life; the sun of the microcosm, even as the sun in his turn might well be designated the heart of the world; for it is the heart by whose virtue and pulse the blood is moved, perfected, made apt to nourish, and is preserved from corruption and coagulation; it is the household divinity which, discharging its function, nourishes, cherishes, quickens the whole body, and is indeed the foundation of life, the source of all action.

From *The Works of William Harvey*, trans. from the original Latin by Robert Willis (London: Lydenham Society Publications, 1847).

The New Physics

[FROM "Preface to Sir Isaac Newton's *Principia*"]

ROGER COTES

1713

Those who have treated of natural philosophy may be nearly reduced to three classes. Of these some have attributed to the several species of things specific and occult qualities, on which, in a manner unknown, they make the operations of the several bodies to depend. The sum of the doctrine of the Schools derived from Aristotle and the Peripatetics is herein contained. They affirm that the several effects of bodies arise from the particular natures of those bodies. But whence it is that bodies derive those natures they don't tell us; and therefore they tell us nothing. And being entirely employed in giving names to things, and not in searching into things themselves, we may say that they have invented a philosophical way of speaking, but not that they have made known to us true philosophy. . . .

There is left then the third class, which profess experimental philosophy. These indeed derive the causes of all things from the most simple principles possible; but then they assume nothing as a principle that is not proved by phenomena. They frame no hypotheses, nor receive them into philosophy otherwise than as questions whose truth may be disputed. They proceed therefore in a twofold method, synthetical and analytical. From some select phenomena they deduce by analysis the forces of nature, and the more simple laws of forces; and from thence by synthesis show the constitution of the rest. This is that incomparably best way of philosophizing, which our renowned author most justly embraced before the rest; and thought alone worthy to be cultivated and adorned by his excellent labours. Of this he has given us a most illustrious example, by the explication of the System of the World, most happily deduced from the Theory of Gravity. That the virtue of gravity was found in all bodies, others suspected, or imagined before him; but he was the only and the first philosopher that could demonstrate it from appearances, and make it a solid foundation to the most noble speculations.

Therefore that we may begin our reasoning from what is most simple and nearest to us, let us consider a little what is the nature of gravity with us on Earth, that we may proceed the more safely when we come to consider it in the heavenly bodies that lie at so vast a distance from us. It is now agreed by all philosophers that all circumterrestrial bodies gravitate towards the Earth. That no bodies really light are to be found is now confirmed by manifold experience. That which is relative levity is not true levity, but apparent only, and arises from the preponderating gravity of the contiguous bodies.

Moreover, as all bodies gravitate towards the Earth, so does the Earth again towards bodies. That the action of gravity is mutual, and equal on both sides, is thus proved. . . .

This is the nature of gravity upon Earth; let us now see what it is in the Heavens.

That every body perseveres in its state either of rest, or of moving uniformly in a right line, unless insofar as it is compelled to change that state by forces impressed, is a law of nature universally received by all philosophers. But from thence it follows that bodies which move in curve lines, and are therefore continually going off from the right lines that are tangents to their orbits, are by some continued force retained in those curvilinear paths. Since then the planets move in curvilinear orbits, there must be some force operating by whose repeated actions they are perpetually made to deflect from the tangents. . . .

From what has been hitherto said, it is plain that the planets are retained in their orbits by some force perpetually acting upon them; it is plain that that force is always directed towards the centres of their orbits; it is plain that its efficacy is augmented with the nearness to the centre, and diminished with the same; and that it is augmented in the same proportion with which the square of the distance is diminished, and diminished in the same proportion with which the square of the distance is augmented. . . .

Because the revolutions of the primary planets about the Sun, and of the secondary about Jupiter and Saturn, are phenomena of the same kind with the revolution of the Moon about the Earth; and because it has been moreover demonstrated that the centripetal forces of the primary planets are directed towards the centre of the Sun, and those of the secondary towards the centres of Jupiter and Saturn, in the same manner as the centripetal force of the Moon is directed towards the centre of the Earth; and since besides, all these forces are reciprocally as the squares of the distances from the centres, in the same manner as the centripetal force of the Moon is as the square of the distance from the Earth; we must of course conclude that the nature of all is the same. Therefore as the Moon gravitates towards the Earth, and the Earth again towards the Moon; so also all the secondary planets will gravitate towards their primary, and the primary planets again towards their secondary; and so all the primary towards the Sun; and the Sun again towards the primary.

Therefore the Sun gravitates towards all the planets, and all the planets towards the Sun. . . .

That the attractive virtue of the Sun is propagated on all sides to prodigious distances, and is diffused to every part of the wide space that surrounds it, is most evidently shown by the motion of the comets; which coming from places immensely distant from the Sun, approach very near to it; and sometimes so near, that in their perihelia they almost touch its body. The theory of these bodies was altogether unknown to astronomers, till in our own times our excellent author most happily discovered it, and demonstrated the truth of it by most certain observations. So that it is now apparent that the comets move in conic sections having their foci in the Sun's centre, and by radii drawn to the Sun describe areas proportional to the times. But from these phenomena it is manifest, and mathematically demonstrated, that those forces, by which the comets are retained in their orbits, respect the Sun, and are reciprocally proportional to the squares of the distances from its centre. Therefore the comets gravitate towards the Sun; and therefore the attractive force of the Sun not only acts on the bodies of the planets, placed at given distances and very nearly in the same plane, but reaches also to the comets in the most different parts of the heavens, and at the most different

distances. This therefore is the nature of gravitating
bodies, to propagate their force at all distances to all
other gravitating bodies.

The foregoing conclusions are grounded on this
axiom which is received by all philosophers; namely
that effects of the same kind, that is, whose known
properties are the same, take their rise from the same
causes and have the same unknown properties also.
For who doubts, if gravity be the cause of the descent
of a stone in Europe, but that it is also the cause of the
same descent in America? . . .

Since then all bodies, whether upon Earth or in the
heavens, are heavy, so far as we can make any experiments or observations concerning them; we must certainly allow that gravity is found in all bodies universally. And in like manner as we ought not to suppose that any bodies can be otherwise than extended,
moveable or impenetrable, so we ought not to conceive
that any bodies can be otherwise than heavy. The
extension, mobility, and impenetrability of bodies become known to us only by experiments; and in the very
same manner their gravity becomes known to us. All
bodies we can make any observations upon are extended, moveable, and impenetrable; and thence we
conclude all bodies, and those we have no observations
concerning, to be extended and moveable and impenetrable. So all bodies we can make observations on
we find to be heavy; and thence we conclude all
bodies, and those we have no observations of, to be
heavy also. If anyone should say that the bodies of the
fixed stars are not heavy because their gravity is not
yet observed; they may say for the same reason that
they are neither extended nor moveable nor impene-

trable, because these affections of the fixed stars are not yet observed. In short, either gravity must have a place among the primary qualities of all bodies, or extension, mobility and impenetrability must not.

In *Main Currents of Western Thought*, ed. *Franklin* Le Van Baumer (New York: Alfred A. Knopf, Inc., 1952).

On a Tortoise and Certain Birds

[FROM *The Natural History and Antiquities of Selbourne*]

GILBERT WHITE

TO THE HONOURABLE DAINES BARRINGTON

April 12, 1772.

DEAR SIR,

While I was in Sussex last autumn my residence was at the village near Lewes, from whence I had formerly the pleasure of writing to you. On the first of November I remarked that the old tortoise, formerly mentioned, began first to dig the ground in order to the forming its hybernaculum, which it had fixed on just beside a great tuft of hepaticas. It scrapes out the ground with its forefeet and throws it up over its back with its hind; but the motion of its legs is ridiculously slow, little exceeding the hour hand of a clock; and suitable to the composure of an animal said to be a whole

month in performing one feat of copulation. Nothing
can be more assiduous than this creature night and day
in scooping the earth, and forcing its great body into
the cavity; but, as the noons of that season proved
unusually warm and sunny, it was continually interrupted, and called forth by the heat in the middle of
the day; and though I continued there till the thir-
teenth of November, yet the work remained unfinished.
Harsher weather, and frosty mornings, would have
quickened its operations. No part of its behaviour ever
struck me more than the extreme timidity it always
expresses with regard to rain; for though it has a shell
that would secure it against the wheel of a loaded
cart, yet does it discover as much solicitude about rain
as a lady dressed in all her best attire, shuffling away
on the first sprinklings, and running its head up in a
corner. If attended to, it becomes an excellent weather-
glass; for as sure as it walks elate, and as it were on
tiptoe, feeding with great earnestness in a morning, so
sure will it rain before night. It is totally a diurnal
animal, and never pretends to stir after it becomes
dark. The tortoise, like other reptiles, has an arbitrary
stomach as well as lungs, and can refrain from eating
as well as breathing for a great part of the year. When
first awakened it eats nothing; nor again in the autumn
before it retires: through the height of the summer it
feeds voraciously, devouring all the food that comes
in its way. I was much taken with its sagacity in discerning those that do it kind offices: for, as soon as
the good old lady comes in sight who has waited on
it for more than thirty years, it hobbles towards its
benefactress with awkward alacrity; but remains inat-
tentive to strangers. Thus not only "the ox knoweth his
owner, and the ass his master's crib," but the most
abject reptile and torpid of beings distinguishes the

hand that feeds it, and is touched with the feelings of gratitude!

P.S. In about three days after I left Sussex the tortoise retired into the ground under the hepatica.

They who write on natural history cannot too frequently advert to *instinct,* that wonderful limited faculty, which, in some instances, raises the brute creation as it were above *reason,* and in others leaves them so far below it. Philosophers have defined instinct to be that secret influence by which every species is impelled naturally to pursue, at all times, the same way or track, without any teaching or example; whereas reason, without instruction, would often vary and do that by many methods which instinct effects by one alone. Now this maxim must be taken in a qualified sense; for there are instances in which instinct does vary and conform to the circumstances of place and convenience.

It has been remarked that every species of bird has a mode of nidification peculiar to itself; so that a schoolboy would at once pronounce on the sort of nest before him. This is the case among fields and woods, and wilds; but, in the villages round London, where mosses and gossamer, and cotton from vegetables, are hardly to be found, the nest of the *chaffinch* has not that elegant finished appearance, nor is it so beautifully studded with lichens, as in a more rural district: and the *wren* is obliged to construct its house with straws and dry grasses, which do not give it that rotundity and compactness so remarkable in the edifices of that little architect. Again, the regular nest of the *house martin* is hemispheric; but where a rafter, or a joist, or a cornice may happen to stand in the way, the nest is so contrived as to conform to the obstruction, and becomes flat or oval, or compressed.

In the following instances instinct is perfectly uniform and consistent. There are three creatures, the *squirrel*, the *fieldmouse*, and the bird called the *nuthatch* (*sitta Europeæa*), which live much on hazelnuts; and yet they open them each in a different way. The first, after rasping off the small end, splits the shell in two with his long foreteeth, as a man does with his knife; the second nibbles a hole with his teeth, so regular as if drilled with a wimble, and yet so small that one would wonder how the kernel can be extracted through it; while the last picks an irregular ragged hole with its bill: but as this artist has no paws to hold the nut firm while he pierces it, like an adroit workman, he fixes it, as it were in a vice, in some cleft of a tree, or in some crevice; when, standing over it, he perforates the stubborn shell. We have often placed nuts in the chink of a gatepost where nut-hatches have been known to haunt, and have always found that those birds have readily penetrated them. While at work they make a rapping noise that may be heard at a considerable distance.

You that understand both the theory and practical part of music may best inform us why *harmony* or *melody* should so strangely affect some men, as it were by recollection, for days after a concert is over. What I mean the following passage will most readily explain:

"Moreover he preferred the music of birds to human voices, and to musical instruments; not that those also failed to give him pleasure, but because human music left in the mind a certain agitation, seizing the attention and disturbing repose, while it goes to and fro, up and down the scale in reverie with changing pitch and interval—while no such impression could be left by the warbling of birds, which, because we cannot equally imitate them, are incapable of so exciting our minds." (Gassendi)

This curious quotation strikes me much by so well representing my own case, and by describing what I have so often felt but never could so well express. When I hear fine music I am haunted with passages therefrom night and day; and especially at first waking, which, by their importunity, give me more uneasiness than pleasure: elegant lessons still tease my imagination, and recur irresistibly to my recollection at seasons, and even when I am desirous of thinking of more serious matters.

(London: Routledge, 1894.)

❖ ❖ ❖

The Rat

[FROM *The Natural History of Animals,
Vegetables, and Minerals*]

GEORGES LOUIS LECLERC,
COMTE DE BUFFON

1767

If we descend by degrees from the great to the small, from the strong to the weak, we shall find that Nature has uniformly maintained a balance; that, attentive only to the preservation of each species, she creates a profusion of individuals, and is supported by the numbers which she has formed of a diminutive size, and which she has denied weapons, denied either strength or courage; and that she has not only taken care that these inferior species should be in a condition to resist, or to maintain their ground by the abundance of their own number, but has likewise provided a supplement, as it were, to each, by multiplying the species which nearly resemble or approach them. The rat, the mouse, the *mulot,* or field-mouse, the water-rat, the *campagnol,* or little field rat, the *loir,* or great dor-mouse, the *lerot,* or middle dor-mouse; the *muscardin,* or small dor-mouse, the *musaraigne,* or shrew-mouse, with many others which I shall not enumerate here, as they are strangers to our climate, form so many distinct and separate species, but yet so little varied, that should any of the others fail, they might so well supply their places that their absence would be hardly perceptible. It is this great number of approximate species that first gave naturalists the idea of *genera;* an idea which can never be employed unless when we view objects in the gross, and which vanishes when we come to consider Nature minutely, and as she really is.

Men began by appropriating different names to things which appeared to them absolutely distinct and different, and at the same time they gave general denominations to such as seemed to bear a near resemblance to each other. Among nations rude and unenlightened, and in all infant languages, there are hardly any but general names, that is to say, vague and unformed expressions of things which, though of the same order, are yet in themselves highly different. Thus, the oak, the beech, the linden, the fir, the yew, the pine, had at first no name but that of tree; afterwards the oak, the beech, the linden, were all three called *oak,*

when they came to be distinguished from the fir, the
pine, and the yew, which in like manner would be distinguished by the name of *fir*. Particular names proceeded solely, in process of time, from the comparison
and minute examination of things. Of these the number was encreased in proportion as the works of Nature were more studied, and better understood; and
the more we shall continue to examine and compare
them, the greater number there will be of proper
names, and of particular denominations. When in these
days, therefore, Nature is presented to us by general
denominations, that is, by genera, it is sending us back
to the ABC, or first rudiments of all knowledge, and
to the infant-darkness of mankind. Ignorance produced
genera, and science produced, and will continue to
produce, proper names; nor of these shall we be afraid
to encrease the number, whenever we shall have occasion to denote different species.

Under the generical name of rat, people have comprised and confounded several species of little animals.
This name we shall solely appropriate to the common
rat, which is black, and lives in our houses. Each of
the other species shall have its particular denomination;
for as neither of them couple together, each is, in
reality, different from all the rest. The rat is well
enough known by the trouble he gives us. It generally
inhabits barns, and other places where corn and fruit
are stored; and from these it proceeds, and invades our
dwellings. This animal is carnivorous, and even, if the
expression is allowable, *omnivorous*. Hard substances,
however, it prefers to soft ones: it devours wool, stuffs,
and furniture of all sorts; eats through wood, makes
hiding places in walls, thence issues in search of prey,
and frequently returns with as much as it is able to
drag along with it, forming, especially when it has

young ones to provide for, a magazine of the whole. The females bring forth several times in the year, though mostly in the summer season; and they usually produce five or six at a birth. They search for warm places; and in winter they generally shelter themselves about the chimnies of houses, or among hay and straw.

In defiance of the cats, and notwithstanding the poison, the traps, and every other method that is used to destroy these creatures, they multiply so fast as frequently to do considerable damage. In old houses in the country especially, where great quantities of corn are kept, and where the neighbouring barns and hay-stacks favour their retreat, as well as their multiplication, they are often so numerous that the inhabitants would be obliged to remove with their furniture, were they not to devour each other. This we have often by experience found to be the case when they have been in any degree straitened for provisions; and the method they take to lessen their numbers is for the stronger to fall upon the weaker. This done, they lay open their skulls, and first eat up the brains, afterwards the rest of the body. The next day hostilities are renewed in the same manner; nor do they suspend their havoc till the majority are destroyed. For this reason it is that after any place has for a long while been infested with rats, they often seem to disappear of a sudden, and sometimes for a considerable time. It is the same with the field-mice, whose prodigious encrease is checked solely by their cruelties towards each other, when they begin to be in want of food. Aristotle attributes this sudden destruction to the rain; but rats are not exposed to the weather, and field-mice know well how to secure themselves from it, their subterranean habitations being never even moistened.

The rat is an animal as salacious as it is voracious.

They have a kind of yelp when they engender; and when they fight, they cry. They prepare a bed for their young, and provide them immediately with food. On their first quitting the hole, she watches over, defends, and will even fight the cats, in order to save them. A large rat is more mischievous, and almost as strong, as a young cat. Its foreteeth are long and strong; and as the cat does not bite so hard, as she can do little execution except with her claws, she must be not only vigorous, but well experienced to conquer. The weasel, though smaller in size, is yet a more dangerous enemy to the rat, and is more feared by it, because he is capable of following it into its hiding-places. The combat between these two animals is generally sharp and long; their strength is at least equal, but their manner of fighting is different. The rat cannot inflict any wounds but by snatches, and with its foreteeth, which, however, being rather calculated for gnawing than for biting, have but little strength; whereas the weasel bites fiercely with the force of its whole jaw at once, and instead of letting go its hold, sucks the blood through the wound. In every conflict with an enemy so formidable, it is no wonder, therefore, that the rat should fall a victim.

There are many varieties in this as in every other species of which the individuals are very numerous. Beside the common black rat there are some which are brown, and some almost black; some which are grey, inclining to white or red, and some altogether white. The white rat, like the white mouse, the white rabbit, and all other animals which are entirely of that colour, has red eyes. The white species, with all its varieties, appears to belong to the temperate climates of our continent, and have been diffused in much greater abundance over hot countries than cold ones. Originally

they had none in America; and those which are to be
found there in such numbers at this day are the produce of rats which accidentally obtained a footing on
the other side of the Atlantic with the first European
settlers. Of these the encrease was so great that the rat
was long considered as the pest of the colonies; where
indeed it had hardly an enemy to oppose it but the
large adder, which swallows it up alive. The European
ships have likewise carried these animals to the East
Indies, into all the islands of the Indian Archipelago, as
well as into Africa, where they are found in great
numbers. In the North, on the contrary, they have
hardly multiplied beyond Sweden; and those which are
called Norway rats, in Lapland, etc., are animals different from our rats.

Trans. W. Kenrick and J. Murdoch (London: T. Bell, 1775).

He Snatched the Thunder
from the Skies

[FROM *Autobiography*]

BENJAMIN FRANKLIN

1771

In 1746, being at Boston, I met there with a Dr.
Spence, who was lately arrived from Scotland, and
show'd me some electric experiments. They were imperfectly perform'd, as he was not very expert; but,

being on a subject quite new to me, they equally sur-
pris d and pleased me. Soon after my return to Philadelphia, our library company receiv'd from Mr. P. Collinson, Fellow of the Royal Society of London, a
present of a glass tube, with some account of the use
of it in making such experiments. I eagerly seized the
opportunity of repeating what I had seen at Boston;
and, by much practice, acquir'd great readiness in performing those, also, which we had an account of from
England, adding a number of new ones. I say much
practice, for my house was continually full, for some
time, with people who came to see these new wonders.

To divide a little this incumbrance among my
friends, I caused a number of similar tubes to be
blown at our glass-house, with which they furnish'd
themselves, so that we had at length several performers.
Among these, the principal was Mr. Kinnersley, an
ingenious neighbour, who, being out of business, I
encouraged to undertake showing the experiments for
money, and drew up for him two lectures, in which
the experiments were rang'd in such order, and accompanied with such explanations in such method, as that
the foregoing should assist in comprehending the following. He procur'd an elegant apparatus for the
purpose, in which all the little machines that I had
roughly made for myself were nicely form'd by instru-
ment-makers. His lectures were well attended, and gave
great satisfaction; and after some time he went thro' the
colonies, exhibiting them in every capital town, and
pick'd up some money. In the West India islands, indeed, it was with difficulty the experiments could be
made, from the general moisture of the air.

Oblig'd as we were to Mr. Collinson for his present
of the tube, etc., I thought it right he should be
inform'd of our success in using it, and wrote him

several letters containing accounts of our experiments. He got them read in the Royal Society, where they were not at first thought worth so much notice as to be printed in their Transactions. One paper, which I wrote for Mr. Kinnersley, on the sameness of lightning with electricity, I sent to Dr. Mitchel, an acquaintance of mine, and one of the members also of that society, who wrote me word that it had been read, but was laughed at by the connoisseurs. The papers, however, being shown to Dr. Fothergill, he thought them of too much value to be stifled, and advis'd the printing of them. Mr. Collinson then gave them to Cave for publication in his *Gentleman's Magazine;* but he chose to print them separately in a pamphlet, and Dr. Fothergill wrote the preface. Cave, it seems, judged rightly for his profit, for by the additions that arrived afterwards they swell'd, to a quarto volume, which has had five editions, and cost him nothing for copy-money.

It was, however, some time before those papers were much taken notice of in England. A copy of them happening to fall into the hands of the Count de Buffon, a philosopher deservedly of great reputation in France, and, indeed, all over Europe, he prevailed with M. Dalibard to translate them into French, and they were printed at Paris. The publication offended the Abbé Nollet, preceptor in Natural Philosophy to the royal family, and an able experimenter, who had form'd and publish'd a theory of electricity, which then had the general vogue. He could not at first believe that such a work came from America, and said it must have been fabricated by his enemies at Paris, to decry his system. Afterwards, having been assur'd that there really existed such a person as Franklin at Philadelphia, which he had doubted, he wrote and published a volume of Letters, chiefly address'd to me, defending his theory, and denying the verity of my experiments, and of the positions deduc'd from them.

I once purpos'd answering the abbé, and actually began the answer; but, on consideration that my writings contain'd a description of experiments which any one might repeat and verify, and if not to be verified, could not be defended; or of observations offer'd as conjectures, and not delivered dogmatically, therefore not laying me under any obligation to defend them; and reflecting that a dispute between two persons, writing in different languages, might be lengthened greatly by mistranslations, and thence misconceptions of one another's meaning, much of one of the abbé's letters being founded on an error in the translation, I concluded to let my papers shift for themselves, believing it was better to spend what time I could spare from public business in making new experiments, than in disputing about those already made. I therefore never answered M. Nollet, and the event gave me no cause to repent my silence; for my friend M. le Roy, of the Royal Academy of Sciences, took up my cause and refuted him; my book was translated into the Italian, German, and Latin languages; and the doctrine it contain'd was by degrees universally adopted by the philosophers of Europe, in preference to that of the abbé; so that he lived to see himself the last of his sect, except Monsieur B——, of Paris, his *élève* and immediate disciple.

What gave my book the more sudden and general celebrity was the success of one of its proposed experiments, made by Messrs. Dalibard and De Lor at Marly, for drawing lightning from the clouds. This engag'd the public attention everywhere. M. de Lor, who had an apparatus for experimental philosophy, and lectur'd in that branch of science, undertook to repeat what he

called the *Philadelphia Experiments;* and, after they
were performed before the king and court, all the curious of Paris flocked to see them. I will not swell this
narrative with an account of that capital experiment,
nor of the infinite pleasure I receiv'd in the success
of a similar one I made soon after with a kite at Philadelphia as both are to be found in the histories of
electricity.

From *The Writings of Benjamin Franklin*, Vol. I, ed. A. H.
Smyth (New York: The Macmillan Co., 1905).

III. *Nature and Nature's God:* RELIGION

The Great Wager, Cleopatra's Nose, and Other Matters

[FROM *Pensées*]

BLAISE PASCAL

1670

Man's greatness lies in his power of thought.

All man's dignity lies in thought.
But what is thought? Mere folly!
Thought, then, is something admirable, incomparable by its very nature. Strange defects would be needed to render thought contemptible; those it has are such as render it ridiculous. How noble by nature! How base by its defects!

339

Man is obviously made for thought; that is all his dignity and all his merit; and all his duty is to think as he ought. Now the order of thought is to begin with self, and go on to its Author and its destiny. Now of what does the world think? Never of *that*, but of dancing, lute-playing, singing, writing verses, running at the ring, etc., fighting, making oneself King without a thought of what it is to be a king, or to be a man.

Man is but a reed, the weakest thing in nature; but a thinking reed. It does not need the universe to take up arms to crush him; a vapour, a drop of water, is enough to kill him. But, though the universe should crush him, man would still be nobler than his destroyer, because he knows that he is dying, knows that the universe has got the better of him; the universe knows naught of that.

All our dignity then consists in thought. We must look to that in order to rise aloft; not to space or time which we can never fill. Strive we then to think aright: that is the first principle of moral life.

It is natural for the mind to believe, and for the will to love; so, failing real objects, they must fix on false ones.

How is it that a cripple does not irritate us, while a crooked mind does? Because the cripple recognizes that we walk straight, while the crooked mind says that it is we who limp; were it not for this, we should feel pity rather than anger for him.

With far greater point Epictetus asks: "Why are we not vext to be told we have a head-ache, and yet are vext to be told we think or decide amiss?" The reason is that we are quite certain that we have no headache and do not limp, but are not so certain that we decide aright. Hence, the cause of our confidence being simply that we see the thing clearly with our own eyes, when another sees the contrary quite as clearly, it gives us pause and creates perplexity; still more so when a whole multitude derides our decision; for we cannot but prefer our own view to that of all the rest, and that is difficult and dangerous. The senses never experience this contradiction over a cripple.

When we do not know the truth of a thing, it is well there should be a common error to occupy the mind, e.g., the moon, to which are attributed changes of season, progress of sickness, etc. For man's chief disease is curiosity about things he cannot know; and error is not so bad a state for him as idle curiosity.

. . . "I know not who sent me into the world, nor what the world is, nor what I am; my ignorance of everything is appalling. I know not what my body is, what my senses, what my soul, nor what this part of me even which thinks my words, which meditates on all things and on itself, and yet is as ignorant of itself as of all the rest.

"I see the formidable regions of the universe which enclose me, and I find myself penned in one corner of this vast expanse, without knowing why I am set in this spot rather than another, nor why the little span of life granted me is assigned to this point of time rather than another of the whole eternity which went before or which shall follow after. I see nothing but infinities on every hand, closing me in as if I were an atom or a shadow which lasts but a moment and returns no more. All I know is that I must shortly die, but what I know least of all about is this very death which I cannot escape.

"As I know not whence I come, neither do I know

whither I am bound; all I know is that, when I quit this world, I fall forever either into nothingness or into the hands of an angry God, without knowing which of these two states is to be forever my lot. Such is my condition, full of weakness and uncertainty. And it leads me to conclude that I must after all pass my whole life without a thought of enquiring into the issue. Perhaps I may find some light amid my doubts; but I am not going to take the trouble to look for it, nor take one step to do so, and then, scorning those who vex themselves with the business, I will proceed without forethought or fear to try the great venture and slip smoothly into death, uncertain as to the eternity of my future state."

Who would care to have as friend a man who talked like that? Who would choose him to be his confidant? Who would have recourse to him in affliction? And finally to what purpose in life could he be put?

. . . Let us now speak according to the light of nature.

If there is a God, He is infinitely incomprehensible, since, having neither parts nor limits, He has no relation to us. We are therefore incapable of knowing what He is, or whether He is. This being so, who will dare to solve the problem? Not we who have no relation to Him.

Who then will blame Christians for inability to give a reason for their belief, professing as they do a religion for which they can give no reason? When they expound it they declare it to be folly, *stultitiam*, and then you complain that they do not prove it! If they proved it they would belie themselves; their lack of proof shows that they do not lack common sense. Agreed; but although that excuses those who present religion as they do, and clears them from blame for setting it forth without supporting reason, it does not excuse those who accept it." Let us then examine this point and say, "God is or is not." But which way shall we lean? Reason can settle nothing here; there is an infinite gulf between us. A game is on, at the other end of this infinite distance, and heads or tails will turn up. What will you wager? According to reason you cannot do either; according to reason you cannot leave either undone.

Do not then condemn those who have made a choice, for you know nothing about it. "I won't, but I shall blame them for making not this choice but any choice; for, although he who calls 'heads' and the other are equally wrong, they are both of them wrong: the right thing is not to wager."

Yes, but wager you must; there is no option, you have embarked on it. So which will you have? Come. Since you must choose, let us see what concerns you least. You have two things to lose: truth and good, and two things to stake: your reason and your will, your knowledge and your happiness. And your nature has two things to shun: error and misery. Your reason does not suffer by your choosing one more than the other, for you must choose. That is one point cleared. But your happiness? Let us weigh gain and loss in calling heads that God is. Reckon these two chances: if you win, you win all; if you lose, you lose naught. Then do not hesitate, wager that He is. "Admirable! Yes, I must wager; but I stake perhaps too much." Now, now. Since there is equal chance of gain and loss, if you had only two lives to gain for one, you might still wager; but were there three to win you would have to play (since play you must) and you would be foolish, when you are forced to play, not to risk your life to

win three at a game, where the chances of loss and
gain are equal. But here there is an eternity of life and
happiness. And this being so, though there should be
an infinity of chances and only one for you, you would
still be right to stake one in order to win two, and
you would be stupid, being obliged to play, did you
refuse to stake one life against three at a game in
which out of an infinity of chances there is one for
you, if there were an infinite amount of infinitely happy
life to gain. But here there *is* an infinity of infinitely
happy life to gain, one chance of gain against a finite
number of chances of loss, and your stake is finite. That
settles it; wherever there is infinity, and not an infinity
of chances of loss against the chance of gain, there can
be no hesitation, you must stake all. And thus, when
you are forced to play, you must renounce reason in
order to keep life, rather than risk it for infinite gain
which is as likely to happen as the loss of naught.

For it is no use saying that our gain is uncertain and
our risk certain, and that the infinite distance between
the *certainty* of what we stake and the *uncertainty* of
what we gain, equals the finite good which is certainly
staked against the uncertain infinite. This is not the
case. Every gambler risks a certainty to gain an
uncertainty; and yet he stakes a finite certainty to gain
a finite uncertainty, and that without transgressing
reason. There is not an infinite distance between the
certain stake and the uncertain gain; that is quite
wrong. There is, in truth, an infinity between certainty
of gain and certainty of loss. But the uncertainty of
gain is proportioned to the certainty of the stake, according to the proportion of the chances of gain and
loss. Hence it comes that, where there are as many
risks on one side as on the other, the game is even;
and then the certainty of the stake is equal to the

uncertainty of the gain; they are far from being infinitely separated. And so our argument is of infinite force when there is the finite to stake in a game in which the chances of gain and loss are equal, and the winnings are infinite. This is demonstrable; and if men are capable of any truth, this is one.

"I confess and admit it. But still is there no way of seeing the face of the cards?" Yes, Scripture and the rest, etc. "Yes, but my hands are tied and my lips are closed; I am forced to wager, and I am not free; I am not released, and I am so made that I cannot believe. What am I to do?"

You speak true. But at least get to understand your inability to believe, since reason leads you to belief, and yet you cannot believe. Do your best then to gain conviction, not by an increase of divine proofs, but by a decrease of human passions. You would fain reach faith, but you know not the way? You would cure yourself of unbelief, and you ask for a remedy? Take a lesson from those who have been bound like you, and who now stake all they possess. These are they who know the road you would follow, who are cured of a disease of which you would be cured. Follow the way by which they began, that is by making believe that they believed, by taking holy water, by hearing mass, etc. This will quite naturally bring you to believe, and will calm you . . . will stupefy you. "But that is just what I fear." Pray why? What have you to lose?

But to show you that this is the way, this is what will lessen your passions, which are your great stumbling block.

Now what harm will you get in following this line? You will be faithful, honest, humble, grateful, beneficent, a good friend, true. Certainly you will be freed from poisonous pleasures, such as ambition and luxury; but will you not have others?

I tell you that you will gain in this life, and that at every step you take on this road you will see such certainty of gain, such nothingness in what you risk, that you will at last recognize that you have wagered on something certain and infinite, for which you have risked naught.

"Oh, your words transport me, delight me, etc."

If they please you and seem cogent, know that they are the utterance of a man who has been on his knees before and after, beseeching that Being, infinite and without parts, to whom he submits all his being, that He may likewise bring into submission all your being for your good and for His glory; that so strength may come to the help of weakness.

We know Truth not only through reason, but also by the heart; it is in this way that we have knowledge of first principles, and it is in vain that Reason, which has no share in them, tries to dispute them. Pyrrhonians, who have no other object, pursue it to no purpose. We know we do not dream; however helpless we are to prove it by reason, our impotence merely demonstrates the weakness of our reason, not the uncertainty of all our knowledge, as they falsely aver. For knowledge of first principles, such as the existence of space, time, motion, numbers, is as sound as any knowledge furnished by our reasoning. And it is on the knowledge supplied by the heart and intuition that reason rests, founding thereon all its utterances. (The heart feels that there are three dimensions in space and that numbers are infinite, and reason goes on to show that there are no square numbers one of which is double the other. Principles are felt, propositions are deduced;

and the whole result is certitude, reached by different routes.) And it is as useless and absurd for reason to ask the heart to prove its first principles before agreeing to them, as it would be for the heart to ask reason to feel all the propositions it demonstrates before accepting them.

This impotence can only serve to humble reason (which would fain rule the roost), but not to assail our certitude, as though reason alone were capable of teaching us. Would to God on the contrary, that we never had need of it, and that we knew everything by intuition and feeling! But nature has refused us this blessing; she has on the contrary given us very little knowledge of this kind; the rest can be acquired only by reason.

And therefore those upon whom God has bestowed religion by cordial feeling are very fortunate, and are quite fairly convinced. But to those who lack religion we can only give it by process of reason, waiting till God makes it felt by the heart, without which faith is but human, and unavailing for salvation.

Do not wonder to see simple folk believe without reasoning. God gives them love of Him and hatred of self. He inclines their heart to believe. We shall never believe with a belief that avails and springs from faith, unless God inclines the heart; and we believe as soon as He inclines it. David knew this: *"O God incline my heart."*

He who would fully know human vanity has but to consider the causes and effects of love. The cause is a *je ne sais quoi* (Corneille), and the effects are fearful. This *je ne sais quoi,* so slight a thing it cannot be further identified, moves earth, princes, armies, the whole world.

Cleopatra's nose: if it had been shorter, the whole face of the earth would have been changed.

From *Pascal's Pensées*, trans., with brief notes and introduction, by H. F. Stewart (New York: Pantheon, 1950).

Sinners in the Hands of an Angry God

[From the sermon of the same title]

JONATHAN EDWARDS

1741

The use of this awful subject may be for awakening unconverted persons in this congregation. This that you have heard is the case of every one of you that are out of Christ. That world of misery, that lake of burning brimstone, is extended abroad under you. There is the dreadful pit of the glowing flames of the wrath of God; there is hell's wide gaping mouth open; and you have nothing to stand upon, nor anything to take hold of; there is nothing between you and hell but the air; it is only the power and mere pleasure of God that holds you up.

You probably are not sensible of this; you find you are kept out of hell, but do not see the hand of God in it; but look at other things, as the good state of your bodily constitution, your care of your own life, and the means you use for your own preservation. But indeed these things are nothing; if God should withdraw his hand, they would avail no more to keep you from falling, than the thin air to hold up a person that is suspended in it.

Your wickedness makes you as it were heavy as lead, and to tend downwards with great weight and pressure towards hell; and if God should let you go, you would immediately sink and swiftly descend and plunge into the bottomless gulf, and your healthy constitution, and your own care and prudence, and best contrivance, and all your righteousness, would have no more influence to uphold you and keep you out of hell, than a spider's web would have to stop a fallen rock. Were it not for the sovereign pleasure of God, the earth would not bear you one moment; for you are a burden to it; the creation groans with you; the creature is made subject to the bondage of your corruption, not willingly; the sun does not willingly shine upon you to give you light to serve sin and Satan; the earth does not willingly yield her increase to satisfy your lusts; nor is it willingly a stage for your wickedness to be acted upon; the air does not willingly serve you for breath to maintain the flame of life in your vitals, while you spend your life in the service of God's enemies. God's creatures are good, and were made for men to serve God with, and do not willingly subserve to any other purpose, and groan when they are abused to purposes so directly contrary to their nature and end. And the world would spew you out, were it not for the sovereign hand of him who hath subjected it in hope. There are black clouds of God's wrath now hanging directly over your heads, full of the dreadful storm, and big with thunder; and were it not for the restraining hand of God, it would immediately burst forth upon you. The sovereign pleasure of God, for the present, stays his rough wind; otherwise it would come with fury, and your destruction would come like a whirl-wind, and you would be like the chaff of the summer threshing floor.

The wrath of God is like great waters that are dammed for the present; they increase more and more, and rise higher and higher, till an outlet is given; and the longer the stream is stopped, the more rapid and mighty is its course, when once it is let loose. It is true that judgment against your evil works has not been executed hitherto; the floods of God's vengeance have been withheld; but your guilt in the meantime is constantly increasing, and you are every day treasuring up more wrath; the waters are constantly rising, and waxing more and more mighty; and there is nothing but the mere pleasure of God, that holds the waters back, that are unwilling to be stopped, and press hard to go forward. If God should only withdraw his hand from the flood-gate, it would immediately fly open, and the fiery floods of the fierceness and wrath of God, would rush forth with inconceivable fury, and would come upon you with omnipotent power; and if your strength were ten thousand times greater than it is, yea, ten thousand times greater than the strength of the stoutest, sturdiest devil in hell, it would be nothing to withstand or endure it.

The bow of God's wrath is bent, and the arrow made ready on the string, and justice bends the arrow at your heart, and strains the bow, and it is nothing but the mere pleasure of God, and that of an angry God, without any promise or obligation at all, that keeps the arrow one moment from being made drunk with your blood. Thus all you that never passed under a great change of heart, by the mighty power of the Spirit of God upon your souls; all you that were never born again, and made new creatures, and raised from being dead in sin, to a state of new, and before altogether unexperienced light and life, are in the hands of an angry God. However you may have reformed your life in many things, and may have had religious affections, and may keep up a form of religion in your families and closets, and in the house of God, it is nothing but his mere pleasure that keeps you from being this moment swallowed up in everlasting destruction. However unconvinced you may now be of the truth of what you hear, by and by you will be fully convinced of it. Those that are gone from being in the like circumstances with you, see that it was so with them; for destruction came suddenly upon most of them; when they expected nothing of it, and while they were saying, Peace and safety: now they see, that those things on which they depended for peace and safety, were nothing but thin air and empty shadows.

The God that holds you over the pit of hell, much as one holds a spider, or some loathsome insect over the fire, abhors you, and is dreadfully provoked: his wrath towards you burns like fire; he looks upon you as worthy of nothing else, but to be cast into the fire; he is of purer eyes than to bear to have you in his sight; you are ten thousand times more abominable in his eyes, than the most hateful venomous serpent is in ours. You have offended him infinitely more than ever a stubborn rebel did his prince; and yet it is nothing but his hand that holds you from falling into the fire every moment. It is to be ascribed to nothing else, that you did not go to hell the last night; that you was suffered to awake again in this world, after you closed your eyes to sleep. And there is no other reason to be given, why you have not dropped into hell since you arose in the morning, but that God's hand has held you up. There is no other reason to be given why you have not gone to hell,

since you have sat here in the house of God, provoking his pure eyes by your sinful wicked manner of
attending his solemn worship. Yea, there is nothing
else that is to be given as a reason why you do not
this very moment drop down into hell.

O sinner! Consider the fearful danger you are in:
it is a great furnace of wrath, a wide and bottomless
pit, full of the fire of wrath, that you are held over in
the hand of that God, whose wrath is provoked and
incensed as much against you, as against many of the
damned in hell. You hang by a slender thread, with
the flames of divine wrath flashing about it, and ready
every moment to singe it, and burn it asunder; and
you have no interest in any Mediator, and nothing to
lay hold of to save yourself, nothing to keep off the
flames of wrath, nothing of your own, nothing that you
ever have done, nothing that you can do, to induce God
to spare you one moment. . . .

How dreadful is the state of those that are daily
and hourly in the danger of this great wrath and infinite
misery! But this is the dismal case of every soul in this
congregation that has not been born again, however
moral and strict, sober and religious, they may otherwise be. Oh that you would consider it, whether you
be young or old! There is reason to think, that there
are many in this congregation now hearing this discourse, that will actually be the subjects of this very
misery to all eternity. We know not who they are, or
in what seats they sit, or what thoughts they now have.
It may be they are now at ease, and hear all these
things without much disturbance, and are now flattering
themselves that they are not the persons, promising
themselves that they shall escape. If we knew that
there was one person, and but one, in the whole congregation, that was to be the subject of this misery,

what an awful thing would it be to think of! If we knew who it was, what an awful sight would it be to see such a person! How might all the rest of the congregation lift up a lamentable and bitter cry over him! But, alas! instead of one, how many is it likely will remember this discourse in hell? And it would be a wonder, if some that are now present should not be in hell in a very short time, even before this year is out. And it would be no wonder if some persons, that now sit here, in some seats of this meeting-house, in health, quiet and secure, should be there before tomorrow morning. Those of you that finally continue in a natural condition, that shall keep out of hell longest will be there in a little time! your damnation does not slumber; it will come swiftly, and, in all probability, very suddenly upon many of you. You have reason to wonder that you are not already in hell. It is doubtless the case of some whom you have seen and known, that never deserved hell more than you, and that heretofore appeared as likely to have been now alive as you. Their case is past all hope; they are crying in extreme misery and perfect despair; but here you are in the land of the living and in the house of God, and have an opportunity to obtain salvation. What would not those poor damned hopeless souls give for one day's opportunity such as you now enjoy!

And now you have an extraordinary opportunity, a day wherein Christ has thrown the door of mercy wide open, and stands in calling and crying with a loud voice to poor sinners; a day wherein many are flocking to him, and pressing into the kingdom of God. Many are daily coming from the east, west, north and south; many that were very lately in the same miserable condition that you are in, are now in a happy state, with their hearts filled with love to him who has loved them, and washed

them from their sins in his own blood, and rejoicing in
hope of the glory of God. How awful is it to be left
behind at such a day! To see so many others feasting,
while you are pining and perishing! To see so many
rejoicing and singing for joy of heart, while you have
cause to mourn for sorrow of heart, and howl for vexation of spirit! How can you rest one moment in such a
condition? Are not your souls as precious as the souls
of the people at Suffield,* where they are flocking
from day to day to Christ?

Are there not many here who have lived long in
the world, and are not to this day born again? and so
are aliens from the commonwealth of Israel, and have
done nothing ever since they have lived, but treasure
up wrath against the day of wrath? Oh, sirs, your case,
in an especial manner, is extremely dangerous. Your
guilt and hardness of heart is extremely great. Do you
not see how generally persons of your years are passed
over and left, in the present remarkable and wonderful
dispensation of God's mercy? You had need to consider
yourselves, and awake thoroughly out of sleep. You
cannot bear the fierceness and wrath of the infinite
God. And you, young men, and young women, will
you neglect this precious season which you now enjoy,
when so many others of your age are renouncing all
youthful vanities, and flocking to Christ? You especially
have now an extraordinary opportunity; but if you
neglect it, it will soon be with you as with those persons who spent all the precious days of youth in sin,
and are now come to such a dreadful pass in blindness
and hardness. And you, children, who are unconverted,
do not you know that you are going down to hell, to
bear the dreadful wrath of that God, who is now
angry with you every day and every night? Will you

* A town in the neighbourhood. [Edwards' note.]

be content to be the children of the devil, when so many other children in the land are converted, and are become the holy and happy children of the King of kings?

And let everyone that is yet of Christ, and hanging over the pit of hell, whether they be old men and women, or middle aged, or young people, or little children, now hearken to the loud calls of God's word and providence. This acceptable year of the Lord, a day of such great favours to some, will doubtless be a day of as remarkable vengeance to others. Men's hearts harden, and their guilt increases apace at such a day as this, if they neglect their souls; and never was there so great danger of such persons being given up to hardness of heart and blindness of mind. God seems now to be hastily gathering in his elect in all parts of the land; and probably the greater part of adult persons that ever shall be saved, will be brought in now in a little time, and that it will be as it was on the great out-pouring of the Spirit upon the Jews in the apostles' days; the election will obtain, and the rest will be blinded. If this should be the case with you, you will eternally curse this day, and will curse the day that ever you was born, to see such a season of the pouring out of God's Spirit, and will wish that you had died and gone to hell before you had seen it. Now undoubtedly it is, as it was in the days of John the Baptist, the axe is in an extraordinary manner laid at the root of the trees, that every tree which brings not forth good fruit, may be hewn down and cast into the fire.

Therefore, let every one that is out of Christ, now awake and fly from the wrath to come. The wrath of Almighty God is now undoubtedly hanging over a great part of this congregation: Let every one fly out of

Sodom: "Haste and escape for your lives, look not behind you, escape to the mountain, lest you be consumed."

(Boston, 1742.)

❖ ❖ ❖

A Reasonable Plea
for an Emotional Faith

[FROM "A Short Address to the Inhabitants of Ireland"]

JOHN WESLEY

1749

1. There has lately appeared (as you cannot be ignorant) a set of men preaching up and down in several parts of this kingdom, who for ten or twelve years have been known in England by the title of Methodists. The vulgar in Ireland term them Swaddlers—a name first given them in Dublin, from one of them preaching on those wods: "Ye shall find the young child wrapped in swaddling clothes, lying in a manger."

2. Extremely various have been the reports concerning them. Some persons have spoken favourably: but the generality of men treat them in a different manner, with utter contempt, if not detestation; and relate abundance of things in order to prove that they are not fit to live upon the earth.

3. A question, then, which you may naturally ask, is this: "In what manner ought a man of religion, a

man of reason, a lover of mankind, and a lover of his country, to act on this occasion?"

4. Before we can properly answer this, it should be inquired, concerning the persons in question, what they are; what they teach; and what are the effects which are generally observed to attend their teaching.

5. It should first be inquired, what they are. In order to reach a speedy determination of this, we may set aside whatever will admit of any dispute, as, whether they are good men or bad, rich or poor, fools, madmen, and enthusiasts, or sober, rational men. Now, waiving all this, one point is indisputable: it is allowed on all hands, they are men who spend all their time and strength in teaching those doctrines, the nature and consequences whereof are described in the following pages.

6. The doctrines they constantly teach are these: that religion does not consist in negatives only—in not taking the name of God in vain, in not robbing or murdering our neighbour, in bare abstaining from evil of any or every kind; but is a real, positive thing: that it does not consist in externals only—in attending the church and sacrament (although all these things they approve and recommend), in using all the means of grace, or in works of charity (commonly so called), superadded to works of piety; but that it is, properly and strictly, a principle within, seated in the inmost soul, and thence manifesting itself by these outward fruits, on all suitable occasions.

7. They insist, that nothing deserves the name of religion, but a virtuous heart, producing a virtuous life: a complication of justice, mercy, and truth, of every right and amiable temper, beaming forth from the deepest recesses of the mind, in a series of wise and generous actions. . . .

8. These are their constant doctrines. It is true, they occasionally touch on abundance of other things. Thus they frequently maintain, that there is an inseparable connection between virtue and happiness; that none but a virtuous (or, as they usually express it, a religious) man can be happy; and that every man is happy in the same proportion as he is truly religious; seeing a contented mind (according to them), a cheerful, thankful, joyous acquiescence in every disposal of that Sovereign Wisdom who governs both heaven and earth, if it be not an essential branch of religion, is, at least, a necessary consequence of it. On all proper occasions they strongly recommend, on the one hand, the most intense love of our country; on the other, the firmest loyalty to our Prince, abstracted from all views of private interest. They likewise take every opportunity of enforcing the absolute necessity of sobriety and temperance; of unwearied industry in the works of our calling; of moral honesty in all its branches; and, particularly, in the discharge of all relative duties, without which, they say, religion is vain. But all these they recommend on that one single ground—the love of God and of all mankind; declaring them to be of no avail, if they do not spring from this love, as well as terminate and centre therein.

9. Whoever is at the pains of hearing these Preachers, or of reading what they have wrote, with any degree of attention and impartiality, must perceive that these are their doctrines. And it is equally easy to discern what the effects of their preaching have been. These doctrines they spread wherever they come. They convince many in every place, that religion does not consist (as they imagined once) either in negatives or externals, in barely doing no harm, or even doing good; but in the tempers of the heart, in right dispositions of

mind towards God and man, producing all right words
and actions.

10. And these dispositions of mind are, more or less,
the continual consequence of their preaching (that is,
if we may know the tree by its fruit, which is doubtless
the most rational way of judging): the lives of many
who constantly attend it show, that God has wrought
a real change in their heart; and that the grand principle of love to God and man already begins to take
root therein.

11. Hence those who were before of quite the opposite temper, are now generous, disinterested lovers of
their country; and faithful, loyal subjects to their
Prince, His sacred Majesty King George: they are now
sober and temperate in all things, and punctually honest in all their dealings: they are strict in every relative
duty, and laborious and diligent in their callings, notwithstanding the continual discouragement they receive from many who still cry out, "Ye are idle, ye are
idle; therefore ye say, Let us go and serve the Lord."
They are content in every state, whether of plenty or
want, and thankful to God and man. These are plain,
glaring, undeniable facts, whereof, if any Magistrate
will be at the trouble to take them, numerous affidavits
may be made, in Dublin, Cork, Limerick, and many
other places.

But if these things are so, it is easy to conceive in
what manner every man of religion, every man of
reason, every lover of mankind, every lover of his
country, ought to act on this occasion.

12. For, first, ought not every man of religion, with
all the earnestness of his soul, to praise God, who, after
so long a night of ignorance and error had overspread
our country, has poured light on so many of those that sat
in darkness and the shadow of death? has shown such

numbers even of the lowest and most brutish of men, wherein true religion lies; has taught them both to lay the right foundation, and to build the whole fabric thereon; has convinced them, "Other foundation can no man lay than that which is laid, even Jesus Christ;" and, "The end of the commandment is love," of the whole commandment or law of Christ; love, the life, the soul, the spirit of religion, the river that makes glad the city of God, the living water continually springing up into everlasting life?

13. Admit that they do not exactly judge right as to some of the appendages of religion; that you have a clearer and juster conception than they of several things pertaining to the beauty of holiness; yet ought you not to bless God for giving these outcasts of men to see at least the essence of it? nay, to be living witnesses of the substance of religion, though they may still mistake as to some of the circumstances of it.

14. Ought not every man of reason (whether he assents, or no, to that system of opinions commonly called Christianity) sincerely and heartily to rejoice in the advancement of solid, rational virtue? in the propagation, not of this or that set of opinions, but of genuine pure morality? of disinterested benevolence, of tender affections, to the whole of the human race? Ought you not to be glad, that there are any instruments found, till others appear who are more equal to the task, whose one employment it is (from whatever motive) to diffuse generous honesty throughout the land?

From *Works*, Vol. IX (London: John Mason, 1856).

❖ ❖ ❖

The Great Chain of Being

[FROM *An Essay on Man*, EPISTLE I]

ALEXANDER POPE

1733

VII. What would this Man? Now upward will he
    soar,
And little less than Angel, would be more;
Now looking downwards, just as griev'd appears
To want the strength of bulls, the fur of bears.
Made for his use all creatures if he call,
Say what their use, had he the powers of all?
Nature to these without profusion kind,
The proper organs, proper powers assign'd;
Each seeming want compensated of course,
Here with degrees of swiftness, there of force;
All in exact proportion to the state;
Nothing to add, and nothing to abate;
Each beast, each insect, happy in its own:
Is Heav'n unkind to man, and man alone?
Shall he alone, whom rational we call,
Be pleas'd with nothing if not bless'd with all?
    The bliss of man (could pride that blessing find)
Is not to act or think beyond mankind;
No powers of body or of soul to share,
But what his nature and his state can bear.
Why has not man a microscopic eye?
For this plain reason, man is not a fly.

Say, what the use, were finer optics giv'n,
T' inspect a mite, not comprehend the Heav'n?
Or touch, if tremblingly alive all o'er,
To smart and agonize at every pore?
Or quick effluvia darting thro' the brain,
Die of a rose in aromatic pain?
If Nature thunder'd in his opening ears,
And stunn'd him with the music of the spheres,
How would he wish that Heav'n had left him still
The whisp'ring zephyr and the purling rill?
Who finds not Providence all good and wise,
Alike in what it gives and what denies?

    VII. Far as creation's ample range extends,
The scale of sensual, mental powers ascends.
Mark how it mounts to man's imperial race
From the green myriads in the peopled grass:
What modes of sight betwixt each wide extreme,
The mole's dim curtain and the lynx's beam:
Of smell, the headlong lioness between
And hound sagacious on the tainted green:
Of hearing, from the life that fills the flood
To that which warbles thro' the vernal wood.
The spider's touch, how exquisitely fine,
Feels at each thread, and lives along the line:
In the nice bee what sense so subtly true,
From pois'nous herbs extracts the healing dew!
How instinct varies in the grovelling swine,
Compared, half-reas'ning elephant, with thine!
'Twixt that and reason what a nice barrier!
For ever separate, yet for ever near!
Remembrance and reflection how allied!
What thin partitions Sense from Thought divide!
And middle natures how they long to join,
Yet never pass th' insuperable line!
Without this just gradation could they be

Subjected these to those, or all to thee!
The powers of all subdued by thee alone,
Is not thy Reason all these powers in one?
  viii. See thro' this air, this ocean, and this earth
All matter quick, and bursting into birth:
Above, how high progressive life may go!
Around, how wide! how deep extend below!
Vast chain of being! which from God began;
Natures ethereal, human, angel, man,
Beast, bird, fish, insect, who no eye can see,
No glass can reach; from infinite to thee;
From thee to nothing.—On superior powers
Were we to press, inferior might on ours;
Or in the full creation leave a void,
Where, one step broken, the great scale's destroy'd:
From Nature's chain whatever link you like,
Tenth, or ten thousandth, breaks the chain alike.
  And if each system in gradation roll,
Alike essential to th' amazing Whole,
The least confusion but in one, not all
That system only, but the Whole must fall.
Let earth unbalanced from her orbit fly,
Planets and stars run lawless thro' the sky;
Let ruling angels from their spheres be hurl'd,
Being on being wreck'd, and world on world;
Heav'n's whole foundations to their centre nod,
And Nature tremble to the throne of God!
All this dread order break—for whom? for thee?
Vile worm!—O madness! pride! impiety!
  ix. What if the foot, ordain'd the dust to tread,
Or hand to toil, aspired to be the head?
What if the head, the eye, or ear repin'd
To serve mere engines to the ruling mind?
Just as absurd for any part to claim
To be another in this gen'ral frame;

Just as absurd to mourn the tasks or pains
The great directing Mind of All ordains.

   All are but parts of one stupendous Whole,
Whose body Nature is, and God the soul;
That changed thro' all, and yet in all the same,
Great in the earth as in th' ethereal frame,
Warms in the sun, refreshes in the breeze,
Glows in the stars, and blossoms in the trees;
Lives thro' all life, extends thro' all extent,
Spreads undivided, operates unspent;
Breathes in our soul, informs our mortal part,
As full, as perfect, in a hair as heart;
As full, as perfect, in vile man that mourns,
As the rapt Seraph that adores and burns.
To him no high, no low, no great, no small;
He fills, he bounds, connects, and equals all!

   x. Cease, then, nor Order imperfection name;
Our proper bliss depends on what we blame.
Know thy own point: this kind, this due degree
Of blindness, weakness, Heav'n bestows on thee.
Submit: in this or any other sphere,
Secure to be as bless'd as thou canst bear;
Safe in the hand of one disposing Power,
Or in the natal or the mortal hour.
All Nature is but Art unknown to thee;
All chance, direction, which thou canst not see;
All discord, harmony not understood;
All partial evil, universal good:
And spite of Pride, in erring Reason's spite,
One truth is clear, *Whatever is, is right*.

   From *Poetical Works*, ed. H. F. Cary (London: Routledge, 1872).

❖ ❖ ❖

The Augustan Heavens

[Hymn, Psalm XIX]

JOSEPH ADDISON

1712

The spacious firmament on high,
With all the blue ethereal sky,
And spangled heavens, a shining frame,
Their great Original proclaim.
The unwearied Sun from day to day
Does his Creator's power display;
And publishes to every land
The work of an Almighty hand.

Soon as the evening shades prevail,
The moon takes up the wondrous tale;
And nightly to the listening Earth
Repeats the story of her birth:
Whilst all the stars that round her burn,
And all the planets in their turn,
Confirm the tidings as they roll,
And spread the truth from pole to pole.

What though in solemn silence all
Move round the dark terrestrial ball;
What though nor real voice nor sound
Amidst their radiant orbs be found?
In Reason's ear they all rejoice,

And utter forth a glorious voice;
Forever singing as they shine,
"The Hand that made us is divine."

In *The Spectator*, No. 465, August 23, 1712.

"He Would Have to Be Invented"

François Marie Arouet de
VOLTAIRE

1770
TO FREDERICK WILLIAM, PRINCE OF PRUSSIA

Monseigneur, the royal family of Prussia has excellent reasons for not wishing the annihilation of the soul. It has more right than anyone to immortality.

It is very true that we do not know any too well what the soul is: no one has ever seen it. All that we do know is that the eternal Lord of nature has given us the power of thinking, and of distinguishing virtue. It is not proved that this faculty survives our death: but the contrary is not proved either. It is possible, doubtless, that God has given thought to a particle to which, after we are no more, He will still give the power of thought: there is no inconsistency in this idea.

In the midst of all the doubts which we have discussed for four thousand years in four thousand ways, the safest course is to do nothing against one's conscience. With this secret, we can enjoy life and have nothing to fear from death.

There are some charlatans who admit no doubts. We know nothing of first principles. It is surely very presumptuous to define God, the angels, spirits, and to pretend to know precisely why God made the world, when we do not know why we can move our arms at our pleasure.

Doubt is not a pleasant condition, but certainty is an absurd one.

What is most repellent in the *System of Nature* [of Holbach]—after the recipe to make eels from flour—is the audacity with which it decides that there is no God, without even having tried to prove the impossibility. There is some eloquence in the book: but much more rant, and no sort of proof. It is a pernicious work, alike for princes and people:

"*Si Dieu n'existait pas, il faudrait l'inventer.*" [If God did not exist, it would be necessary to invent him.]

But all nature cries aloud that He does exist: that there *is* a supreme intelligence, an immense power, an admirable order, and everything teaches us our own dependence on it.

From the depth of our profound ignorance, let us do our best: this is what I think, and what I have always thought, amid all the misery and follies inseparable from seventy-seven years of life.

Your Royal Highness has a noble career before you. I wish you, and dare prophesy for you, a happiness worthy of yourself and of your heart. I knew you when you were a child, monseigneur: I visited you in your sick room when you had smallpox: I feared for your life. Your father honoured me with much goodness: you condescend to shower on me the same favours which are the honour of my old age, and the consolation of those sufferings which must shortly end it. I am, with deep respect, etc.

In *Voltaire in His Letters* trans. S. G. Tallentyre (New York: G. P. Putnam's Sons, 1919).

❖ ❖ ❖

A Warm Deist

[FROM *Emile*]

JEAN JACQUES ROUSSEAU

1762

I believe, therefore, that the world is governed by a wise and powerful *Will*. I see it, or rather I feel it; and this is of importance for me to know. But is the world eternal, or is it created? Are things derived from one self-existent principle, or are there two or more, and what is their essence? Of all this I know nothing, nor do I see that it is necesary I should. In proportion as such knowledge may become interesting I will endeavor to acquire it: but further than this I give up all such idle disquisitions, which serve only to make me discontented with myself, which are useless in practice, and are above my understanding.

You will remember, however, that I am not dictating my sentiments to you, but only explaining what they are. Whether matter be eternal or only created, whether it have a passive principle or not, certain it is that the whole universe is one design, and sufficiently displays one intelligent agent: for I see no part of this system that is not under regulation, or that does not concur to one and the same end; viz., that of preserving the present and established order of things. That Being, whose will is his deed, whose principle of action is in himself—that Being, in a word, whatever it be, that gives motion to all parts of the universe, and governs all things, I call GOD.

To this term I affix the ideas of intelligence, power, and will, which I have collected from the order of things; and to these I add that of goodness, which is a necessary consequence of their union. But I am not at all the wiser concerning the essence of the Being to which I give these attributes. He remains at an equal distance from my senses and my understanding. The more I think of him, the more I am confounded. I know of a certainty that he exists, and that his existence is independent of any of his creatures. I know also that my existence is dependent on his, and that every being I know is in the same situation as myself. I perceive the deity in all his works, I feel him within me, and behold him in every object around me: but I no sooner endeavour to contemplate what he is in himself —I no sooner enquire where he is, and what is his substance, than he eludes the strongest efforts of my imagination; and my bewildered understanding is convinced of its own weakness.

For this reason I shall never take upon me to argue about the nature of God further than I am obliged to do by the relation he appears to stand in to myself. There is so great a temerity in such disquisitions that a wise man will never enter on them without trembling, and feeling fully assured of his incapacity to proceed far on so sublime a subject: for it is less injurious to entertain no ideas of the deity at all, than to harbour those which are unworthy and unjust.

After having discovered those of his attributes by

which I am convinced of his existence, I return to myself and consider the place I occupy in that order of things, which is directed by him and subjected to my examination. Here I find my species stand incontestibly in the first rank; as man, by virtue of his will and the instruments he is possessed of to put it in execution, has a greater power over the bodies by which he is surrounded than they, by mere physical impulse, have over him. By virtue of his intelligence, I also find, he is the only created being here below that can take a general survey of the whole system. Is there one among them, except man, who knows how to observe all others? to weigh, to calculate, to foresee their motions, their effects, and to join, if I may so express myself, the sentiment of a general existence to that of the individual? What is there so very ridiculous then in supposing everything made for man, when he is the only created being who knows how to consider the relation in which all things stand to himself?

It is then true that man is lord of the creation, that he is, at least, sovereign over the habitable earth; for it is certain that he not only subdues all other animals, and even disposes by his industry of the elements at his pleasure, but he alone of all terrestrial beings knows how to subject to his convenience, and even by contemplation to appropriate to his use, the very stars and planets he cannot approach. Let anyone produce me an animal of another species who knows how to make use of fire, or hath faculties to admire the sun. What! am I able to observe, to know other beings and their relations; am I capable of discovering what is order, beauty, virtue, of contemplating the universe, of elevating my ideas to the hand which governs the whole; am I capable of loving what is good and doing it, and shall I compare myself to the brutes? Abject soul! it is your gloomy philosophy alone that renders you at all like them. Or, rather, it is in vain you would debase yourself. Your own genius rises up against your principles; your benevolent heart gives the lie to your absurd doctrines, and even the abuse of your faculties demonstrates their excellence in spite of yourself.

For my part, who have no system to maintain, who am only a simple, honest man, attached to no party, unambitious of being the founder of any sect, and contented with the situation in which God hath placed me, I see nothing in the world, except the deity, better than my own species; and were I left to choose my place in the order of created beings, I see none that I could prefer to that of man.

This reflection, however, is less vain than affecting; for my state is not the effect of choice, and could not be due to the merit of a being that did not before exist. Can I behold myself, nevertheless thus distinguished, without thinking myself happy in occupying so honourable a post; or without blessing the hand that placed me here? From the first view I thus took of myself, my heart began to glow with a sense of gratitude towards the author of our being; and hence arose my first idea of the worship due to a beneficent deity. I adore the supreme power, and melt into tenderness at his goodness. I have no need to be taught artificial forms of worship; the dictates of nature are sufficient. Is it not a natural consequence of self-love to honour those who protect us, and to love such as do us good?

But when I come afterwards to take a view of the particular rank and relation in which I stand, as an individual, among the fellow creatures of my species;

to consider the different ranks of society and the persons by whom they are filled; what a scene is presented to me! Where is that order and regularity before observed? The scenes of nature present to my view the most perfect harmony and proportion: those of mankind nothing but confusion and disorder. The physical elements of things act in concert with each other; the moral world alone is a chaos of discord. Mere animals are happy; but man, their lord and sovereign, is miserable! Where, Supreme Wisdom! are thy laws? Is it thus, O Providence! thou governest the world? What is become of thy power, thou Supreme Beneficence, when I behold evil thus prevailing upon the earth?

Would you believe, my good friend, that from such gloomy reflections and apparent contradictions, I should form to myself more sublime ideas of the soul than ever resulted from my former researches? In meditating on the nature of man, I conceived that I discovered two distinct principles; the one raising him to the study of eternal truths, the love of justice and moral beauty—bearing him aloft to the regions of the intellectual world, the contemplation of which yields the truest delight to the philosopher—the other debasing him even below himself, subjecting him to the slavery of sense, the tyranny of the passions, and exciting these to counteract every noble and generous sentiment inspired by the former. When I perceived myself hurried away by two such contrary powers, I naturally concluded that man is not one simple and individual substance. I will, and I will not; I perceive myself at once free, and a slave; I see what is good, I admire it, and yet I do the evil: I am active when I listen to my reason, and passive when hurried away by my passions; while my greatest uneasiness is to find, when fallen under temptations, that I had the power of resisting them.

Attend, young man, with confidence to what I say; you will find I shall never deceive you. If conscience be the offspring of our prejudices, I am doubtless in the wrong, and moral virtue is not to be demonstrated; but if self-love, which makes us prefer ourselves to everything else, be natural to man, and if nevertheless an innate sense of justice be found in his heart, let those who imagine him to be a simple uncompounded being reconcile these contradictions, and I will give up my opinion and acknowledge him to be one substance.

You will please to observe that by the word substance I here mean, in general, a being possessed of some primitive quality, abstracted from all particular or secondary modifications. Now, if all known primitive qualities may be united in one and the same being, we have no need to admit of more than one substance; but if some of these qualities are incompatible with, and necessarily exclusive of each other, we must admit of the existence of as many different substances as there are such incompatible qualities. You will do well to reflect on this subject. For my part, notwithstanding what Mr. Locke hath said on this head, I need only to know that matter is extended and divisible, to be assured that it cannot think; and when a philosopher comes and tells me that trees and rocks have thought and perception, he may, perhaps, embarrass me with the subtlety of his arguments, but I cannot help regarding him as a disingenuous sophist, who had rather attribute sentiment to stocks and stones than acknowledge man to have a soul.

Let us suppose that a man, born deaf, should deny

the reality of sounds, because his ears were never sensible of them. To convince him of his error, I place a violin before his eyes; and, by playing on another, concealed from him, give a vibration to the strings of the former. This motion, I tell him, is effected by sound.

"Not at all," says he, "the cause of the vibration of the string is in the string itself: it is a common quality in all bodies so to vibrate."

"Show me then," I reply, "the same vibration in other bodies; or, at least, the cause of it in this string."

"I cannot," the deaf man may reply, "but wherefore must I, because I do not conceive how this string vibrates, attribute the cause to your pretended sounds, of which I cannot entertain the least idea? This would be to attempt an explanation of one obscurity by another still greater. Either make your sounds perceptible to me, or I shall continue to doubt their existence."

The more I reflect on our capacity of thinking, and the nature of the human understanding, the greater is the resemblance I find between the arguments of our materialists and that of such a deaf man. They are, in effect, equally deaf to that internal voice which, nevertheless, calls to them so loud and emphatically. A mere machine is evidently incapable of thinking, it has neither motion nor figure productive of reflection: whereas in man there exists something perpetually prone to expand, and to burst the fetters by which it is confined. Space itself affords not bounds to the human mind: the whole universe is not extensive enough for man; his sentiments, his desires, his anxieties, and even his pride, take rise from a principle different from that body within which he perceives himself confined.

No material being can be self-active, and I perceive that I am so. It is in vain to dispute with me so clear a point. My own sentiment carries with it a stronger conviction than any reason which can ever be brought against it. I have a body on which other bodies act, and which acts reciprocally upon them. This reciprocal action is indubitable; but my will is independent of my senses. I can either consent to, or resist, their impressions. I am either vanquished or victor, and perceive clearly within myself when I act according to my will, and when I submit to be governed by my passions. I have always the power to will, though not the force to execute it. When I give myself up to any temptation, I act from the impulse of external objects. When I reproach myself for my weakness in so doing, I listen only to the dictates of my will. I am a slave in my vices, and free in my repentance. The sentiment of my liberty is effaced only by my depravation, and when I prevent the voice of the soul from being heard in opposition to the laws of the body. . . .

Enquire no longer then, who is the author of evil. Behold him in yourself. There exists no other evil in nature than what you either do or suffer, and you are equally the author of both. A general evil could exist only in disorder, but in the system of nature I see an established order, which is never disturbed. Particular evil exists only in the sentiment of the suffering being; and this sentiment is not given to man by nature, but is of his own acquisition. Pain and sorrow have but little hold on those who, unaccustomed to reflection, have neither memory nor foresight. Take away our fatal improvements, take away our errors and our vices, take away, in short, everything that is the work of man, and all that remains is good.

Where everything is good, nothing can be unjust,

justice being inseparable from goodness. Now goodness is the necessary effect of infinite power and self-love essential to every being conscious of its existence. An omnipotent Being extends its existence also, if I may so express myself, with that of its creatures. Production and preservation follow from the constant exertion of its power: it does not act on non-existence. God is not the God of the dead, but of the living. He cannot be mischievous or wicked without hurting himself. A being capable of doing everything cannot *will* to do anything but what is good. He who is infinitely good, therefore, because he is infinitely powerful, must also be supremely just, otherwise he would be inconsistent with himself. For that love of order which produces it we call goodness, and that love of order which preserves it is called justice.

God, it is said, owes nothing to his creatures. For my part, I believe he owes them everything he promised them when he gave them being. Now what is less than to promise them a blessing, if he gives them an idea of it, and has so constituted them as to feel the want of it? The more I look into myself, the more plainly I read these words written in my soul: *Be just and thou wilt be happy.* I see not the truth of this, however, in the present state of things, wherein the wicked triumph and the just are trampled on and oppressed. What indignation, hence, arises within us to find that our hopes are frustrated! Conscience itself rises up and complains of its maker. It cries out to him, lamenting, *Thou hast deceived me!*

"I have deceived thee, rash man? Who hath told thee so? Is thy soul annihilated? Dost thou cease to exist? Oh, Brutus! stain not a life of glory in the end. Leave not thy honour and thy hopes with thy body in the fields of Philippi. Wherefore dost thou say, virtue is a shadow, when thou wilt yet enjoy the reward of thine own? Dost thou imagine thou art going to die? No! thou art going to live! and then will I make good every promise I have made to thee."

From *Profession of Faith of a Savoyard Vicar* [part of *Emile*], trans. Olive Schreiner (New York: Peter Eckler, 1889).

❖ ❖ ❖

A Cautious Deist

BENJAMIN FRANKLIN

TO EZRA STILES

Philad^a, March 9, 1790.
REVEREND AND DEAR SIR,

You desire to know something of my Religion. It is the first time I have been questioned upon it. But I cannot take your curiosity amiss, and shall endeavour in a few words to gratify it. Here is my creed. I believe in one God, Creator of the universe. That he governs it by his Providence. That he ought to be worshipped. That the most acceptable service we render to him is doing good to his other children. That the soul of Man is immortal, and will be treated with justice in another life respecting its conduct in this. These I take to be the fundamental principles of all sound religion, and I regard them as you do in whatever sect I meet with them.

As to Jesus of Nazareth, my opinion of whom you particularly desire, I think the system of morals and his religion, as he left them to us, the best the world ever saw or is likely to see; but I apprehend it has received various corrupting changes, and I have, with most of the present dissenters in England, some doubts as to his divinity; tho' it is a question I do not dogmatize upon, having never studied it, and think it needless to busy myself with it now, when I expect soon an opportunity of knowing the truth with less trouble. I see no harm, however, in its being believed, if that belief has the good consequence, as probably it has, of making his doctrines more respected and better observed; especially as I do not perceive that the Supreme takes it amiss, by distinguishing the unbelievers in his government of the world with any peculiar marks of his displeasure.

I shall only add, respecting myself, that, having experienced the goodness of that Being in conducting me prosperously thro' a long life, I have no doubt of its continuance in the next, though without the smallest conceit of meriting such goodness. My sentiments on this head you will see in the copy of an old letter enclosed, which I wrote in answer to one from a zealous religionist, whom I had relieved in a paralytic case by electricity, and who, being afraid I should grow proud upon it, sent me his serious though rather impertinent caution. I send you also the copy of another letter, which will shew something of my disposition relating to religion. With great and sincere esteem and affection, I am, Your obliged old friend and most obedient humble servant

B. FRANKLIN

P.S. Had not your College [Yale] some present of books from the King of France? Please to let me know if you had an expectation given you of more, and the nature of that expectation? I have a reason for the enquiry. I confide that you will not expose me to criticism and censure by publishing any part of this communication to you. I have ever let others enjoy their religious sentiments, without reflecting on them for those that appeared to me unsupportable and even absurd. All sects here, and we have a great variety, have experienced my good will in assisting them with subscriptions for building their new places of worship; and, as I have never opposed any of their doctrines, I hope to go out of the world in peace with them all.

From *The Writings of Benjamin Franklin*, Vol. X, ed. A. H. Smyth (New York: The Macmillan Co., 1905-1907).

On Church and State

[FROM "The Fundamental Constitutions of Carolina"]

JOHN LOCKE[1]

1669

xcv. No man shall be permitted to be a freeman of Carolina, or to have any estate or habitation within it, that doth not acknowledge a God; and that God is publicly and solemnly to be worshipped.

xcvii. But since the natives of that place, who will be concerned in our plantation, are utterly strangers to Christianity, whose idolatry, ignorance, or mistake, gives us no right to expel, or use them ill; and those who

---

[1] Although not actually signed by Locke, these clauses are almost certainly from his pen. [C.B.'s note.]

remove from other parts to plant there, will unavoidably be of different opinions concerning matters of religion, the liberty whereof they will expect to have allowed them, and it will not be reasonable for us on this account to keep them out: the civil peace may be maintained amidst the diversity of opinions, and our agreement and compact with all men may be duly and faithfully observed; the violation whereof, upon what pretense soever, cannot be without great offense to Almighty God, and great scandal to the true religion, which we profess; and also that Jews, heathens, and other dissenters from the purity of the Christian religion, may not be scared and kept at a distance from it, but by having an opportunity of acquainting themselves with the truth and reasonableness of its doctrines, and the peaceableness and inoffensiveness of its professors, may by good usage and persuasion, and all those convincing methods of gentleness and meekness, suitable to the rules and design of the Gospel, be won over to embrace and unfeignedly receive the truth; therefore any seven or more persons, agreeing in any religion, shall constitute a church or profession, to which they shall give some name, to distinguish it from others.

xcviii. The terms of admittance and communion with any church or profession shall be written in a book, and therein be subscribed by all the members of the said church or profession; which book shall be kept by the public register of the precinct where they reside.

xcix. The time of everyone's subscription and submittance shall be dated in the said book or religious record.

c. In the terms of communion of every church or profession, these following shall be three; without which no agreement or assembly of men, upon pretense of

religion, shall be accounted a church or profession
within these rules:

1. "That there is a GOD.

2. "That GOD is publicly to be worshipped.

3. "That it is lawful, and the duty of every man,
being thereunto called by those that govern, to bear
witness to truth; and that every church or profession
shall in their terms of communion set down the external
way wheieby they witness a truth as in the presence of
GOD, whether it be by laying hands on, or kissing the
Bible, as in the Church of England, or by holding up
the hand, or any other sensible way."

CI. No person above seventeen years of age shall
have any benefit or protection of the law, or be capable
of any place of profit or honour, who is not a member
of some church or profession, having his name recorded
in some one, and but one religious record at once.

CII. No person of any other church or profession shall
disturb or molest any religious assembly.

CIII. No person whatsoever shall speak anything in
their religious assembly, irreverently or seditiously of the
government or governors, or state matters.

CIV. Any person subscribing the terms of communion
in the record of the said church or profession, before
the precinct register, and any five members of the said
church or profession, shall be thereby made a member
of the said church or profession.

CV. Any person striking out his own name out of
any religious record, or his name being struck out by
any officer thereunto, authorized by each church or
profession respectively, shall cease to be a member of
that church or profession.

CVI. No man shall use any reproachful, reviling or
abusive language against any religion of any church

or profession; that being the certain way of disturbing the peace, and of hindering the conversion of any to the truth, by engaging them in quarrels and animosities, to the hatred of the professors and that profession, which otherwise they might be brought to assent to.

CVII. Since charity obliges us to wish well to the souls of all men, and religion ought to alter nothing in any man's civil estate or right, it shall be lawful for slaves, as well as others, to enter themselves, and be of what church or profession any of them shall think best, and thereof be as fully members as any freeman. But yet no slave shall hereby be exempted from that civil dominion his master hath over him, but be in all other things in the same state and conditions he was in before.

CVIII. Assemblies, upon what pretense soever of religion, not observing and performing the abovesaid rules, shall not be esteemed as churches, but unlawful meetings, and be punished as other riots.

CIX. No person whatsoever shall disturb, molest, or persecute another for his speculative opinions in religion, or his way of worship.

From *On Politics and Education*, ed. Howard R. Penniman (New York: D. Van Nostrand Co., 1947).

A Parable of Toleration

[FROM *Nathan the Wise*]

GOTTHOLD EPHRAIM LESSING

1779

NATHAN

In days of yore a man lived in the East,
Who owned a ring of marvellous worth,
Given to him by a hand beloved.
The stone was opal, and shed a hundred lovely rays,
But chiefly it possessed the secret power
To make the owner loved of God and man,
If he but wore it in this faith and confidence;
What wonder then that this man in the East
Ne'er from his finger took the ring,
And so arranged it should forever with his house
    remain,
Namely, thus: He bequeathed it to
The most belovèd of his sons,
Firmly prescribing that he in turn
Should leave it to the dearest of his sons;
And always thus the dearest, without respect to birth,
Became the head and chieftain of the house
By virtue of the ring alone.
You understand me, Sultan?

SALADIN

I understand. Proceed.

NATHAN

The ring, descending thus from son to son,
Came to the father of three sons at last,
All three of whom obeyed him equally,
And all of whom he therefore loved alike.
From time to time indeed, now one seemed worthiest
    of the ring,
And now another, now the third,
Just as it happened one or other with him were alone,
And his o'erflowing heart was not divided with the
    other two;
And so to each one of the three he gave
The promise—in pious weakness done—
He should possess the wondrous ring.
This then went on long as it could;
But then at last it came to dying,
Which brings the father into sore perplexity.
It pains him much to practise such deceit
Upon two sons who rested so upon his word.
What can be done? In secret
He seeks out a skilful artist,
And from him orders yet two other rings,
Just to the pattern of his own,
And urges him to spare neither pains nor gold,
To make a perfect match.
The artist so succeeded in his task,
That, when he brought the jewels home,
The father even failed to tell which was the pattern
    ring.
Now, glad and joyous, he calls his sons—
But separately of course—gives each
A special blessing with his ring, and dies.
You hear me, Sultan?

SALADIN

(*Who, somewhat moved, turns from him*)

I hear, I hear;
But pray get ended with your tale.
You soon will be?

NATHAN

I'm at the end,
For what still follows is self-understood.
Scarce was the father dead,
When each one with his ring appears
Claiming each the headship of the house.
Inspections, quarrelling, and complaints ensue;
But all in vain, the veritable ring
Was not distinguishable—

(*After a pause, during which he expects the
Sultan's answer*)

Almost as indistinguishable as to us,
Is now—the true religion.

SALADIN

What? Is that meant as answer to my question?

NATHAN

'Tis meant but to excuse myself, because
I lack the boldness to discriminate between the rings,
Which the father by express intent had made
So that they might not be distinguished.

SALADIN

The rings! Don't play with me.
I thought the faiths which I have named

Were easily distinguishable,
Even to their raiment, even to meat and drink.

NATHAN

But yet not as regards their proofs;
For do not all rest upon history, written or traditional?
And history can also be accepted
Only on faith and trust. Is it not so?
Now, whose faith and confidence do we least mis-
    doubt?
That of our relatives? Of those whose flesh and blood
    we are,
Of those who from our childhood
Have lavished on us proofs of love,
Who ne'er deceived us, unless 'twere wholesome for
    us so?
How can I place less faith in my forefathers
Than you in yours? or the reverse?
Can I desire of you to load your ancestors with lies,
So that you contradict not mine? Or the reverse?
And to the Christian the same applies.
Is that not so?

SALADIN

[By the living God, the man is right. I must be dumb.]

NATHAN

Let us return unto our rings.
As said, the sons accused each other,
And each one swore before the judge
He had received his ring directly
From his father's hand—which was quite true—
And that, indeed, after having long his promise held,
To enjoy eventually the ring's prerogative,
Which was no less the truth.

Each one insisted that it was impossible
His father could play false with him,
And ere he could suspect so dear and true a father,
He was compelled, howe'er inclined to think
The best of them, to accuse his brothers
Of this treacherous act, to unmask the traitors,
And avenge himself.

SALADIN

                    Well, and the judge?
I'm curious to hear what you will give
The judge to say. Go on.

NATHAN

The judge said this: Produce your father here
At once, or I'll dismiss you from this court.
Think you I'm here but to solve riddles?
Or would you wait till the true ring itself will speak?
But stop: I've just been told that the right ring,
Contains the wondrous gift to make its wearer loved,
Agreeable alike to God and man.
That must decide, for the false rings will not have this
       power.
Now which one do the other two love most?
Come, speak out; you're silent?
Do the rings work only backwards and not outwardly?
Does each one love himself the best?
Then you're all three deceived deceivers:
None of your rings are genuine.
The genuine ring is no doubt lost.
To hide the loss and to supply its place
The father ordered other three.

SALADIN

Splendid, splendid!

NATHAN

The judge went further on to say:
If you will have my judgment, not my advice,
Then go. But my advice is this:
You take the matter as it stands.
If each one had his ring straight from his father,
So let each believe *his* ring the true one.
'Tis possible your father would no longer tolerate
The tyranny of this one ring in his family,
And surely loved you all—and all alike,
And that he would not two oppress
By favouring the third.
Now then, let each one emulate in affection
Untouched by prejudice. Let each one strive
To gain the prize of proving by results
The virtue of his ring, and aid its power
With gentleness and heartiest friendliness,
With benevolence and true devotedness to God;
And if the virtue of the ring will then
Have proved itself among your children's children,
I summon them to appear again
Before this judgment seat,
After a thousand thousand years.
Here then will sit a judge more wise than I,
Who will pronounce. Go you.
So said the modest judge.

SALADIN

                                    God, oh God!

NATHAN

Saladin, if now you feel yourself to be
That promised sage—

SALADIN

*(Who rushes to him and seizes his hand, which to
the end he does not let go)*

         I dust? I nothing? Oh God!

NATHAN

What ails thee, Sultan?

SALADIN

Nathan, dear Nathan, your judge's thousand
Thousand years have not yet fled,
His judgment seat's not become mine.
Go, go; but be my friend.

Trans. William Jacks (Glasgow: James Maclehose & Sons, 1894).

An Early Piece
of the Higher Criticism

[FROM *Dictionary*]

PIERRE BAYLE

1697

SARAH

   Sarah, sister and wife of Abraham, was his faithful
companion in all his travels.

   This is so clear from the xxth chapter of Genesis,
that were it not for the ill habit contracted by some,

of sacrificing the natural sense of the words of Scripture to the least difficulties that arise, there could not be two different opinions about the matter. Let us take right the circumstances of the fact. Abraham being come into the country of the Philistines, made Sarah pass there for his sister. Whereupon Abimelech taking her to be a maid, or a widow, so that nothing could hinder him from making her one of his wives, caused her to be brought to him. But knowing by revelation that she was Abraham's wife, he restored her, complaining of their lies, which had exposed him to great mischief. I say, *their lies;* for, on the one side, Abraham had said of his wife, "she is my sister"; and Sarah had said of her husband, "he is my brother." Abraham excused himself, in the first place, on account of the fear he was in for his life, if he had said "she is my wife"; in the second place, because she was truly his sister, "the daughter of my father," said he, "though she is not the daughter of my mother." After this, he endeavoured to justify his wife by saying, that he had asked of her as a favour, that wheresoever they came she should declare that he was her brother. I am surprised that they do not see in this discourse, that Sarah was Abraham's sister, not by the mother's side, but by the father's side. These are my reasons.

1. In the first place, if Sarah had not been the sister of Abraham in this manner, the apology of her husband would only have still more deceived the good prince, who upbraided him with his former dissimulation; for if the Patriarch's excuses found credit, it was impossible to take Sarah for any other than the true and real sister of Abraham by the father's side, nor could any man living gather from such discourse that she was only his niece. I leave all knowing people to judge whether Abimelech could form any other ideas from

Abraham's apology. But then I require that they be capable of placing themselves in the exact situation, and in all the circumstances of this adventure. It is to no purpose to suppose that Sarah was the daughter of Haran, and consequently the grandchild of the father of Abraham; and to add, that a nephew is sometimes called *brother,* and that a grandson is sometimes called *son;* that, I say, is to no purpose in this affair, for the circumstances required that Abraham should use the words in the most literal sense; for if he had not, he must have passed for a man who designed to impose upon Abimelech.

II. Besides to what purpose should he make use of this distinction, "Daughter of my father, daughter of my mother," if he meant only that he was the uncle of Sarah? Put the case that he might have called sister, her that was only his niece; to what purpose should he say that his mother was not the grandmother of this niece? It is, will some say, to represent ingeniously the degree of his kindred in respect to Sarah. But why did he use the word *daughter* in an ambiguous sense? Why does he not use it in its right sense, as I suppose he did. Besides, the ingenuity spoken of would have been very unseasonable; it would have weakened the apology of the Patriarch; for it would make the bonds of kinship appear less strong. If it be objected, that in my supposition that same ingenuity weakens the apology more than it strengthens it, I will give a reason why Abraham declared that Sarah was not his sister by the mother's side. They made a difference between the marriage of a man with his sister both by the father's and mother's side, and the marriage of a man with his half-sister. The Athenians who permitted the marrying of the sister by the father's side, forbade the marrying of the sister by the mother's. Solon decided

it so. On the contrary, Lycurgus permitted the Lacede-
monians to marry the sister by the mother, and not by
the father. Some have said, that as the community of
blood is more certain between a brother and a sister
by the mother, than between a brother and a sister by
the father; the permission of Solon was, generally
speaking, less odious than the permission of Lycurgus.
Will anyone say, after this, that, on my supposition,
Abraham would have said without any necessity, that
his wife was not his sister by the mother's side; as by
the contrary supposition it would have been to no
purpose to say, that his mother was not the grandmother of Sarah?

III. Add to this, that if Abraham meant nothing else
but that his father Terah was the grandfather of Sarah,
he took the terms of father and sister in a large and
less proper meaning. Why therefore did he declare that
his mother was not the mother of Sarah. Was she not
so, in the sense that he took the word *father* in relation
to Terah; that is to say, was she not the grandmother
of Sarah, just as Terah was her grandfather? Some
think to clear the difficulty by supposing that Haran
was the father of Sarah, and that he was not the
brother of Abraham by the mother: they assign therefore two wives to Terah, and they suppose he had
Haran by the one and Abraham by the other. Consequently if Sarah was the daughter of Haran, her grandfather was the father of Abraham; but her grandmother
was different from the mother of Abraham. I answer,
all this falls to the ground as soon as it is supposed
that this Patriarch made use of the words *sister* and
daughter in a broader sense; for upon this foot it is
certain, that the mother of Abraham is grandmother
to the children of Haran, whether she bore Haran, or
whether she was only the wife of him who begat him.

As soon as you leave the proper and strict meaning of the words which denote relationship, and follow the custom observed in families, the word *mother* applies to the wives in relation to all the children of their husbands, and by consequence that of grandmother, with respect to all the children of all the children of their husbands: so that if Abraham had taken the terms in their large meaning, which the style of friendship or civility has introduced into families, he could not have denied, as he did, that his mother was the grandmother of Sarah. . . .

IV. My fourth reason is taken from thence, viz., that it cannot be supposed upon any good grounds that Sarah was adopted by Terah. If it were so, Abraham might have made use of his distinction without departing from exactness of speaking; for in that case his father might have been called the father of Sarah in a literal enough sense. But see here what ruins this evasion: they have recourse to it only to avoid the imputation of incest, and they do not avoid it by that; for a fraternity or brotherhood, founded upon adoption, properly so called, was no less an obstacle to marriage than a natural fraternity. According to the laws, a brother who should marry his adopted sister, committed incest, properly so called. "Marriage is prohibited between a sister and brother, whether they have both parents or only one in common: if the woman be a sister by adoption, so long as that adoption continues, marriage is likewise prohibited: but if the adoption should happen to be dissolved, then they may lawfully marry."

From *Selections from Bayle's Dictionary*, ed. E. A. Beller and M. duP. Lee, Jr. (Princeton: Princeton University Press, 1952).

❖ ❖ ❖

Reason against Miracles

[FROM *Enquiries
Concerning the Human Understanding*]

DAVID HUME

1741

A miracle is a violation of the laws of nature; and
as a firm and unalterable experience has established
these laws, the proof against a miracle, from the very
nature of the fact, is as entire as any argument from
experience can possibly be imagined. Why is it more
than probable, that all men must die; that lead cannot,
of itself, remain suspended in the air; that fire consumes wood, and is extinguished by water; unless it
be, that these events are found agreeable to the laws
of nature, and there is required a violation of these
laws, or in other words a miracle to prevent them?
Nothing is esteemed a miracle, if it ever happen in the
common course of nature. It is no miracle that a man,
seemingly in good health, should die on a sudden: because such a kind of death, though more unusual than
any other, has yet been frequently observed to happen.
But it is a miracle, that a dead man should come to
life; because that has never been observed in any age
or country. There must, therefore, be a uniform experience against every miraculous event, otherwise the
event would not merit that appellation. And as a uniform experience amounts to a proof, there is here a

direct and full *proof*, from the nature of the fact, against the existence of any miracle; nor can such a proof be destroyed, or the miracle rendered credible, but by an opposite proof, which is superior.

The plain consequence is (and it is a general maxim worthy of our attention), "That no testimony is sufficient to establish a miracle, unless the testimony be of such a kind, that its falsehood would be more miraculous than the fact which it endeavours to establish; and even in that case there is a mutual destruction of arguments, and the superior only gives us an assurance suitable to that degree of force, which remains, after deducting the inferior." When anyone tells me, that he saw a dead man restored to life, I immediately consider with myself, whether it be more probable, that this person should either deceive or be deceived, or that the fact, which he relates, should really have happened. I weigh the one miracle against the other; and according to the superiority, which I discover, I pronounce my decision, and always reject the greater miracle. If the falsehood of his testimony would be more miraculous than the event which he relates; then, and not till then, can he pretend to command my belief or opinion.

In the foregoing reasoning we have supposed, that the testimony, upon which a miracle is founded, may possibly amount to an entire proof, and that the falsehood of that testimony would be a real prodigy: But it is easy to show, that we have been a great deal too liberal in our concession, and that there never was a miraculous event established on so full an evidence.

For *first*, there is not to be found, in all history, any miracle attested by a sufficient number of men, of such unquestioned good sense, education, and learning, as to secure us against all delusion in themselves; of such undoubted integrity, as to place them beyond all suspicion of any design to deceive others; of such credit and reputation in the eyes of mankind, as to have a great deal to lose in case of their being detected in any falsehood; and at the same time, attesting facts performed in such a public manner and in so celebrated a part of the world, as to render the detection unavoidable: All which circumstances are requisite to give us a full assurance in the testimony of men.

Secondly. We may observe in human nature a principle which, if strictly examined, will be found to diminish extremely the assurance which we might, from human testimony, have in any kind of prodigy. The maxim, by which we commonly conduct ourselves in our reasonings, is, that the objects of which we have no experience, resemble those of which we have; that what we have found to be most usual is always most probable; and that where there is an opposition of arguments, we ought to give the preference to such as are founded on the greatest number of past observations. But though, in proceeding by this rule, we readily reject any fact which is unusual and incredible in an ordinary degree; yet in advancing farther, the mind observes not always the same rule; but when anything is affirmed utterly absurd and miraculous, it rather the more readily admits of such a fact, upon account of that very circumstance, which ought to destroy all its authority. The passion of *surprise* and *wonder,* arising from miracles, being an agreeable emotion, gives a sensible tendency towards the belief of those events, from which it is derived. And this goes so far, that even those who cannot enjoy this pleasure immediately, nor can believe those miraculous events, of which they are informed, yet love to partake of the satisfaction at second-hand or by rebound, and place a pride and delight in exciting the admiration of others.

With what greediness are the miraculous accounts of travellers received, their descriptions of sea and land monsters, their relations of wonderful adventures, strange men, and uncouth manners? But if the spirit of religion join itself to the love of wonder, there is an end of common sense; and human testimony, in these circumstances, loses all pretensions to authority. A religionist may be an enthusiast, and imagine he sees what has no reality: he may know his narrative to be false, and yet persevere in it, with the best intentions in the world, for the sake of promoting so holy a cause: or even where this delusion has not place, vanity, excited by so strong a temptation, operates on him more powerfully than on the rest of mankind in any other circumstances; and self-interest with equal force. His auditors may not have, and commonly have not, sufficient judgment to canvass his evidence: what judgment they have, they renounce by principle, in these sublime and mysterious subjects: or if they were ever so willing to employ it, passion and a heated imagination disturb the regularity of its operations. Their credulity increases his impudence: and his impudence overpowers their credulity.

Eloquence, when at its highest pitch, leaves little room for reason or reflection; but addressing itself entirely to the fancy or the affections, captivates the willing hearers, and subdues their understanding. Happily, this pitch it seldom attains. But what a Tully or a Demosthenes could scarcely effect over a Roman or Athenian audience, every Capuchin, every itinerant or stationary teacher can perform over the generality of mankind, and in a higher degree, by touching such gross and vulgar passions.

The many instances of forged miracles, and prophecies, and supernatural events, which, in all ages, have
either been detected by contrary evidence, or which
detect themselves by their absurdity, prove sufficiently
the strong propensity of mankind to the extraordinary
and the marvellous, and ought reasonably to beget a
suspicion against all relations of this kind. This is our
natural way of thinking, even with regard to the most
common and most credible events. For instance: There
is no kind of report which rises so easily, and spreads
so quickly, especially in country places and provincial
towns, as those concerning marriages; insomuch that
two young persons of equal condition never see each
other twice, but the whole neighbourhood immediately
join them together. The pleasure of telling a piece of
news so interesting, of propagating it, and of being the
first reporters of it, spreads the intelligence. And this
is so well known, that no man of sense gives attention
to these reports, till he find them confirmed by some
greater evidence. Do not the same passions, and others
still stronger, incline the generality of mankind to believe and report, with the greatest vehemence and assurance, all religious miracles?

Thirdly. It forms a strong presumption against all
supernatural and miraculous relations, that they are
observed chiefly to abound among ignorant and barbarous nations; or if a civilized people has ever given
admission to any of them, that people will be found to
have received them from ignorant and barbarous ancestors, who transmitted them with that inviolable
sanction and authority which always attend received
opinions. When we peruse the first histories of all nations, we are apt to imagine ourselves transported into
some new world; where the whole frame of nature is
disjointed, and every element performs its operations in

a different manner from what it does at present. Battles, revolutions, pestilence, famine and death, are never the effect of those natural causes, which we experience. Prodigies, omens, oracles, judgments, quite obscure the few natural events that are intermingled with them. But as the former grow thinner every page, in proportion as we advance nearer the enlightened ages, we soon learn, that there is nothing mysterious or supernatural in the case, but that all proceeds from the usual propensity of mankind towards the marvellous, and that, though this inclination may at intervals receive a check from sense and learning, it can never be thoroughly extirpated from human nature.

It is strange, a judicious reader is apt to say, upon the perusal of these wonderful historians, *that such prodigious events never happen in our days.* But it is nothing strange, I hope, that men should lie in all ages. You must surely have seen instances enough of that frailty. You have yourself heard many such marvellous relations started, which, being treated with scorn by all the wise and judicious, have at last been abandoned even by the vulgar. Be assured, that those renowned lies, which have spread and flourished to such a monstrous height, arose from like beginnings; but being sown in a more proper soil, shot up at last into prodigies almost equal to those which they relate. . . .

It was a wise policy in that false prophet, Alexander, who though now forgotten, was once so famous, to lay the first scene of his impostures in Paphlagonia, where, as Lucian tells us, the people were extremely ignorant and stupid, and ready to swallow even the grossest delusion. People at a distance, who are weak enough to think the matter at all worth enquiry, have no opportunity of receiving better information. The stories come magnified to them by a hundred circumstances. Fools are industrious in propagating the imposture; while the wise and learned are contented, in general, to deride its absurdity, without informing themselves of the particular facts, by which it may be distinctly refuted. And thus the impostor above mentioned was enabled to proceed, from his ignorant Paphlagonians, to the enlisting of votaries, even among the Grecian philosophers, and men of the most eminent rank and distinction in Rome: nay, could engage the attention of that sage emperor Marcus Aurelius; so far as to make him trust the success of a military expedition to his delusive prophecies.

The advantages are so great, of starting an imposture among an ignorant people, that, even though the delusion should be too gross to impose on the generality of them (*which, though seldom, is sometimes the case*), it has a much better chance for succeeding in remote countries, than if the first scene had been laid in a city renowned for arts and knowledge. The most ignorant and barbarous of these barbarians carry the report abroad. None of their countrymen have a large correspondence, or sufficient credit and authority to contradict and beat down the delusion. Men's inclination to the marvellous has full opportunity to display itself. And thus a story, which is universally exploded in the place where it was first started, shall pass for certain at a thousand miles distance. But had Alexander fixed his residence at Athens, the philosophers of that renowned mart of learning had immediately spread, throughout the whole Roman empire, their sense of the matter; which, being supported by so great authority, and displayed by all the force of reason and eloquence, had entirely opened the eyes of mankind. It is true; Lucian, passing by chance through

Paphlagonia, had an opportunity of performing this good office. But, though much to be wished, it does not always happen, that every Alexander meets with a Lucian, ready to expose and detect his impostures.

I may add as a *fourth* reason, which diminishes the authority of prodigies, that there is no testimony for any, even those which have not been expressly detected, that is not opposed by an infinite number of witnesses; so that not only the miracle destroys the credit of testimony, but the testimony destroys itself. To make this the better understood, let us consider that, in matters of religion, whatever is different is contrary; and that it is impossible the religions of ancient Rome, of Turkey, of Siam, and of China should, all of them, be established on any solid foundation. Every miracle, therefore, pretended to have been wrought in any of these religions (and all of them abound in miracles), as its direct scope is to establish the particular system to which it is attributed; so has it the same force, though more indirectly, to overthrow every other system. In destroying a rival system, it likewise destroys the credit of those miracles on which that system was established; so that all the prodigies of different religions are to be regarded as contrary facts, and the evidences of these prodigies, whether weak or strong, as opposite to each other. According to this method of reasoning, when we believe any miracle of Mahomet or his successors, we have for our warrant the testimony of a few barbarous Arabians: And on the other hand, we are to regard the authority of Titus Livius, Plutarch, Tacitus, and, in short, of all the authors and witnesses, Grecian, Chinese, and Roman Catholic, who have related any miracle in their particular religion; I say, we are to regard their testimony in the same light as if they had mentioned that Mahometan miracle, and

❖ ❖ ❖

The Man Who Believes in Nothing

[FROM "A Philosophical Conversation"]

DENIS DIDEROT

1777

Having some business with the Maréchal de ——, I called on him one morning; he was out, but I waited for him and was shown in to the Maréchale. She is a charming woman, an angel of beauty and piety; sweet temper is depicted on her countenance, the tone of her voice and the simplicity of her conversation agree perfectly with the expression of her features. She was still at her toilet table; I was asked to sit down, and we began to talk. At some remark of mine which edified and surprised her (for she believed that a man who denies the Holy Trinity is a rogue who will end at the gallows), she said:

La Maréchale: Are you not Monsieur Crudéli?

Crudéli: Yes, Madam.

L.M.: Then you are the man who believes in nothing?

Cr.: The same.

L.M.: Nevertheless you profess the same moral principles as a believer.

Cr.: Why should I not, if I am an honest man?

L.M.: And do you put these principles in practice?

Cr.: As well as I can.

L.M.: What! you never steal; you are neither a murderer nor a robber?

Cr.: Very rarely.

L.M.: Then what do you gain by your unbelief?

Cr.: Nothing; is one to believe because of something to be gained thereby?

L.M.: That I can hardly say; but the motive of personal interest is not amiss in the business either of this world or of the next. I am rather sorry for the credit of poor humanity; it is not saying much for us. But, really! do you never steal?

Cr.: Never, on my word.

L.M.: If you are neither a murderer nor a thief, you must own that your conduct is unreasonable and inconsistent.

Cr.: How so?

L.M.: Because it seems to me that if I had nothing to hope or to fear when I am out of this world, there are many little indulgences which I should not deprive myself of now that I am in it. I own to investing my good works in expectation of repayment with enormous interest.

Cr.: You think you do.

L.M.: I do not merely think so; it is a fact.

Cr.: And might I ask you what things you would permit yourself if you were an unbeliever?

L.M.: If you please, no; I keep that subject for the confessional.

Cr.: My investment of good works is a poor speculation; I shall never see my capital again.

L.M.: That is an unthrifty investment.

Cr.: Would you rather I should be a usurer?

L.M.: Well, yes; you may practise usury to any extent in your dealings with God, you cannot ruin him. I know that it is a rather shabby proceeding, but what does that matter? The point is to get into heaven by hook or by crook; we must make the best of everything and neglect nothing which can bring us in a return. Alas! whatever we do, our investment will always be pitifully small in comparison with the handsome return we expect for it. And so you expect no return?

Cr.: Nothing.

L.M.: How sad! You must own that you are either very wicked or very foolish?

Cr.: Indeed I cannot say which.

L.M.: What motive for being good can an unbeliever have if he is in his right mind? Please tell me that.

Cr.: I can tell you.

L.M.: I shall be glad to know.

Cr.: Do you not think it possible that one may be so fortunately born as to find a natural pleasure in doing good?

L.M.: I think it is possible.

Cr.: That one may have received an excellent education which strengthens the natural inclination towards good deeds?

L.M.: Certainly.

Cr.: And that in after-life experience may have convinced us that, taking everything into consideration, it is better for one's happiness in this world to be an honest man than a rogue?

L.M.: Yes indeed; but can one be honest supposing that bad principles combine with the passions to lead us towards evil?

Cr.: One may not act in consequence; and what do we more commonly see than actions at variance with principles?

L.M.: Alas! it is unfortunately so; believers constantly act as if they did not believe.

Cr.: And without believing one may act nearly as well as if one believed.

L.M.: I am glad to hear you say so; but what inconvenience would there be in having a reason the more, religion, for doing good, and a reason the less, unbelief, for doing evil?

Cr.: None, if religion were a motive for doing good and unbelief a motive for doing evil.

L.M.: Can there be any doubt on that point? Does not the spirit of religion incessantly thwart the promptings of this vile, corrupted human nature, and does not the spirit of unbelief abandon it to its evil ways by relieving it from all fear?

Cr.: Madame la Maréchale, this will lead us into a long discussion.

L.M.: And what if it does? The Marshal will not be back for some time, and we are better employed talking sense than taking away our neighbours' good names.

Cr.: You see that I shall have to take up the subject rather far back.

L.M.: As far back as you like, provided I understand you.

Cr.: If you do not understand me it will certainly be my fault.

L.M.: I thank you for the compliment; but you must know that I have never read anything but my prayer book, and that my occupations have been exclusively confined to putting the Gospel in practice and looking after my children.

Cr.: Two duties that you have well fulfilled.

L.M.: Yes, as regards the children. But begin.

Cr.: Madame la Maréchale, is there in this world any good without some drawback?

L.M.: None.

Cr.: What, then, do you call good and evil?

L.M.: Evil must be that in which the drawbacks are greater than the advantages, while good must, on the contrary, be that which has advantages greater than the drawbacks.

Cr.: Will you please to bear in mind your definition of good and evil?

L.M.: I will remember it. Do you call that a definition?

Cr.: Yes.

L.M.: This is philosophy, then?

Cr.: Excellent philosophy.

L.M.: The last thing I should have thought myself capable of.

Cr.: So you are persuaded that religion has more advantages than drawbacks, and that for this reason you call it good?

L.M.: Yes.

Cr.: For my own part I do not doubt that your steward robs you somewhat less on Good Friday than on Easter Monday; and that now and then religion prevents a number of little evils and produces a number of little benefits.

L.M.: Little by little, the sum mounts up.

Cr.: But do you believe that such wretched little advantages can sufficiently compensate the terrible ravages which religion has caused in past times, and which it will still cause in times to come? Consider the violent antipathy which it has created between nations, and which it still keeps up. There is not a Mussulman who would not imagine he was doing an act agreeable to God and the holy prophet in exterminating all the Christians, who, on their side, are hardly more tolerant. Consider the dissensions which it has created and perpetuated in the midst of nearly every nation, dissensions which have rarely been stifled without bloodshed. Our own history offers us examples which are only too recent and too disastrous. Consider that it has created, and still keeps up, the most violent and undying hatred between the members of society, between the individuals of a family. Christ said he had come to divide the man from his wife, the mother from her children, the brother from his sister, the friend from the friend, and his prediction has only been too completely fulfilled.

L.M.: That may be the abuse of the thing without being the thing itself.

Cr.: It is the thing itself, if the abuses are inseparable from it.

L.M.: And how can you show me that the abuses of religion are inseparable from religion?

Cr.: Very easily. Tell me this: supposing a man-hater had desired to render the human race as unhappy as possible, what could he have invented for the purpose better than belief in an incomprehensible being about whom men could never be able to agree, and whom they should regard as more important than their own lives? And is it possible to form a conception of a deity without attaching to it the deepest incomprehensibility and the highest importance?

L.M.: No.

Cr.: Then draw your conclusion.

L.M.: I conclude that it is an idea not without serious consequence in the mind of fools.

Cr.: And add that fools always have been and always will be the majority of mankind, that the most dangerous fools are those rendered so by religion, and that these are the men whom the disturbers of society know how to work when they have need of them.

L.M.: But we must have something to frighten men from such bad actions as escape the severity of the law; and, if you destroy religion, what can you substitute for it?

Cr.: Even if I had nothing to substitute for it, there would be always a terrible prejudice the less, without counting that in no age and in no country have religious opinions formed the basis of national manners. The gods adored by the old Greeks and Romans, the finest people on earth, were a most dissolute set of rascals; a Jupiter who deserved the faggot and the stake, a Venus worthy of the House of Correction, a Mercury whose proper place was in jail.

L.M.: And so you think that it is quite a matter of indifference whether we be Christians or pagans; that as pagans we should be equally good and that as Christians we are no better?

Cr.: Indeed I am convinced of it; excepting that as pagans we should be rather merrier.

L.M.: It is impossible.

Cr.: But, Madame la Maréchale, are there any Christians? I have never seen any.

L.M.: That is a nice thing to say to me.

Cr.: I am not saying it to you: I was thinking of a lady who is a neighbour of mine, good and pious as you are, and who believed herself in all sincerity to be a Christian, just as you do.

L.M.: And you showed her that she was mistaken?
Cr.: At once.
L.M.: How did you manage that?
Cr.: I opened a New Testament, a well-read one, for it was considerably worn. I read her the Sermon on

the Mount, and at each article of it I asked her: "Do you act up to this?" I went on further. She is a beautiful woman, and although very pious she is not unconscious of her attraction; she has a most delicate fair complexion, and although she does not attach much value to this perishable charm, she is not displeased if it excites admiration; her bust is perfect, and, although very modest, she is not averse to its beauty being observed.

L.M.: Provided, of course, that she and her husband should alone be aware of this.

Cr.: I believe that her husband knows it much better than anyone else; but for a woman who prides herself on high Christian principles that is not enough. I said to her: "Is it not written in the Gospel that he who has coveted his neighbour's wife has committed adultery already in his heart?"

L.M.: I suppose she answered yes?

Cr.: I said to her: "And does not adultery committed in the heart damn as surely as a more complete adultery?"

L.M.: I suppose she answered yes?

Cr.: I said: "And if the man is damned for adultery committed in the heart, what will be the fate of the woman who invites all those who come near her to commit that crime?" This last question rather embarrassed her.

L.M.: I understand; she did not cover up that perfect bust as completely as she might.

Cr.: Not quite. She answered that it was a custom, as if nothing was more customary than to call oneself Christian and yet not to be so; that it was wrong to dress in a ridiculous manner, as if there could be any comparison between a petty ridiculous act and the eternal damnation of one's self and one's neighbours;

that she did not interfere with her dressmaker, as if it were not better to change one's dressmaker than to be false to one's religion; that it was her husband's fancy, as if a husband could be mad enough to demand that his wife should push obedience to a wrong-headed husband so far as to disobey the will of God and to contemn the threats of her Redeemer!

L.M.: I was well aware of all those childish reasons; I might even have answered as your neighbour did; but both she and I would have been taken at a disadvantage. However, what conduct did she adopt, after your remonstrance?

Cr.: The day after this conversation was a holy day; I was going upstairs to my room, when my neighbour was coming downstairs on her way to Mass.

L.M.: Dressed as usual?

Cr.: Dressed as usual. I smiled, she smiled; and we passed one another without speaking. This was a good woman! a Christian! a pious woman! After this example and a hundred thousand others of the same sort, what real influence on conduct can I grant religion to have? Hardly any: and so much the better.

L.M.: How so much the better?

Cr.: Yes, I mean it. Supposing that twenty thousand of the inhabitants of Paris took it into their heads to conform strictly to the precepts of the Sermon on the Mount—

L.M.: There would be some ladies' shoulders better covered than at present.

Cr.: And so many lunatics that the police would be at their wits' end to find room for them all in the madhouses. In all inspired books there are two kinds of morality; one general and common to every nation, to every religion, and which is followed pretty nearly; another peculiar to each nation and to each religion, in which men believe, which they preach in their churches, which they teach in their homes, and which they do not follow at all.

L.M.: What is the reason of this contradiction?

Cr.: In the impossibility of subjecting a people to a rule which only agrees with a few melancholy men who have drawn it from a model found in their own character. Religions are like monastic rules; all become relaxed in time. They are follies which cannot hold ground against the constant efforts of nature to bring us back to her laws. Let the statesman take care that the welfare of individuals should be so bound up with the common weal that a citizen can hardly harm society without hurting himself; let virtue be rewarded as certainly as wickedness is punished; let merit, in whatever position it exist, and without distinction of sect, be eligible for state employment, and only count as wicked the small number of men whom an incorrigible perversity of nature has dragged into vice. Temptation is too near and hell is too far off; it is not worth the while of a legislator to take in hand a system of crooked opinions which can only keep children under its yoke, which encourages crime by the facility of its expiation; which sends the culprit to ask pardon from God for the injuries inflicted on man, and which degrades the order of natural and moral duties by making it subordinate to an order of chimerical duties.

L.M.: I do not understand you.

Cr.: I will explain; but I think I hear the Marshal's carriage coming, just in time to prevent me from saying something which you might think impudent.

L.M.: If what you are about to say is impudent, I shall not hear it; I have a good habit of only hearing what I choose.

Cr.: Madame la Maréchale, ask the curate of your parish which is the more atrocious crime: to defile one of the eucharistic vessels or to blacken the good name of an honest woman? He will shudder with horror at the first, he will cry sacrilege; and the civil law which takes hardly any notice of calumny while it punishes sacrilege by the stake, will finish the confusion of moral ideas and the corruption of the public mind.

L.M.: I know more than one woman who would scruple to eat meat on a Friday, and yet would— I was also going to say my piece of impudence. Continue.

Cr.: But, Madam, I must really go and see the Marshal.

L.M.: Another minute, and then we will go together and see him. I don't know how to answer you, and yet you do not persuade me.

Cr.: I had no intention of persuading you. It is the same with religion as with marriage. Although marriage has caused misery to so many others, it has given happiness to you and the Marshal. Religion which has made, which still makes, and will yet make so many men wicked, has rendered you better than before; you do well in keeping to it. It pleases you to imagine, above your head, a great and powerful being, who watches your journey through life; this idea strengthens your steps. Continue, Madam, to enjoy the thought of this august keeper of your mind, at once a spectator and a sublime model of your actions.

L.M.: I see that you are not possessed by the mania of proselytism.

Cr.: By no means.

L.M.: And I esteem you the more for it.

Cr.: I permit everyone to think in his way, provided

he does not interfere with mine; and, besides, those who are destined to deliver themselves from these prejudices have no need of being catechized.

L.M.: Do you think that man can do without superstition?

Cr.: No; not as long as he remains ignorant and timorous.

L.M.: Well then, superstition for superstition, as well ours as another.

Cr.: I do not think so.

L.M.: Tell me truly, have you no repugnance for the idea of being nothing after death?

Cr.: I would prefer to retain my existence; notwithstanding that I see no reason why a Being who has already been able to render me unhappy without any reason, might not amuse himself again in the same way.

L.M.: If, notwithstanding that drawback, the hope of a life to come appears sweet and consoling, even to you, why tear it from us?

Cr.: I have no such hope, for my desire does not imply an expectation which I know to be vain; but I take it away from no one. If any person can believe that he will see when he has no eyes, that he will hear when he has no ears, that he will think when he has no brain, that he will love when he has no heart, that he will feel when he has no sensation, that he will exist when he will be nowhere, that he will be a something without measure or place—I have no objection.

L.M.: But this world, who made it?

Cr.: Perhaps you can inform me.

L.M.: God.

Cr.: And what is God?

L.M.: A spirit.

Cr.: If a spirit can make matter, why should not matter make a spirit?

L.M.: And why should it?

Cr.: Because I see it do so every day. Do you believe that animals have souls?

L.M.: Certainly I believe so.

Cr.: And could you tell me what becomes, for instance, of the soul of the Peruvian serpent which is hung up in a chimney to dry, and remains in the smoke for one or two years?

L.M.: Let it go where it pleases; what does that matter to me?

Cr.: You are probably not aware that this serpent, smoked and dried, revives, and comes to life again.

L.M.: I don't believe it.

Cr.: Nevertheless, a clever man, Bouguer, asserts that it is so.

L.M.: Your clever man has told a story.

Cr.: Suppose what he says were true?

L.M.: Well, I should have to believe that animals are machines.

Cr.: Remembering that man is only a rather more perfect animal than the rest. But I think the Marshal is—

L.M.: One more question; the last. Are you at ease in your unbelief?

Cr.: Impossible to be more so.

L.M.: Yet, if it turned out that you were mistaken?

Cr.: Well, and if I were mistaken?

L.M.: All that you believe to be false would come true, and you would be cast amongst the damned. Monsieur Crudéli, it is a terrible thing to be condemned to hell, to burn there for all eternity!

Cr.: La Fontaine believed that we should be as comfortable there as fish in the water.

L.M.: You may laugh now; but remember that La Fontaine became very serious at his last moments; and this is the point where I make my stand against you.

Cr.: I answer for nothing when my head will be no longer right; but if I die from one of those diseases which leave the expiring man his whole reason, I shall not be more disturbed at the moment you mention than I am at present.

L.M.: I am confounded at your boldness.

Cr.: I think there is much more boldness in the man who dies believing in a severe judge who weighs our most secret thoughts and in whose scales the most upright man would be lost through vanity, did he not tremble through fear of being found wanting; if this dying man had then the choice either of annihilation or of judgment, his boldness would impress me more should he hesitate to choose the former alternative; unless he were more insane than the companion of St. Bruno, or more intoxicated with his own merits than Bohola.

L.M.: I have read the story of St. Bruno's companion, but I have never heard of Bohola.

Cr.: He was a Jesuit of the college of Pinsk in Lithuania, who left at his death a coffer full of money, with a memorandum which he had written and signed.

L.M.: And what was the memorandum about?

Cr.: It ran thus: "I request the dear brother to whom I have confided this coffer, to open it when I shall have performed miracles. The money which it contains will pay the expenses of my canonization. 1 have left some authentic memoirs for the confirmation of my virtues and the guidance of those who undertake to write my life."

L.M.: What a ridiculous story!

Cr.: It may be so to me, Madam, but in your case a joke on such a subject may offend God

L.M.: Indeed, you are right.

Cr.: It is so easy to sin grievously against your law.

L.M.: I admit that it is.

Cr.: The justice which will decide your fate is very rigorous.

L.M.: True.

Cr.: And if you believe the oracles of your religion on the number of the elect, it will be very small.

L.M.: Oh! but I am not a Jansenist; I only look at the consoling side of the question; the blood of Jesus Christ covers, in my eyes, a multitude of sins; and it would seem to me very singular if the Devil had the best share of mankind, although he did not give up a son to death.

Cr.: Do you damn Socrates, Phocion, Aristides, Cato, Trajan, Marcus Aurelius?

L.M.: Certainly not; no one but a wild beast could think of such a thing. St. Paul says that every man shall be judged by the law which he has known, and St. Paul is right.

Cr.: And by what law is the unbeliever to be judged?

L.M.: Your case is rather different. You are one of the accursed inhabitants of Chorazin and Bethsaida, who shut their eyes to the light which shone on them and stopped their ears so as not to hear the voice of truth speaking to them.

Cr.: The people of Chorazin and Bethsaida were men such as never existed elsewhere, if they were free to believe or not to believe.

L.M.: They saw mighty works which would have made sackcloth and ashes more valuable than gold, had they been done in Tyre and Sidon.

Cr.: Well, you see, the inhabitants of Tyre and Sidon were clever people, while those of Chorazin and Bethsaida were fools. I told you a story just now, I should like to tell you another. Once upon a time, a young Mexican— But the Marshal—

L.M.: I will send and find out if he is disengaged. Well, what about the young Mexican?

Cr.: Feeling weary of his work, was walking one day along the seashore. He saw a plank, one end of which was floating while the other was aground. He sat down on the plank, and then, gazing over the vast expanse of sea, said to himself: "My grandmother must be doting when she tells that story about those people, who at some long time ago landed here from somewhere or other beyond the seas. What nonsense! is it not plain that the sea and the sky join in the distance? Can I believe, against the evidence of my senses, an old story the date of which is unknown, which everyone tells in his own fashion, and which is nothing but a tissue of absurd traditions about which people tear their own hearts and one another's eyes?" While he was thus meditating, the rippling waters were rocking him as he lay on the plank, and he soon fell asleep. The wind rose and the tide carried the plank out to sea with our young reasoner still lying asleep on it.

L.M.: Alas! that is a true image of mankind: we are each of us floating on a plank, the wind rises and the tide carries us out to sea.

Cr.: When he awoke he was already far from the land. Much as he was surprised to find himself out at sea, he was still more surprised when the land disappeared and the sea joined with the sky over the place where he had not long ago been walking. Then he began to suspect that he might very possibly have been mistaken in his incredulity, and that if the wind continued from the same point, he might perhaps be carried to the coast inhabited by the people of whom his grandmother had so often spoken to him.

L.M.: You say nothing about the anxiety he must have felt.

Cr.: He had none. He said to himself: "What does it matter, provided I get to land? I have reasoned rather clumsily, I must own; but I was sincere, and that is all that can be expected of me. If cleverness is not a virtue, stupidity cannot be a crime." In the meantime the wind continued to blow, the plank and its freight floated on, the unknown shore soon began to appear, and before very long he arrived there and landed.

L.M.: We shall meet on that shore one day, Monsieur Crudéli.

Cr.: I hope so, Madame la Maréchale; wherever it be I shall always be delighted at an opportunity of paying my respects to you. Scarcely had he left the plank and set foot on shore, when he perceived a venerable old man standing at his side. He asked where he was and to whom he had the honour of speaking. "I am the sovereign of this country," replied the old man. "You denied my existence?" "True, I did." "And that of my empire?" "True, I did." "I pardon you, because I am He who sees to the bottom of hearts, and I have read in yours that you were in good faith; but all your thoughts and deeds have not been so innocent." Whereupon the old man took him gently by the ear, recalled to him all the faults of his life, and at each one the young Mexican bowed down, beat his breast, and asked forgiveness. Now, Madame la Maréchale, put yourself for a moment in the place of the old man and tell me what you would have done? Would you have seized this young fool and taken a pleasure in dragging him round the beach by the hair for all eternity?

L.M.: Indeed, no.

Cr.: If one of those pretty children of yours had escaped from the house, and after doing all sorts of foolish things, came back repentant?

L.M.: I should rush to meet him, I should take him in my arms and embrace him with tears. But his father, the Marshal, would not take things so gently.

Cr.: The Marshal is not exactly a tiger.

L.M.: Not by any means.

Cr.: He would require a little persuasion, but he would certainly end by forgiving.

L.M.: Certainly.

Cr.: Especially if he came to think that, before causing the birth of this child, he knew its whole life, and that the punishment of its faults would be useless, either for himself, for the culprit, or for the other children.

L.M.: But the old man and the Marshal are two very different persons.

Cr.: Do you mean that the Marshal is kinder than the old man?

L.M.: God forbid! I only mean that if my justice is not the same as the Marshal's, his may not be the same as the old man's.

Cr.: Ah! Madam, you do not foresee the consequences of that answer. Either the general definition of justice is equally applicable to you, to the Marshal, to me, to the young Mexican, and to the old man, or else I don't know what justice is and am totally in the dark as to the means by which the old man is pleased or displeased.

At this point of our conversation we were told that the Marshal was waiting for us. As I shook hands with the Maréchale, she said: "It is enough to make one giddy, isn't it?"

Cr.: Why should it, if the head is firm?

L.M.: After all, the shortest way is to behave as if the old man existed.

Cr.: Even if one doesn't believe it.

L.M.: And if you do believe it, not to count on his goodness.

Cr.: If that is not the politest conduct, at least it is the safest.

L.M.: By the way, suppose you were taken before the magistrates to give an account of your religious principles, would you confess them?

Cr.: I should do my best to save the authorities from committing an atrocious act.

L.M.: Ah! you are a coward! And if you were at the point of death, would you submit to receive the sacraments of the church?

Cr.: I would not fail to do so.

L.M.: For shame! you wicked hypocrite!

Trans. E. N., in *Scott's Tracts*, Vol. I (London: Thomas Scott, 1875).

IV. *Sense and Sensibility:*

LITERATURE

The Foundling Found

[FROM *The History of Tom Jones, a Foundling*]

HENRY FIELDING

1749

Mr. Allworthy had been absent a full quarter of a year in London, on some very particular business, though I know not what it was; but judge of its importance by its having detained him so long from home, whence he had not been absent a month at a time during the space of many years. He came to his house very late in the evening, and after a short supper with his sister, retired much fatigued to his chamber. Here, having spent some minutes on his knees—a custom which he never broke through on any account—he was preparing to step into bed, when, upon opening the clothes, to his great surprise he beheld an infant, wrapt

423

up in some coarse linen, in a sweet and profound sleep, between his sheets. He stood some time lost in astonishment at this sight; but, as good nature had always the ascendant in his mind, he soon began to be touched with sentiments of compassion for the little wretch before him. He then rang his bell, and ordered an elderly woman-servant to rise immediately, and come to him; and in the meantime was so eager in contemplating the beauty of innocence, appearing in those lively colours with which infancy and sleep always display it, that his thoughts were too much engaged to reflect that he was in his shirt when the matron came in. She had indeed given her master sufficient time to dress himself; for out of respect to him, and regard to decency, she had spent many minutes in adjusting her hair at the looking-glass, notwithstanding all the hurry in which she had been summoned by the servant, and though her master, for aught she knew, lay expiring in an apoplexy, or in some other fit.

It will not be wondered at that a creature who had so strict a regard to decency in her own person, should be shocked at the least deviation from it in another. She therefore no sooner opened the door, and saw her master standing by the bedside in his shirt, with a candle in his hand, than she started back in a most terrible fright, and might perhaps have swooned away, had he not now recollected his being undrest, and put an end to her terrors by desiring her to stay without the door till he had thrown some clothes over his back, and was become incapable of shocking the pure eyes of Mrs. Deborah Wilkins, who, though in the fifty-second year of her age, vowed she had never beheld a man without his coat. Sneerers and profane wits may perhaps laugh at her first fright; yet my grave reader, when he considers the time of night, the summons from her bed, and the situation in which she found her master, will highly justify and applaud her conduct, unless the prudence which must be supposed to attend maidens at that period of life at which Mrs. Deborah had arrived, should a little lessen his admiration.

When Mrs. Deborah returned into the room, and was acquainted by her master with the finding the little infant, her consternation was rather greater than his had been; nor could she refrain from crying out, with great horror of accent as well as look, "My good sir! what's to be done?" Mr. Allworthy answered, she must take care of the child that evening, and in the morning he would give orders to provide it a nurse. "Yes, sir," says she; "and I hope your worship will send out your warrant to take up the hussy its mother, for she must be one of the neighbourhood; and I should be glad to see her committed to Bridewell, and whipt at the cart's tail. Indeed, such wicked sluts cannot be too severely punished. I'll warrant 'tis not her first, by her impudence in laying it to your worship." "In laying it to me, Deborah!" answered Allworthy: "I can't think she hath any such design. I suppose she hath only taken this method to provide for her child; and truly I am glad she hath not done worse." "I don't know what is worse," cries Deborah, "than for such wicked strumpets to lay their sins at honest men's doors; and though your worship knows your own innocence, yet the world is censorious; and it hath been many an honest man's hap to pass for the father of children he never begot; and if your worship should provide for the child, it may make the people the apter to believe; besides, why should your worship provide for what the parish is obliged to maintain? For my own part, if it was an honest man's child, indeed—but for my own part, it goes against me to touch these misbegotten wretches, whom I don't look upon as my fellow creatures. Faugh! how it stinks! It doth not smell like a Christian. If I might be so bold to give my advice, I would have it put in a basket, and sent out and laid at the church-warden's door. It is a good night, only a little rainy and windy; and if it was well wrapt up, and put in a warm basket, it is two to one but it lives till it is found in the morning. But if it should not, we have discharged our duty in taking proper care of it; and it is, perhaps, better for such creatures to die in a state of innocence, than to grow up and imitate their mothers; for nothing better can be expected of them."

There were some strokes in this speech which perhaps would have offended Mr. Allworthy, had he strictly attended to it; but he had now got one of his fingers into the infant's hand, which, by its gentle pressure, seeming to implore his assistance, had certainly outpleaded the eloquence of Mrs. Deborah, had it been ten times greater than it was. He now gave Mrs. Deborah positive orders to take the child to her own bed, and to call up a maid-servant to provide it pap, and other things, against it waked. He likewise ordered that proper clothes should be procured for it early in the morning, and that it should be brought to himself as soon as he was stirring.

Such was the discernment of Mrs. Wilkins, and such the respect she bore her master, under whom she enjoyed a most excellent place, that her scruples gave way to his peremptory commands; and she took the child under her arms, without any apparent disgust at the illegality of its birth; and declaring it was a sweet little infant, walked off with it to her own chamber.

Allworthy here betook himself to those pleasing slumbers which a heart that hungers after goodness is apt to enjoy when thoroughly satisfied. As these are of those we love. A man enjoys the happiness he feels; a woman the happiness she gives. This essential difference, so rarely noted, has a bearing on everything that either one of them does. The pleasure of the man is to satisfy desires, that of the woman to rouse them. To please is for him but a way towards success; for her it *is* success. Coquetry, so often made a reproach to woman, is simply the abuse of this feeling, and by that very fact a proof of its existence. Finally, this exclusiveness of desire, which especially distinguishes love, is in the man no more than a preference which serves at most to add to his pleasure. Another love affair at the same time might diminish his pleasure in the first one, but it would not destroy it. But in women love for one man is so profoundly exclusive that all possibilities of enjoying any other love are extinguished. Indeed, stronger than our physical nature itself, and therefore freed from its laws, a woman's love makes her feel repugnance and disgust at the thought of possibilities otherwise calculated to rouse voluptuous anticipations.

Do not think that the more or less numerous specific exceptions that can be brought against these general truths invalidate them! They have the support of public opinion, which distinguishes between infidelity and inconstancy only among men—a distinction on which they pride themselves although they should be ashamed of it, a distinction which among us has been adopted only by those depraved women who are the shame of our sex, and to whom any motive seems good which can save them from feeling their own degradation.

I thought, my dear, that it might be useful for you to have these reflections to oppose to the chimerical ideas of perfect happiness with which love never fails to delude our imagination. Such ideas give us a deceptive hope, to which we cling even when we see ourselves obliged to abandon it, and the loss of which irritates and multiplies the all too real difficulties inseparable from a strong passion! This task of softening your troubles, or of diminishing their number, is all I want to do at the moment, indeed all I can do. In afflictions without remedy, advice can be given only as to palliatives. I ask you to remember that to pity a sick person is not to blame him. Ah! what are we, to blame one another? Let us leave the right to judge to Him who alone can read our hearts; and I dare to believe that in his fatherly eyes a host of virtues can make up for a single weakness.

But, I beg of you, my dear, avoid above all those violent resolutions which are not so much evidence of strength as of complete discouragement. Do not forget that in making another the possessor of your whole life (to use your own phrase), you cannot deprive your friends of what they possessed before, which they will continue to claim.

Farewell, my dear daughter; think sometimes of your fond mother, and believe that you will be always and above everything the object of her dearest thoughts.

From *Les liaisons dangéreuses* (Amsterdam [Paris]: 1782); trans. C.B.

❖ ❖ ❖

A Burgundian Patriarch

[FROM *The Life of My Father*]

NICOLAS EDME RESTIF DE LA BRETONNE

1779

Each evening at supper, which was the only meal at which all the family could be assembled, my father [Edme R.], was a venerable patriarch at the head of a large household. Ordinarily there were twenty-two at the table, including the ploughmen, and the vineyard-men (who in the winter were threshers), the oxkeeper, the shepherd, and two maid-servants, one of whom aided the vineyardmen, while the other took charge of the dairy. All these were seated at the same table: father at the end next to the fireplace; his wife at his side within reach of the serving dishes (because she alone was in charge of the cooking; the maid-servants who had worked all day were seated and ate tranquilly); then the children of the house according to their age, which alone determined their rank; then the oldest of the ploughmen and his comrades; then the vineyardmen. After these came the oxkeeper and the shepherd, and the two maid-servants completed the group. These were at the other end of the table, directly across from their mistress, from whom they could hide none of their movements.

Everyone ate the same bread. The hateful distinction between white bread and brown bread was never

made in this house. Moreover, the latter would not
have constituted a saving, since the bran, being a bit
fatty, was necessary to the horses, the milk cows, the
swine which fattened on it, and even the sheep after
lambing time.

As for wine, since the head of the great family drank
little of it, and since he had acquired the habit
exceedingly late, he drank only old vintages. Mother
drank only water. Her husband had no little trouble
keeping her from blushing at the very thought of wine.
All the children without exception drank water. The
ploughmen and the vineyardists drank a wine which
they preferred to their master's; it was wine of the
second pressing, passed through the leavings of the
already pressed grapes. Everyone knows that peasants
like a wine with strength in it; and this general pre-
dilection is considerably reinforced at Saci, where
the human race has a rudeness and massiveness not
often equalled, even east of the Rhine. Germain, the
first ploughman, had the appearance of a real Teuton.
He was a large man whose face, without being fat, was
excessively long and wide. He gave an impression of
incredible strength; but despite this, there was visible
in his features a certain reassuring goodness that
made the children seek him out in their play. After
the master and the mistress, Germain was the most
respected. The other servants did nothing without
taking his advice; and he always gave it without an
air of command. He was an excellent fellow; happy
the houses where there are such servants! Happy the
good servants who find masters capable of appreciating
them fully! The oxkeeper and the shepherd, who were
likely to be young men, respected the ploughmen and
the vineyardmen. The two maid-servants were well
disposed towards all of them, and their mistress charged

them with the laundry and sewing of the men. These women had, in addition, certain fixed times when they could work for themselves.

It had not been possible for Edme R. to keep a certain order in the working day for prayers, or even for meals. The duties of the different hired people were absolutely different. It was only at breakfast, at five o'clock in the morning, that they were all more or less assembled. In summer the oxkeeper and the shepherd had by this time already left for the pasture. There was only a short prayer in common, based on the Sunday sermon; then everyone separated, not to be re-assembled until evening. At that time, however, no one was missing. It was after supper that father read from the Holy Scriptures. He began with Genesis, and read with fervour three or four chapters according to their length, accompanying them with several short observations. These were infrequent, depending on what he judged to be absolutely necessary. I cannot recall except with great emotion how attentively that reading was followed; how it communicated to each one in the large family a tone of equanimity and fraternity (by "in the family," I understand the servants too). My father always began with these words: "Let us meditate devoutly, my children. It is the Holy Ghost that is going to speak." The next day during work, the reading of the preceding evening was a subject of conversation, especially among the plough-men. . . .

In winter, when the evenings are longer in the country (because in the city the weather is always the same), after the reading and the catechism, father told stories, either ancient or modern. He introduced into them as part of the story the wisest maxims of the ancients. That was our recreation. Our eagerness for

these instructive stories was extreme; and because
everyone could laugh and express his opinions, the
story hour was delicious entertainment for both the
peasants and the children, who never knew anything
more agreeable. These discussions and readings must
have pleased them immensely. We had often had in
our house the sons of our best neighbours as servants;
and when their parents asked them what made them
so eager to enter our household, they gave no other
explanation than the readings and discussions of the
evening. If my father had been capable of nourishing
political ambitions, he would have been well advised
to maintain exactly this way of life.

As to the work of the day, father occupied himself
with indefatigable zeal, and preached more by example
than by words. There was never a better master or one
dearer to the people who served him. That was because
the work was accomplished mutually whenever possible.
Father often quoted this maxim of the masters of wisdom: "If thou hast a good servant, let him be as thy
soul; treat him as if he were thy brother" (Ecclesiasticus: 33). And this other: "Do not overburden a servant
who does what he can and who employs his soul in
thy service" (Ecclesiasticus: 7).[1] He rose early in the
morning and guided one of the ploughs himself. He
was a perfect ploughman. His servants did all they
could to imitate him, and none of them, not even Germain, could flatter himself at having equalled him. It

[1] These passages from Ecclesiasticus are literally translated
from Restif. They appear in the authorized version of the
Old Testament Apocrypha of the English Bible in Ecclesiasticus 33:31 ("If thou have a servant, entreat him as a
brother; for thou hast need of him, and of thine own soul")
and in Ecclesiasticus 7:20 ("Whenas thy servant worketh
truly, entreat him not evil, nor the hireling that bestoweth
himself wholly for thee"). [C.B.'s note.]

was in exercising this special skill that he was in his glory. It was plain from a soft smile on his always gracious and gentle face how much he was flattered when we told him that he was an "excellent plough-man." "It is the art of arts," he often answered, "and any man might be justifiably proud to excel in it." He had a repugnance for work on the vines, and he did not busy himself in his own vineyards except during the vintage. But he visited them as a good master and knew perfectly well when anything was amiss. This repugnance was not a fault. If he had had a passion for working his vines, then, together with his other occupations—the notaryship, the magistracy, consultations, and arbitrations—it would have been necessary for him to abandon ploughing, which he prized above everything else.

He was never seen idle for a single instant, unless it was on Sunday or on holidays; and even then he had a book in his hand while walking, provided he was alone. The book was on either ethics or jurisprudence, and he would study some passage in it relative to the cases which he had to judge during the week. He said that in these cases, his "French Book of Right Practice" ["Practicien français"] was an excellent book of devotion, because in it he learned his duty.

He was always readily accessible to his sons, but a bit more reserved with his daughters, whom he never addressed with the familiar "thou."

With his intention of uniting his first family with his second (he was twice married) by all possible ties, he made the oldest children the godfathers and god-mothers of the younger ones. The worthy vicar of Courgis, and Anne, the eldest of the daughters, chris-tened me. So it went all the way down the line to the very youngest of them all, for whom I was in turn a godfather, while the youngest daughter of the first marriage was a godmother. That was in 1745, at which time my father was fifty-three years old.

The following year, the prosperity of Edme R., despite the burden of fourteen living children, excited the envy of one inhabitant of Saci, the tax collector. He assigned my father an exorbitant tax. Edme R. complained moderately, but no one paid any attention to him. Nettled, perhaps a bit too much (these were his own expressions), he decided to seek remedy from the law which gave advantages to fathers of twelve living children. He presented a petition to M. de Brou, who was then the *Intendant* at Tonnerre. It simply set forth the facts without complaining against anyone. The *Intendant* wrote in his own hand: "Edme R., father of fourteen children, will pay six livres." And he told him personally: "You need not pay anything at all. But since you asked for a tax, I am giving you this one, which will be the same each year. I know, moreover, that you are too good a subject of the King to wish to be exempted entirely."

I was told that in the early days of my mother's marriage, her extreme vivacity and the rather permissive education she had received did not make it easy for her to choose the means most certain to capture the affection of her husband. With any other man she would have been unhappy. But Edme R., as a wise and prudent husband, studied the character of his new wife and behaved towards her in a manner designed to impress her spirit. He appealed to her sentiments in persuading her to restrain her vivacity. Then he solidly instructed her as to her real duties, but in private, and without anyone in the family ever suspecting what he was doing. On the contrary, in front of his children and before strangers he showed her the highest consideration. Here is some of the advice he gave her. It was my mother herself who reported it to me after my father's death. She cited his opinions to me in order to make me realize how thankful she was to him, and how impossible it was for anything to mitigate the sorrow caused by the loss of such a husband.

"My dear wife, the most dangerous fault in a husband is to be a weak husband, one who does not know how to take hold of the sceptre of conjugal authority. That is the fault I have observed in Parisian husbands. I want you to be happy. I would not have married you if I had not had our common advantage in mind. But I do not wish it blindly. I foresaw the solution from the moment I decided to offer you my hand. The solution is the very purpose I had in marrying you, to be your helper and defender, not your slave. Tell me, where does the strength come from that nature gave to man? How came he, moreover, always to be free in his activities, bold, courageous, even audacious? Was it in order to cringe as a weak adulator? Whence came the nature that made you so charming and at the same time weak and fearful? Whence came the sweet tone of voice it gave you; these delicate and dainty inflections? Was it to command with severity and arrogance? No, my dear wife, it is to charm; and, let me speak frankly, to make the stronger person bend, and to influence him in your favour. Your lot is to please and mollify by the charm of your caresses the arduous labours which the strong person undertakes for you, he who is united to you, and he who is one with you. This charming smile was made only to relieve him in one instant from the burden of all his labours, and to induce him to undertake others even more arduous.

"If a wife finds her husband weak, she commands and believes herself happier thereby. She is imperious, but the command is never a joy, although it satisfies one passion of the human heart. But that passion, being one of those which places her at odds with her fellows, brings her more trouble than real pleasure. Let us imagine that you persist in playing the part of a man. Then I, not being a tyrant, will have to play the woman's part—and however ridiculous I may appear in it, with these male traits and this thick beard, you will have to endure it until you allow me to return to my original role. You smile, but on my word of honour, I speak in earnest. The first way for a couple to be happy, the one that gives value to all others, is for the man to command, and for the wife, tender and dear, to do out of love what one has the right to demand from every other person than a wife—that is, obey."

"You coat the pill with sugar, but I understand."

"For that reason I spoke clearly, my dear wife, because one should speak only to be understood. Do not counter with the argument that you had been happy in your first marriage while observing entirely opposite principles. Your first husband began by committing fundamental errors in his treatment of you. Later he felt that he could never do enough to make it up to you. I approve of that. It was wise conduct. In his place, I would have done the same. But the position between us two is different. We are no longer children who must flatter each other. We are adults, husband and wife, who must act seriously, each of us fulfilling his role in its entirety. Man can only be happy when he follows nature. The role of the stronger is direction; the natural role of the weaker, the most lovable, is to temper the hardness not only for herself but for all the family. My dear wife, I have firmly resolved to conform to the will of nature. Be gentle. Receive and do not demand. On the other hand, you have as much authority as I over the whole house, because man and wife are only one. But you are not the leader. When there are two, one must be first. He whom nature gave the strength to be master must occupy that place by virtue of the deference that is shown to him by his mate. In turn he must show her that he is aware of her merit in yielding to him; he must exercise his authority as a friend and as a father. . . .

"Regulate your conduct on the basis of these principles. If it were only a question of my happiness, I would use my strength to make many sacrifices for you. But I know by experience that the husband who also plays the role of wife is the least happy of all. Women resemble Oriental peoples, and their imagination is just as lively. Easy to terrify, they prefer, without doubt, a government they obey without reasoning, to one that gives them the choice of obeying or not. Always undecided, they would pass their lives in a fatiguing perplexity. Moreover, if someone were to free the Asiatics from a despot, they would have another on the morrow. I read that the Romans had at one time experimented with the peoples of Cappadocia, and that nation preferred an absolute sovereign to liberty."

"But, my husband, I do not ask to dominate you."

"Nor do I you, my dear wife. I only ask that each of us remain exactly in his place: that there reign between you and me an accord, a harmony like that which exists between all the parts of the same body. Listen: each time you wish something, tell me impartially what it is. I will examine it with you calmly, and if the thing is useful to us both . . . or even if it be useful to you alone, it will be something irrevocably decided."

"I promise you."

From *La Vie de mon père*, third edition (Paris: 1788); trans. L.S.G.

❖ ❖ ❖

A Famous Simple Life

[FROM *Paul and Virginia*]

JACQUES HENRI
BERNARDIN DE SAINT-PIERRE

1788

Every day was to these families a day of happiness and of tranquillity. Neither ambition nor envy disturbed their repose. They did not seek to obtain a useless reputation out of doors, which may be procured by artifice, and lost by calumny; but were contented to be the sole witnesses and judges of their own actions. In this island, where, as is the case in most colonies, scandal forms the principal topic of conversation, their virtues, and even their names, were unknown. The passer-by on the road to the Shaddock Grove, indeed, would sometimes ask the inhabitants of the plain, who lived in the cottages up there? and was always told, even by those who did not know them, "They are good people." The modest violet thus, concealed in thorny places, sheds all unseen its delightful fragrance around.

Slander, which, under an appearance of justice, naturally inclines the heart to falsehood or to hatred, was entirely banished from their conversation; for it is impossible not to hate men if we believe them to be wicked, or to live with the wicked without concealing that hatred under a false pretence of good feeling. Slander thus puts us ill at ease with others and with ourselves. In this little circle, therefore, the conduct of individuals was not discussed, but the best manner of doing good to all; and although they had but little in their power, their unceasing goodwill and kindness of heart made them constantly ready to do what they could for others. Solitude, far from having blunted these benevolent feelings, had rendered their dispositions even more kindly. Although the petty scandals of the day furnished no subject of conversation to them, yet the contemplation of nature filled their minds with enthusiastic delight. They adored the bounty of that Providence which, by their instrumentality, had spread abundance and beauty amid these barren rocks, and had enabled them to enjoy those pure and simple pleasures, which are ever grateful and ever new.

Paul, at twelve years of age, was stronger and more intelligent than most European youths are at fifteen; and the plantations, which Domingo merely cultivated, were all embellished by him. He would go with the old Negro into the neighbouring woods, where he would root up the young plants of lemon, orange, and tamarind trees, the round heads of which are of so fresh a green, together with date-palm trees, which produce fruit filled with a sweet cream, possessing the fine perfume of the orange flower. These trees, which had already attained to a considerable size, he planted round their little enclosure. He had also sown the seeds of many trees which the second year bear flowers or fruit; such as the agathis, encircled with long clusters of white flowers, which hang from it like the crystal pendants of a chandelier; the Persian lilac, which lifts high in air its grey flax-coloured branches; the papaw tree, the branchless trunk of which forms a column studded with green melons, surmounted by a capital of broad leaves similar to those of the fig tree.

The seeds and kernels of the gum tree, terminalia, mango, alligator pear, the guava, the breadfruit tree, and the narrow-leaved rose-apple, were also planted by him with profusion; and the greater number of these trees already afforded their young cultivator both shade and fruit. His industrious hands diffused the riches of nature over even the most barren parts of the plantation. Several species of aloes, the Indian fig, adorned with yellow flowers spotted with red, and the thorny torch-thistle, grew upon the dark summits of the rocks, and seemed to aim at reaching the long lianas, which, laden with blue or scarlet flowers, hung scattered over the steepest parts of the mountain. . . .

But perhaps the most delightful spot of this enclosure was that called Virginia's Resting Place. At the foot of the rock which bore the name of The Discovery of Friendship is a small crevice, whence issues a fountain, forming, near its source, a little spot of marshy soil in the middle of a field of rich grass.

At the time of Paul's birth I had made Margaret a present of an Indian cocoa which had been given me, and which she planted on the border of this fenny ground, in order that the tree might one day serve to mark the epoch of her son's birth. Madame de la Tour planted another cocoa, with the same view, at the birth of Virginia. These nuts produced two cocoa trees, which formed the only records of the two families: one was called Paul's tree, the other, Virginia's. Their growth was in the same proportion as that of the two young persons, not exactly equal; but they rose, at the end of twelve years, above the roofs of the cottages. Already their tender stalks were interwoven, and clusters of young cocoas hung from them over the basin of the fountain. With the exception of these two trees, this nook of the rock was left as it had been decorated by nature.

On its embrowned and moist sides broad plants of maidenhair glistened with their green and dark stars; and tufts of wave-leaved hart's-tongue, suspended like long ribands of purpled green, floated on the wind. Near this grew a chain of the Madagascar periwinkle, the flowers of which resembled the red gillyflower; and the long-podded capsicum, the seed-vessels of which are of the colour of blood, and more resplendent than coral. Near them, the herb balm, with its heart-shaped leaves, and the sweet basil, which has the odour of the clove, exhaled the most delicious perfumes. From the precipitous side of the mountain hung the graceful lianas, like floating draperies, forming magnificent canopies of verdure on the face of the rocks. The sea birds, allured by the stillness of these retreats, resorted here to pass the night.

At the hour of sunset we could perceive the curlew and the stint skimming along the seashore; the frigat bird poised high in air; and the white bird of the tropic, which abandons, with the star of day, the solitudes of the Indian Ocean. Virginia took pleasure in resting herself upon the border of this fountain, decorated with wild and sublime magnificence. She often went thither to wash the linen of the family beneath the shade of the two cocoa trees, and thither too she sometimes led her goats to graze. While she was making cheeses of their milk, she loved to see them browse on the maidenhair fern which clothed the steep sides of the rock, and hung suspended by one of its cornices, as on a pedestal. Paul, observing that Virginia was fond of this spot, brought thither, from the neighbouring forest, a great variety of birds' nests. The old birds, following their young, soon established themselves in this new colony. Virginia, at stated times, distributed amongst them grains of rice, millet, and maize. As soon as she appeared, the whistling blackbird, the amadavid bird, whose note is so soft, the cardinal, with its flame-coloured plumage, forsook their bushes; the parroquet, green as an emerald, descended from the neighbouring fan-palms; the partridge ran along the grass: all advanced promiscuously towards her, like a brood of chickens: and she and Paul found an exhaustless source of amusement in observing their sports, their repasts, and their loves.

Amiable children! thus passed your earlier days in innocence, and in obeying the impulses of kindness. How many times, on this very spot, have your mothers, pressing you in their arms, blessed Heaven for the consolations your unfolding virtues prepared for their declining years, while they at the same time enjoyed the satisfaction of seeing you begin life under the happiest auspices! How many times, beneath the shade of those rocks, have I partaken with them of your rural repasts, which never cost any animal its life! Gourds full of milk, fresh eggs, cakes of rice served upon plantain leaves, with baskets of mangoes, oranges, dates, pomegranates, pineapples, furnished a wholesome repast, the most agreeable to the eye, as well as delicious to the taste, that can possibly be imagined. . . .

You Europeans, whose minds are imbued from infancy with prejudices at variance with happiness, cannot imagine all the instruction and pleasure to be derived from nature. Your souls, confined to a small sphere of intelligence, soon reach the limit of its artificial enjoyments; but nature and the heart are inexhaustible. Paul and Virginia had neither clock, nor almanack, nor books of chronology, history, or philosophy. The periods of their lives were regulated by those of the operations of nature, and their familiar conversation had a constant reference to the changes of the seasons. They knew the time of day by the shadows of the trees; the seasons, by the times when those trees bore flowers or fruit; and the years, by the number of their harvests. These soothing images diffused an inexpressible charm over their conversation. "It is time to dine," said Virginia, "the shadows of the plantain trees are at their roots"; or, "Night approaches; the tamarinds are closing their leaves." "When will you come and see us?" inquired some of her companions in the neighbourhood. "At the time of the sugarcanes," answered Virginia. "Your visit will be then still more delightful," resumed her young acquaintances. When she was asked what was her own age, and that of Paul—"My brother," said she, "is as old as the great cocoa tree of the fountain; and I am as old as the little one: the mangoes have borne fruit twelve times, and the orange trees have flowered four-and-twenty times, since I came into the world."

Their lives seemed linked to that of the trees, like those of fauns or dryads. They knew no other historical epochs than those of the lives of their mothers, no other chronology than that of their orchards, and no other philosophy than that of doing good, and resigning themselves to the will of Heaven.

What need, indeed, had these young people of riches or learning such as ours? Even their necessities and their ignorance increased their happiness. No day passed in which they were not of some service to one another, or in which they did not mutually impart some instruction. Yes, instruction; for if errors mingled with it, they were, at least, not of a dangerous character. A pure-minded being has none of that description to fear. Thus grew these children of nature. No care had troubled their peace, no intemperance had corrupted their blood, no misplaced passion had depraved their hearts. Love, innocence, and piety possessed their souls; and those intellectual graces were unfolding daily in their features, their attitudes, and their movements. Still in the morning of life, they had all its blooming freshness; and surely such in the Garden of Eden appeared our first parents, when, coming from the hands of God, they first saw and approached each other, and conversed together, like brother and sister. Virginia was gentle, modest, and confiding as Eve; and Paul, like Adam, united the stature of manhood with the simplicity of a child.

Trans. from the French [no translator named] (Boston: Estes and Lauriat, n.d.).

A Very Reasonable Boy

[FROM *The History of Sandford and Merton*]

THOMAS DAY

1783

After dinner, Mrs. Merton filled a large glass of wine, and, giving it to Harry, bade him drink it up; but he thanked her, and said he was not thirsty. "But, my dear," said she, "this is very sweet and pleasant, and as you are a good boy, you may drink it up."

"Ay! but, madam, Mr. Barlow says that we must only eat when we are hungry, and drink when we are thirsty; and that we must eat and drink only such things as are easily met with; otherwise we shall grow peevish and vexed when we can't get them. And this was the way that the Apostles did, who were all very good men."

Mr. Merton laughed at this. "And pray," said he, "little man, do you know who the Apostles were?"

"Oh, yes, sir, to be sure I do."

"And who were they?"

"Why, sir, there was a time when people had grown so very wicked, that they did not care what they did; and the great folk were all proud, and minded nothing but eating, drinking, and sleeping, and amusing themselves; and took no care of the poor, and would not give a morsel of bread to hinder a beggar from starving; and the poor were all lazy, and loved to be idle better than to work; and little boys were disobedient to their parents, and their parents took no care to teach them anything that was good; and all the world was very bad, very bad indeed. And then there came a very good man indeed, a man from Heaven, whose name was Christ; and he went about doing good to everybody, and curing people of all sorts of diseases, and taught them what they ought to do; and he chose out twelve other very good men, and called them Apostles; and these Apostles went about the world, doing as he did, and teaching people as he taught them. And they never minded what they ate or drank, but lived upon dry bread and water; and when anybody offered them money, they would not take it, but told them to be good, and give it to the poor and the sick; and so they made the world a great deal better. And therefore it is not fit to mind what we live upon, but we should take what we can get, and be contented; just as the beasts and birds do, who lodge in the open air, and live upon herbs, and drink nothing but water; and yet they are strong, and active, and healthy."

"Upon my word," said Mr. Merton, "this little man is a great philosopher; and we should be much obliged to Mr. Barlow, if he would take our Tommy under his care; for he grows a great boy, and it is time that he should know something. What say you, Tommy, should you like to be a philosopher?"

"Indeed, Papa, I don't know what a philosopher is; but I should like to be a king; because he's finer and richer than anybody else, and has nothing to do, and everybody waits upon him, and is afraid of him."

"Well said, my dear," replied Mrs. Merton; and rose and kissed him; "and a king you deserve to be with such a spirit; and here's a glass of wine for you for making such a pretty answer. And should not you like to be a king, too, little Harry?"

"Indeed, madam, I don't know what that is; but I hope I shall soon be big enough to go to plough, and get my own living; and then I shall want nobody to wait upon me."

"What a difference there is between the children of farmers and gentlemen!" whispered Mrs. Merton to her husband, looking rather contemptuously upon Harry.

"I am not sure," said Mr. Merton, "that for this time the advantage is on the side of our son. But should not you like to be rich, my dear?" said he, turning to Harry.

"No, indeed, sir."

"No, simpleton!" said Mrs. Merton; "and why not?"

"Because the only rich man I ever saw is Squire Chase, who lives hard by; and he rides among people's corn, and breaks down their hedges, and shoots their poultry, and kills their dogs, and lames their cattle, and abuses the poor; and they say he does all this because he's rich; but everybody hates him, though they dare not tell him so to his face: and I would not be hated for anything in the world."

"But should you not like to have a fine laced coat, and a coach to carry you about, and servants to wait upon you?"

"As to that, madam, one coat is as good as another, if it will but keep one warm; and I don't want to ride, because I can walk wherever I choose; and, as to servants, I should have nothing for them to do, if I had a hundred of them."

Mrs. Merton continued to look at him with a sort of contemptuous astonishment, but did not ask him any more questions.

In the evening, little Harry was sent home to his father, who asked him what he had seen at the great house, and how he liked being there.

"Why," replied Harry, "they were all very kind to me, for which I'm much obliged to them; but I had rather have been at home, for I never was so troubled in all my life to get a dinner. There was one man to take away my plate, and another to give me drink, and another to stand behind my chair, just as though I had been lame or blind, and could not have waited upon myself: and then there was so much to do with putting this thing on, and taking another off, I thought it would never have been over: and, after dinner, I was obliged to sit two whole hours without ever stirring, while the lady was talking to me, not as Mr. Barlow does, but wanting me to love fine clothes, and to be a king, and to be rich, that I might be hated like Squire Chase."

Ed. Cecil Hartley (New York: Hurd & Houghton, 1865).

FROM A Modest Proposal

FOR PREVENTING THE CHILDREN OF POOR PEOPLE FROM BEING A BURTHEN TO THEIR PARENTS OR COUNTRY, AND FOR MAKING THEM BENEFICIAL TO THE PUBLIC

JONATHAN SWIFT

1729

It is a melancholy object to those who walk through this great town, or travel in the country, when they see the streets, the roads, and cabin-doors crowded with beggars of the female sex, followed by three, four, or six children, *all in rags,* and importuning every passenger for an alms. These mothers, instead of being able to work for their honest livelihood, are forced to employ all their time in strolling, to beg sustenance for their helpless infants, who, as they grow up, either turn thieves for want of work, or leave their dear Native Country to fight for the Pretender in Spain, or sell themselves to the Barbadoes.

I think it is agreed by all parties that this prodigious number of children, in the arms, or on the backs, or at the heels of their mothers, and frequently of their fathers, is in the present deplorable state of the kingdom a very great additional grievance; and therefore whoever could find out a fair, cheap, and easy method of making these children sound useful members of the commonwealth would deserve so well of the public as to have his statue set up for a preserver of the nation.

But my intention is very far from being confined to provide only for the children of professed beggars; it is of a much greater extent, and shall take in the whole number of infants at a certain age who are born of parents in effect as little able to support them as those who demand our charity in the streets.

As to my own part, having turned my thoughts, for many years, upon this important subject, and maturely weighed the several schemes of other projectors, I have always found them grossly mistaken in their computation. It is true a child, just dropped from its dam, may be supported by her milk for a solar year with little other nourishment, at most not above the value of two shillings, which the mother may certainly get, or the value in scraps, by her lawful occupation of begging, and it is exactly at one year old that I propose to provide for them, in such a manner as, instead of being a charge upon their parents, or the parish, or wanting food and raiment for the rest of their lives, they shall, on the contrary, contribute to the feeding and partly to the clothing of many thousands.

There is likewise another great advantage in my scheme, that it will prevent those voluntary abortions, and that horrid practice of women murdering their bastard children, alas, too frequent among us, sacrificing the poor innocent babes, I doubt, more to avoid the expense than the shame, which would move tears and pity in the most savage and inhuman breast.

The number of souls in this kingdom being usually reckoned one million and a half, of these I calculate there may be about two hundred thousand couples whose wives are breeders, from which number I subtract thirty thousand couples who are able to maintain their own children, although I apprehend there cannot be so many under the present distresses of the kingdom, but this being granted, there will remain an hundred and seventy thousand breeders. I again subtract fifty thousand for those women who miscarry, or whose children die by accident or disease within the year. There only remain an hundred and twenty thousand children of poor parents annually born: The question therefore is, how this number shall be reared, and provided for, which, as I have already said, under the present situation of affairs, is utterly impossible by all the methods hitherto proposed, for we can neither employ them in handicraft, or agriculture; we neither build houses (I mean in the country), nor cultivate land: they can very seldom pick up a livelihood by stealing till they arrive at six years old, except where they are of towardly parts, although, I confess they learn the rudiments much earlier, during which time they can however be properly looked upon only as *probationers,* as I have been informed by a principal gentleman in the County of Cavan, who protested to me that he never knew above one or two instances under the age of six, ever in a part of the kingdom so renowned for the quickest proficiency in that art.

I am assured by our merchants that a boy or a girl, before twelve years old, is no saleable commodity, and even when they come to this age, they will not yield above three pounds, or three pounds and half-a-crown at most on the Exchange, which cannot turn to account either to the parents or the kingdom, the charge of nutriment and rags having been at least four times that value.

I shall now therefore humbly propose my own thoughts, which I hope will not be liable to the least objection.

I have been assured by a very knowing American of my acquaintance in London, that a young healthy child well nursed is at a year old a most delicious, nourishing, and wholesome food, whether stewed, roasted, baked, or boiled, and I make no doubt that it will equally serve in a fricassee, or a ragout.

I do therefore humbly offer it to public consideration, that of the hundred and twenty thousand children already computed, twenty thousand may be reserved for breed, whereof only one-fourth part to be males, which is more than we allow to sheep, black-cattle, or swine, and my reason is that these children are seldom the fruits of marriage, a circumstance not much regarded by our savages, therefore one male will be sufficient to serve four females. That the remaining hundred thousand may at a year old be offered in sale to the persons of quality, and fortune, through the kingdom, always advising the mother to let them suck plentifully in the last month, so as to render them plump, and fat for a good table. A child will make two dishes at an entertainment for friends, and when the family dines alone, the fore or hind quarter will make a reasonable dish, and seasoned with a little pepper or salt will be very good boiled on the fourth day, especially in winter.

I have reckoned upon a medium, that a child just born will weigh 12 pounds, and in a solar year if tolerably nursed increaseth to 28 pounds.

I grant this food will be somewhat dear, and therefore very proper for landlords, who, as they have already devoured most of the parents, seem to have the best title to the children.

Infants' flesh will be in season throughout the year, but more plentiful in March, and a little before and after, for we are told by a grave author, an eminent French physician, that fish being a prolific diet, there are more children born in Roman Catholic countries about nine months after Lent than at any other season; therefore reckoning a year after Lent, the markets will be more glutted than usual, because the number of Popish infants is at least three to one in this kingdom, and therefore it will have one other collateral advantage by lessening the number of Papists among us.

I have already computed the charge of nursing a beggar's child (in which list I reckon all cottagers, labourers, and four-fifths of the farmers) to be about two shillings *per annum*, rags included, and I believe no gentleman would repine to give ten shillings for the carcass of a good fat child, which, as I have said, will make four dishes of excellent nutritive meat, when he hath only some particular friend or his own family to dine with him. Thus the Squire will learn to be a good landlord, and grow popular among his tenants, the mother will have eight shillings net profit, and be fit for work till she produces another child.

Those who are more thrifty (as I must confess the times require) may flay the carcass; the skin of which, artificially dressed, will make admirable gloves for ladies, and summer boots for fine gentlemen.

As to our City of Dublin, shambles may be appointed for this purpose, in the most convenient parts of it, and butchers we may be assured will not be wanting, although I rather recommend buying the children alive, and dressing them hot from the knife, as we do roasting pigs.

A very worthy person, a true lover of this country, and whose virtues I highly esteem, was lately pleased, in discoursing on this matter, to offer a refinement upon my scheme. He said that many gentlemen of this kingdom, having of late destroyed their deer, he conceived that the want of venison might be well supplied by the bodies of young lads and maidens, not exceeding fourteen years of age, nor under twelve, so great a number of both sexes in every country being now ready to starve, for want of work and service: and these to be disposed of by their parents if alive, or otherwise by their nearest relations. But with due deference to so excellent a friend, and so deserving a patriot, I cannot be altogether in his sentiments; for as to the males, my American acquaintance assured me from frequent experience that their flesh was generally tough and lean, like that of our schoolboys, by continual exercise, and their taste disagreeable, and to fatten them would not answer the charge. Then as to the females, it would, I think with humble submission, be a loss to the public, because they soon would become breeders themselves: And besides, it is not improbable that some scrupulous people might be apt to censure such a practice (although indeed very unjustly) as a little bordering upon cruelty, which, I confess, hath always been with me the strongest objection against any project, however so well intended.

From *Works*, Vol. VIII (London: J. Nichols, 1808).

❖ ❖ ❖

Two Portraits

[FROM *Absalom and Achitophel*]

JOHN DRYDEN

1681

BUCKINGHAM

Such were the tools: but a whole Hydra more
Remains of sprouting heads too long to score.
Some of their chiefs were princes of the land;
In the first rank of these did Zimri stand;
A man so various, that he seem'd to be
Not one, but all mankind's epitome:
Stiff in opinions, always in the wrong;
Was every thing by starts, and nothing long;
But, in the course of one revolving moon,
Was chymist, fidler, statesman, and buffoon:
Then all for women, painting, rhiming, drinking,
Besides ten thousand freaks that dy'd in thinking.
Blest madman, who could every hour employ,
With something new to wish, or to enjoy!
Railing and praising were his usual themes;
And both, to shew his judgment, in extremes:
So over violent, or over civil,
That every man with him was God or Devil.
In squandering wealth was his peculiar art:
Nothing went unrewarded but desert.
Beggar'd by fools, whom still he found too late;
He had his jest, and they had his estate.

He laugh'd himself from court; then sought relief
By forming parties, but could ne'er be chief:
For, spite of him, the weight of business fell
On Absalom, and wise Achitophel:
Thus, wicked but in will, of means bereft,
He left not faction, but of that was left.

TITUS OATES

To speak the rest who better are forgot,
Would tire a well-breath'd witness of the plot.
Yet Corah, thou shalt from oblivion pass;
Erect thyself, thou monumental brass,
High as the serpent of thy metal made,
While nations stand secure beneath thy shade.
What, though his birth were base, yet comets rise
From earthly vapours, ere they shine in skies.
Prodigious actions may as well be done
By weaver's issue, as by prince's son.
This arch-attestor for the public good
By that one deed ennobles all his blood.
Who ever ask'd the witnesses' high race,
Whose oath with martyrdom did Stephen grace?
Ours was a Levite, and as times went then,
His tribe were God Almighty's gentlemen.
Sunk were his eyes, his voice was harsh and loud,
Sure signs he neither choleric was, nor proud:
His long chin prov'd his wit; his faint-like grace
A church vermillion, and a Moses' face.
His memory, miraculously great,
Could plots, exceeding man's belief, repeat;
Which therefore cannot be accounted lies,
For human wit could never such devise.
Some future truths are mingled in his book;
But where the witness fail'd, the prophet spoke:
Some things like visionary flights appear;

The spirit caught him up the Lord knows where;
And gave him his rabbinical degree,
Unknown to foreign university.
His judgment yet his memory did excel;
Which piec'd his wonderous evidence so well,
And suited to the temper of the times,
Then groaning under Jebusitic crimes.
Let Israel's foes suspect his heavenly call,
And rashly judge his writ apocryphal;
Our laws for such affronts have forfeits made:
He takes his life who takes away his trade.
Were I myself in witness Corah's place,
The wretch who did me such a dire disgrace,
Should whet my memory, though once forgot,
To make him an appendix of my plot.
His zeal to heaven made him his prince despise,
And load his person with indignities.
But zeal peculiar privilege affords,
Indulging latitude to deeds and words:
And Corah might for Agag's murder call,
In terms as coarse as Samuel us'd to Saul.
What others in his evidence did join,
The best that could be had for love or coin,
In Corah's own predicament will fall;
For witness is a common name to all.

From *Poetical Works*, Vol. I, ed. J. Warton (London: 1811).

Two More Portraits

[FROM "Epistle to Dr. Arbuthnot"]

ALEXANDER POPE

1735

ADDISON

Peace to all such! but were there One whose fires
True Genius kindles, and fair Fame inspires;
Blest with each talent and each art to please,
And born to write, converse, and live with ease:
Should such a man, too fond to rule alone,
Bear, like the Turk, no brother near the throne,
View him with scornful, yet with jealous eyes,
And hate for arts that caused himself to rise;
Damn with faint praise, assent with civil leer,
And without sneering, teach the rest to sneer;
Willing to wound, and yet afraid to strike,
Just hint a fault, and hesitate dislike;
Alike reserved to blame, or to commend,
A timorous foe, and a suspicious friend;
Dreading even fools, by Flatterers besieged,
And so obliging, that he ne'er obliged;
Like *Cato*, give his little Senate laws,
And sit attentive to his own applause;
While Wits and Templars every sentence raise,
And wonder with a foolish face of praise—

Who but must laugh, if such a man there be?
Who would not weep, if ATTICUS were he?

HERVEY

   Let *Sporus* tremble— *A.*[1] What? that thing of silk,
Sporus, that mere white curd of Ass's milk?
Satire or sense, alas! can *Sporus* feel?
Who breaks a butterfly upon a wheel?
P. Yet let me flap this bug with gilded wings,
This painted child of dirt, that stinks and stings;
Whose buzz the witty and the fair annoys,
Yet wit ne'er tastes, and beauty ne'er enjoys:
So well-bred spaniels civilly delight
In mumbling of the game they dare not bite.
Eternal smiles his emptiness betray,
As shallow streams run dimpling all the way.
Whether in florid impotence he speaks,
And, as the prompter breathes, the puppet squeaks;
Or at the ear of *Eve*, familiar Toad,
Half froth, half venom, spits himself abroad,
In puns, or politics, or tales, or lies,
Or spite, or smut, or rhymes, or blasphemies.
His wit all seesaw, between *that* and *this*,
Now high, now low, now master up, now miss,
And he himself one vile Antithesis.
Amphibious thing! that acting either part,
The trifling head, or the corrupted heart,
Fop at the toilet, flatterer at the board,
Now trips a Lady, and now struts a Lord.
Eve's tempter thus the Rabbins have exprest,
A Cherub's face, a reptile all the rest;

---

   [1] Dr. John Arbuthnot (1667-1735), to whom this epistle
was addressed. [C.B.'s note.]

Beauty that shocks you, parts that none will trust,
Wit that can creep, and pride that licks the dust.

From *Poetical Works*, ed. H. F. Cary (London: Routledge, 1871).

❖ ❖ ❖

Wit in Verse

François Marie Arouet de
VOLTAIRE

1730-74

On a Garden Statue of Love

Whoe'er thou be, thy master see;
He is, he was, or has to be.

On a Figure of Christ in the Jesuit Habit

Consider, pray, the artfulness
    Industrious monks like these can show.
My God, they've clothed Thee in their dress,
    Lest men should love Thee here below!

On the Placing of His Portrait
between Two Others

'Twixt Fréron and La Beaumelle me!
    What can Le Jay by this have meant?
It were indeed a Calvary,
    Had either thief been penitent.

The Snake That Bit Fréron

One day, down in the vale below,
A snake bit Fréron on the toe.
And what ensued, I ask you? Why,
It was the snake that had to die.

All in J. G. Legge, *Chanticleer; A Study of the French Muse*
New York: E. P. Dutton & Company, 1935).

To Madame Lullin

Are you astonished to be told
That though I'm past my eightieth year,
My muse, albeit frail and old,
Still quavers verse for you, my dear?

At times a little green will smile
In fields beneath the frosted grass;
It comforts nature a brief while,
Only to wither soon, alas!

We oft may hear a bird pipe long
After the summer days are over:
There's nothing tender in his song,
For now he sings not as a lover.

Thus too with failing, trembling fingers
I touch the strings upon my lyre;
I'd wake my song just as the singer's
Voice is ready to expire.

"I would, when I'm about to die,"
Tibullus to his love said, "hold thee

And cling to thee with eye to eye
And in my dying arms enfold thee."

But when we're breathing our last sighs
And when the spirit ebbs apace,
Then have we eyes for Delia's eyes
And have we arms for an embrace!

At that hour we forget to do
Whate'er we did when we were well;
What man e'er gave a rendez-vous
To love bidding a last farewell?

When Delia's turn comes to repair
From day into eternal night,
She'll not remember she was fair
And only lived for love's delight.

We're born, we live, my shepherdess,
We die, just how is not too clear:
We come here out of nothingness:
Where to we? . . . God alone knows, dear.

In *A Treasury of French Poetry*, trans. Alan Conder (London: Cassell & Company, 1950).

❖ ❖ ❖

Selections from a Witty Tale

[FROM *Candide*]

FRANÇOIS MARIE AROUET DE
VOLTAIRE

1759

CANDIDE GOES TO WAR

Nothing could be smarter, more splendid, more brilliant, better drawn up than the two armies. Trumpets, fifes, hautboys, drums, cannons, formed a harmony such as has never been heard even in hell. The cannons first of all laid flat about six thousand men on each side; then the musketry removed from the best of worlds some nine or ten thousand blackguards who infested its surface. The bayonet also was the sufficient reason for the death of some thousands of men. The whole might amount to thirty thousand souls.

Candide, who trembled like a philosopher, hid himself as well as he could during this heroic butchery. At last, while the two Kings each commanded a Te Deum in his camp, Candide decided to go elsewhere to reason about effects and causes. He clambered over heaps of dead and dying men and reached a neighboring village, which was in ashes; it was an Abare village which the Bulgarians had burned in accordance with international law. Here, old men dazed with blows watched the dying agonies of their murdered wives who clutched their children to their bleeding breasts; there, disemboweled girls who had been made to satisfy the natural appetites of heroes gasped their last sighs; others, half-burned, begged to be put to death. Brains were scattered on the ground among dismembered arms and legs.

Candide fled to another village as fast he could; it belonged to the Bulgarians, and Abarian heroes had treated it in the same way. Candide, stumbling over quivering limbs or across ruins, at last escaped from the theatre of war, carrying a little food in his knapsack, and never forgetting Mademoiselle Cunegonde.

His provisions were all gone when he reached Holland; but, having heard that everyone in that country was rich and a Christian, he had no doubt at all but that he would be as well treated as he had been in the Baron's castle before he had been expelled on account of Mademoiselle Cunegonde's pretty eyes. He asked an alms of several grave persons, who all replied that if he continued in that way he would be shut up in a house of correction to teach him how to live.

CANDIDE IN THE LAND OF ELDORADO

Cacambo informed the host of his curiosity, and the host said: "I am a very ignorant man and am all the better for it; but we have here an old man who has retired from the court and who is the most learned and most communicative man in the kingdom." And he at once took Cacambo to the old man. Candide now played only the second part and accompanied his valet. They entered a very simple house, for the door was only of silver and the paneling of the apartments in gold, but so tastefully carved that the richest decorations did not surpass it. The antechamber indeed was only encrusted with rubies and emeralds; but the order with which everything was arranged atoned for this extreme simplicity. The old man received the two strangers on a sofa padded with colibri feathers, and presented them with drinks in diamond cups; after which he satisfied their curiosity in these words: "I am a hundred and seventy-two years old and I heard from my late father, the King's equerry, the astonishing revolutions of Peru of which he had been an eye-witness. The kingdom where we now are is the ancient country of the Incas, who most imprudently left it to conquer part of the world and were at last destroyed by the Spaniards. The princes of their family who remained in their native country had more wisdom; with the consent of the nation, they ordered that no inhabitants should ever leave our little kingdom, and this it is that has preserved our innocence and our felicity. The Spaniards had some vague knowledge of this country, which they called Eldorado, and about a hundred years ago an Englishman named Raleigh came very near to it; but, since we are surrounded by inaccessible rocks and precipices, we have hitherto been exempt from the rapacity of the nations of Europe, who have an inconceivable lust for the pebbles and mud of our land and would kill us to the last man to get possession of them."

The conversation was long; it touched upon the form of the government, manners, women, public spectacles, and the arts. Finally Candide, who was always interested in metaphysics, asked through Cacambo whether the country had a religion. The old man blushed a little. "How can you doubt it?" said he. "Do you think we are ingrates?" Cacambo humbly asked what was the religion of Eldorado. The old man blushed again. "Can there be two religions?" said he.

"We have, I think, the religion of everyone else; we adore God from evening until morning." "Do you adore only one God?" said Cacambo, who continued to act as the interpreter of Candide's doubts. "Manifestly," said the old man, "there are not two or three or four. I must confess that the people of your world ask very extraordinary questions." Candide continued to press the old man with questions; he wished to know how they prayed to God in Eldorado. "We do not pray," said the good and respectable sage, "we have nothing to ask from him; he has given us everything necessary and we continually give him thanks." Candide was curious to see the priests; and asked where they were. The good old man smiled. "My friends," said he, "we are all priests; the King and all the heads of families solemnly sing praises every morning, accompanied by five or six thousand musicians." "What! Have you no monks to teach, to dispute, to govern, to intrigue and to burn people who do not agree with them?" "For that, we should have to become fools," said the old man; "here we are all of the same opinion and do not understand what you mean with your monks." At all this Candide was in an ecstasy and said to himself: "This is very different from Westphalia and the castle of His Lordship the Baron; if our friend Pangloss had seen Eldorado, he would not have said that the castle of Thunder-tentronckh was the best of all that exists on the earth; certainly, a man should travel."

After this long conversation the good old man ordered a carriage to be harnessed with six sheep and gave the two travellers twelve of his servants to take them to court. "You will excuse me," he said, "if my age deprives me of the honour of accompanying you. The King will receive you in a manner which will not displease you and doubtless you will pardon the cus-

none, and that nobody ever went to law. He asked if there were prisons and was told there were none. He was still more surprised and pleased by the palace of sciences, where he saw a gallery two thousand feet long, filled with instruments of mathematics and physics. After they had explored all the afternoon about a thousandth part of the town, they were taken back to the King. Candide sat down to table with his Majesty, his valet Cacambo, and several ladies. Never was better cheer, and never was anyone wittier at supper than his Majesty. Cacambo explained the King's witty remarks to Candide and even when translated they still appeared witty. Among all the things which amazed Candide, this did not amaze him the least.

They enjoyed this hospitality for a month. Candide repeatedly said to Cacambo: "Once again, my friend, it is quite true that the castle where I was born cannot be compared with this country; but then Mademoiselle Cunegonde is not here, and you probably have a mistress in Europe. If we remain here, we shall only be like everyone else; but if we return to our own world with only twelve sheep laden with Eldorado pebbles, we shall be richer than all the kings put together; we shall have no more Inquisitors to fear, and we can easily regain Mademoiselle Cunegonde." Cacambo agreed with this; it is so pleasant to be on the move, to show off before friends, to make a parade of the things seen on one's travels, that these two happy men resolved to be so no longer and to ask his Majesty's permission to depart. "You are doing a very silly thing," said the King. "I know my country is small; but when we are comfortable anywhere we should stay there; I certainly have not the right to detain foreigners, that is a tyranny which does not exist either in our manners or our laws; all men are free, leave when you please, but the way out is very difficult. It is impossible to ascend the rapid river by which you miraculously came here and which flows under arches of rock. The mountains which surround the whole of my kingdom are ten thousand feet high and are perpendicular like walls; they are more than ten leagues broad, and you can only get down from them by way of precipices. However, since you must go, I will give orders to the directors of machinery to make a machine which will carry you comfortably. When you have been taken to the other side of the mountains, nobody can proceed any farther with you; for my subjects have sworn never to pass this boundary, and they are too wise to break their oath. Ask anything else of me you wish." "We ask nothing of your Majesty," said Cacambo, "except a few sheep laden with provisions, pebbles, and the mud of this country." The King laughed. "I cannot understand," said he, "the taste you people of Europe have for our yellow mud; but take as much as you wish, and much good may it do you."

He immediately ordered his engineers to make a machine to hoist these two extraordinary men out of his kingdom. Three thousand learned scientists worked at it; it was ready in a fortnight and only cost about twenty million pounds sterling in the money of that country. Candide and Cacambo were placed on the machine; there were two large red sheep saddled and bridled for them to ride on when they had passed the mountains, twenty sumpter sheep laden with provisions, thirty carrying presents of the most curious productions of the country, and fifty laden with gold, precious stones, and diamonds. The King embraced the two vagabonds tenderly. Their departure was a splendid sight, and so was the ingenious manner in which they and their sheep were hoisted onto the top of the mountains. The scientists took leave of them after having landed them safely, and Candide's only desire and object was to go and present Mademoiselle Cunegonde with his sheep. "We have sufficient to pay the governor of Buenos Aires," said he, "if Mademoiselle Cunegonde can be bought. Let us go to Cayenne, and take ship, and then we will see what kingdom we will buy."

CANDIDE IN ENGLAND

"You know England" [said Candide]; "are the people there as mad as they are in France?" " 'Tis another sort of madness," said Martin. "You know these two nations are at war for a few acres of snow in Canada, and that they are spending more on this fine war[1] than all Canada is worth. It is beyond my poor capacity to tell you whether there are more madmen in one country than in the other; all I know is that in general the people we are going to visit are extremely melancholic." Talking thus, they arrived at Portsmouth. There were multitudes of people on the shore, looking attentively at a rather fat man with his eyes bandaged, who was kneeling down on the deck of one of the ships in the fleet; four soldiers placed opposite this man each shot three bullets into his brain in the calmest manner imaginable; and the whole assembly returned home with great satisfaction. "What is all this?" said Candide. "And what Demon exercises his power everywhere?" He asked who was the fat man who had just been killed so ceremoniously. "An admiral" [John Byng], was the reply. "And why kill the admiral?" "Because," he was told, "he did not kill enough people. He fought a battle with a French admiral and it was held that the

[1] The Seven Years War, 1756-63, known to us as the French and Indian War. [C.B.'s note.]

English, admiral was not close enough to him." "But," said Candide, "the French admiral was just as far from the English admiral!" "That is indisputable," was the answer, "but in this country it is a good thing to kill an admiral from time to time to encourage the others."

Trans. Richard Aldington (London: Routledge, 1927).

A Pseudo-Persian Stick
to Beat with

[FROM *Persian Letters*]

CHARLES DE SECONDAT, BARON DE LA BREDE ET DE MONTESQUIEU

1721

INTRODUCTION

I am not about to write a dedication, nor do I solicit protection for this work. It will be read, if it is good; and if it is bad, I am not anxious that it should be read.

I have issued these first letters in order to gauge the public taste; in my portfolio I have a goodly number more which I may hereafter publish.

This, however, depends upon my remaining unknown: let my name once be published and I cease to write. I know a lady who walks well enough, but who limps if she is watched. Surely the blemishes of my book are sufficient to make it needless that I should submit those of my person to the critics. Were I known, it would be said, "His book is at odds with his character; he might have employed his time to better purpose; it is not worthy of a serious man." Critics are never at a loss for such remarks, because there goes no great expense of brains to the making of them.

The Persians who wrote these letters lodged at my house, and we spent our time together: they looked upon me as a man belonging to another world, and so they concealed nothing from me. Indeed, people so far from home could hardly be said to have secrets. They showed me most of their letters, and I copied them. I also intercepted some, mortifying to Persian vanity and jealousy, which they had been particularly careful to conceal from me.

I am therefore nothing more than a translator: all my endeavour has been to adapt the work to our taste and manners. I have relieved the reader as much as possible of Asiatic phraseology, and have spared him an infinitude of sublime expressions which would have driven him wild.

Nor does my service to him end there. I have curtailed those tedious compliments of which the Orientals are as lavish as ourselves; and I have omitted a great many trifling matters which barely survive exposure to the light, and ought never to emerge from the obscurity proper to "small beer."

Had most of those who have given the world collections of letters done likewise, their works would have disappeared in the editing. . . .

LETTER XLVIII: USBEK TO RHEDI, AT VENICE

. . . I spent some days in the country near Paris at the house of a man of some note, who delights in having company with him. He has a very amiable wife, who, along with great modesty, possesses what the secluded life they lead stifles in our Persian women, a charming gaiety.

Stranger as I was, I had nothing better to do than to study the crowd of people who came and went without ceasing, affording me a constant change of subject for contemplation. I noticed at once one man, whose simplicity pleased me; I allied myself with him, and he with me, in such a manner that we were always together.

One day, as we were talking quietly in a large company, leaving the general conversation to the others, I said, "You will perhaps find in me more inquisitiveness than good manners; but I beg you to let me ask some questions, for I am wearied to death doing nothing, and of living with people with whom I have nothing in common. My thoughts have been busy these two days; there is not one among these men who has not put me to the torture two hundred times; in a thousand years I would never understand them; they are more invisible to me than the wives of our great king." "You have only to ask," replied he, "and I will tell you all you desire—the more willingly because I think you a discreet man, who will not abuse my confidence."

"Who is that man," said I, "who has told us so much about the banquets at which he has entertained the great, who is so familiar with your dukes, and who talks so often to your ministers, who, they tell me, are so difficult of access? He ought surely to be a man of quality; but his aspect is so mean that he is hardly an honour to the aristocracy; and, besides, I find him deficient in education. I am a stranger; but it seems to me that there is, generally speaking, a certain tone of good breeding common to all nations, and I do not find it in him. Can it be that your upper classes are not so well trained as those of other nations?" "That man," answered he, laughing, "is a farmer-general; he is as much above others in wealth, as he is inferior to us all by birth. He might have the best people in Paris at his table, if he could make up his mind never to eat in his own house. He is very impertinent, as you see; but he excels in his cook, and is not ungrateful, for you heard how he praised him today."

"And that big man dressed in black," said I, "whom that lady has placed next her? How comes he to wear a dress so solemn, with so jaunty an air, and such a florid complexion? He smiles benignly when he is addressed; his attire is more modest, but not less carefully adjusted than that of your women." "That," answered he, "is a preacher, and, which is worse, a confessor. Such as he is, he knows more of their own affairs than the husbands; he is acquainted with the women's weak side, and they also know his." "Ha!" cried I, "he talks forever of something he calls Grace?" "No, not always," was the reply; "in the ear of a pretty woman he speaks more willingly of the Fall: in public, he is a son of thunder; in private, as gentle as a lamb." "It seems to me," said I, "that he receives much attention, and is held in great respect."

"In great respect! Why! he is a necessity; he is the sweetener of solitude; then there are little lessons, officious cares, set visits; he cures a headache better than any man in the world; he is incomparable."

"But, if I may trouble you again, tell me who that ill-dressed person is opposite us? He makes occasional grimaces, and does not speak like the others; and without wit enough to talk, he talks that he may have wit." "That," answered he, "is a poet, the grotesquest of human kind. These sort of people declare that they

are born what they are; and, I may add, what they
will be all their lives, namely, almost always, the most
ridiculous of men; and so nobody spares them; contempt is cast upon them from every quarter. Hunger
has driven that one into this house. He is well received
by its master and mistress, as their good nature and
courtesy are always the same to everybody. He wrote
their epithalamium when they were married, and it is
the best thing he has done, for the marriage has been
as fortunate as he prophesied it would be.

"You will not believe, perhaps," added he, "prepos-
sessed as you are in favour of the East, that there are
among us happy marriages, and wives whose virtue is
a sufficient guard. This couple, here, enjoy untroubled
peace; everybody loves and esteems them; only one
thing is amiss: in their good nature they receive all
kinds of people, which makes the company at their
house sometimes not altogether unexceptionable. I,
of course, have nothing to say against it; we must live
with people as we find them; those who are said to be
well bred are often only those who are exquisite in
their vices; and perhaps it is with them as with poisons,
the more subtle, the more dangerous."

"And that old man," I whispered, "who looks so
morose? I took him at first for a foreigner; because, in
addition to being dressed differently from the rest,
he condemns everything that is done in France, and
disapproves of your government." "He is an old soldier," said he, "who makes himself memorable to all
his hearers by the tedious story of his exploits. He cannot endure the thought that France has gained any
battles without him, nor hear a siege bragged of at
which he did not mount the breach. He believes himself so essential to our history that he imagines it came
to an end when he retired; some wounds he has re-

ceived mean, simply, the dissolution of the monarchy; and, unlike the philosophers who maintain that enjoyment is only in the present, and that the past is as if it had not been, he, on the contrary, delights in nothing but the past, and exists only in his old campaigns; he breathes the air of the age that has gone by, just as heroes ought to live in that which is to come." "But why," I asked, "has he quitted the service?" "He has not quitted it, but it has quitted him. He has been employed in a small post, where he will retail his adventures for the rest of his days; but he will never get any further; the path of honour is closed to him." "And why?" asked I. "It is a maxim in France," replied he, "never to advance officers whose patience has been worn out as subalterns; we look upon them as men whose minds have been narrowed by detail; and who, through a constant application to small things, are become incapable of great ones." . . .

A moment after, curiosity again seized me, and I said, "I promise not to ask another question if you will only answer this one. Who is that tall young man who wears his own hair, and has more impertinence than wit? How comes it that he speaks louder than the others, and is so charmed with himself for being in the world?" "That is a great lady-killer," he replied. With these words some people entered, others left, and all rose. Someone came to speak to my acquaintance, and I remained in my ignorance. But shortly after, I know not by what chance, the young man in question found himself beside me, and began to talk. "It is fine weather," he said. "Will you take a turn with me in the garden?" I replied as civilly as I could, and we went out together. "I have come to the country," said he, "to please the mistress of the house, with whom I am not on the worst of terms. There is a certain woman in the world who will be rather out of humour; but what can one do? I visit the finest women in Paris; but I do not confine my attentions to one; they have plenty to do to look after me, for, between you and me, I am a sad dog." "In that case, sir," said I, "you doubtless have some office or employment which prevents you from waiting on them more assiduously?" "No, sir; I have no other business than to provoke husbands, and drive fathers to despair; I delight in alarming a woman who thinks me hers, and in bringing her within an ace of losing me. A set of us young fellows divide up Paris among us in this pursuit, and keep it wondering at everything we do." "From what I understand," said I, "you make more stir than the most valorous warrior, and are more regarded than a grave magistrate. If you were in Persia, you would not enjoy all these advantages; you would be held fitter to guard our women than to please them." The blood mounted to my face; and I believe, had I gone on speaking, I could not have refrained from affronting him.

What say you to a country where such people are tolerated, and where a man who follows such a profession is allowed to live? Where faithlessness, treachery, rape, deceit, and injustice lead to distinction? Where a man is esteemed because he has bereaved a father of his daughter, a husband of his wife, and distresses the happiest and purest homes? Happy the children of Hali who protect their families from outrage and seduction! Heaven's light is not purer than the fire that burns in the hearts of our wives; our daughters think only with dread of the day when they will be deprived of that purity, in virtue of which they rank with the angels and the spiritual powers. My beloved land, on which the morning sun looks first, thou art unsoiled by those horrible crimes which compel that star to hide his beams as he approaches the dark West!

Paris, the 5th of the moon of Rhamazan, 1713.

LETTER CXXXIII: RICA TO ———

The other day I visited a great library in a convent of dervishes, to whose care it has been entrusted, and who are obliged to admit all comers at certain hours.

On entering I saw a grave-looking man, who walked up and down in the midst of a prodigious number of volumes which surrounded him. I approached him, and asked him to tell me what books those were which I saw better bound than others. "Sir," he replied, "I live here in a strange land, where I know no one. Many people ask me similar questions; but you can easily understand how I cannot read all these books to satisfy them; my librarian will tell you all you wish, for he employs himself night and day in deciphering all you see here; he is a good-for-nothing, and is a great expense to us, because he does no work for the convent. But I hear the refectory bell. Those who, like me, are at the head of a community, ought to be foremost in all its exercises." With that, the monk pushed me out, shut the door, and vanished from my sight as if he would have flown.

Paris, the 21st of the moon of Rhamazan, 1719.

LETTER CXXXVIII: RICA TO IBBEN, AT SMYRNA

Ministers succeed and destroy each other here like the seasons; during three years I have seen the financial system change four times. Today taxes are levied in Turkey and Persia as they were levied by the founders of these empires; a state of affairs very different from that which exists here. It is true that we do not set about it so intelligently as the people of the west. We imagine that there is no more difference between the administration of the revenues of a prince and the fortune of a private person, than there is between counting a hundred thousand tomans and counting only a hundred; but the matter is very much more delicate and mysterious. It requires the greatest geniuses to work night and day, inventing endless new schemes with all the pains of travail; they must listen to the advice of a multitude of people, who, unasked, meddle in their affairs; they have to retire and live shut up in closets inaccessible to the great, and worshipped by the small; they must always have their heads full of important secrets, miraculous plans, and new systems; and, being absorbed in thought, it behoves them to be deprived of the use of speech, and sometimes even of the ability to be polite.

No sooner had the late king died, than they thought of setting up a new administration. They felt that things were in a bad way; but knew not how to bring about a better state. They did not believe in the unlimited authority of the preceding ministers; they wished the power to be divided. For that purpose five or six councils were created, and that ministry was perhaps the wisest of all those which have governed France; it did not last long, and neither did the good which it brought to pass.

France, at the death of the late king, was a body overcome by a thousand disorders: N——[1] took the knife in hand, cut away the useless flesh, and applied some local remedies. But there always remained an

[1] The duc de Noailles. [All notes are C.B.'s.]

internal disease. A stranger came who undertook its cure.[2] After many violent remedies, he imagined he had put it into good condition, whereas it had only become unhealthily stout.

All who were rich six months ago are now paupers, and those who lacked bread are rolling in wealth. These two extremities never before approached so near. This foreigner has turned the state as an old-clothes man turns a coat; he causes that to appear uppermost which was under, and that which was above he places beneath. What unexpected fortunes, incredible even to those who made them! God creates men out of nothing with no greater expedition. How many valets are now waited on by their fellows, and may tomorrow be served by their former masters!

The oddest things happen as a result of all this. Lacqueys, who made their fortune in the last reign, brag today of their birth: they avenge themselves upon those who have just doffed their livery in a certain street,[3] for all the contempt poured out upon themselves six months before; they cry with all their might, "The nobility is ruined! What a chaotic condition the state is in! What confusion of ranks! Only nameless people now make fortunes!" And these nameless ones, you may be sure, will take their revenge on those who come after them; in thirty years as people of quality they will make sufficient noise in the world.

Paris, the 1st of the moon of Zilcade, 1720.

Trans. John Davidson (London: Routledge, 1924).

[2] John Law, the Scottish financier, responsible for the orgy of speculation known as the Mississippi Bubble (1717-1720).

[3] The rue Quincampoix, at that time the rendezvous of stockbrokers.

❖ ❖ ❖

A Pseudo-Chinese Stick
to Beat with

[FROM *The Citizen of the World*]

OLIVER GOLDSMITH

1762

LETTER XCVIII: FROM LIEN CHI ALTANGI TO FUM HOAM, FIRST PRESIDENT OF THE CEREMONIAL ACADEMY AT PEKIN, IN CHINA

I had some intentions lately of going to visit Bedlam, the place where those who go mad are confined. I went to wait upon the man in black to be my conductor; but I found him preparing to go to Westminster Hall, where the English hold their courts of justice. It gave me some surprise to find my friend engaged in a law-suit, but more so when he informed me that it had been depending for several years. "How is it possible," cried I, "for a man who knows the world to go to law? I am well acquainted with the courts of justice in China; they resemble rat traps, every one of them— nothing more easy than to get in, but to get out again is attended with some difficulty, and more cunning than rats are generally found to possess."

"Faith," replied my friend, "I should not have gone to law but that I was assured of success before I began; things were presented to me in so alluring a light that

I thought by barely declaring myself a candidate for the prize I had nothing more to do than to enjoy the fruits of the victory. Thus have I been upon the eve of an imaginary triumph every term these ten years— have travelled forward with victory ever in my view, but ever out of reach; however, at present, I fancy we have hampered our antagonist in such a manner that, without some unforeseen demur, we shall this day lay him fairly on his back."

"If things be so situated," said I, "I do not care if I attend you to the courts, and partake in the pleasure of your success. But prithee," continued I, as we set forward, "what reasons have you to think an affair at last concluded which has given you so many former disappointments?" "My lawyer tells me," returned he, "that I have Salkeld and Ventris strong in my favour, and that there are no less than fifteen cases in point." "I understand," said I: "those are two of your judges who have already declared their opinions." "Pardon me," replied my friend, "Salkeld and Ventris are lawyers who, some hundred years ago, gave their opinions on cases similar to mine; these opinions which make for me my lawyer is to cite, and those opinions which look another way are cited by the lawyer employed by my antagonist; as I observed, I have Salkeld and Ventris for me, he has Coke and Hale for him; and he that has most opinions is most likely to carry his cause." "But where is the necessity," cried I, "of prolonging a suit by citing the opinions and reports of others, since the same good sense which determined lawyers in former ages may serve to guide your judges at this day? They at that time gave their opinions only from the light of reason; your judges have the same light at present to direct them; let me even add, a greater, as in former ages there were many prejudices from which the present is happily free. If arguing from authorities be exploded from every other branch of learning, why should it be particularly adhered to in this? I plainly foresee how such a method of investigation must embarrass every suit, and even perplex the student; ceremonies will be multiplied, formalities must increase, and more time will thus be spent in learning the arts of litigation than in the discovery of right."

"I see," cries my friend, "that you are for a speedy administration of justice; but all the world will grant that the more time that is taken up in considering any subject, the better it will be understood. Besides, it is the boast of an Englishman that his property is secure, and all the world will grant that a deliberate administration of justice is the best way to secure his property. Why have we so many lawyers but to secure our property? why so many formalities but to secure our property? Not less than one hundred thousand families live in opulence, elegance, and ease merely by securing our property."

"To embarrass justice," returned I, "by a multiplicity of laws, or to hazard it by a confidence in our judges, are, I grant, the opposite rocks on which legislative wisdom has ever split: in one case the client resembles that emperor who is said to have been suffocated with the bedclothes which were only designed to keep him warm; in the other, to that town which let the enemy take possession of its walls, in order to show the world how little they depended upon aught but courage for safety. But, bless me! what numbers do I see here, all in black—how is it possible that half this multitude find employment?" "Nothing so easily conceived," returned my companion; "they live by watching each other. For instance, the catchpole watches the man in debt, the attorney watches the catchpole, the counsellor watches the attorney, the solicitor the counsellor, and all find sufficient employment." "I conceive you," interrupted I; "they watch each other, but it is the client that pays them all for watching. It puts me in mind of a Chinese fable, which is entitled 'Five Animals at a Meal.'

"A grasshopper filled with dew was merrily singing under a shade; a whangam, that eats grasshoppers, had marked it for its prey, and was just stretching forth to devour it; a serpent, that had for a long time fed only on whangams, was coiled up to fasten on the whangam; a yellow bird was just upon the wing to dart upon the serpent; a hawk had just stooped from above to seize the yellow bird; all were intent on their prey, and unmindful of their danger; so the whangam ate the grasshopper, the serpent ate the whangam, the yellow bird the serpent, and the hawk the yellow bird; when, sousing from on high, a vulture gobbled up the hawk, grasshopper, whangam, and all in a moment."

I had scarce finished my fable when the lawyer came to inform my friend that his cause was put off till another term; that money was wanted to retain, and that all the world was of opinion that the very next hearing would bring him off victorious. "If so, then," cries my friend, "I believe it will be my wisest way to continue the cause for another term; and, in the meantime, my friend here and I will go and see Bedlam." Adieu.

From *The Works of Oliver Goldsmith*, ed. Peter Cunningham, Vol. II (New York: Harper & Brothers, 1881).

❖ ❖ ❖

An Emperor in Love

[FROM *Berenice*]

JEAN RACINE

1670

BERENICE

Leave me, I say! you cannot keep me back,
I must speak with him. So, Lord, you are here!
Well, is it true that Titus casts me off?
That we must part, that Titus orders it?

TITUS

Lady, have pity on a wretched Prince.
We must not here give way to tenderness;
I have sufficient bitterness at heart
Without your tears to torture me still more.
Recall that heart, which many times of old
Showed me my duty; for the time has come;
But by your love, look simply at my duty
And fortify my heart against yourself,
And help me overcome my love for you.
Duty demands that we must separate.

BERENICE

You tell me this! I felt sure that you loved me!
My soul that loved you only lived for you.
Were you then ignorant of your Roman laws
When for the first time I confessed my love?

Why did you not, then, say, "Oh, wretched Queen,
There is no hope! Why pledge your love to me?
Give not your heart to one who cannot take it."
But no, you took it, but to fling it back,
When that poor heart was living but for you.
Full twenty times they have conspired against us:
Then was the time—why not have cast me then?
There were a thousand things against me then
That might have helped console me in my grief.
I could have blamed your Father, all the Romans,
The Senate and the Empire, all the world,
Rather than this dear hand.
I should not then have had this cruel blow,
Even when I hoped to be most happy here.
Here, when your love can do all that it wishes
When Rome is silent and your Father dead
And all the world is bowing at your feet—
When I have nothing more to fear—then you—
You spurn me.

TITUS

It was myself who thus destroyed myself,
I was content to live, to let myself
Be charmed; my heart would never search the future
For what might one day disunite us two.
I willed that nothing should o'er come my wishes.
Examined nothing, hoped the impossible;
Perhaps for death rather than these farewells.
The very obstacles increased my love.
And Empire spoke, but glory had not spoken
As yet, within my heart, in the clear tone
With which it stirs the hearts of Emperors.
I know the torments that this parting brings,
I know too well I cannot live without you.

But this is not a question now of living;
I have to reign.

BERENICE

Then reign, harsh King, and be content with glory.
I will not vex you. No; I only waited
Before I would believe that those same lips
After a thousand oaths of love for me,
Would order me away forevermore.
I wished to hear you say it in this place.
Now nothing more. Good-bye forever, then.
Forever, Sir, it is a cruel word
When one's in love.
A month will come, a year will come, and we—
We shall be parted by a world of seas.
How shall we suffer when the day begins
And the sun climbs the sky and then declines,
And Titus will not see his Berenice.
And all day long she will not look on Titus!
Perhaps you will not feel those days so long;
They may be long for me, too short for you.

TITUS

Lady, I shall not live for many days;
I hope that presently news of my death
Will show you that I cannot live without you,
Will make you own, that you were loved indeed.

BERENICE

If that be true, why should we separate?
I do not speak of marriage with you now:
Rome had condemned me not to see you more:
But do you envy me the air you breathe?

TITUS

You can do all things, Lady. Stay, if you wish;
I'll not forbid it; but I feel my weakness;
It would be endless struggle, endless fear,
And endless watching to restrain my steps
From turning towards your beauty all day long.
I cannot speak, my heart forgets itself,
Remembering only that it loves you dearly.

BERENICE

Well, Lord, and what could happen if I stayed?
Would all your Romans rise against me, Lord?

TITUS

Who knows? Suppose they did? Suppose they clam-
    oured?
I should be forced to back my choice by blood;
And if they did not speak and did not rise,
They would expect that some day I should pay them.
What would they not demand for their complaisance?
How can I guard the laws I cannot keep?

BERENICE

You count the tears of Berenice for nothing?

TITUS

That is unjust.

BERENICE

Unjust? For unjust laws, that you can change,
You would condemn yourself to lifelong grief.
You say Rome has her rights. Have you not yours?
And are Rome's interests dearer than our own?
Come, speak!

TITUS

Alas, my Queen, you torture me!

BERENICE

You are the Emperor, Lord, and yet you weep.

TITUS

Yes, Lady, it is true. I weep. I shudder.
When I accepted here the Emperor's purple,
Rome made me swear to maintain all her laws.
I must maintain them. Already many times
Rome has most strictly proved her Emperors;
They have obeyed her orders to the death,
To their sons' deaths. Rome and the glory of Rome
Have won the victory in those Roman hearts;
And I, in leaving you, do as they did,
But think I pass them in austerity.

BERENICE

All things seem easy to your barbarism.
I will not speak again of staying here.
Think you I would have wished, ashamed, despised,
To stay among the mocks of those who hate me?
Do not expect me to break out against you,
But if the gods have pity of my tears,
And if your harsh injustice touches them,
And if before I die I, the sad Queen,
Wish for some bold avenger of my death,
I seek that bold avenger in your heart—
My love, my love that cannot be effaced,
My present grief and my past happiness,
Are the enemies that I will leave you, Lord.
I leave my vengeance unto them. Good-bye.

(Exit)

PAULINUS

Lord, she has gone. Will she then leave the country?

TITUS

Paulinus, follow her. I think she is dying.
Run to her help.

PAULINUS

My Lord, her women will be round her there,
They'll turn her thoughts. Fear not, the worst is over.
Go on, my Lord, the victory is yours:
I know you could not hear her without pity;
I couldn't keep from pity even in seeing her—
But you must take long views, and you must know
That happiness will come from this brief pain:
All the wide world will ring with praise of you.

TITUS

I hate myself! I am a brute! Even Nero
Was not so cruel. Oh, I cannot bear it!
If Berenice should die!
Come, let Rome say what it may.

PAULINUS

What, Lord?

TITUS

I know not what I say.
Excess of trouble overwhelms my spirit.

PAULINUS

Do not be troubled for what Rome will say.
The news that she has gone is spread abroad;
Rome, which was murmuring, is triumphing,

The altars are all smoking in your honour,
And in the streets the crowd, singing your virtues,
Crown all your statues with eternal laurel.

TITUS

Ah, Rome! Ah, Berenice! Unhappy fate,
To be a lover and an Emperor!

Trans. John Masefield, in *Esther and Berenice: Two Plays* (New York: The Macmillan Co., 1922).

❖ ❖ ❖

Honesty at Court

[FROM *The Misanthrope*]

JEAN BAPTISTE POQUELIN DE
MOLIÈRE

1666

ORONTE (*to Alceste*)

    The servants told me at the door
That Eliante and Célimène were out,
But when I heard, dear Sir, that you were about,
I came to say, without exaggeration,
That I hold you in the vastest admiration,
And that it's always been my dearest desire
To be the friend of one I so admire.
I hope to see my love of merit requited,
And you and I in friendship's bond united.
I'm sure you won't refuse—if I may be frank—
A friend of my devotedness—and rank.

(During this speech of Oronte's, Alceste is abstracted, and seems unaware that he is being spoken to. He only breaks off his reverie when Oronte says:)

It was for you, if you please, that my words were in-
    tended.

ALCESTE

For me, Sir?

ORONTE

    Yes, for you. You're not offended?

ALCESTE

By no means, But this much surprises me. . . .
The honor comes most unexpectedly. . . .

ORONTE

My high regard should not astonish you;
The whole world feels the same. It is your due.

ALCESTE

Sir . . .

ORONTE

    Why, in all the State there isn't one
Can match your merits; they shine, Sir, like the sun.

ALCESTE

Sir . . .

ORONTE

    You are higher in my estimation
Than all that's most illustrious in the nation.

ALCESTE

Sir . . .

ORONTE

     If I lie, may heaven strike me dead!
To show you that I mean what I have said,
Permit me, Sir, to embrace you most sincerely,
And swear that I will prize our friendship dearly.
Give me your hand. And now, Sir, if you choose,
We'll make our vows.

ALCESTE

Sir . . .

ORONTE

               What! You refuse?

ALCESTE

Sir, it's a very great honor you extend:
But friendship is a sacred thing, my friend;
It would be profanation to bestow
The name of friend on one you hardly know.
All parts are better played when well-rehearsed;
Let's put off friendship, and get acquainted first.
We may discover it would be unwise
To try to make our natures harmonize.

ORONTE

By heaven! You're sagacious to the core;
This speech has made me admire you even **more**.
Let time, then, bring us closer day by day;
Meanwhile, I shall be yours in every way.
If, for example, there should be anything

You wish at court, I'll mention it to the King.
I have his ear, of course; it's quite well known
That I am much in favor with the throne.
In short, I am your servant. And now, dear friend,
Since you have such fine judgment, I intend
To please you, if I can, with a small sonnet
I wrote not long ago. Please comment on it,
And tell me whether I ought to publish it.

ALCESTE

You must excuse me, Sir; I'm hardly fit
To judge such matters.

ORONTE

Why not?

ALCESTE

I am, I fear,
Inclined to be unfashionably sincere.

ORONTE

Just what I ask; I'd take no satisfaction
In anything but your sincere reaction.
I beg you not to dream of being kind.

ALCESTE

Since you desire it, Sir, I'll speak my mind.

ORONTE

Sonnet. It's a sonnet. . . . *Hope* . . . The poem's addressed
To a lady who wakened hopes within my breast.
Hope . . . this is not the pompous sort of thing,
Just modest little verses, with a tender ring.

ALCESTE

Well, we shall see.

ORONTE

   Hope . . . I'm anxious to hear
Whether the style seems properly smooth and clear,
And whether the choice of words is good or bad.

ALCESTE

We'll see, we'll see.

ORONTE

   Perhaps I ought to add
That it took me only a quarter-hour to write it.

ALCESTE

The time's irrelevant, Sir: kindly recite it.

ORONTE (*reading*)

Hope comforts us awhile, 'tis true,
Lulling our cares with careless laughter,
And yet such joy is full of rue,
My Phyllis, if nothing follows after.

PHILINTE

I'm charmed by this already; the style's delightful.

ALCESTE (*sotto voce, to Philinte*)

How can you say that? Why, the thing is frightful.

ORONTE

Your fair face smiled on me awhile,
But was it kindness so to enchant me?

> 'Twould have been fairer not to smile,
> If hope was all you meant to grant me.

PHILINTE

What a clever thought! How handsomely you phrase
it!

ALCESTE (*sotto voce, to Philinte*)

You know the thing is trash. How dare you praise it?

ORONTE

> If it's to be my passion's fate
> Thus everlastingly to wait,
> Then death will come to set me free:
> For death is fairer than the fair;
> Phyllis, to hope is to despair
> When one must hope eternally.

PHILINTE

The close is exquisite—full of feeling and grace.

ALCESTE (*sotto voce, aside*)

Oh, blast the close; you'd better close your face
Before you send your lying soul to hell.

PHILINTE

I can't remember a poem I've liked so well.

ALCESTE (*sotto voce, aside*)

Good Lord!

ORONTE (*to Philinte*)

I fear you're flattering me a bit.

Oh, no!

ALCESTE *(sotto voce, aside)*

What else d'you call it, you hypocrite?

ORONTE *(to Alceste)*

But you, Sir, keep your promise now: don't shrink
From telling me sincerely what you think.

ALCESTE

Sir, these are delicate matters; we all desire
To be told that we've the true poetic fire.
But once, to one whose name I shall not mention,
I said, regarding some verse of his invention,
That gentlemen should rigorously control
That itch to write which often afflicts the soul;
That one should curb the heady inclination
To publicize one's little avocation;
And that in showing off one's works of art
One often plays a very clownish part.

ORONTE

Are you suggesting in a devious way
That I ought not . . .

ALCESTE

Oh, that I do not say.
Further, I told him that no fault is worse
Than that of writing frigid, lifeless verse,
And that the merest whisper of such a shame
Suffices to destroy a man's good name.

ORONTE

D'you mean to say my sonnet's dull and trite?

ALCESTE

I don't say that. But I went on to cite
Numerous cases of once-respected men
Who came to grief by taking up the pen.

ORONTE

And am I like them? Do I write so poorly?

ALCESTE

I don't say that. But I told this person, "Surely
You're under no necessity to compose;
Why you should wish to publish, heaven knows.
There's no excuse for printing tedious rot
Unless one writes for bread, as you do not.
Resist temptation, then, I beg of you;
Conceal your pastimes from the public view;
And don't give up, on any provocation,
Your present high and courtly reputation,
To purchase at a greedy printer's shop
The name of silly author and scribbling fop."
These were the points I tried to make him see.

ORONTE

I sense that they are also aimed at me;
But now—about my sonnet—I'd like to be told . . .

ALCESTE

Frankly, that sonnet should be pigeonholed.
You've chosen the worst models to imitate.
The style's unnatural. Let me illustrate:

For example, *Your fair face smiled on me awhile,*
Followed by, *'Twould have been fairer not to smile!*
Or this: *Such joy is full of rue;*
Or this: *For death is fairer than the fair:*
Or, *Phyllis, to hope is to despair*
   When one must hope eternally!
This artificial style, that's all the fashion,
Has neither taste, nor honesty, nor passion;
It's nothing but a sort of wordy play,
And nature never spoke in such a way.
What, in this shallow age, is not debased?
Our fathers, though less refined, had better taste;
I'd barter all that men admire today
For one old love-song I shall try to say:

   If the King had given me for my own
   Paris, his citadel,
   And I for that must leave alone
   Her whom I love so well,
   I'd say then to the Crown,
   Take back your glittering town;
   My darling is more fair, I swear,
   My darling is more fair.

The rhyme's not rich, the style is rough and old,
But don't you see that it's the purest gold
Beside the tinsel nonsense now preferred,
And that there's passion in its every word?

   If the King had given me for my own
   Paris, his citadel,
   And I for that must leave alone
   Her whom I love so well,
   I'd say then to the Crown,
   Take back your glittering town;
   My darling is more fair, I swear,
   My darling is more fair.

There speaks a loving heart. (*To Philinte*) You're
     laughing, eh?
Laugh on, my precious wit. Whatever you say,
I hold that song's worth all the bibelots
That people hail today with ah's and oh's.

ORONTE

And I maintain my sonnet's very good.

ALCESTE

It's not at all surprising that you should.
You have your reasons; permit me to have mine
For thinking that you cannot write a line.

ORONTE

Others have praised my sonnet to the skies.

ALCESTE

I lack their art of telling pleasant lies.

ORONTE

You seem to think you've got no end of wit.

ALCESTE

To praise your verse, I'd need still more of it.

ORONTE

I'm not in need of your approval, Sir.

ALCESTE

That's good; you couldn't have it if you were.

ORONTE

Come now, I'll lend you the subject of my sonnet,
I'd like to see you try to improve upon it.

ALCESTE

I might, by chance, write something just as shoddy;
But then I wouldn't show it to everybody.

ORONTE

You're most opinionated and conceited.

ALCESTE

Go find your flatterers, and be better treated.

ORONTE

Look here, my little fellow, pray watch your tone.

ALCESTE

My great big fellow, you'd better watch your own.

PHILINTE *(stepping between them)*

Oh, please, please, gentlemen! This will never do.

ORONTE

The fault is mine, and I leave the field to you.
I am your servant, Sir, in every way.

ALCESTE

And I, Sir, am your most abject valet.

❖ ❖ ❖

*(In a later scene, Philinte explains how the matter
ended—with no duel.)*

PHILINTE

Madam, he acted like a stubborn child;
I thought they never would be reconciled;
In vain we reasoned, threatened, and appealed;

He stood his ground and simply would not yield.
The Marshals, I feel sure, have never heard
An argument so splendidly absurd.
"No, gentlemen," said he, "I'll not retract.
His verse is bad: extremely bad, in fact.
Surely it does the man no harm to know it.
Does it disgrace him, not to be a poet?
A gentleman may be respected still,
Whether he writes a sonnet well or ill.
That I dislike his verse should not offend him;
In all that touches honor, I commend him;
He's noble, brave, and virtuous—but I fear
He can't in truth be called a sonneteer.
I'll gladly praise his wardrobe; I'll endorse
His dancing, or the way he sits a horse;
But, gentlemen, I cannot praise his rhyme.
In fact, it ought to be a capital crime
For anyone so sadly unendowed
To write a sonnet, and read the thing aloud."
At length he fell into a gentler mood
And, striking a concessive attitude,
He paid Oronte the following courtesies:
"Sir, I regret that I'm so hard to please,
And I'm profoundly sorry that your lyric
Failed to provoke me to a panegyric."
After these curious words, the two embraced,
And then the hearing was adjourned—in haste.

Trans. Richard Wilbur (New York: Harcourt, Brace & Co., 1955).

❖ ❖ ❖

Marriage à la Mode

[FROM *The Way of the World*]

WILLIAM CONGREVE

1700

MIRABELL: "Like Daphne she, as lovely and as coy." Do you lock yourself up from me, to make my search more curious? Or is this pretty artifice contrived to signify that here the chase must end, and my pursuits be crowned? For you can fly no further.

MILLAMANT: Vanity! no—I'll fly, and be followed to the last moment. Though I am upon the very verge of matrimony, I expect you should solicit me as much as if I were wavering at the grate of a monastery, with one foot over the threshold. I'll be solicited to the very last, nay, and afterwards.

MIRABELL: What, after the last?

MILLAMANT: Oh, I should think I was poor and had nothing to bestow, if I were reduced to an inglorious ease, and freed from the agreeable fatigues of solicitations.

MIRABELL: But do not you know, that when favours are conferred upon instant and tedious solicitation, that they diminish in their value, and that both the giver loses the grace, and the receiver lessens his pleasure?

MILLAMANT: It may be in things of common application; but never sure in love. Oh, I hate a lover that can dare to think he draws a moment's air, independent of the bounty of his mistress. There is not so impudent a thing in nature, as the saucy look of an assured man, confident of success. The pedantic arrogance of a very husband has not so pragmatical an air. Ah! I'll never marry, unless I am first made sure of my will and pleasure.

MIRABELL: Would you have 'em both before marriage? Or will you be contented with the first now, and stay for the other till after grace?

MILLAMANT: Ah! don't be impertinent. My dear liberty, shall I leave thee? My faithful solitude, my darling contemplation, must I bid you then adieu? Ay-h adieu —my morning thoughts, agreeable wakings, indolent slumbers, ye *douceurs,* ye *sommeils du matin,* adieu?— I can't do't, 'tis more than impossible—positively, Mirabell, I'll lie abed in a morning as long as I please.

MIRABELL: Then I'll get up in a morning as early as I please.

MILLAMANT: Ah! idle creature, get up when you will —and d'ye hear, I won't be called names after I'm married; positively I won't be called names.

MIRABELL: Names!

MILLAMANT: Ay, as wife, spouse, my dear, joy, jewel, love, sweetheart, and the rest of that nauseous cant, in which men and their wives are so fulsomely familiar— I shall never bear that—good Mirabell, don't let us be familiar or fond, nor kiss before folks, like my Lady Fadler and Sir Francis: nor go to Hyde-park together the first Sunday in a new chariot, to provoke eyes and whispers, and then never to be seen there together again; as if we were proud of one another the first week, and ashamed of one another ever after. Let us never visit together, nor go to a play together; but let us be very strange and well bred: let us be as strange as if we had been married a great while; and as well bred as if we were not married at all.

MIRABELL: Have you any more conditions to offer? Hitherto your demands are pretty reasonable.

MILLAMANT: Trifles! As liberty to pay and receive visits to and from whom I please; to write and receive letters, without interrogatories or wry faces on your part; to wear what I please; and choose conversation with regard only to my own taste; to have no obligation upon me to converse with wits that I don't like, because they are your acquaintance; or to be intimate with fools, because they may be your relations. Come to dinner when I please; dine in my dressing-room when I'm out of humour, without giving a reason. To have my closet inviolate; to be sole empress of my tea-table, which you must never presume to approach without first asking leave. And lastly, wherever I am, you shall always knock at the door before you come in. These articles subscribed, if I continue to endure you a little longer, I may by degrees dwindle into a wife.

From *The Works of Mr. William Congreve*, Vol. III (London: Tonson, 1730).

❖ ❖ ❖

A Soliloquy That Foreshadows the French Revolution

[FROM *The Marriage of Figaro*]

PIERRE AUGUSTIN CARON DE BEAUMARCHAIS

1778

FIGARO (*Alone, walking in the darkness, speaks in sombre tones*): . . . No, Monsieur le Comte, you shan't have her! You shan't have her. Because you are a great noble, you think you are a great genius! Nobility, a fortune, a rank, appointments to office: all this makes a man so proud! What did you do to earn all this? You took the trouble to get born—nothing more. Moreover, you're really a pretty ordinary fellow! While as for me, lost in the crowd, I've had to use more knowledge, more brains, just to keep alive than your likes have had to spend on governing Spain and the Empire for a century. And you want to contest with me— Someone's coming, it's she—no, nobody— The night is black as the devil, and here I am plying the silly trade of husband, though I'm only half a husband. (*He sits down on a bench*) Is there anything stranger than my fate? Son of I don't know whom, kidnapped by robbers, brought up in their ways, I got disgusted with them, and tried to follow an honest career; and everywhere I met with rebuffs. I learned chemistry,

pharmacy, surgery, and all the credit of a great noble
barely succeeded in putting a veterinary's lancet in my
hand! Tired of making sick beasts sadder, I turned to
a very different trade, and threw myself into the life
of the theatre. What a stone I hung around my neck
that time! I sketched a comedy about harem life; being a Spanish writer, I assumed I could be irreverent
towards Mohammed without any scruples: but at once
an Envoy from somewhere complained that my verses
offended the Sublime Porte, Persia, a part of India, all
Egypt, the kingdoms of Barca, Tripoli, Tunis, Algiers
and Morocco; and there was my comedy burned, to
please some Mohammedan princes not one of whom I
suppose knows how to read, and who keep cursing
away at us all as "Christian dogs"—not being able to
degrade the human spirit, they take revenge by abusing it. A question came up about the nature of wealth:
and since it isn't necessary to own a thing to reason
about it, I, penniless, wrote on the value of money and
the *produit net:* at once I saw, from the inside of a
cab, the lowered drawbridge of a fortress prison at
the entrance to which I left hope and liberty! (*He gets
up*) How I'd love to get one of these powerful men
of four days' standing, so ready with such penalties,
just after some good disgrace had fermented his pride!
I'd tell him—that printed foolishness has no importance, except for those who try to suppress it; that
without freedom to blame, there can be no flattering
eulogies; and that only little men fear little writings.
(*He sits down again*) Tired of feeding an obscure
boarder, they let me out of prison. I was told that
during my economic retreat, there had been established
in Madrid a system of free sale of products which included even the press. To profit by this sweet liberty,
I announced a periodical, and, thinking to offend no

one, I called it *The Useless Journal*. Whew! I had a thousand poor devils of scribblers rise up against me: I was suppressed; and there I was once more among the unemployed. I began almost to despair; I was thought of for a government post, but unfortunately I was qualified for it. They needed an accountant: a dancer got the job. All that was left for me was stealing; I set up a faro game; and now, good folk, I supped in society, and people known as *comme il faut* opened their houses to me politely, on condition they kept three-quarters of the profits. I might have gone pretty far, for I was beginning to understand that to gain wealth it is better to have know-how [*savoir-faire*] than to have knowledge [*savoir*]. But as everybody about me stole, while insisting I stay honest, I should have failed once more. I should have left this world and put a watery grave between me and it, but a kindly God recalled me to my first condition. I took up once more my barber's case and my English leather strop. I travelled about, shaving, from town to town, living at last a carefree life.

From *Le Mariage de Figaro* (Paris: Lemerre, 1872); trans. C.B.

❖ ❖ ❖

The Lion, the Wolf, and the Fox

[Fable III, Book VIII]

JEAN DE LA FONTAINE

1673

A careworn lion, all bones and pained in each paw,
Craved a cure lest his disabilities progress.
(Better not gainsay a king or you are an outlaw.)
    In this case, to relieve his distress
The king had practitioners of any description
Come to attend him, from every direction,
Till all varieties of cure in the world had been brought
    To afford him the one that he sought.
But the fox paid no heed and sat at home, safely
    denned.
In paying court, the wolf said the fox had meant to
    offend,
Slandering the poor beast and creating a stir.
Plucked forth in embarrassment, the fox dared not
    demur,
So at last drew near and said what he had to say,
Aware that it was the wolf who was the slanderer.
He pled, "Sire, though I have been called malingerer
    As one the wolf wished to betray,
    My service to you has been delayed
    Since vows for you had to be paid,
Involving a hard journey day after day.
    Wherever my loyalty led,

I told surgeons and sage that you barely can prick
              up an ear
Lest your vestige of vigor should fail you some night.
              They said the blood cools from year to year,
              And since you lack heat through an over-
                    sight,
Wrap a live wolf's skin about the flesh you'd redeem—
              At the height of its natural heat—
              That should compensate, it would seem.
              For energy years can deplete.
              To make a long story short,
              Try a wolfskin dressing gown."
              The king welcomed the report;
              The wolf was flayed, torn up, choked down.
       The king devoured his former escort
              And found the skin a constant comfort.

Courtiers, don't be slanderers; better turn a deaf ear.
Why must one compromise a fair career?
Evil hurries home faster than good we have done.
This is sure; slanders are laid at the slanderer's door.
              Courts are places, furthermore,
              Where nothing is forgiven one.

From *The Fables of La Fontaine*, trans. Marianne Moore (New York: The Viking Press, 1954).

❖ ❖ ❖

The Man and the Flea

[Fable XLIX]

JOHN GAY

1727

Whether on earth, in air, or main,
Sure ev'ry thing alive is vain!
  Does not the hawk all fowls survey,
As destin'd only for his prey?
And do not tyrants, prouder things,
Think men were born for slaves to kings?
  When the crab views the pearly strands,
Or *Tagus,* bright with golden sands,
Or crawles beside the coral grove,
And hears the ocean roll above;
Nature is too profuse, says he,
Who gave all these to pleasure me!
  When bord'ring pinks and roses bloom,
And ev'ry garden breathes perfume,
When peaches glow with sunny dyes,
Like *Laura's* cheek, when blushes rise;
When with huge figs the branches bend;
When clusters from the vine depend;
The snail looks round on flow'r and tree,
And cries, all these were made for me!
  What dignity's in human nature,
Says Man, the most conceited creature,
As from a cliff he cast his eye,

And view'd the sea and arched sky!
The sun was sunk beneath the main,
The moon, and all the starry train
Hung the vast vault of heav'n. The Man
His contemplation thus began.

When I behold this glorious show,
And the wide wat'ry world below,
The scaly people of the main,
The beasts that range the wood or plain,
The wing'd inhabitants of air,
The day, the night, the various year,
And know all these by heav'n design'd
As gifts to pleasure human kind,
I cannot raise my worth too high;
Of what vast consequence am I!

Not of th' importance you suppose,
Replies a Flea upon his nose:
Be humble, learn thyself to scan;
Know, pride was never made for man.
'Tis vanity that swells thy mind.
What, heav'n and earth for thee design'd!
For thee! made only for our need;
That more important Fleas might feed.

From *Poetical Works*, ed. G. C. Faber (London: Oxford University Press, 1926).

Elegies

ANDRÉ MARIE DE CHÉNIER

About 1785-90

I

Every man has his sorrows; yet each still
Hides under a calm forehead his own will.
Each pities but himself. Each in his grief
Envies his neighbor: he too seeks a relief;
For one man's pain is of no other known:
They hide their sorrows as he hides his own;
And each, with tears and aching heart, can sigh:
All other men are happy, but not I.
They are unhappy all. They, desolate,
Cry against heaven and bid heaven change their fate.
Their fate is changed; they soon, with fresh tears, know
They have but changed one for another woe.

II

A white nymph wandering in the woods by night
Spies a swift satyr, and pretends a flight;
She runs, and, running, feigns to call him back!
The goat-foot, following on her flying track,
Falls down and flounders in the stagnant pool:
Whereat they, while he whimpers, mock the fool.

III

Well, I would have it so. I should have known
How many times I made her will my own.

For once, at least, I should have let her be,
And waited, till I made her come to me.
No. I forget what fretful cries last night
Drove me to bitter silence and to flight;
This morning, O weak heart, I long
To have her back, yet do her pride no wrong.

I fly to her, take all her wrongs, but she
Whom I would pardon will not pardon me.
I it is who am false, unjust, and seek
To show my horrid strength where she is weak.
And floods and tempest come, and tears that flow
Obediently, as she would have them go.
And I, to have some peace, must own defeat,
Kneel down, and take her pardon at her feet.

Trans. Arthur Symons, in *Knave of Hearts* (New York: Dodd,
Mead & Company, 1913).

❖ ❖ ❖

On Taste and Fashion

[FROM *The Theory of Moral Sentiments*]

ADAM SMITH

1759

Dress and furniture are allowed by all the world to
be entirely under the dominion of custom and fashion.
The influence of those principles, however, is by no
means confined to so narrow a sphere, but extends itself to whatever is in any respect the object of taste,
to music, to poetry, to architecture. The modes of

dress and furniture are continually changing; and that fashion appearing ridiculous today which was admired five years ago, we are experimentally convinced that it owed its vogue chiefly or entirely to custom and fashion. Clothes and furniture are not made of very durable materials. A well-fancied coat is done in a twelve-month, and cannot continue longer to propagate, as the fashion, that form according to which it was made. The modes of furniture change less rapidly than those of dress; because furniture is commonly more durable. In five or six years, however, it generally undergoes an entire revolution, and every man in his own time sees the fashion in this respect change many different ways. The productions of the other arts are much more lasting, and, when happily imagined, may continue to propagate the fashion of their make for a much longer time. A well-contrived building may endure many centuries: a beautiful air may be delivered down, by a sort of tradition, through many successive generations: a well-written poem may last as long as the world: and all of them continue for ages together, to give the vogue to that particular style, to that particular taste or manner, according to which each of them was composed. Few men have an opportunity of seeing in their own times the fashion in any of these arts change very considerably. Few men have so much experience and acquaintance with the different modes which have obtained in remote ages and nations, as to be thoroughly reconciled to them, or to judge with impartiality between them, and what takes place in their own age and country. Few men therefore are willing to allow, that custom or fashion have much influence upon their judgments concerning what is beautiful, or otherwise, in the productions of any of those arts: but imagine, that all the rules, which they think ought to be observed in each of them, are founded upon reason and nature, not upon habit or prejudice. A very little attention, however, may convince them of the contrary, and satisfy them, that the influence of custom and fashion over dress and furniture is not more absolute than over architecture, poetry, and music.

Can any reason, for example, be assigned why the Doric capital should be appropriated to a pillar, whose height is equal to eight diameters; the Ionic volute to one of nine; and the Corinthian foliage to one of ten? The propriety of each of those appropriations can be founded upon nothing but habit and custom. The eye having been used to see a particular proportion, connected with a particular ornament, would be offended if they were not joined together. Each of the five orders has its peculiar ornament, which cannot be changed for any other, without giving offence to all those who know anything of the rules of architecture. According to some architects, indeed, such is the exquisite judgment with which the ancients have assigned to each order its proper ornaments, that no others can be found which are equally suitable. It seems, however, a little difficult to be conceived that these forms, though, no doubt, extremely agreeable, should be the only forms which can suit those proportions, or that there should not be five hundred others, which, antecedent to established custom, would have fitted them equally well. When custom, however, has established particular rules of building, provided they are not absolutely unreasonable, it is absurd to think of altering them for others which are only equally good, or even for others which, in point of elegance and beauty, have naturally some little advantage over them. A man would be ridiculous who should appear in public with a suit of clothes quite different from those which are commonly worn, though the new dress should in itself be ever so graceful or convenient. And there seems to be an absurdity of the same kind in ornamenting a house after a quite different manner from that which custom and fashion have prescribed; though the new ornaments should in themselves be somewhat superior to the common ones.

According to the ancient rhetoricians, a certain measure or verse was by nature appropriated to each particular species of writing, as being naturally expressive of that character, sentiment, or passion which ought to predominate in it. One verse, they said was fit for grave, and another for gay works, which could not, they thought, be interchanged without the greatest impropriety. The experience of modern times, however, seems to contradict this principle, though in itself it would appear to be extremely probable. What is the burlesque verse in English, is the heroic verse in French. The tragedies of Racine and the Henriad of Voltaire, are nearly in the same verse with,

Let me have your advice in a weighty affair.

The burlesque verse in French, on the contrary, is pretty much the same with the heroic verse of ten syllables in English. Custom has made the one nation associate the ideas of gravity, sublimity, and seriousness, to that measure which the other has connected with whatever is gay, flippant, and ludicrous. Nothing would appear more absurd in English, than a tragedy written in the alexandrine verses of the French; or in French, than a work of the same kind in verses of ten syllables.

(Philadelphia: Anthony Finley, 1817.)

❖ ❖ ❖

Augustan Criticism

[FROM *The Spectator*]

JOSEPH ADDISON

1711

The English writers of tragedy are possessed with a notion that when they represent a virtuous or innocent person in distress, they ought not to leave him till they have delivered him out of his troubles, or made him triumph over his enemies. This error they have been led into by a ridiculous doctrine in modern criticism, that they are obliged to an equal distribution of rewards and punishments, and an impartial execution of poetical justice. Who were the first that established this rule I know not; but I am sure it has no foundation in nature, in reason, or in the practice of the ancients. We find that good and evil happen alike to all men on this side the grave; and as the principal design of tragedy is to raise commiseration and terror in the minds of the audience, we shall defeat this great end if we always make virtue and innocence happy and successful. Whatever crosses and disappointments a good man suffers in the body of the tragedy, they will make but small impression on our minds, when we know that in the last act he is to arrive at the end of his wishes and desires. When we see him engaged in the depth of his afflictions, we are apt to comfort ourselves, because we are sure he will find his way out of them, and that his grief, how great soever it may be at present, will soon terminate in gladness. For this reason the ancient writers of tragedy treated men in their plays, as they are dealt with in the world, by making virtue sometimes happy and sometimes miserable, as they found it in the fable which they made choice of, or as it might affect their audience in the most agreeable manner. Aristotle considers the tragedies that were written in either of these kinds, and observes that those which ended unhappily had always pleased the people, and carried away the prize in the public disputes of the stage, from those that ended happily. Terror and commiseration leave a pleasing anguish in the mind, and fix the audience in such a serious composure of thought, as is much more lasting and delightful than any little transient starts of joy and satisfaction. Accordingly we find that more of our English tragedies have succeeded, in which the favourites of the audience sink under their calamities, than those in which they recover themselves out of them. The best plays of this kind are *The Orphan, Venice Preserved, Alexander the Great, Theodosius, All for Love, Œdipus, Oroonoko, Othello*, etc. *King Lear* is an admirable tragedy of the same kind, as Shakespeare wrote it; but as it is reformed according to the chimerical notion of poetical justice, in my humble opinion it has lost half its beauty. At the same time I must allow that there are very noble tragedies which have been framed upon the other plan, and have ended happily; as indeed most of the good tragedies, which have been written since the starting of the above-mentioned criticism, have taken this turn: as *The Mourning Bride, Tamerlane, Ulysses, Phædra and Hippolitus*, with most of Mr. Dryden's. I must also allow that many of Shakespeare's, and several of the celebrated tragedies

of the same person. His words are as follow: "And hence, perhaps, may be given some reason of that common observation, that men who have a great deal of wit, and prompt memories, have not always the clearest judgment or deepest reason. For wit lying most in the assemblage of ideas, and putting those together with quickness and variety wherein can be found any resemblance or congruity, thereby to make up pleasant pictures, and agreeable visions in the fancy; judgment, on the contrary, lies quite on the other side, in separating carefully one from another ideas wherein can be found the least difference, thereby to avoid being misled by similitude, and by affinity to take one thing for another. This is a way of proceeding quite contrary to metaphor and allusion, wherein, for the most part, lies that entertainment and pleasantry of wit, which strikes so lively on the fancy, and is therefore so acceptable to all people."

This is, I think, the best and most philosophical account that I have ever met with of wit, which generally, though not always, consists in such a resemblance and congruity of ideas as this author mentions. I shall only add to it, by way of explanation, that every resemblance of ideas is not that which we call wit, unless it be such a one that gives delight and surprise to the reader. These two properties seem essential to wit, more particularly the last of them. In order therefore, that the resemblance in the ideas be wit, it is necessary that the ideas should not lie too near one another in the nature of things; for where the likeness is obvious, it gives no surprise. To compare one man's singing to that of another, or to represent the whiteness of any object by that of milk and snow, or the variety of its colours by those of the rainbow, cannot be called wit, unless, besides this obvious resemblance, there be some further congruity discovered in the two ideas, that is capable of giving the reader some surprise. Thus when a poet tells us the bosom of his mistress is as white as snow, there is no wit in the comparison; but when he adds, with a sigh, it is as cold too, it then grows into wit. Every reader's memory may supply him with innumerable instances of the same nature. For this reason the similitudes in heroic poets, who endeavour rather to fill the mind with great conceptions than to divert it with such as are new and surprising, have seldom anything in them that can be called wit. Mr. Locke's account of wit, with this short explanation, comprehends most of the species of wit—as metaphors, similitudes, allegories, enigmas, mottos, parables, fables, dreams, visions, dramatic writings, burlesque, and all the methods of allusion. There are many other species of wit, how remote soever they may appear at first sight from the foregoing description, which upon examination will be found to agree with it.

As true wit generally consists in this resemblance and congruity of ideas, false wit chiefly consists in the resemblance and congruity, sometimes of single letters, as in anagrams, chronograms, lipograms, and acrostics; sometimes of syllables, as in echoes and doggerel rhymes; and sometimes of whole sentences or poems, cast into the figures of eggs, axes, or altars. Nay, some carry the notion of wit so far as to ascribe it even to external mimicry, and to look upon a man as an ingenious person that can resemble the tone, posture, or face of another.

As true wit consists in the resemblance of ideas, and false wit in the resemblance of words, according to the foregoing instances, there is another kind of wit which consists partly in the resemblance of ideas, and partly in the resemblance of words, which for distinction sake

I shall call mixed wit. This kind of wit is that which abounds in Cowley, more than in any other author that ever wrote. Mr. Waller has likewise a great deal of it. Mr. Dryden is very sparing in it. Milton had a genius much above it. Spenser is in the same class with Milton. The Italians, even in their epic poetry, are full of it. Monsieur Boileau, who formed himself upon the ancient poets, has everywhere rejected it with scorn. . . .

Out of the innumerable branches of mixed wit, I shall choose one instance which may be met with in all the writers of this class. The passion of love in its nature has been thought to resemble fire, for which reason the words *fire* and *flame* are made use of to signify love. The witty poets therefore have taken an advantage from the double meaning of the word fire, to make an infinite number of witticisms. Cowley, observing the cold regard of his mistress's eyes, and at the same time their power of producing love in him, considers them as burning-glasses made of ice; and, finding himself able to live in the greatest extremities of love, concludes the torrid zone to be habitable. When his mistress has read his letter written in juice of lemon, by holding it to the fire, he desires her to read it over a second time by love's flame. When she weeps, he wishes it were inward heat that distilled those drops from the limbeck. When she is absent, he is beyond eighty—that is, thirty degrees nearer the Pole than when she is with him. His ambitious love is a fire that naturally mounts upwards; his happy love is the beams of heaven, and his unhappy love flames of hell. When it does not let him sleep, it is a flame that sends up no smoke; when it is opposed by counsel and advice, it is a fire that rages the more by the winds blowing upon it. Upon the dying of a tree in which he had

cut his loves, he observed that his written flames had
burnt up and withered the tree. When he resolves to
give over his passion, he tells us that one burnt like
him forever dreads the fire. His heart is an Ætna, that,
instead of Vulcan's shop, encloses Cupid's forge in it.
His endeavouring to drown his love in wine is throwing oil upon the fire. He would insinuate to his mistress that the fire of love, like that of the sun (which
produces so many living creatures), should not only
warm, but beget. Love, in another place, cooks pleasure at his fire. Sometimes the poet's heart is frozen in
every breast, and sometimes scorched in every eye.
Sometimes he is drowned in tears and burnt in love,
like a ship set on fire in the middle of the sea.

The reader may observe in every one of these instances, that the poet mixes the qualities of fire with
those of love; and, in the same sentence, speaking of
it both as a passion and as real fire, surprises the reader
with those seeming resemblances or contradictions that
make up all the wit in this kind of writing. Mixed wit
is therefore a composition of pun and true wit, and is
more or less perfect as the resemblance lies in the
ideas or in the words. Its foundations are laid partly
in falsehood and partly in truth; reason puts in her
claim for one half of it, and extravagance for the other.
The only province, therefore, for this kind of wit is
epigram, or those little occasional poems that in their
own nature are nothing else but a tissue of epigrams.
I cannot conclude this head of mixed wit without
owning that the admirable poet out of whom I have
taken the examples of it, had as much true wit as any
author that ever writ, and indeed all other talents of
an extraordinary genius. . . .

Bouhours, whom I look upon to be the most penetrating of all the French critics, has taken pains to

show that it is impossible for any thought to be beautiful which is not just, and has not its foundation in the nature of things; that the basis of all wit is truth; and that no thought can be valuable of which good sense is not the ground work. Boileau has endeavoured to inculcate the same notion in several parts of his writings, both in prose and verse. This is that natural way of writing, that beautiful simplicity, which we so much admire in the compositions of the ancients, and which nobody deviates from but those who want strength of genius to make a thought shine in its own natural beauties. Poets who want this strength of genius to give that majestic simplicity to nature which we so much admire in the works of the ancients, are forced to hunt after foreign ornaments, and not to let any piece of wit of what kind soever escape them. I look upon these writers as Goths in poetry, who, like those in architecture, not being able to come up to the simplicity of the old Greeks and Romans, have endeavoured to supply its place with all the extravagancies of an irregular fancy. . . . Were I not supported by so great an authority as that of Mr. Dryden, I should not venture to observe that the taste of most of our English poets, as well as readers, is extremely Gothic. . . .

From No. 40 (April 16, 1711) and No. 62 (May 11, 1711).

❖ ❖ ❖

On Shakespeare, Voltaire, and Others

[FROM "Notes from the Hamburg Dramaturgy"]

GOTHOLD EPHRAIM LESSING

1767-69

The sixteenth evening *Zaire* by Voltaire was performed. "To those who care for literary history," says M. de Voltaire, "it will not be displeasing to know how this play originated. Various ladies had reproached the author because his tragedies did not contain enough about love. He replied, that in his opinion, tragedy was not the most fitting place for love; still if they would insist on having enamoured heroes he also could create them. The play was written in eighteen days and received with applause. In Paris it is named a Christian tragedy and has often been played in place of *Polyeucte*."

To the ladies therefore we are indebted for this tragedy, and it will long remain the favourite play of the ladies. A young ardent monarch, only subjugated by love; a proud conqueror only conquered by love; a Sultan without polygamy; a seraglio converted into the free and accessible abode of an absolute mistress; a foresaken maiden raised to the highest pinnacle of fortune, thanks solely to her lovely eyes; a heart for which religion and tenderness contest, that is divided between its god and its idol, that would like to be pious if only it need not cease loving; a jealous man who recognizes his error and avenges it on himself: if these flattering ideas do not bribe the suffrages of the fair sex, then what indeed could bribe them?

Love itself dictated *Zaire* to Voltaire! said a polite art critic. He would have been nearer the truth had he said gallantry; I know but one tragedy at which love itself has laboured, and that is *Romeo and Juliet* by Shakespeare. It is incontestable, that Voltaire makes his enamoured Zaire express her feelings with much nicety and decorum. But what is this expression compared with that living picture of all the smallest, most secret, artifices whereby love steals into our souls, all the imperceptible advantages it gains thereby, all the subterfuges with which it manages to supersede every other passion until it succeeds in holding the post of sole tyrant of our desires and aversions? Voltaire perfectly understands the—so to speak—official language of love; that is to say the language and the tone love employs when it desires to express itself with caution and dignity, when it would say nothing but what the prudish female sophist and the cold critic can justify. Still even the most efficient government clerk does not always know the most about the secrets of his government; or else if Voltaire had the same deep insight as Shakespeare into the essence of love, he would not exhibit it here, and therefore the poem has remained beneath the capacities of the poet.

Almost the same might be said of jealousy. His jealous Orosman plays a sorry figure beside the jealous Othello of Shakespeare. And yet Othello has unquestionably furnished the prototype of Orosman. Cibber says Voltaire avails himself of the brand that lighted the tragic pile of Shakespeare. I should have said: a brand from out of this flaming pile, and moreover one that smoked more than it glowed or warmed. In Orosman we hear a jealous man speak and we see him commit a rash deed of jealousy, but of jealousy itself we learn neither more nor less than what we knew before. Othello on the contrary is a complete manual of this deplorable madness; there we can learn all that refers to it and awakens it and how we may avoid it.

But is it always Shakespeare, always and eternally Shakespeare, who understood everything better than the French, I hear my readers ask? That annoys us, because we cannot read him. I seize this opportunity to remind the public of what it seems purposely to have forgotten. We have a translation of Shakespeare. It is scarcely finished and yet seems already forgotten. Critics have spoken ill of it. I have a mind to speak very well of it. Not in order to contradict these learned men, nor to defend the faults they have discovered, but because I believe there is no need to make so much ado about these faults. The undertaking was a difficult one, and any other person than Herr Wieland would have made other slips in their haste, or have passed over more passages from ignorance or laziness, and what parts he has done well few will do better. Anyway, his rendering of Shakespeare is a book that cannot be enough commended among us. We have much to learn yet from the beauties he has given to us, before the blemishes wherewith he has marred them offend us so greatly that we require a new translation. . . .

To what end the hard work of dramatic form? Why build a theatre, disguise men and women, torture their memories, invite the whole town to assemble at one place, if I intend to produce nothing more with my work and its representation than some of those emotions that would be produced as well by any good story that everyone could read by his chimney corner at home?

The dramatic form is the only one by which pity and fear can be excited, at least in no other form can these passions be excited to such a degree. Nevertheless it is preferred to excite all others rather than these; nevertheless it is preferred to employ it for any purpose but this, for which it is so especially adapted.

The public will put up with it; this is well, and yet not well. One has no special longing for the board at which one always has to put up with something.

It is well known how intent the Greek and Roman people were upon their theatres; especially the former on their tragic spectacles. Compared with this, how indifferent, how cold, is our people towards the theatre! Whence this difference if it does not arise from the fact that the Greeks felt themselves animated by their stage with such intense, such extraordinary emotions, that they could hardly await the moment to experience them again and again, whereas we are conscious of such weak impressions from our stage that we rarely deem it worth time and money to attain them. We most of us go to the theatre from idle curiosity, from fashion, from ennui, to see people, from desire to see and be seen, and only a few, and those few very seldom, go from any other motive.

I say we, our people, our stage, but I do not mean the Germans only. We Germans confess openly enough that we do not as yet possess a theatre. What many of our critics who join in this confession and are great admirers of the French theatre think when they make

it I cannot say, but I know well what I think. I think
that not alone we Germans, but also that those who
boast of having had a theatre for a hundred years, ay,
who boast of having the best theatre in all Europe,
even the French have as yet no theatre, certainly no
tragic one. The impressions produced by French tragedy
are so shallow, so cold. Let us hear a Frenchman himself speak of them.

M. de Voltaire says: "Combined with the surpassing
beauties of our theatre is connected a hidden fault
which remained unobserved because the public of its
own accord could have no higher ideas than those
imparted to it by the models of the great masters. Only
Saint-Evremond has discovered this fault; he says
that our dramatic works do not make sufficient impression, that that which should excite our pity only
awakens tenderness, that emotion takes the place of
agitation, and surprise the place of fear—in short, that
our impressions do not penetrate deeply enough. It
cannot be denied that Saint-Evremond has put his
finger to the secret sore of the French theatre. Let no
one rejoin that Saint-Evremond is the author of a
miserable comedy, *Sir Politic Wouldbe,* and of another
equally miserable one called *The Operas;* that his small
social poems are the shallowest and commonest we
possess of this kind, that he is nothing but a phrase-
monger; one may have no spark of genius and yet
possess much wit and taste. His taste was unquestionably very subtle, since he accurately hit the cause why
most of our plays are weak and cold; we have always
lacked a degree of warmth, but we possess everything
else." Which means we possessed everything, only not
that which we ought to have had; our tragedies were
excellent, only they were no tragedies. How was it that
they were none? Voltaire continues: "This coldness,

this monotonous weakness arose in part from the petty spirit of gallantry that reigned at that time among our courtiers and ladies, and transformed tragedy into a succession of amorous conversations after the taste of Cyrus and Clelie. The plays that may be excepted therefrom consisted of long political reasonings such as have spoiled Sertorius, made Otho cold and Surena and Attila wretched. There was yet another cause that kept back high pathos from our stage and prevented the action from becoming truly tragic, and that was the narrow miserable theatre with its poor scenery. What could be done on a few dozen boards that were besides filled with spectators! How could the eyes of the spectators be bribed and enchained, deceived by any display of pomp, by any artifice? What great tragic action could be performed there? What liberty could the imagination of the poet have there? The plays had to consist of long narratives, and they thus became rather dialogues than plays. Every actor wished to shine in a long monologue, and every play that did not contain these was rejected. In this form all theatrical action, the great expressions of passion, fell away; there were no powerful pictures of human misery; all traits of the terrible that could penetrate to the innermost soul were absent; the heart was scarcely touched instead of being torn."

The first cause alleged is very true; gallantry and politics always leave us cold, and as yet no poet in the world has succeeded in combining with them the excitation of pity and fear. The former only exhibits the *fat* or the schoolmaster, the latter requires that we should have nothing but the human being.

But the second cause, how about that? Is it possible that the want of a large theatre and good scenery should have such an influence on the genius of the poet? Is it true that every tragic action demands pomp and display; ought not the poet rather so to arrange his play that it can produce its full effect without these appendages?

It certainly ought to do so, according to Aristotle. The philosopher says: "Pity and fear may be excited by vision; they may also be produced by the connection of the events themselves—the latter plan is more excellent and after the manner of the best poets. The fable must be so arranged that it must excite pity and fear in him who merely listens to the relation of its events; such is the fable of Œdipus that only requires to be heard to produce this effect. To attain this aim by the organs of sight requires far less art and is the business of those who have undertaken the business of the representation of the play."

Shakespeare's plays are said to afford a curious proof how needless are scenic decorations. We are asked what plays could more need the assistance of scenery and the whole art of the decorator than these, with their constant interruptions and change of scene; yet there was a time when the stages on which they were performed consisted of nothing but a curtain of poor coarse stuff, which when it was drawn up showed either the walls bare or else hung with matting or tapestry. Here was nothing for the imagination, nothing to assist the comprehension of the spectator or to help the actor, and yet it is said that, notwithstanding, Shakespeare's plays were at that time more intelligible without scenery than they became afterwards with it.

If therefore the poet need take no notice of decorations, if the decorations may be omitted even where they appear necessary without any disadvantage to his play, why should the narrow miserable theatre be the reason that the French poets have furnished us with no touching plays? Not so, this was not the cause, the cause lay in themselves.

And experience has proved this. Nowadays the French have a beautiful roomy stage, no spectators are tolerated on it, the *coulisses* are empty, the scene painter has a free field; he paints and builds all the poet requires of him, yet where are they now, those warmer plays which they have attained since? Does M. de Voltaire flatter himself that his *Semiramis* is such a play? It contains pomp and decoration enough; a ghost into the bargain, and yet I know no chillier play than his *Semiramis*.

From "Notes . . . , Nos. 15 and 80," in *Selected Prose Works*, ed. Edward Bell, trans. (1879) E. C. Beasley and Helen Zimmern (London: G. Bell & Sons, 1913).

Style—a Classical View

[FROM *Discourse on Style*]

GEORGES LOUIS LECLERC,
COMTE DE BUFFON

1753

Style is nothing but the order and movement according to which a man arranges his thoughts. If he ties them closely together, if he tightens them up, the style becomes firm, lively, and concise; if he lets them pile themselves loosely one upon another, and unites them only by means of words, however elegant these may be, the style will be diffuse, loose, dragging. . . .

And yet, every subject is a whole; and, however

LITERATURE

great it may be, it can be covered in a single discourse.
Breaks, rests, internal divisions, should be employed
only in the treatment of diverse subjects or when, since
it has to deal with vast, thorny, and disparate subjects,
the march of the mind is interrupted by a multiplicity
of obstacles and constrained by force of circumstances;
otherwise, multiple divisions, far from making a work
more solid, destroy it as a structural whole; the book
may seem clear at a glance, but the author's plan remains obscure; he cannot make an impression on the
mind of the reader, he cannot even make himself felt,
save by the continuity of the thread of the work, by the
harmonic interdependence of its ideas, by a successive
development, a sustained gradation, a uniform movement which any interruption destroys or weakens.

Why are the works of nature so perfect? It is because
each one of her works is a whole, and because she
labours according to an immutable plan from which
she never departs; she prepares in silence the seeds
of her productions; she sketches by a unique act the
original form of each living thing; she develops it,
perfects it in a continuous movement within a prescribed time. The finished work astounds: but it is
the divine imprint whose mark it carries that should
impress us. The human mind can create nothing; it
will produce only after having been made fecund by
experience and reflection; the information it has
amassed furnishes but the seeds of its end-products;
but if the human mind will imitate nature in its movement and in its labour, if it will rise to the contemplation of the most sublime truths; if it will gather them
together in due order, if it will make a whole of them,
a system, by reflection, it will establish on unshakeable
foundations immortal monuments.

It is for lack of a plan, for not having reflected sufficiently on his purpose, that an intelligent man finds
himself embarrassed and unable to decide where to
begin to write. He entertains a great number of ideas;
and since he has neither compared them, nor sub-
ordinated them one to another, nothing determines him
to prefer one over another; he remains in perplexity.
But once he has made a plan, once he has assembled
and put in order all the thoughts essential to his subject,
he will be readily aware of the exact moment to take
up his pen, he will recognize the point at which the
mind is ready to produce, he will be anxious to hasten
its work, he will indeed have no other pleasure than
that of writing; ideas will follow one another easily
and the style will be natural and unconstrained; warmth
will be born of this pleasure, will spread throughout
and give life to each expression; everything will grow
livelier; the tone will be raised, objects will take on
colour; and emotion thus joined to penetration, will
increase it, carry it further, make it pass from what is
said to what is going to be said, and the style becomes
interesting and luminous.

Nothing is more opposed to this warmth of style
than the desire to put striking traits everywhere; nothing is more contrary to the penetrating light that ought
to embody itself and spread itself evenly throughout
a work than those sparks which are made only by
force in the mutual shock of words, and which dazzle
us for an instant only to leave us afterwards in the dark.
These are the thoughts that shine only by artificial opposition; one aspect only of the object is shown, the
others left in the shadow; and ordinarily the aspect
chosen is a point, an angle, over which the mind may
play with the more facility in that the great aspects

on which good sense customarily dwells are pushed into the background. . . .

To write well, a man must, then, possess his subject fully; he must reflect upon it sufficiently to see clearly the order of his thoughts, and to make of them a sequence, a continuous chain, of which each point represents an idea; and when he has taken up his pen, he must guide it with due sequence along this chain, without letting it wander, or bear too heavily anywhere, or make any movement save that which will be determined by the ground it has to cover. It is in this that severity of style consists, and it is this also that will make unity of style, and regulate its flow; and this alone also will suffice to make the style precise and simple, even and clear, lively and consecutive. If to the observance of this first rule, dictated by the very nature of things, there is added delicacy of taste, scrupulous attention to the choice of words, care to name things only by the most general term possible, then the style will have nobility. If there is added further a distrust of first impulses, a scorn for what is no more than brilliant, and a steady repugnance for the equivocal and the jesting, the style will have graveness, even, indeed, majesty. Finally, if a man write as he thinks, if he believe what he seeks to get believed, this good faith with himself, which insures propriety in the eyes of others, and makes for the truth of a style, will give style all its effect, provided that this interior conviction is not marked by a too violent enthusiasm, and that everywhere there is displayed more candour than assurance, more reason than heat.

From *Discours sur le style* (Paris: 1894); trans. C.B.

❖ ❖ ❖

Ne'er So Well Expressed:
Aphorisms and Maxims

❖ ❖ ❖

[FROM *The Memoirs*]

JEAN FRANÇOIS PAUL DE GONDI,
CARDINAL DE RETZ

1660-79

This is the unhappiness of civil wars; through right conduct one often commits errors.

. . . in great affairs there is no little step.

. . . blind rashness and extreme fear produce the same effects when the danger is not known.

. . . one has more difficulty within parties, in living with those who are of them, than in acting against opponents.

. . . civil war is one of those complicated ills, in which the remedy that you intend for the cure of one symptom sometimes increases three or four others.

. . . in factions the chiefs are masters only so far as they know how to prevent or appease the murmurs [of discontent], . . .

. . . the talent of insinuating is more useful than that of persuading, because you can insinuate to everybody and you can almost never persuade anybody.

From *Mémoires du Cardinal de Retz* (Paris: Etienne Ledoux, 1820); trans. L. J. Henderson.

[FROM *The Maxims*]

FRANÇOIS, DUC DE LA ROCHEFOUCAULD

1678

The desire of appearing to be wise often prevents our becoming so.

We should often be ashamed of our best actions, were the world witness to the motives which produce them.

In the distress of our best friends we always find something that does not displease us.

Love is one and the same in the original; but there are a thousand different copies of it.

There are people who would never have been in love, had they never heard talk of it.

Strength and weakness of mind are improper terms; they are in reality only the good or ill disposition of the organs of the body.

It is a common fault to be never satisfied with our fortune, nor dissatisfied with our understanding.

The duration of our passions is as little in our power as the duration of our lives.

Absence destroys small passions, and increases great ones: the wind extinguishes tapers, but kindles fires.

We are by no means aware of the influence of our passions.

Death and the sun are not to be looked at steadily.

Sobriety is either the love of health, or an incapacity for debauch.

Those who think themselves persons of merit, take a pride often in being unlucky: they make themselves, as well as others, believe that they are worthy to be the butt of Fortune.

From *Maxims and Moral Reflections* (London: printed for Lockyer Davis, 1781).

[FROM *The Characters*]

JEAN DE LA BRUYÈRE

1688

The pleasure of criticism takes away from us the pleasure of being deeply moved by very fine things.

It is the glory and the merit of some men to write well, and of others not to write at all.

There are more tools than workmen, and of the latter more bad than good ones. What would you think of a man who would use a plane to saw, and his saw to plane?

If it be usual to be strongly impressed by things that are scarce, why are we so little impressed by virtue?

I have heard some people say they should like to be a girl, and a handsome girl, too, from thirteen to two-and-twenty, and after that age again to become a man.

Women become attached to men through the favours they grant them, but men are cured of their love through those same favours.

When a woman no longer loves a man, she forgets the very favours she has granted him.

I do not know who is more to be pitied, either a woman in years who needs a young man, or a young man who needs an old woman.

Women run to extremes; they are either better or worse than men.

A man keeps another person's secret better than his own; a woman, on the contrary, keeps her own secrets better than any other person's.

Children are overbearing, supercilious, passionate, envious, inquisitive, egotistical, idle, fickle, timid, intemperate, liars, and dissemblers; they laugh and weep easily, are excessive in their joys and sorrows, and that about the most trifling objects; they bear no pain, but like to inflict it on others; already they are men.

Children begin among themselves with a democracy, where everyone is master; and what is very natural, it does not suit them for any length of time, and then they adopt a monarchy. One of them distinguishes himself from among the rest, either by greater vivacity, strength, and comeliness, or by a more exact knowledge of their various sports and of the little laws which regulate them; all the others submit to him, and then an absolute government is established, but only in matters of pleasure.

Hatred is so lasting and stubborn, that reconciliation on a sick-bed certainly forebodes death.

Trans. Henri van Laun (London: John C. Nimmo, 1885).

[FROM *Reflections and Maxims*]

LUC DE CLAPIERS,
MARQUIS DE VAUVENARGUES

1746

It is easier to say original things than to reconcile with one another things already said.

The mind of man is more intuitive than logical, and comprehends more than it can co-ordinate.

When an idea is not robust enough to stand expression in simple terms, it is a sign that it should be rejected.

Lucidity adds beauty to profound thoughts.

Obscurity is the realm of error.

All erroneous ideas would perish of their own accord if given clear expression.

Prosperity makes few friends.

Courage is more helpful than reason in combating humiliations.

Before setting out to attack an abuse, we should see if we can undermine its foundations.

Inevitable abuses are part of nature's law.

We have no right to make unhappy those whom we cannot make good.

There is perhaps no truth, which is not a cause of error to some misguided mind.

Women and young people never separate their esteem from their liking.

Habit is all powerful, even in love.

It is difficult to esteem anyone as he wishes to be esteemed.

Should peace of mind be accepted as a sure proof of virtue? No, it is the gift of good health.

The wicked are always surprised to discover ability in the just.

Children break windows and pull chairs to pieces when their nurses are not present. Soldiers fire the camp they quit, in spite of the general's orders; they love to trample under foot the promise of the harvest, and ruin proud buildings. What prompts them to leave everywhere such enduring evidence of their savagery? Is it mere delight in mischief? or is it not rather that feeble spirits find in wantonness some notion of audacity and power?

A thoroughly new and original work would be one which familiarized us with long-established truths.

Few maxims admit of no exception.

Trans. F. G. Stevens (London: Oxford University Press, 1940).

[FROM *Poor Richard*]

BENJAMIN FRANKLIN

1733-58

He's a fool that makes his doctor his heir.

Men and melons are hard to know.

Where there's marriage without love, there will be love without marriage.

A learned blockhead is a greater blockhead than an ignorant one.

The ancients tell us what is best; but we must learn of the moderns what is fittest.

Sin is not hurtful because it is forbidden, but it is forbidden because it is hurtful.

Beware of little expences; a small leak will sink a great ship.

A man without ceremony has need of great merit in its place.

Philosophy as well as foppery often changes fashion.

The wit of conversation consists more in finding it in others, than shewing a great deal yourself.

In a corrupt age, the putting the world in order would breed confusion; then e'en mind your own business.

To serve the publick faithfully, and at the same time please it entirely is impracticable.

Men often mistake themselves, seldom forget themselves.

From *The Writings of Benjamin Franklin*, ed. A. H. Smyth (New York: The Macmillan Co., 1905-1907).

[FROM *The Maxims*]

SÉBASTIEN ROCH NICOLAS CHAMFORT

1805

Most of those who make collections of verse or epigrams are like men eating cherries or oysters: they choose out the best at first, and end by eating all.

There are two classes of Moralists and Politicians: those, and they are the more numerous, who have only looked at human nature on its odious or ridiculous side: Lucian, Montaigne, La Bruyère, La Rochefoucauld, Swift, Mandeville, Helvetius, and the rest: and those, such as Shaftesbury and a few others, who have only regarded her on the fair side, and seen her perfections. The first know nothing of the palace, because they have only seen its privies. The second are enthusiasts who turn their eyes away from what offends them; but the offence remains. *Est in medio verum.*

Philosophy, like Medicine, has many drugs, a very few good remedies, and practically no specifics.

Our Reason sometimes makes us as unhappy as our passions may; and we can say of a man, when this is so, that he is a patient poisoned by his doctor.

The mind is often to the heart only what the library of a country house is to its owner.

I cannot conceive of a wisdom without diffidence. The Scriptures say that the beginning of wisdom is the fear of God, but I believe it is the fear of man.

Each thing among things is *composite*, each man among men is *patchwork*. Whether on the moral or physical plane, all things are compound. Nothing is one thing only, nothing is pure.

Society and the World are like a library where at first glance all seems in order, for the books are arranged according to their shapes and sizes, but where, on closer scrutiny, there is seen to be utter confusion, because there has been no grouping under subject matter, class, or author.

All is true and all is false in love; love is the only thing about which it is impossible to say anything absurd.

It has been made a subject for remark that writers on Natural History, Physics, Physiology, and Chemistry are usually men of mild and equable character, and of a happy disposition; while writers on Law and Politics, and even on Moral Philosophy, are of a dismal and melancholy temper. The reason is not far to seek: the former consider Nature and survey the work of the great Being, while the latter observe Society and meditate upon the works of man. Their studies are bound to affect them differently.

I would say of metaphysicians what Scaliger said of the Basques: they are supposed to understand each other, but I do not believe it.

"I have utterly lost my taste for mankind," said Monsieur de L——. "Then you have not lost your taste," said Monsieur de N——.

Paris: a city of pleasures and amusements where four-fifths of the people die of grief.

The phrase which Saint Teresa used to describe Hell is equally applicable to Paris: *A place that stinks, and where there is no love.*

The Revolution is like a lost dog that nobody dares to stop.

[Of the Jacobin of the Terror]: He says: Be my brother or I will kill you.

From *Maxims and Considerations,* trans. E. Powys Mathers, Waltham Saint Lawrence, Berkshire, England: Golden Cockerel Press, 1926).

v. *Self-Revelation:*

MEMOIRS
AND LETTERS

A Pepys Sample

[FROM *The Diary*]

SAMUEL PEPYS

Nov. 9, 1663.

Thence I took leave of them, and so having taken up something at my wife's tailor's, I home by coach and there to my office, whither Shales came and I had much discourse with him about the business of the victualling, and thence in the evening to the Coffee-house, and there sat till by and by, by appointment Will brought me word that his uncle Blackburne was ready to speak with me. So I went down to him, and he and I to a taverne hard by, and there I begun to speak to Will friendlily, advising him how to carry

himself now he is going from under my roof, without
any reflections upon the occasion from whence his removal arose. This his uncle seconded, and after laying
down to him his duty to me, and what I expect of
him, in a discourse of about a quarter of an houre or
more, we agreed upon his going this week, towards the
latter [end] of the week, and so dismissed him, and
Mr. Blackburne and I fell to talk of many things,
wherein I did speak so freely to him in many things
agreeing with his sense that he was very open to me:
first, in that of religion, he makes it great matter of
prudence for the King and Council to suffer liberty of
conscience; and imputes the losse of Hungary to the
Turke from the Emperor's denying them this liberty
of their religion. He says that many pious ministers of
the word of God, some thousands of them, do now
beg their bread: and told me how highly the present
clergy carry themselves every where, so as that they
are hated and laughed at by every body; among other
things, for their excommunications, which they send
upon the least occasions almost that can be. And I am
convinced in my judgment, not only from his discourse,
but my thoughts in general, that the present clergy will
never heartily go down with the generality of the commons of England; they have been so used to liberty and
freedom, and they are so acquainted with the pride
and debauchery of the present clergy. He did give me
many stories of the affronts which the clergy receive
in all places of England from the gentry and ordinary
persons of the parish. He do tell me what the City
thinks of General Monk, as of a most perfidious man
that hath betrayed every body, and the King also; who,
as he thinks, and his party, and so I have heard other
good friends of the King say, it might have been

better for the King to have had his hands a little bound for the present, than be forced to bring such a crew of poor people about him, and be liable to satisfy the demands of every one of them. He told me that to his knowledge (being present at every meeting at the Treaty at the Isle of Wight), that the old King did confess himself over-ruled and convinced in his judgement against the Bishopps, and would have suffered and did agree to exclude the service out of the churches, nay his own chappell; and that he did always say, that this he did not by force, for that he would never abate one inch by any vyolence; but what he did was out of his reason and judgement. He tells me that the King by name, with all his dignities, is prayed for by them that they call Fanatiques, as heartily and powerfully as in any of the other churches that are thought better: and that, let the King think what he will, it is them that must helpe him in the day of warr. For as they are the most, so generally they are the most substantiall sort of people, and the soberest; and did desire me to observe it to my Lord Sandwich, among other things, that of all the old army now you cannot see a man begging about the street; but what? You shall have this captain turned a shoemaker; the lieutenant, a baker; this a brewer; that a haberdasher; this common soldier, a porter; and every man in his apron and frock, &c., as if they never had done anything else: whereas the others go with their belts and swords, swearing and cursing, and stealing; running into people's houses, by force oftentimes, to carry away something; and this is the difference between the temper of one and the other; and concludes (and I think with some reason) that the spirits of the old parliament soldiers are so quiett and contented with God's providences, that the King is safer from any evil meant him by them one thousand times more than from his own discontented Cavalier.

Feb. 6, 1668.

. . . and my wife being gone before, i to the Duke of York's playhouse; where a new play of Etherige's, called "She Would if she Could"; and though I was there by two o'clock, there was 1000 people put back that could not have room in the pit: and I at last, because my wife was there, made shift to get into the 18d. box, and there saw; but, Lord! how full was the house, and how silly the play, there being nothing in the world good in it, and few people pleased in it. The King was there; but I sat mightily behind, and could see but little, and hear not all. The play being done, I into the pit to look [for] my wife, and it being dark and raining, I to look my wife out, but could not find her; and so staid going between the two doors and through the pit an hour and half, I think, after the play was done; the people staying there till the rain was over, and to talk with one another. And, among the rest, here was the Duke of Buckingham to-day openly sat in the pit; and there I found him with my Lord Buckhurst, and Sidly, and Etherige, the poet; the last of whom I did hear mightily find fault with the actors, that they were out of humour, and had not their parts perfect, and that Harris did do nothing, nor could so much as sing a ketch in it; and so was mightily concerned: while all the rest did, through the whole pit, blame the play as a silly, dull thing, though there was something very roguish and witty; but the design of the play, and end, mighty insipid. At last I did find my wife staying for me in the entry; and with her was Betty Turner, Mercer, and Deb. So I got a

coach, and a humour took us, and I carried them to
Hercules Pillars, and there did give them a kind of a
supper of about 7s., and very merry, and home round
the town, not through the ruines; and it was pretty
how the coachman by mistake drives us into the ruines
from London-wall into Coleman Street: and would
persuade me that I lived there. And the truth is, I did
think that he and the linkman had contrived some
roguery; but it proved only a mistake of the coachman;
but it was a cunning place to have done us a mischief
in, as any I know, to drive us out of the road into the
ruines, and there stop, while nobody could be called
to help us. But we come safe home, and there, the girls
being gone home, I to the office, where a while busy,
my head not being wholly free of my trouble about
my prize business, I home to bed. This evening coming
home I did put my hand under the coats of Mercer
and did touch her thigh, but then she did put by my
hand and no hurt done, but talked and sang and was
merry.

Ed. Henry B. Wheatley (London: George Bell & Sons, 1893,
1896).

❖ ❖ ❖

The Last Days
of the Grand Monarque

[FROM *Memoirs*]

LOUIS DE ROUVROY,
DUC DE SAINT-SIMON

After 1721

This same Monday, 26th of August, after the two
Cardinals had left the room, the King dined in his bed
in the presence of those who were privileged to enter.
As the things were being cleared away, he made them
approach and addressed to them these words, which
were stored up in their memory: "Gentlemen, I ask
your pardon for the bad example I have given you. I
have much to thank you for the manner in which you
have served me, and for the attachment and fidelity
you have always shown for me. I am very sorry I have
not done for you all I should have wished to do; bad
times have been the cause. I ask for my grandson the
same application and the same fidelity you have had
for me. He is a child who may experience many re-
verses. Let your example be one for all my other
subjects. Follow the orders my nephew will give you;
he is to govern the realm; I hope he will govern it
well; I hope also that you will all contribute to keep up
union, and that if anyone falls away you will aid in
bringing him back. I feel that I am moved, and that

I move you also. I ask your pardon. Adieu, gentlemen, I hope you will sometimes remember me."

A short time after, he called the Maréchal de Villeroy to him, and said he had made him governor of the Dauphin. He then called to him M. le Duc and M. le Prince de Conti, and recommended to them the advantages of union among princes. Then, hearing women in the cabinet, questioned who were there, and immediately sent word they might enter. Madame la Duchesse de Berry, Madame la Duchesse d'Orleans, and the Princesses of the blood forthwith appeared, crying. The King told them they must not cry thus, said a few friendly words to them, and dismissed them. They retired by the cabinet, weeping and crying very loudly, which caused people to believe outside that the King was dead; and, indeed, the rumour spread to Paris, and even to the provinces.

Sometime after, the King requested the Duchesse de Ventadour to bring the little Dauphin to him. He made the child approach, and then said to him, before Madame de Maintenon and the few privileged people present, "My child, you are going to be a great king; do not imitate me in the taste I have had for building, or in that I have had for war; try, on the contrary, to be at peace with your neighbours. Render to God what you owe him; recognize the obligations you are under to him; make him honoured by your subjects. Always follow good counsels; try to comfort your people, which I unhappily have not done. Never forget the obligation you owe to Madame de Ventadour. Madame (*addressing her*), let me embrace him (*and while embracing him*), my dear child, I give you my benediction with my whole heart."

As the little Prince was about to be taken off the bed, the King redemanded him, embraced him again, and raising hands and eyes to Heaven, blessed him once more. This spectacle was extremely touching.

On Tuesday the 27th of August, the King said to Madame de Maintenon, that he had always heard, it was hard to resolve to die; but that as for him, seeing himself upon the point of death, he did not find this resolution so difficult to form. She replied that it was very hard when we had attachments to creatures, hatred in our hearts, or restitutions to make. "Ah," rejoined the King, "as for restitutions, to nobody in particular do I owe any; but as for those I owe to the realm, I hope in the mercy of God."

The night which followed was very agitated. The King was seen at all moments joining his hands, striking his breast, and was heard repeating the prayers he ordinarily employed.

On Wednesday morning, the 28th of August, he paid a compliment to Madame de Maintenon, which pleased her but little, and to which she replied not one word. He said that what consoled him in quitting her was that, considering the age she had reached, they must soon meet again!

About seven o'clock in the morning, he saw in the mirror two of his valets at the foot of the bed weeping, and said to them, "Why do you weep? Is it because you thought me immortal? As for me, I have not thought myself so, and you ought, considering my age, to have been prepared to lose me."

A very clownish Provençal rustic heard of the extremity of the King, while on his way from Marseille to Paris, and came this morning to Versailles with a remedy which, he said, would cure the gangrene. The King was so ill, and the doctors so at their wits' ends, that they consented to receive him. Fagon tried to say something, but this rustic, who was named Le Brun, abused him very coarsely, and Fagon, accustomed to abuse others, was confounded. Ten drops of Le Brun's mixture in Alicante wine were therefore given to the King about eleven o'clock in the morning. Sometime after he became stronger, but the pulse falling again and becoming bad, another dose was given to him about four o'clock, to recall him to life, they told him. He replied, taking the mixture, "To life or to death as it shall please God."

Le Brun's remedy was continued. Someone proposed that the King should take some broth. The King replied that it was not broth he wanted, but a confessor, and he sent for him. One day, recovering from loss of consciousness, he asked Père Tellier to give him absolution for all his sins. Père Tellier asked him if he suffered much? "No," replied the King, "that's what troubles me: I should like to suffer more for the expiation of my sins."

On Thursday, the 29th of August, he grew a little better; he even ate two little biscuits steeped in wine, with a certain appetite. The news immediately spread abroad that the King was recovering. I went that day to the apartments of M. le Duc d'Orleans, where, during the previous eight days, there had been such a crowd that, speaking exactly, a pin would not have fallen to the ground. Not a soul was there! As soon as the Duc saw me he burst out laughing, and said I was the first person who had been to see him all the day! And until the evening he was entirely deserted. Such is the world!

In the evening it was known that the King had only recovered for the moment. In giving orders during the day, he called the young Dauphin "the young King." He saw a movement amongst those around him. "Why not?" said he, "that does not trouble me." Towards eight o'clock he took the elixir of the rustic. His brain appeared confused; he himself said he felt very ill. Towards eleven o'clock his leg was examined. The gangrene was found to be in the foot and the knee; the thigh much inflamed. He swooned during this examination. He had perceived with much pain that Madame de Maintenon was no longer near him. She had in fact gone off on the previous day with very dry eyes to St. Cyr, not intending to return. He asked for her several times during the day. Her departure could not be hidden. He sent for her to St. Cyr, and she came back in the evening.

Friday, August the 30th, was a bad day preceded by a bad night. The King continually lost his reason. About five o'clock in the evening Madame de Maintenon left him, gave away her furniture to the domestics, and went to St. Cyr never to leave it.

On Saturday, the 31st of August, everything went from bad to worse. The gangrene had reached the knee and all the thigh. Towards eleven o'clock at night the King was found to be so ill that the prayers for the dying were said. This restored him to himself. He repeated the prayers in a voice so strong that it rose above all the other voices. At the end he recognized Cardinal de Rohan, and said to him, "These are the last favours of the church." This was the last man to whom he spoke. He repeated several times, *Nunc et in hora mortis,* then said, "Oh my God, come to my aid: hasten to succour me."

These were his last words. All the night he was without consciousness and in a long agony, which finished on Sunday, the 1st Sept., 1715, at a quarter past eight in the morning, three days before he had accomplished his seventy-seventh year, and in the seventy-second of his reign. He had survived all his sons and his grandsons, except the King of Spain. Europe never saw so long a reign or France a King so old.

Louis XIV was made for a brilliant Court. In the midst of other men, his figure, his courage, his grace, his beauty, his grand mien, even the tone of his voice and the majestic and natural charm of all his person, distinguished him till his death as the King Bee, and showed that if he had only been born a simple private gentleman, he would equally have excelled in fetes, pleasures, and gallantry, and would have had the greatest success in love. The intrigues and adventures which early in life he had been engaged in—when the Comtesse de Soissons lodged at the Tuileries, as superintendent of the Queen's household, and was the centre figure of the Court group—had exercised an unfortunate influence upon him: he received those impressions with which he could never after successfully struggle. From his time, intellect, education, nobility of sentiment, and high principle, in others, became objects of suspicion to him, and soon of hatred. The more he advanced in years the more this sentiment was confirmed in him. He wished to reign by himself. His jealousy on this point unceasingly, became weakness. He reigned, indeed, in little things; the great he could never reach: even in the former, too, he was often governed. The superior ability of his early ministers and his early generals soon wearied him. He liked nobody to be in any way superior to him. Thus he chose his ministers, not for their knowledge, but for their ignorance; not for their capacity, but for their want of it. He liked to form them, as he said; liked to teach them even the most trifling things. It was the same with his generals. He took credit to himself for instructing them; wished it to be thought that from his cabinet he commanded and directed all his armies. Naturally fond of trifles, he unceasingly occupied himself with the most petty details of his troops, his household, his mansions; would even instruct his cooks, who received, like novices, lessons they had known by heart for years. This vanity, this unmeasured and unreasonable love of admiration, was his ruin. His ministers, his generals, his mistresses, his courtiers, soon perceived his weakness. They praised him with emulation and spoiled him. Praises, or, to say truth, flattery, pleased him to such an extent that the coarsest was well received, the vilest even better relished. It was the sole means by which you could approach him. Those whom he liked owed his affection for them to their untiring flatteries. This is what gave his ministers so much authority, and the opportunities they had for adulating him, of attributing everything to him, and of pretending to learn everything from him. Suppleness, meanness, an admiring, dependent, cringing manner—above all, an air of nothingness—were the sole means of pleasing him.

This poison spread. It spread, too, to an incredible extent, in a prince who, although of intellect beneath mediocrity, was not utterly without sense, and who had had some experience. Without voice or musical knowledge, he used to sing, in private, the passages of the opera prologues that were fullest of his praises! He was drowned in vanity; and so deeply, that at his public suppers—all the Court present, musicians also— he would hum these self-same praises between his teeth, when the music they were set to was played!

And yet, it must be admitted, he might have done better. Though his intellect, as I have said, was beneath mediocrity, it was capable of being formed. He loved glory, was fond of order and regularity; was

by disposition prudent, moderate, discreet, master of
his movements and his tongue. Will it be believed? He
was also by disposition good and just! God had sufficiently gifted him to enable him to be a good King;
perhaps even a *tolerably great King!* All the evil came
to him from elsewhere. His early education was so
neglected that nobody dared approach his apartment.
He has often been heard to speak of those times with
bitterness, and even to relate that, one evening, he was
found in the basin of the Palais Royale garden fountain,
into which he had fallen! He was scarcely taught how
to read or write, and remained so ignorant, that the
most familiar historical and other facts were utterly
unknown to him! He fell, accordingly, and sometimes
even in public, into the grossest absurdities.

From Vol. III, trans. Bayle St. John (London: Chapman & Hall,
1857).

The Death of Queen Caroline

[FROM *Some Materials towards Memoirs of
the Reign of King George II*]

JOHN, LORD HERVEY

After 1737

Busier not being immediately to be found, and the
King very impatient, he bid Ranby go and bring the
first surgeon of any note and credit he could find; and
whilst Ranby was absent on this errand, the King told
Lord Hervey the whole history of this rupture.

"The first symptoms I ever perceived of it," said he, "were fourteen years ago, just after the Queen lay in of Louisa; and she then told me, when I spoke to her of it, that it was nothing more than what was common for almost every woman to have after a hard labour, or having many children. This made me easy, and it grew better, and continued better afterwards for several years. When it grew worse again, I persuaded her to consult some surgeon, which she declined, and was so uneasy whenever I spoke to her on this subject that I knew not how to press her; but when I came from Hanover the last time but one, I found it so much worse than ever that I again spoke to her, told her it was certainly a rupture, and that she ran great risks in taking no care of it. She was so very uneasy upon my saying this, telling me it was no such thing, and that I fancied she had a nasty distemper which she was sure she had not, and spoke so much more peevishly to me on this occasion than she had ever done in her life upon any other, that upon my renewing my solicitations to her to let somebody see it, and her growing everytime I mentioned it more and more hurt and angry, I at last told her I wished she might not repent her obstinacy, but promised her I never would mention this subject to her again as long as I lived."

The King, in as plain insinuations as he could without saying it in direct terms, did intimate to Lord Hervey that the Queen had received what he had said to her on this subject, upon his return from Hanover, as if she had reproached him with being grown weary of her person, and endeavouring to find blemishes in it that did not belong to her.

I do firmly believe she carried her abhorrence to being known to have a rupture so far that she would have died without declaring it, or letting it be known,

had not the King told it in spite of her; and though
people may think this weakness little of a piece with
the greatness of the rest of her character, yet they will
judge partially who interpret this delicacy to be merely
an ill-timed coquetry at fifty-four that would hardly
have been excusable at twenty-five. She knew better
than anybody else that her power over the King was
not preserved independent, as most people thought,
of the charms of her person; and as her power over him
was the principal object of her pursuit, she feared, very
reasonably, the loss or the weakening of any tie by
which she held him. Several things she afterwards said
to the King in her illness, which both the King and
the Princess Caroline told me again, plainly demonstrated how strongly these apprehensions of making her
person distasteful to the King worked upon her.

Nobody now remained in the room with the Queen
but the King, the Duke, and her four daughters, of
whom she took leave in form, desiring they would not
leave her till she expired. She told the King she had
nothing to say to him. "For as I have always," said
she, "told you my thoughts of things and people as
fast as they arose, I have nothing left to communicate
to you. The people I love and those I do not, the people I like and dislike, and those I would wish you to
be kind to, you know as well as myself; and I am
persuaded it would therefore be a useless trouble both
to you and me at this time to add any particular recom-
mendations."

To the Princess Emily she said nothing very particular; to the Princess Caroline she recommended the care
of her two younger sisters, and said: "Poor Caroline,
it is a fine legacy I leave you—the trouble of educating
these two young things. As for you, William," continued

she to the Duke, "you know I have always loved you tenderly, and placed my chief hope in you; show your gratitude to me in your behaviour to the King; be a support to your father, and double your attention to make up for the disappointment and vexation he must receive from your profligate and worthless brother. It is in you only I hope for keeping up the credit of our family when your father shall be no more. Attempt nothing ever against your brother, and endeavour to mortify him no way but by showing superior merit."

She then spoke of the different tempers and dispositions of her two youngest daughters, and the different manner in which they ought to be treated, cautioning the Princess Caroline not to let the vivacity of the Princess Louisa (the youngest) draw her into any inconveniences, and desiring her to give all the aid she could to support the meek and mild disposition of the Princess Mary.

She then took a ruby ring off her finger, which the King had given her at her coronation, and, putting it upon his, said: "This is the last thing I have to give you—naked I came to you, and naked I go from you. I had everything I ever possessed from you, and to you whatever I have I return. My will you will find a very short one; I give all I have to you." She then asked for her keys, and gave them to him.

All this and many more things of the like nature, whilst she expatiated on the several rules and instructions she gave to her children, according to their different ages, situations, and dispositions, passed in this interview, which the King and the Princess Caroline repeated to me, who told me there were during this conference no dry eyes in the room but the Queen's, who, as they could perceive, shed in all this touching scene not one tear.

It is not necessary to examine whether the Queen's reasoning was good or bad in wishing the King, in case she died, should marry again. It is certain she did wish it, had often said so when he was present, and when he was not present, and when she was in health, and gave it now as her advice to him when she was dying; upon which his sobs began to rise and his tears to fall with double vehemence. Whilst in the midst of this passion, wiping his eyes, and sobbing between every word, with much ado he got out this answer: "*Non . . . j'aurai . . . des . . . maîtresses*" [No . . . I'll take . . . mistresses]. To which the Queen made no other reply than: "*Ah! mon Dieu! cela n'empêche pas*" [Good Lord! that will be no hindrance (to taking a wife)]. I know this episode will hardly be credited, but it is literally true.

When she had finished all she had to say on these subjects, she said she fancied she could sleep. The King said many kind things to her and kissed her face and her hands a hundred times; but even at this time, on her asking for her watch, which hung by the chimney, in order to give it him to take care of her seal, the natural brusquerie of his temper, even in these moments, broke out, which showed how addicted he was to snapping without being angry, and that he was often capable of using those worst whom he loved best. For on this proposal of giving him the watch to take care of the seal with the Queen's arms, in the midst of sobs and tears he raised and quickened his voice, and said: "Ah! my God! let it alone; the Queen has always such strange fancies. Who should meddle with your seal? Is it not as safe there as in my pocket?"

From Vol. II, ed. J. W. Croker (London: John Murray, 1848).

❖ ❖ ❖

Oxford, Rome, and a Life Work

[FROM *Memoirs*]

EDWARD GIBBON

After 1788

A traveller, who visits Oxford or Cambridge, is surprised and edified by the apparent order and tranquillity that prevail in the seats of the English muses. In the most celebrated universities of Holland, Germany, and Italy, the students, who swarm from different countries, are loosely dispersed in private lodgings at the houses of the burghers: they dress according to their fancy and fortune; and in the intemperate quarrels of youth and wine, their *swords,* though less frequently than of old, are sometimes stained with each other's blood. The use of arms is banished from our English universities; the uniform habit of the academics, the square cap, and black gown, is adapted to the civil and even clerical professions; and from the doctor in divinity to the under-graduate, the degrees of learning and age are externally distinguished. Instead of being scattered in a town, the students of Oxford and Cambridge are united in colleges; their maintenance is provided at their own expense, or that of the founders; and the stated hours of the hall and chapel represent the discipline of a regular, and, as it were, a religious community. The eyes of the traveller are attracted by the size or beauty of the public edifices; and the principal colleges appear to be so many palaces, which a liberal nation has erected and endowed for the habitation of science. My own introduction to the university of Oxford forms a new æra in my life; and at the distance of forty years I still remember my first emotions of surprise and satisfaction. In my fifteenth year I felt myself suddenly raised from a boy to a man: the persons, whom I respected as my superiors in age and academical rank, entertained me with every mark of attention and civility; and my vanity was flattered by the velvet cap and silk gown, which distinguish a gentleman commoner from a plebeian student. A decent allowance, more money than a schoolboy had ever seen, was at my own disposal; and I might command, among the tradesmen of Oxford, an indefinite and dangerous latitude of credit. A key was delivered into my hands, which gave me the free use of a numerous and learned library, my apartment consisted of three elegant and well-furnished rooms in the new building, a stately pile, of Magdalen College, and the adjacent walks, had they been frequented by Plato's disciples, might have been compared to the Attic shade on the banks of the Ilissus. Such was the fair prospect of my entrance (April 3, 1752) into the university of Oxford.

. . . It may indeed be observed, that the atmosphere of Oxford did not agree with Mr. Locke's constitution; and that the philosopher justly despised the academical bigots, who expelled his person and condemned his principles. The expression of gratitude is a virtue and a pleasure: a liberal mind will delight to cherish and celebrate the memory of its parents; and the teachers of science are the parents of the minds. I applaud the filial piety, which it is impossible for me to imitate; since I must not confess an imaginary

debt, to assume the merit of a just or generous retribu-
tion. To the university of Oxford *I* acknowledge no
obligation; and she will as cheerfully renounce me for
a son, as I am willing to disclaim her for a mother.
I spent fourteen months at Magdalen College; they
proved the fourteen months the most idle and un-
profitable of my whole life: the reader will pronounce
between the school and the scholar; but I cannot affect
to believe that Nature had disqualified me for all
literary pursuits. The specious and ready excuse of my
tender age, imperfect preparation, and hasty departure,
may doubtless be alleged; nor do I wish to defraud
such excuses of their proper weight. Yet in my sixteenth year I was not devoid of capacity or application; even my childish reading had displayed an early
though blind propensity for books; and the shallow
flood might have been taught to flow in a deep channel
and a clear stream. In the discipline of a well-consti-
tuted academy, under the guidance of skilful and
vigilant professors, I should gradually have risen from
translations to originals, from the Latin to the Greek
classics, from dead languages to living science: my
hours would have been occupied by useful and agreeable studies, the wanderings of fancy would have been
restrained, and I should have escaped the temptations
of idleness, which finally precipitated my departure
from Oxford.

. . . The schools of Oxford and Cambridge were
founded in a dark age of false and barbarous science;
and they are still tainted with the vices of their origin.
Their primitive discipline was adapted to the education of priests and monks; and the government still
remains in the hands of the clergy, an order of men
whose manners are remote from the present world, and
whose eyes are dazzled by the light of philosophy. The

legal incorporation of these societies by the charters of popes and kings had given them a monopoly of the public instruction; and the spirit of monopolists is narrow, lazy, and oppressive; their work is more costly and less productive than that of independent artists; and the new improvements so eagerly grasped by the competition of freedom, are admitted with slow and sullen reluctance in those proud corporations, above the fear of a rival, and below the confession of an error. We can scarcely hope that any reformation will be a voluntary act; and so deeply are they rooted in law and prejudice, that even the omnipotence of Parliament would shrink from an inquiry into the state and abuses of the two universities. . . .

In all the universities of Europe, excepting our own, the languages and sciences are distributed among a numerous list of effective professors: the students, according to their taste, their calling, and their diligence, apply themselves to the proper masters; and in the annual repetition of public and private lectures, these masters are assiduously employed. Our curiosity may inquire what number of professors has been instituted at Oxford? (for I shall now confine myself to my own university;) by whom are they appointed, and what may be the probable chances of merit or incapacity; how many are stationed to the three faculties, and how many are left for the liberal arts? what is the form, and what the substance, of their lessons? But all these questions are silenced by one short and singular answer, "That in the university of Oxford, the greater part of the public professors have for these many years given up altogether even the pretence of teaching." Incredible as the fact may appear, I must rest my belief on the positive and impartial evidence of a master of moral and political wisdom, who had himself resided at Oxford. Dr. Adam Smith assigns as the cause of their indolence, that, instead of being paid by voluntary contributions, which would urge them to increase the number, and to deserve the gratitude of their pupils, the Oxford professors are secure in the enjoyment of a fixed stipend, without the necessity of labour, or the apprehension of control. It has indeed been observed, nor is the observation absurd, that excepting in experimental sciences, which demand a costly apparatus and a dexterous hand, the many valuable treatises, that have been published on every subject of learning, may now supersede the ancient mode of oral instruction. Were this principle true in its utmost latitude, I should only infer that the offices and salaries, which are become useless, ought without delay to be abolished. But there still remains a material difference between a book and a professor; the hour of the lecture enforces attendance; attention is fixed by the presence, the voice, and the occasional questions of the teacher; the most idle will carry something away; and the more diligent will compare the instructions, which they have heard in the school, with the volumes, which they peruse in their chamber. The advice of a skilful professor will adapt a course of reading to every mind and every situation; his authority will discover, admonish, and at last chastise the negligence of his disciples; and his vigilant inquiries will ascer ain the steps of their literary progress. Whatever science he professes he may illustrate in a series of discourses, composed in the leisure of his closet, pronounced on public occasions, and finally delivered to the press. I observe with pleasure, that in the university of Oxford, Dr. Lowth, with equal eloquence and erudition, has executed this task in his incomparable *Prælections* on the Poetry of the Hebrews.

The college of St. Mary Magdalen was founded in the fifteenth century by Wainfleet, bishop of Winchester; and now consists of a president, forty fellows, and a number of inferior students. It is esteemed one of the largest and most wealthy of our academical corporations, which may be compared to the Benedictine abbeys of Catholic countries; and I have loosely heard that the estates belonging to Magdalen College, which are leased by those indulgent landlords at small quit-rents and occasional fines, might be raised, in the hands of private avarice, to an annual revenue of nearly thirty thousand pounds. Our colleges are supposed to be schools of science as well as of education; nor is it unreasonable to expect that a body of literary men, devoted to a life of celibacy, exempt from the care of their own subsistence, and amply provided with books, should devote their leisure to the prosecution of study, and that some effects of their studies should be manifested to the world. The shelves of their library groan under the weight of the Benedictine folios, of the editions of the fathers, and the collections of the middle ages, which have issued from the single abbey of St. Germain de Prez at Paris. A composition of genius must be the offspring of one mind; but such works of industry as may be divided among many hands, and must be continued during many years, are the peculiar province of a laborious community. If I inquire into the manufactures of the monks of Magdalen, if I extend the inquiry to the other colleges of Oxford and Cambridge, a silent blush, or a scornful frown, will be the only reply. The fellows or monks of my time were decent easy men, who supinely enjoyed the gifts of the founder; their days were filled by a series of uniform employments; the chapel and the hall, the coffee-house and the common room, till they retired, weary and well satisfied, to a long slumber. From the toil of reading, or thinking, or writing, they had absolved their conscience; and the first shoots of learning and ingenuity withered on the ground, without yielding any fruits to the owners or the public. As a gentleman commoner, I was admitted to the society of the fellows, and fondly expected that some questions of literature would be the amusing and instructive topics of their discourse. Their conversation stagnated in a round of college business, Tory politics, personal anecdotes, and private scandal: their dull and deep potations excused the brisk intemperance of youth; and their constitutional toasts were not expressive of the most lively loyalty for the house of Hanover. A general election was now approaching: the great Oxfordshire contest already blazed with all the malevolence of party zeal. Magdalen College was devoutly attached to the old interest! and the names of Wenman and Dashwood were more frequently pronounced than those of Cicero and Chrysostom. The example of the senior fellows could not inspire the undergraduates with a liberal spirit or studious emulation; and I cannot describe, as I never knew, the discipline of college. Some duties may possibly have been imposed on the poor scholars, whose ambition aspired to the peaceful honours of a fellowship (*ascribi quietis ordinibus . . . Deorum*); but no independent members were admitted below the rank of a gentleman commoner, and our velvet cap was the cap of liberty. A tradition prevailed that some of our predecessors had spoken Latin declamations in the hall, but of this ancient custom no vestige remained: the obvious methods of public exercises and examinations were totally unknown; and I have never heard that either the president or the society interfered in the private economy of the tutors and their pupils.

The silence of the Oxford professors, which deprives the youth of public instruction, is imperfectly supplied by the tutors, as they are styled, of the several colleges. Instead of confining themselves to a single science, which had satisfied the ambition of Burman, or Bernoulli, they teach, or promise to teach, either history or mathematics, or ancient literature, or moral philosophy; and as it is possible that they may be defective in all, it is highly probable that of some they will be ignorant. They are paid, indeed, by voluntary contributions; but their appointment depends on the head of the house: their diligence is voluntary, and will consequently be languid, while the pupils themselves, or their parents, are not indulged in the liberty of choice or change. The first tutor into whose hands I was resigned appears to have been one of the best of the tribe: Dr. Waldegrave was a learned and pious man, of a mild disposition, strict morals and abstemious life, who seldom mingled in the politics or the jollity of the college. But his knowledge of the world was confined to the university; his learning was of the last, rather than the present age; his temper was indolent; his faculties, which were not of the first rate, had been relaxed by the climate, and he was satisfied, like his fellows, with the slight and superficial discharge of an important trust. As soon as my tutor had sounded the insufficiency of his pupil in school-learning, he proposed that we should read every morning from ten to eleven the comedies of Terence. The sum of my improvement in the university of Oxford is confined to three or four Latin plays; and even the study of an elegant classic, which might have been illustrated by

a comparison of ancient and modern theatres, was reduced to a dry and literal interpretation of the author's
text.

. . . My temper is not very susceptible of enthusiasm; and the enthusiasm which I do not feel, I have
ever scorned to affect. But, at the distance of twenty-
five years, I can neither forget nor express the strong
emotions which agitated my mind as I first approached
and entered the *eternal city*. After a sleepless night, I
trod, with a lofty step, the ruins of the Forum; each
memorable spot where Romulus *stood*, or Tully spoke,
or Cæsar fell, was at once present to my eye; and
several days of intoxication were lost or enjoyed before
I could descend to a cool and minute investigation.
My guide was Mr. Byers, a Scotch antiquary of experience and taste; but, in the daily labour of eighteen
weeks, the powers of attention were sometimes fatigued, till I was myself qualified, in a last review, to
select and study the capital works of ancient and
modern art. Six weeks were borrowed for my tour of
Naples, the most populous of cities, relative to its size,
whose luxurious inhabitants seem to dwell on the con-
fines of paradise and hell-fire. I was presented to the
boy-king by our new envoy, Sir William Hamilton;
who, wisely diverting his correspondence from the
Secretary of State to the Royal Society and British
Museum, has elucidated a country of such inestimable
value to the naturalist and antiquarian. On my return,
I fondly embraced, for the last time, the miracles of
Rome; but I departed without kissing the feet of
Rezzonico (Clement XIII), who neither possessed the
wit of his predecessor Lambertini, nor the virtues of
his successor Ganganelli.

. . . It was at Rome, on the 15th of October, 1764, as I sat musing amidst the ruins of the Capitol, while the bare-footed fryars were singing vespers in the Temple of Jupiter, that the idea of writing the decline and fall of the city first started to my mind. But my original plan was circumscribed to the decay of the city rather than of the empire, and though my reading and reflections began to point towards that object, some years elapsed, and several avocations intervened, before I was seriously engaged in the execution of that laborious work.

It was not till after many designs, and many trials, that I preferred, as I still prefer, the method of grouping my picture by nations; and the seeming neglect of chronological order is surely compensated by the superior merits of interest and perspicuity. The style of the first volume is, in my opinion, somewhat crude and elaborate; in the second and third it is ripened into ease, correctness, and numbers; but in the three last I may have been seduced by the facility of my pen, and the constant habit of speaking one language and writing another may have infused some mixture of Gallic idioms. Happily for my eyes, I have always closed my studies with the day, and commonly with the morning; and a long, but temperate, labour has been accomplished, without fatiguing either the mind or body; but when I computed the remainder of my time and my task, it was apparent that, according to the season of publication, the delay of a month would be productive of that of a year. I was now straining for the goal, and in the last winter many evenings were borrowed from the social pleasures of Lausanne. I could now wish that a pause, an interval, had been allowed for a serious revisal.

I have presumed to mark the moment of conception: I shall now commemorate the hour of my final deliverance. It was on the day, or rather night, of the 27th of June, 1787, between the hours of eleven and twelve, that I wrote the last lines of the last page, in a summer-house in my garden. After laying down my pen, I took several turns in a *berceau,* or covered walk of acacias, which commands a prospect of the country, the lake, and the mountains. The air was temperate, the sky was serene, the silver orb of the moon was reflected from the waters, and all nature was silent. I will not dissemble the first emotions of joy on the recovery of my freedom, and, perhaps, the establishment of my fame. But my pride was soon humbled, and a sober melancholy was spread over my mind, by the idea that I had taken an everlasting leave of an old and agreeable companion, and that whatsoever might be the future date of my History, the life of the historian must be short and precarious. I will add two facts, which have seldom occurred in the composition of six, or at least of five quartos. 1. My first rough manuscript, without any intermediate copy, has been sent to the press. 2. Not a sheet has been seen by any human eyes, excepting those of the author and the printer; the faults and the merits are exclusively my own.

I cannot help recollecting a much more extraordinary fact, which is affirmed of himself by Restif de la Bretonne, a voluminous and original writer of French novels. He laboured, and may still labour, in the humble office of corrector to a printing-house; but this office enabled him to transport an entire volume from his mind to the press; and his work was given to the public without ever having been written with a pen.

From *The Memoirs of the Life of Edward Gibbon*, ed. G. B. Hill (London: Methuen & Co., 1900).

❖ ❖ ❖

Wild Life in Venice

[FROM *Memoirs*]

GIOVANNI JACOPO CASANOVA DE SEINGALT

After 1785

It was written that I should return to Venice as I left it, a mere ensign. The *proveditor* broke his word to me, and the bastard son of a Venetian nobleman was promoted over my head. From that moment military life became hateful to me, and I determined to abandon it. This chagrin was only an instance of the inconstancy of fortune; everything went against me, I never played but I lost, not at the tables only, but everywhere my luck seemed to have deserted me. When I first returned from Casopo I was the most feted man in Corfu, rich, lucky at cards, beloved by every one, and the favourite of the most beautiful woman in the city. I led the fashion. Then I began to lose health, money, credit, and consideration. My good humour and intelligence, the very faculty of expressing myself, seemed to leave me, to melt with my fortune. I chattered, but my words had no effect, for I was known to be down on my luck! The ascendency I had over Madame F—— went with the rest, the good lady became completely indifferent to me.

So I left the place almost penniless, after having sold or pawned everything I possessed of value. Twice I had gone to Corfu rich, and twice I had left it poor, and I contracted debts which I have never paid, more from carelessness than want of will. When I was rich and happy everyone made much of me, when I was poor and lean no one showed me consideration. With a full purse and an air of confidence I was thought witty and amusing; with an empty purse, and told in a different voice, my stories were stupid and insipid. Had I suddenly grown rich again, I should once more have been considered the eighth wonder of the world. O men! O fortune! I was avoided, as though the ill luck which pursued me had been infectious.

When I got to Venice my first visit was to my guardian, M. Grimani. He received me kindly, but told me that he had my brother François in safe keeping at the fort of Saint Andrew, where he had formerly imprisoned me.

"He is working hard," he said, "copying the battle pieces of Simonetti, which he sells, so he manages to earn his living and study to become a good painter at one and the same time."

On leaving M. Grimani I went to the fort, where I found my brother, brush in hand. He seemed neither happy nor unhappy, and was in excellent health. When I asked him for what crime he was shut up, he answered: "Ask the major, perhaps he can tell you; for my part I have not the least idea."

The major came in just then, and after saluting him I asked by what right he kept my brother in confinement.

"I have no explanation to give you," he answered curtly.

The next day I went to the war office, and laid a complaint before the minister, at the same time notifying him of my desire to resign my commission.

Shortly after, my brother was set at liberty, and the acceptance of my resignation was notified to me. I pocketed a hundred sequins for my commission, laid aside my uniform, and became once more my own master.

I had to think seriously of some means of earning my living. I decided to become a professional gambler; but Dame Fortune did not favour me, and in eight days I found myself without a sol. What could I do? I had no desire to starve, but no one was willing to employ me. It was then that my humble musical talent stood me in good stead. Dr. Gozzi had taught me how to scrape a tune on a fiddle, and M. Grimani got me a place in his theatre of Saint Samuel, where I was paid a crown a day. On this I could manage till something better turned up.

I did not show my nose in any of the houses where I had once been so welcome. I judged that I had fallen too low to be received by the *beau-monde*. I knew I was considered a scapegrace, but I did not care. People despised me, but I knew that I had done nothing despicable. The position humiliated me, but so long as I did not expose myself to slights, I did not feel myself degraded. I had not given up all hopes of better fortune. I was still young, and the volatile goddess smiles on youth. I earned enough by my violin to keep me without asking help from anyone. Happy is the man who can manage to keep himself. I tried to stifle my better nature, and threw myself heart and soul into the pursuits and habits of my low companions. After the play I would go with them to some cabaret, where we would remain till we were drunk, and then depart to finish the night in still lower resorts. We would amuse ourselves with inventing and executing the wildest acts of bravado in different quarters of the town.

In the month of April, the eldest son of the Cornaros married one of the daughters of the house of Saint Pol, and I was bidden to the wedding in my quality of musician. The third day of the feast, as I was going home about an hour before dawn, I saw a senator in his red robes going down the stairs in front of me; as he stepped into his gondola, he dropped a letter from his pocket; I hurried after him to return it. Having thanked me, he asked me where I lived, telling me to get into his gondola and he would take me home. We had hardly been seated a moment when he asked me to shake his left arm, for he felt a strange numbness in it. I worked it up and down vigorously, but he said, in an indistinct voice, that the numbness was spreading up his left side, and that he believed he was dying. I pulled back the curtain, and saw by the lamplight that his mouth was drawn all awry. I knew that it was apoplexy. I called to the gondoliers to stop, while I ran for a doctor. I found one in a few minutes and hurried him away with me in his dressing-gown. He bled the senator, while I tore up my shirt for bandages. This done, the gondoliers rowed in haste to their master's place at San Marino, where we aroused the servants, and I carried him almost lifeless to bed.

Voting myself into the place of command, I sent for another doctor, and took my place at the bedside. By and by two noblemen, friends of the sick man, came in. They were in despair. They questioned me, and I told them what I could. They did not know who I was, and they did not dare to ask. For my part I thought it best to maintain a discreet silence. The sick man gave no sign of life. We remained with him throughout the day. A quiet little dinner was served to us, which we partook of in the sickroom.

In the evening the elder of the friends told me if I had business elsewhere I must not neglect it—they would pass the night with the invalid.

"And I, gentlemen," said I, "will pass the night in this armchair, for if I leave this poor man he will die, whereas so long as I remain he will live."

This sententious reply struck them dumb with surprise; they exchanged glances. We sat down to supper, and in the course of conversation I learned that the patient was M. de Bragadin, celebrated in Venice for his eloquence, his talents as a statesman, and the gallant adventures of his youth. He was handsome, learned, lively, kind-hearted, and about fifty years old. One of his friends belonged to the family of Dandolo; the other was a Barbaro. They were all three devotedly attached to each other, and lived in the closest intimacy.

About midnight our patient became worse, the fever increased, and he seemed hardly able to breathe. I called up his two friends, and told them that I was certain he would die unless we removed a huge mercury plaster with which the doctor had covered his chest: without waiting for their sanction I tore it off and sponged him with warm water. In less than five minutes he began to breathe peacefully, and by and by fell into a quiet sleep. When the doctor came in the morning, M. de Bragadin was well enough to tell him himself what had happened, adding, "Providence has sent me a physician who knows more of medicine than you do."

"In that case I will retire, and leave you in his charge," replied the doctor, and bowing coldly to me, he departed.

I saw that I had bewitched the three worthy friends, and I began to give myself airs, lay down the law, and quote authors whom I had never read.

M. de Bragadin had a weakness for abstract science, and one day he told me he was sure I possessed a superhuman knowledge, I was too learned for a young man. I did not want to shock his vanity by contradicting him, and then and there, in the presence of his friends made a most extravagant statement. I told him an old hermit had taught me how to make certain numerical calculations, by means of which I could obtain an answer to any question if I wrote it down according to a system he had also imparted to me, the words of the question must be represented by numbers, and pyramidal numbers, the answers were given in the same form.

"The answers are sometimes very obscure," I said, "yet if I had not consulted my oracle the other night, I should not now have the pleasure of knowing your excellencies. When I asked if I should meet anyone at the ball whose encounter would be disagreeable to me, I was told, 'You must leave the ball one hour before dawn.' I obeyed, and your excellency knows the rest."

"It is the clavicula of Solomon which you possess," said M. de Bragadin, "which the vulgar call the *cabbala*. It is a veritable treasure. You can, if you like, make your fortune with it."

"I got it," I said, "from a hermit on Mount Carpegna, when I was under arrest in the Spanish army."

I saw I had produced a good effect on my listeners; the difficulty was not to destroy it. M. Dandolo said he would write a question the meaning of which could only be understood by himself. He handed me a slip of paper couched in such obscure language I could make neither head nor tail of it; but it was too late to draw back. I could but trust to effrontery to carry me through. I put down four lines in ordinary figures, and handed them to him with an indifferent air. He read them, reread them, and then pronounced the reply to have been inspired by more than mortal intelligence. I was saved.

It was now the turn of the others. They questioned me on all sorts of subjects. My answers, perfectly incomprehensible to myself as they were, enchanted them. They found in each the solution they chose to find, and they asked me in how short a time I could teach them the rules of my sublime science.

"In a few hours," I said, "and I shall be very glad to do so. Although the hermit assured me that if I communicated the secret to anyone, I should die suddenly within three days—this may, however, have been merely a threat."

On hearing this, M. de Bragadin looked very grave, and said I must believe what the hermit had told me, and obey him implicitly, and from this time forth there was no further question of their learning the secret.

In this way I became the hierophant of the three friends, who, in spite of their education and literary ability, were perfectly infatuated about the occult sciences, and believed in the possibility of all sorts of things contrary to moral and physical laws. These noblemen were not only good Christians, they were devout and scrupulous in the exercise of their religion.

They were none of them married, and they had forever renounced the society of women, whose implacable foes they now were. They maintained that it was the necessary condition of communication and intimate intercourse with spirits.

It was not very commendable of me to deceive them in this way, but I was only twenty, and had been earning my bread in the orchestra of a theatre, and it was none of my business to point out to them the folly of their allusions. I did but add one to the number when I constituted myself their apostle. I procured for them a great deal of innocent pleasure, and for myself some pleasure which was not so innocent, but, as I said before, I was twenty years old and had a fine constitution. What man, given these advantages, does not seek by every possible means to get all the good he can out of life?

No one in Venice could understand how men of their character could associate with a man of mine. They were all heavenly, I was all earthly; they were severe and strict in their lives, I was entirely given up to pleasure. No one guessed the secret, and I daily strengthened the hold I had on them. By the beginning of summer M. de Bragadin was well enough to appear at the Senate. The day before he resumed his seat there he sent for me.

"Whatever you may be," he said, "I owe you my life. Your former protectors who tried to make you a priest, a doctor, a lawyer, or a soldier, only succeeded in making a fiddler of you; they were fools who did not understand you. Your guardian angel has brought you to me; I understand and appreciate you. I shall treat you as my son to the day of my death. Your place will be always laid at my table, your room is ready for you in my palace. You will have a servant to wait entirely on you, a private gondola, and ten sequins a month for pocket money; it is what my father gave me when I was your age. You need have no thought for the future; you have nothing to do but to amuse yourself, and whatever may happen, be sure I shall always be your father and friend."

Such, my dear reader, is the history of my metamorphosis; from the rank of a poor violinist, I was suddenly raised to that of the rich and powerful.

From *The Memoirs of Jacques Casanova* (Garden City, New York: Garden City Publishing Company, 1929).

❖ ❖ ❖

A Few Days of Samuel Johnson

[FROM *Life of Johnson*]

JAMES BOSWELL

1791

On the 30th of September [1769] we dined together at the Mitre. I attempted to argue for the superior happiness of the savage life, upon the usual fanciful topicks. JOHNSON. "Sir, there can be nothing more false. The savages have no bodily advantages beyond those of civilised men. They have not better health; and as to care or mental uneasiness, they are not above it, but below it, like bears. No, Sir; you are not to talk such paradox: let me have no more on't. It cannot entertain, far less can it instruct. Lord Monboddo, one of your Scotch Judges, talked a great deal of such nonsense. I suffered *him;* but I will not suffer *you.*"

BOSWELL. "But, Sir, does not Rousseau talk such non-sense?" JOHNSON. "True, Sir; but Rousseau *knows* he is talking nonsense, and laughs at the world for staring at him." BOSWELL. "How so, Sir?" JOHNSON. "Why, Sir, a man who talks nonsense so well, must know that he is talking nonsense. But I am *afraid,* (chuckling and laughing,) Monboddo dces *not* know that he is talking nonsense." BOSWELL. "Is it wrong then, Sir, to affect singularity, in order to make people stare?" JOHNSON. "Yes, if you do it by propagating errour: and, indeed, it is wrong in any way. There is in human nature a general inclination to make people stare; and every wise man has himself to cure of it, and does cure himself. If you wish to make people stare by doing better than others, why, make them stare till they stare their eyes out. But consider how easy it is to make people stare by being absurd. I may do it by going into a drawing-room without my shoes. You remember the gentleman in *The Spectator,* who had a commission of lunacy taken out against him for his extreme singularity, such as never wearing a wig, but a night-cap. Now, Sir, abstractedly, the night-cap was best; but, relatively, the advantage was overbalanced by his making the boys run after him."

Talking of a London life, he said, "The happiness of London is not to be conceived but by those who have been in it. I will venture to say, there is more learning and science within the circumference of ten miles from where we now sit, than in all the rest of the kingdom." BOSWELL. "The only disadvantage is the great distance at which people live from one another." JOHNSON. "Yes, Sir; but that is occasioned by the largeness of it, which is the cause of all the other advantages." BOSWELL. "Sometimes I have been in the humour of wishing to retire to a desart." JOHNSON. "Sir, you have desart enough in Scotland."

On Tuesday, April 13 [1773], he and Dr. Goldsmith and I dined at General Oglethorpe's. Goldsmith expatiated on the common topick, that the race of our people was degenerated, and that this was owing to luxury. JOHNSON. "Sir, in the first place, I doubt the fact. I believe there are as many tall men in England now, as ever there were. But, secondly, supposing the stature of our people to be diminished, that is not owing to luxury; for, Sir, consider to how very small a proportion of our people luxury can reach. Our soldiery, surely, are not luxurious, who live on sixpence a day; and the same remark will apply to almost all the other classes. Luxury, so far as it reaches the poor, will do good to the race of people; it will strengthen and multiply them. Sir, no nation was ever hurt by luxury; for, as I said before, it can reach but to a very few. I admit that the great increase of commerce and manufactures hurts the military spirit of a people; because it produces a competition for something else than martial honours—a competition for riches. It also hurts the bodies of the people; for you will observe, there is no man who works at any particular trade, but you may know him from his appearance to do so. One part or other of his body being more used than the rest, he is in some degree deformed: but, Sir, that is not luxury. A tailor sits cross-legged; but that is not luxury." GOLDSMITH. "Come, you're just going to the same place by another road." JOHNSON. "Nay, Sir, I say that is not *luxury*. Let us take a walk from Charing-cross to Whitechapel, through, I suppose, the greatest series of shops in the world; what is there in any of these shops (if you except gin-shops,) that can do any human being any harm?" GOLDSMITH. "Well, Sir, I'll accept your challenge. The very next shop to Northumberland-house is a pickle-shop." JOHNSON. "Well, Sir: do we not know that a maid can in one afternoon make pickles sufficient to serve a whole family for a year? nay, that five pickle-shops can serve all the kingdom? Besides, Sir, there is no harm done to any body by the making of pickles, or the eating of pickles."

We drank tea with the ladies; and Goldsmith sung Tony Lumpkin's song in his comedy, *She Stoops to Conquer,* and a very pretty one, to an Irish tune, which he had designed for Miss Hardcastle; but as Mrs. Bulkeley, who played the part, could not sing, it was left out. He afterwards wrote it down for me, by which means it was preserved, and now appears amongst his poems. Dr. Johnson, in his way home, stopped at my lodgings in Piccadilly, and sat with me, drinking tea a second time, till a late hour.

I told him that Mrs. Macaulay said, she wondered how he could reconcile his political principles with his moral; his notions of inequality and subordination with wishing well to the happiness of all mankind, who might live so agreeably, had they all their portions of land, and none to domineer over another. JOHNSON. "Why, Sir, I reconcile my principles very well, because mankind are happier in a state of inequality and subordination. Were they to be in this pretty state of equality, they would soon degenerate into brutes; they would become Monboddo's nation; their tails would grow. Sir, all would be losers were all to work for all: they would have no intellectual improvement. All intellectual improvement arises from leisure; all leisure arises from one working for another."

Talking of the family of Stuart, he said, "It should seem that the family at present on the throne has now established as good a right as the former family, by the long consent of the people; and that to disturb this right might be considered as culpable. At the same time I own, that it is a very difficult question, when considered with respect to the house of Stuart. To oblige people to take oaths as to the disputed right, is wrong. I know not whether I could take them: but I do not blame those who do." So conscientious and so delicate was he upon this subject, which has occasioned so much clamour against him.

Talking of law cases, he said, "The English reports, in general, are very poor: only the half of what has been said is taken down; and of that half, much is mistaken. Whereas, in Scotland, the arguments on each side are deliberately put in writing, to be considered by the Court. I think a collection of your cases upon subjects of importance, with the opinions of the Judges upon them, would be valuable."

On Thursday, April 15, I dined with him and Dr. Goldsmith at General Paoli's. We found here Signor Martinelli, of Florence, authour of a *History of England*, in Italian, printed at London.

I spoke of Allan Ramsay's *Gentle Shepherd*, in the Scottish dialect, as the best pastoral that had ever been written; not only abounding with beautiful rural imagery, and just and pleasing sentiments, but being a real picture of manners; and I offered to teach Dr. Johnson to understand it. "No, Sir, (said he,) I won't learn it. You shall retain your superiority by my not knowing it."

This brought on a question whether one man is lessened by another's acquiring an equal degree of knowledge with him. Johnson asserted the affirmative. I maintained that the position might be true in those kinds of knowledge which produce wisdom, power, and force, so as to enable one man to have the government of others; but that a man is not in any degree lessened by others knowing as well as he what ends in mere pleasure: eating fine fruits, drinking delicious wines, reading exquisite poetry.

The General observed, that Martinelli was a Whig. JOHNSON. "I am sorry for it. It shows the spirit of the times: he is obliged to temporise." BOSWELL. "I rather think, Sir, that Toryism prevails in this reign." JOHNSON. "I know not why you should think so, Sir. You see your friend Lord Lyttelton, a nobleman, is obliged in his *History* to write the most vulgar Whiggism.". . .

We talked of the King's coming to see Goldsmith's new play. "I wish he would," said Goldsmith; adding, however, with an affected indifference, "Not that it would do me the least good." JOHNSON. "Well then, Sir, let us say it would do *him* good, (laughing). No, Sir, this affectation will not pass; it is mighty idle. In such a state as ours, who would not wish to please the Chief Magistrate?" GOLDSMITH. "I *do* wish to please him. I remember a line in Dryden,

'And every poet is the monarch's friend.'

It ought to be reversed." JOHNSON. "Nay, there are finer lines in Dryden on this subject:

'For colleges on bounteous Kings depend,
And never rebel was to arts a friend.'"

General Paoli observed, that "successful rebels

might." MARTINELLI. "Happy rebellions." GOLDSMITH.
"We have no such phrase." GENERAL PAOLI. "But have
you not the *thing?*" GOLDSMITH. "Yes; all our *happy*
revolutions. They have hurt our constitution, and will
hurt it, till we mend it by another HAPPY REVOLU-
TION." I never before discovered that my friend Goldsmith had so much of the old prejudice in him.

(London: Oxford University Press, 1953).

❖ ❖ ❖

A Sévigné Sample

[FROM *Letters*]

MADAME DE SÉVIGNÉ

TO HER DAUGHTER, MADAME DE GRIGNAN

Paris, Friday, March 13, 1671.
To the joy of my heart, I am alone in my own apartment, and writing quietly to you—a most agreeable
situation. I dined today at Madame de Lavardin's after
having been to Bourdaloue, where I saw the mothers of
the church, for so I call the princesses of Conti and
Longueville. All the world was at the sermon, and the
sermon was worthy of the audience. I thought of you
twenty times, and wished as often that you were with
me: you would have been delighted to hear it, and I
should have been still more delighted to have seen
you listening to it. Monsieur de la Rouchefoucauld
was at Madame de Lavardin's, and received with
pleasantry the compliment you sent him: we talked a

great deal about you. Monsieur d'Ambres was there
with his cousin de Brissac: he appeared greatly interested in your supposed shipwreck; and but one opinion prevailed respecting your temerity. Monsieur de
la Rouchefoucauld said that you wished to appear
courageous in the hope that some compassionate person would hinder you from going. . . . We have been
to the fair to see a monster of a woman; she is taller
than Riberpré by a whole head: she was brought to
bed the other day, of two enormous children, who
came into the world abreast, with their arms a-kimbo.
She is a perfect giantess. I have given your compliments to the de Rambouillets, who send you a
thousand in return. I have been at Madame du Puy-
du-Fou's, and at Madame de Maillane's, for the third
time: I often smile to myself at the pleasure I take
in these little things. And now, should you suppose
that the Queen's women are all run mad, you would
not suppose amiss: for about a week since, Mesd. de
Ludres, Coëtlogon, and little Rouvroy, were bitten
by a dog belonging to Theobon, which has since died
mad; so that de Ludres, Coëtlogon, and Rouvroy, are
set out this morning for Dieppe, for the purpose of
bathing in the salt water: it is a melancholy journey
for them, Benserade was quite in despair; Theobon
would not go, though she was slightly bitten; but the
Queen will not let her be in waiting, till it is seen
how this adventure terminates. Can you fancy de
Ludres an Andromeda? For my part, I think I see her
bound to a rock, and Treville on a flying horse, slaying
the monster. *Ah! my Cot, Matame de Grignan, vat a
ting it is to pe trown naket into te sea!* [1]

[1] Madame de Ludres spoke with a heavy German accent.
[C.B.'s note.]

Here is a budget full of nonsense, but not a syllable yet from you: you may suppose that I can guess at what you are doing; but the state of your health and your mind is too precious for me to rest satisfied with mere conjecture. The most trifling circumstances that relate to those we love are as dear to us as the concerns of others about whom we are indifferent are troublesome. In this truth we have often agreed. . . . I send you a letter from Monsieur Condom, which I received enclosed in a very pretty note. Your brother wears the chains of Ninon[2]; I wish they may do him no harm. There are minds that shudder at such ties. This same Ninon corrupted the morals of his father. Let us commend him to God. A Christian, or at least one who wishes to be a Christian, cannot see these irregularities without concern. Ah, Bourdaloue! what divine truths did you tell us today on the subject of death! Madame de la Fayette was there for the first time in her life, and was overcome with admiration: she is highly delighted with your remembrance of her. I have made her a present of a fine copy of your picture; it ornaments a room in which you are never forgotten. If you are still in the same humour you were in at Saint Mary's, and preserve my letters, see if you have not received one dated the 18th of February.

March 30, 1671.

A circumstance took place yesterday at Mademoiselle's, which gave me no small pleasure. Who should

---

[2] This is the very celebrated courtesan, wit, and free-thinker, Ninon de L'Enclos (about 1620-1705), who is said to have had love affairs up to a prodigiously great age. [C.B.'s note.]

come in but Madame de Gêvres, in all her airs and graces! I fancy she expected I should have offered her my place; but, to say the truth, I have owed her a little grudge for her conduct the other day, and now I paid her with interest, for I did not stir. Mademoiselle was in bed; Madame de Gêvres was therefore obliged to place herself at the lower end of the room, a provoking thing to be sure. The princess called for drink; somebody must present the napkin. I perceived Madame de Gêvres drawing the glove from her withered hand, upon which I gave Madame d'Arpajon, who was above me, a push, which she understood; and pulling off her glove, with the best grace in the world, advanced a step, got before the duchess, took the napkin, and presented it. The duchess was perfectly embarrassed; for she had reached the upper end of the room, and had pulled off her gloves, only to have the mortification of being a nearer witness of Madame d'Arpajon's presenting the napkin before her. My dear child, I am very wicked; this pleased me infinitely: it was uncommonly well done. Would anyone have thought of depriving Madame d'Arpajon of a little piece of honour, which is naturally her due, as being one of the bedchamber? Madame de Puisieux was very much diverted at it. As for Mademoiselle, she did not dare look up, and my countenance was not the most settled. After this, a thousand kind things were said to me about you; and Mademoiselle was pleased to order me to tell you, that she is very glad you escaped drowning, and are in good health.

I shall give you the two volumes of La Fontaine; and be as angry as you please, I insist upon it that they have some entertaining passages, and some very dull ones. We are never satisfied with having done

for England to remain in a gross and avowed error, especially in such company; the inconvenience of it was likewise felt by all those who had foreign correspondences, whether political or mercantile. I determined, therefore, to attempt the reformation; I consulted the best lawyers, and the most skilful astronomers, and we cooked up a bill for that purpose. But then my difficulty began; I was to bring in this bill, which was necessarily composed of law jargon and astronomical calculations, to both which I am an utter stranger. However, it was absolutely necessary to make the House of Lords think that I knew something of the matter, and also to make them believe that they knew something of it themselves, which they do not. For my own part, I could just as soon have talked Celtic or Sclavonian to them as astronomy, and they would have understood me full as well; so I resolved to do better than speak to the purpose, and to please instead of informing them. I gave them, therefore, only an historical account of calendars, from the Egyptian down to the Gregorian, amusing them now and then with little episodes; but I was particularly attentive to the choice of my words, to the harmony and roundness of my periods, to my elocution, to my action. This succeeded, and ever will succeed; they thought I informed, because I pleased them; and many of them said, that I had made the whole very clear to them, when, God knows, I had not even attempted it. Lord Macclesfield, who had the greatest share in forming the bill, and who is one of the greatest mathematicians and astronomers in Europe, spoke afterwards with infinite knowledge, and all the clearness that so intricate a matter would admit of; but as his words, his periods, and his utterance were not near so good as mine, the preference was most unanimously, though most unjustly, given to me. This will ever be the case; every numerous assembly is *mob,* let the individuals who compose it be what they will. Mere reason and good sense is never to be talked to a mob; their passions, their sentiments, their senses, and their seeming interests, are alone to be applied to. Understanding they have collectively none; but they have ears and eyes, which must be flattered and seduced; and this can only be done by eloquence, tuneful periods, graceful action, and all the various parts of oratory.

When you come into the House of Commons, if you imagine that speaking plain and unadorned sense and reason will do your business, you will find yourself most grossly mistaken. As a speaker, you will be ranked only according to your eloquence, and by no means according to your matter; everybody knows the matter almost alike, but few can adorn it. I was early convinced of the importance and powers of eloquence, and from that moment I applied myself to it. I resolved not to utter one word, even in common conversation, that should not be the most expressive and the most elegant that the language could supply me with for that purpose; by which means I have acquired such a certain degree of habitual eloquence, that I must now really take some pains, if I would express myself very inelegantly. I want to inculcate this known truth into you, which you seem by no means to be convinced of yet—that ornaments are at present your only objects. Your sole business now is to shine, not to weigh. Weight without lustre is lead. You had better talk trifles elegantly, to the most trifling woman, than coarse inelegant sense to the most solid man. You had better return a dropped fan genteely, than give a thousand pounds awkwardly; and you had better refuse a favour gracefully, than grant it clumsily. Manner is all in everything; it is by manner only that you can please, and consequently rise. All your Greek will never advance you from Secretary to Envoy, or from Envoy to Ambassador; but your address, your manner, your air, if good, very probably may. Marcel can be of much more use to you than Aristotle. I would, upon my word, much rather that you had Lord Bolingbroke's style and eloquence, in speaking and writing, than all the learning of the Academy of Sciences, the Royal Society, and the two Universities united.

From *The Letters of Philip Dormer Stanhope, 4th Earl of Chesterfield*, Vol. IV, ed. Bonamy Dobrée (London: Eyre & Spottiswoode, 1932; New York: The Viking Press, 1932).

Voltaire and Frederick: The Crisis

François Marie Arouet de VOLTAIRE

to Frederick the Great

Paris, 15th October, 1749.

Sire,

I have just made an effort in my present dreadful state of mind to write to M. d'Argens; I will make another to throw myself at your Majesty's feet.

I have lost one who was my friend for twenty-five years, a great man, whose only defect was being a woman, whom all Paris regrets and honours. She did not perhaps receive justice during her life, and you perhaps have not judged her as you would have done, if she had had the honour to be known to your Majesty. But a woman who could translate Newton and Vergil, and who had all the virtues of a man of honour, will no doubt have a share in your regret.

The state I have been in for the last month hardly leaves me a hope of ever seeing you; but I will tell you boldly that if you knew my heart better you might also have the goodness to regret a man who has loved in your Majesty nothing but your person.

Sire, you are a very great king; you dictated peace in Dresden; your name will be great throughout all ages; but all your fame and all your power do not give you the right to distress a heart wholly devoted to you. Were I as well as I am ill, were I but ten leagues from your dominions, I would not stir a foot to visit the court of a great man who did not love me and who only sent for me as a sovereign. But if you knew me, if you had a true kindness for me, I would go to Pekin to throw myself at your feet. I am a man of sensibility, Sire, and nothing but that. I have perhaps only two days left to live, I shall spend them in admiring you but in deploring the injustice you do a soul which was so devoted to yours, and which still loves you as M. de Fénelon loved God—for his own sake. God should not scorn one who offers so rare an incense.

Continue to believe, if you please, that I have no need of petty vanities and that I seek you alone.

Paris, 10th November, 1749.

SIRE,

I received almost at the same time three letters from your Majesty; one dated the 10th September, via

Frankfort, forwarded from Frankfort to Lunéville, sent on to Paris, to Cirey, back to Lunéville and again to Paris, while I was in the country in the most complete retirement; the two others reached me the day before yesterday by the offices of M. Chambrier, who is still I think at Fontainebleau. Alas! Sire, if the first of these letters had reached me in the crisis of my grief, at the time when I ought to have received it, I should only have left that disastrous Lorraine for you; I should have left it to throw myself at your feet; I should have come to hide myself in some corner of Potsdam or Sans Souci; half dead as I was, I should certainly have made this journey; I should have found the strength for it. I should even have had reasons which you may guess, for preferring to die in your dominions rather than in the country where I was born.

What has happened? Your silence made me think that my request had displeased you; that you had really no feeling of kindness towards me; that you took what I proposed as a subterfuge and a determined wish to remain near King Stanislas. His Court, where I saw Mme. du Châtelet die in a way a hundred times more dreadful than you can believe, became for me a horrible dwelling-place, in spite of my tender attachment for that good prince and in spite of his extreme kindness. I therefore returned to Paris; I collected my family about me, I took a house, I found myself the father of a family without having any children. Thus in my grief I have made myself a quiet and honourable establishment, and I am passing the winter in these arrangements and in my business affairs which were mixed up with those of her whom death should not have carried off before me. But, since you are still graciously pleased to love me a little, your Majesty may be very sure that I shall come and throw myself at your feet next summer, if I am still alive. I now need no pretext, I need only the continuation of your kindness. I shall spend a week with King Stanislas, a duty I must fulfill; and the rest shall be for your Majesty.

I beg you will be convinced that I only thought of that black rag because at that time King Stanislas would not have allowed me to leave him. I thought you had conferred that favour upon M. de Maupertuis. I expect new presents from your pen, and I flatter myself that the cargo you will receive immediately from me will bring me one from you. I shall have the honour to continue this little commerce during the winter; and with due respect, Sire, I think that you and I are the only two merchants of that sort in Europe. I shall then come to look over your accounts, to expatiate, to talk of grammar and poetry; I shall bring you Madame du Châtelet's analytical grammar and as much as I can collect of her Vergil; in a word, I shall come with full pockets and I shall find your portfolios well furnished. I have a delicious expectation of these moments; but it is on the express condition that you are graciously pleased to love me a little, for otherwise I shall die at Paris.

From *Letters of Voltaire and Frederick the Great*, trans. Richard Aldington (London: Routledge, 1927).

❖ ❖ ❖

In Defense of Civilization

François Marie Arouet de
VOLTAIRE

TO JEAN JACQUES ROUSSEAU

Les Délices, August 30, 1755.

I have received, sir, your new book against the human species, and I thank you for it. You will please people by your manner of telling them the truth about themselves, but you will not alter them. The horrors of that human society—from which in our feebleness and ignorance we expect so many consolations—have never been painted in more striking colors: no one has ever been so witty as you are in trying to turn us into brutes: to read your book makes one long to go on all fours. Since, however, it is now some sixty years since I gave up the practice, I feel that it is unfortunately impossible for me to resume it: I leave this natural habit to those more fit for it than are you and I. Nor can I set sail to discover the aborigines of Canada, in the first place because my ill health ties me to the side of the greatest doctor in Europe,[1] and I should not find the same professional assistance among the Missouris: and secondly because war is going on in that country, and the example of the civilized nations has made the barbarians almost as wicked as we are

[1] Dr. Theodore Tronchin. [Notes are the trans.]

ourselves. I must confine myself to being a peaceful savage in the retreat I have chosen—close to your country, where you yourself should be.

I agree with you that science and literature have sometimes done a great deal of harm. Tasso's enemies made his life a long series of misfortunes: Galileo's enemies kept him languishing in prison, at seventy years of age, for the crime of understanding the revolution of the earth: and, what is still more shameful, obliged him to forswear his discovery. Since your friends began the Encyclopedia, their rivals attack them as deists, atheists—even Jansenists.

If I might venture to include myself among those whose works have brought them persecution as their sole recompense, I could tell you of men set on ruining me from the day I produced my tragedy *Oedipe:* of a perfect library of absurd calumnies which have been written against me: of an ex-Jesuit[2] priest whom I saved from utter disgrace rewarding me by defamatory libels: of a man yet more contemptible[3] printing my *Century of Louis XIV* with *Notes* in which crass ignorance gave birth to the most abominable falsehoods: of yet another, who sold to a publisher some chapters of a *Universal History* supposed to be by me: of the publisher avaricious enough to print this shapeless mass of blunders, wrong dates, mutilated facts and names: and, finally, of men sufficiently base and craven to assign the production of this farago to me. I could show you all society poisoned by this class of person —a class unknown to the ancients—who, not being able to find any honest occupation—be it manual labour or service—and unluckily knowing how to read and write, become the brokers of literature, live on our

[2] The Abbé Desfontaines.
[3] La Baumelle, who pirated Voltaire's *Louis XIV*.

works, steal our manuscripts, falsify them, and sell them. I could tell of some loose sheets of a gay trifle[4] which I wrote thirty years ago (on the same subject that Chapelain was stupid enough to treat seriously) which are in circulation now through the breach of faith and the cupidity of those who added their own grossness to my *badinage* and filled in the gaps with a dullness only equalled by their malice; and who, finally, after twenty years, are selling everywhere a manuscript which, in very truth, is theirs and worthy of them only.

I may add, last of all, that someone has stolen part of the material I amassed in the public archives to use in my History of the War of 1741 when I was historiographer of France; that he sold that result of my labours to a bookseller in Paris; and is as set on getting hold of my property as if I were dead and he could turn it into money by putting it up to auction. I could show you ingratitude, imposture, and rapine pursuing me for forty years to the foot of the Alps and the brink of the grave. But what conclusion ought I to draw from all these misfortunes? This only: that I have no right to complain: Pope, Descartes, Bayle, Camoëns— a hundred others—have been subjected to the same, or greater, injustice: and my destiny is that of nearly everyone who has loved letters too well.

Confess, sir, that all these things are, after all, but little personal pinpricks, which society scarcely notices. What matter to humankind that a few drones steal the honey of a few bees? Literary men make a great fuss of their petty quarrels: the rest of the world ignores them, or laughs at them.

They are, perhaps, the least serious of all the ills attendant on human life. The thorns inseparable from

[4] *La Pucelle.*

literature and a modest degree of fame are flowers in comparison with the other evils which from all time have flooded the world. Neither Cicero, Varron, Lucretius, Virgil, or Horace had any part in the proscriptions of Marius, Scylla, that profligate Antony, or that fool Lepidus; while as for that cowardly tyrant, Octavius Caesar—servilely entitled Augustus—he only became an assassin when he was deprived of the society of men of letters.

Confess that Italy owed none of her troubles to Petrarch or to Boccaccio: that Marot's jests were not responsible for the massacre of St. Bartholomew: or that tragedy of the *Cid* for the wars of the Fronde. Great crimes are always committed by great ignoramuses. What makes, and will always make, this world a vale of tears is the insatiable greediness and the indomitable pride of men, from Thomas Koulikan, who did not know how to read, to a customhouse officer who can just count. Letters support, refine, and comfort the soul: they are serving you, sir, at the very moment you decry them: you are like Achilles declaiming against fame, and Father Malebranche using his brilliant imagination to belittle imagination.

If anyone has a right to complain of letters, I am that person, for in all times and in all places they have led to my being persecuted: still, we must needs love them in spite of the way they are abused—as we cling to society, though the wicked spoil its pleasantness: as we must love our country, though it treats us unjustly: and as we must love and serve the Supreme Being, despite the superstition and fanaticism which too often dishonour His service.

M. Chappus tells me your health is very unsatisfactory: you must come and recover here in your native place, enjoy its freedom, drink (with me) the milk of its cows, and browse on its grass.

I am yours most philosophically and with sincere esteem.

From *Voltaire in His Letters*, trans. S. G. Tallentyre (New York: G. P. Putnam's Sons, 1919).

❖ ❖ ❖

A Portrait of M. de Voltaire

[FROM *Posthumous Works*]

FREDERICK THE GREAT

1756

M. de Voltaire is very thin in person; not tall, but rather of the middle size. He is constitutionally hot and atrabilarious, meagre-visaged, with an ardent and penetrating look, and a quick and malignant eye. In action, though he is sometimes absurd from vivacity, he appears to be animated with the same fire that inspires his works. Like a meteor, which is momentarily seen, and as often vanishing, he dazzles us with his lustre. A man of such a temperament must necessarily be a valetudinarian. The blade continually lacerates the scabbard. Habitually gay, yet grave from restraint; frank yet not candid; politic yet not artful; knowing the world which he neglects, he is now Aristippus, and anon Diogenes. Loving pomp, yet despising the great, he behaves without restraint to his superiors, but with reserve to his equals. Polite on a first approach, he soon becomes freezingly cold. He delights in yet takes offence at courts. With great sensibility he forms but few friendships, and abstains from pleasure only from the absence of passion. When he attaches himself to anyone, it is rather from levity than choice. He reasons without principles, which is the cause that he, like the herd of mankind, is subject to fits of folly. With a liberal head he has a corrupted heart. He reflects on all, and turns all into ridicule. A libertine without stamina, a moralist destitute of morality, and vain to the most supreme degree. Yet is his vanity inferior to his avarice. He writes less for fame than for money, and may be said to labour only to live. Though formed for enjoyment, he is never weary of amassing.

Such is the man, here follows the author.

No poet ever wrote verses with more facility; but this facility is detrimental, by being abused. None of his works are finished, for he does not give himself sufficient attention to retouch them. His verses are rich, elegant, and full of wit. He would succeed better in writing history, were he less prodigal of his reflections, and more fortunate in his comparisons; for which he has nevertheless merited applause. In his last work, he has criticised, corrected, copied, and imitated Bayle.

An author who wishes to write without passion, and without prejudice, ought, it is said, to have neither religion nor country; and this is nearly the case with Voltaire. No person will tax him with partiality for his own nation. He is rather possessed by the phrenzy of dotards, who are incessantly vaunting of times past at the expence of times present. Voltaire continually praises the different countries of Europe; he complains only of his own. He has not formed any system of religion for himself; and, were it not for a little of the leaven of the anti-Jansenist, which is found in several parts of his writings, he would, without con-

❖ ❖ ❖

Letters

HORACE WALPOLE

TO SIR HORACE MANN

Arlington Street, Dec. 31, 1769.
The licentiousness of abuse surpasses all example.
The most savage massacre of private characters passes
for sport; but we have lately had an attack made on
the King himself, exceeding the *North Briton*. Such a
paper has been printed by the famous Junius, whoever
he is, that it would scarce have been written before
Charles I was in Carisbrook Castle. The Dukes of
Gloucester and Cumberland are as little spared; the
former for having taken a wife for himself—so says
the *North Briton;* observe, *I* do not say so; and the
latter, for having taken another man's. . . .

I have often said, and oftener think, *that this world
is a comedy to those who think, a tragedy to those
who feel*—a solution of why Democritus laughed and
Heraclitus wept. The only gainer is History, which
has constant opportunities of showing the various
ways in which men can contrive to be fools and knaves.

Feb. 2, 1770.
The gaming at Almack's, which has taken the *pas*
of White's, is worthy the decline of our Empire, or
Commonwealth, which you please. The young men of

the age lose five, ten, fifteen thousand pounds in
an evening there. Lord Stavordale, not one-and-twenty,
lost eleven thousand there, last Tuesday, but recovered
it by one great hand at hazard: he swore a great oath
—"Now, if I had been playing *deep,* I might have
won millions." His cousin, Charles Fox, shines equally
there and in the House of Commons. He was twenty-
one yesterday se'nnight; and is already one of our
best speakers. Yesterday he was made a Lord of the
Admiralty.

Strawberry Hill, May 6, 1770.

You have seen the accounts from Boston. The
tocsin seems to be sounded to America. I have many
visions about the country, and fancy I see twenty
empires and republics forming upon vast scales over
all that continent, which is growing too mighty to be
kept in subjection to half a dozen exhausted nations
in Europe. . . .

I have touched before to you on the incredible profusion of our young men of fashion. I know a younger
brother who literally gives a flower-woman half a
guinea every morning for a bunch of roses for the
nosegay in his button-hole. There has lately been an
auction of stuffed birds; and, as natural history is in
fashion, there are physicians and others who paid
forty and fifty guineas for a single Chinese pheasant:
you may buy a live one for five. After this, it is not
extraordinary that pictures should be dear. We have
at present three exhibitions. One West, who paints
history in the taste of Poussin, gets three hundred
pounds for a piece not too large to hang over a
chimney. He has merit, but is hard and heavy, and
far unworthy of such prices. The rage to see these
exhibitions is so great, that sometimes one cannot pass

through the streets where they are. But it is incredible what sums are raised by mere exhibitions of anything; a new fashion, and to enter at which you pay a shilling or half-a-crown.

June 8, 1771.

Strawberry is in the most perfect beauty, the verdure exquisite, and the shades venerably extended. I have made a Gothic gateway to the garden, the piers of which are of artificial stone, and very respectable. The round tower is finished, and magnificent; and the state bedchamber proceeds fast; for you must know the little villa is grown into a superb castle.

. . . My party has succeeded to admiration, and Gothic architecture has received great applause. I will not swear that it has been really admired. I found by Monsieur de Guisnes that, though he had heard much of the house, it was in no favourable light. He had been told it was only built of lath and plaster, and that there were not two rooms together on a level. When I once asked Madame du Deffand what her countrymen said of it, she owned they were not struck with it, but looked upon it as natural enough in a country which had not yet arrived at true taste. In short, I believe, they think all the houses they see are Gothic, because they are not like that single pattern that reigns in every hotel in Paris; and which made me say there, that I never knew whether I was in the house that I was in, or in the house I came out of. Two or three rooms in a row, a naked *salle-à-manger*, a white and gold cabinet, with four looking-glasses, a lustre, a scrap of hanging over against the windows, and two rows of chairs, with no variety in the apartments, but from bigger to less, and more or less gilt, and a bedchamber with a blue or red damask bed; this is that effort of taste to which they think we have not attained—we who have as pure architecture and as classic taste as there was in Adrian's or Pliny's villas.

Arlington Street, Feb. 7, 1772.

Yesterday there was a long debate, for *this* session, in the House of Commons. A petition was offered from two hundred and fifty divines, for abolition of the Thirty-nine Articles, that summary of impertinent folly. It was rejected at eleven at night by a large majority; so much more difficult is it to expel nonsense than sense—for sense makes few martyrs.

From *Private Letters*, Vol. II, ed. R. E. Prothero (London, Murray, 1897).

❖ ❖ ❖

The Death of Hume

ADAM SMITH

TO WILLIAM STRAHAN

Kirkaldy, Fifeshire, Nov. 9, 1776.

DEAR SIR,

It is with a real, though a very melancholy pleasure, that I sit down to give you some account of the behaviour of our late excellent friend, Mr. Hume, during his last illness.

Though in his own judgment his disease was mortal and incurable, yet he allowed himself to be prevailed upon, by the entreaty of his friends, to try what might be the effects of a long journey. . . . Upon his return to Edinburgh, though he found himself much weaker, yet his cheerfulness never abated, and he continued to divert himself, as usual, with correcting his own works for a new edition, with reading books of amusement, with the conversation of his friends; and sometimes in the evening with a party at his favourite game of whist. His cheerfulness was so great, and his conversation and amusements ran so much in their usual strain, that notwithstanding all bad symptoms, many people could not believe he was dying. "I shall tell your friend Colonel Edmonstoune," said Dr. Dundas to him one day, "that I left you much better, and in a fair way of recovery." "Doctor," said he, "as I believe you would not choose to tell anything but the truth, you had better tell him I am dying as fast as my enemies, if I have any, could wish, and as easily and cheerfully as my best friends could desire." Colonel Edmonstoune soon afterwards came to see him, and take leave of him; and on his way home he could not forbear writing him a letter, bidding him once more an eternal adieu, and applying to him, as to a dying man, the beautiful French verses in which the Abbé Chaulieu, in expectation of his own death, laments his approaching separation from his friend the Marquis de la Fare. Mr. Hume's magnanimity and firmness were such, that his most affectionate friends knew that they hazarded nothing in talking and writing to him as to a dying man; and that so far from being hurt by this frankness, he was rather pleased and flattered by it. I happened to come into his room while he was reading this letter, which he had just received, and which he immediately showed me. I told him, that though I was sensible how very much he was weakened, and that appearances were in many respects very bad, yet his cheerfulness was still so

great, the spirit of life seemed still to be so very strong
in him, that I could not help entertaining some faint
hopes. He answered, "Your hopes are groundless. An
habitual diarrhœa of more than a year's standing
would be a very bad disease at any age; at my age it
is a mortal one. When I lie down in the evening I
feel myself weaker than when I rose in the morning;
and when I rise in the morning weaker than when I
lay down in the evening. I am sensible, besides, that
some of my vital parts are affected, so that I must
soon die." "Well," said I, "if it must be so, you have
at least the satisfaction of leaving all your friends,
your brother's family in particular, in great prosperity." He said that he felt that satisfaction so sensibly,
that when he was reading, a few days before, Lucian's
Dialogues of the Dead, among all the excuses which
are alleged to Charon for not entering readily into his
boat, he could not find one that fitted him: he had no
house to finish, he had no daughter to provide for,
he had no enemies upon whom he wished to revenge
himself. "I could not well imagine," said he, "what
excuse I could make to Charon, in order to obtain a
little delay. I have done everything of consequence
which I ever meant to do, and I could at no time
expect to leave my relations and friends in a better
situation than that in which I am now likely to leave
them: I therefore have all reason to die contented."
He then diverted himself with inventing several jocular
excuses, which he supposed he might make to Charon,
and with imagining the very surly answers which it
might suit the character of Charon to return to them.
"Upon further consideration," said he, "I thought I
might say to him, 'Good Charon, I have been correcting my works for a new edition. Allow me a little time
that I may see how the public received the alterations.'

But Charon would answer, 'When you have seen the
effect of these, you will be for making other alterations. There will be no end of such excuses; so, honest
friend, please step into the boat.' But I might still urge,
'Have a little patience, good Charon, I have been
endeavouring to open the eyes of the public. If I live
a few years longer, I may have the satisfaction of seeing the downfall of some of the prevailing systems
of superstition.' But Charon would then lose all temper
and decency. 'You loitering rogue, that will not happen
these many hundred years. Do you fancy I will grant
you a lease for so long a term? Get into the boat this
instant, you lazy loitering rogue.'"

But though Mr. Hume always talked of his approaching dissolution with great cheerfulness, he never affected to make any parade of his great magnanimity.
He never mentioned the subject but when the conversation naturally led to it, and never dwelt longer
upon it than the course of the conversation happened
to require; it was a subject, indeed, which occurred
pretty frequently, in consequence of the inquiries
which his friends, who came to see him, naturally made
concerning the state of his health. . . .

Thus died our most excellent, and never-to-be-for-
gotten friend; concerning whose philosophical opinions
men will no doubt judge variously, everyone approving
or condemning them according as they happen to
coincide, or disagree with his own; but concerning
whose character and conduct there can scarce be a
difference of opinion. His temper, indeed, seemed to
be more happily balanced, if I may be allowed such
an expression, than that perhaps of any other man I
have ever known. Even in the lowest state of his
fortune, his great and necessary frugality never hindered him from exercising, upon proper occasions, acts

both of charity and generosity. It was a frugality founded not upon avarice, but upon the love of independency. The extreme gentleness of his nature never weakened either the firmness of his mind, or the steadiness of his resolutions. His constant pleasantry was the genuine effusion of good nature and good humour, tempered with delicacy and modesty, and without even the slightest tincture of malignity, so frequently the disagreeable source of what is called wit in other men. It never was the meaning of his raillery to mortify; and therefore, far from offending, it seldom failed to please and delight even those who were the objects of it. To his friends, who were frequently the objects of it, there was not perhaps any one of all his great and amiable qualities which contributed more to endear his conversation. And that gaiety of temper, so agreeable in society, but which is so often accompanied with frivolous and superficial qualities, was in him certainly attended with the most severe application, the most extensive learning, the greatest depth of thought, and a capacity in every respect the most comprehensive. Upon the whole, I have always considered him, both in his lifetime, and since his death, as approaching as nearly to the idea of a perfectly wise and virtuous man, as perhaps the nature of human frailty will admit.

From *Letters*, David Hume, ed. J. Y. T. Greig (Oxford: Clarendon Press, 1932).

tion is chiefly in the hands of persons who, from their profession, have an interest in the reputation and the dreams of Plato. They give the tone while at school, and few in their after years have occasion to revise their college opinions. But fashion and authority apart, and bringing Plato to the test of reason, take from him his sophisms, futilities and incomprehensibilities, and what remains? In truth, he is one of the race of genuine sophists, who has escaped the oblivion of his brethren, first, by the elegance of his diction, but chiefly, by the adoption and incorporation of his whimsies into the body of artificial Christianity. . . . The doctrines which flowed from the lips of Jesus himself are within the comprehension of a child; but thousands of volumes have not yet explained the Platonisms engrafted on them; and for this obvious reason, that nonsense can never be explained. Their purposes, however, are answered. Plato is canonized; and it is now deemed as impious to question his merits as those of an Apostle of Jesus. He is peculiarly appealed to as an advocate of the immortality of the soul; and yet I will venture to say, that were there no better arguments than his in proof of it, not a man in the world would believe it. It is fortunate for us, that Platonic republicanism has not obtained the same favour as Platonic Christianity; or we should now have been all living, men, women and children, pell mell together, like beasts of the field or forest. Yet "Plato is a great philosopher," said La Fontaine. But, says Fontenelle, "Do you find his ideas very clear?" "Oh no! he is of an obscurity impenetrable." "Do you not find him full of contradictions?" "Certainly," replied La Fontaine, "he is but a sophist." Yet immediately after he exclaims again, "Oh, Plato was a great philosopher." Socrates had reason, indeed, to complain of the misrepresentations of Plato; for in truth, his dialogues are libels on Socrates.

But why am I dosing you with these antediluvian topics? Because I am glad to have someone to whom they are familiar, and who will not receive them as if dropped from the moon. Our post-revolutionary youth are born under happier stars than you and I were. They acquire all learning in their mother's womb, and bring it into the world ready made. The information of books is no longer necessary; and all knowledge which is not innate, is in contempt, or neglect at least. Every folly must run its round; and so, I suppose, must that of self-learning and self-sufficiency; of rejecting the knowledge acquired in past ages, and starting on the new ground of intuition. When sobered by experience, I hope our successors will turn their attention to the advantages of education. I mean of education on the broad scale, and not that of the petty *academies,* as they call themselves, which are starting up in every neighbourhood, and where one or two men, possessing Latin and sometimes Greek, a knowledge of the globes, and the first six books of Euclid, imagine and communicate this as the sum of science. They commit their pupils to the theatre of the world, with just taste enough of learning to be alienated from industrious pursuits, and not enough to do service in the ranks of science. We have some exceptions, indeed. I presented one to you lately, and we have some others. But the terms I use are general truths. I hope the necessity will, at length, be seen of establishing institutions here, as in Europe, where every branch of science, useful at this day, may be taught in its highest degree. Have you ever turned your thoughts to the plan of such an institution? I mean to a specification of the particular sciences of real use in human affairs, and how they might be so grouped as to require so many professors only as might bring them within the views of a just but enlightened economy? I should be happy in a communication of your ideas on this problem, either loose or digested. But to avoid my being run away with by another subject, and adding to the length and ennui of the present letter, I will here present to Mrs. Adams and yourself, the assurance of my constant and sincere friendship and respect.

From *The Works of Thomas Jefferson*, Vol. XI, ed. P. L. Ford (New York: G. P. Putnam's Sons, 1905).

Debate with Condorcet

JOHN ADAMS

1798-1811

[*Marginalia written on his copy of Condorcet's* Outlines of an Historical View of the Progress of the Human Mind[1]]

Condorcet: Little by little the priests forgot some of the truths hidden behind their allegories, and at last became themselves *the dupes of their own fables.*

Adams: Just as you and yours have become the dupes of your own atheism and profligacy, your nonsensical notions of liberty, equality, and fraternity. . . .

C.: All progress of the sciences came to a halt; and the human mind, a prey to ignorance and prejudice,

---

[1] The English translation, under this title, of Condorcet's *Esquisse d'un tableau historique des progrès de l'esprit humain* which Adams read and annotated was published in London in 1795, within a few months of the work's appearance in French. See also p. 220 ff. [C.B.'s note.]

was condemned to that shameful stagnation which has so long disgraced Asia.

A.: God grant that your extravagances may not introduce another such Age of Darkness.

C.: The Asiatic nations are the only ones where one may still observe this state of civilization and this decadence.

A.: All Europe will be another if your plans are pursued.

C.: Then alphabetical writing was introduced into Greece, among . . . a people which fate had decreed to be the benefactor of all nations and all ages . . .

A.: As much as I love, esteem, and admire the Greeks, I believe the Hebrews have done more to enlighten and civilize the world. Moses did more than all their legislators and philosophers.

C.: Only one other nation has since conceived the idea of leading a revolution new in the destiny of mankind. . . . But let us not seek to penetrate what an uncertain future as yet conceals from us.

A.: Ah! Let us cast a veil over this awful scene.

. . . .

C.: The philosophers could not aspire as yet to found the *super-structure* of a society of equal and free men upon reason, upon the maxims of universal justice.

A.: All authority in one center and that center the nation. Fool!

C.: To guard against change, such institutions were sought for as cherished the love of country, including the love of its legislation and even customs.

A.: What fault do you find in this?

C.: The rich, who alone were in a position to acquire knowledge . . .

A.: Will not knowledge always be confined chiefly to the rich?

C.: . . . could, by seizing the reins of authority, oppress the poor and compel them to throw themselves into the arms of a tyrant.

A.: This is stupid and wicked.

C.: The ignorance and fickleness of the people, and its jealousy of powerful citizens, might suggest to the latter the desire of establishing aristocratic despotism . . .

A.: He knows that nature has ordained an aristocracy, and he wishes only that his men of genius might have the aristocratic despotism.

C.: Modern republics have hardly an institution with which the Greeks were unacquainted. The Amphictyonic League, as well as those of the Aetolians, Arcadians, and Achæans, present examples of federal constitutions and unions more or less close; and there were established more liberal rules of commerce between these different nations.

A.: There is not among them all a form of government which could hold together any modern commercial nation.

C.: A study of existing governments alone was not enough to convert politics into an extensive science. Thus even in the writings of the philosophers it appears to be *a science rather of facts* than a true theory founded upon general principles. . . .

A.: Is there any science, not of facts? Newton's science is empirical. Principles drawn from nature are drawn from facts. What is nature but facts? How can reason acknowledge anything but facts and inferences from facts? Behmen and Swedenborg were not more mystical and unintelligible than this philosophical and mathematical charlatan.

[Adams's comment, dated 1811, on the flyleaf of the volume]

The rapid progress of the mind to perfection has been the commonplace topic of declamation for half a century. But I can see no other end they have in view as their ultimate object than to bring men back to the state of mind so frankly avowed by Tacitus and Quintilian—absolute doubt whether chance or fate governs the world. But it will be found that men must be governed as well as cultivated. Without government, there is not a more savage beast of the forest.

The philosophers of France were too rash and hasty. They were as artful as selfish and as hypocritical as the priests and politicians of Babylon, Persia, Egypt, India, Greece, Rome, Turkey, Germany, Wales, Scotland, Ireland, France, Spain, Italy or England. They understood not what they were about. They miscalculated their forces and resources: and were consequently overwhelmed in destruction with all their theories.

The precipitation and temerity of philosophers has, I fear, retarded the progress of improvement and amelioration in the condition of mankind for at least an hundred years.

The public mind was improving in knowledge and the public heart in humanity, equity, and benevolence; the fragments of feudality, the Inquisition, the rack, the cruelty of punishments, Negro slavery, were giving way, etc. But the philosophers must arrive at perfection *per saltum*. Ten times more furious than Jack in the *Tale of a Tub,* they rent and tore the whole garment to pieces and left not one whole thread in it. They have even been compelled to resort to Napoleon, and Gibbon himself became an advocate for the Inquisition. What an amiable and glorious Equality,

Fraternity, and Liberty they have now established in Europe! . . .

The logos of Plato, the ratio of Manilius, and the mind of Condorcet, all plausible and specious as they are, will be three thousand years longer more delusive than useful. Not one of them takes human nature as it is for his foundation. Equality is one of those equivocal words which the philosophy of the eighteenth century has made fraudulent. The word as it is used is a swindler. In the last twenty-five years it has cheated millions out of their lives and tens of millions out of their property.

From *John Adams and the Prophets of Progress*, Zoltán Haraszti (Cambridge: Harvard University Press, 1952).

Epilogue

REASON BECOMES REVOLUTION

The Festival of Reason
in Notre-Dame de Paris

[FROM *The History of the French Revolution,
1799-1800*[1]]

LOUIS ADOLPHE THIERS

1823

At the requisition of Chaumette, it was resolved that
the metropolitan church of Notre-Dame should be
converted into a republican edifice, called the *Temple
of Reason*. A festival was instituted for all the Décadis

[1] On the whole, this passage, though it was written later
than the period covered by this *Reader*, gives a more
rounded account of what happened to "Reason" in 1794 than
does any contemporary document. [C.B.'s note.]

[tenth days], to supersede the Catholic ceremonies of Sunday. The mayor, the municipal officers, the public functionaries, repaired to the Temple of Reason, where they read the declaration of the rights of man and the constitutional act, analyzed the news from the armies, and related the brilliant actions which had been performed during the decade. A *mouth of truth,* resembling the mouths of denunciation which formerly existed at Venice, was placed in the Temple of Reason, to receive *opinions, censures, advice,* that might be useful to the public. These letters were examined and read every Décadi, a moral discourse was delivered, after which pieces of music were performed, and the ceremonies concluded with the singing of republican hymns. There were in the temple two tribunes—one for aged men, the other for pregnant women, with these inscriptions: *Respect for old age—Respect and attention for pregnant women.*

The first festival of Reason was held with pomp on the 20th of Brumaire (the 10th of November). It was attended by all the sections, together with the constituted authorities. A young woman represented the goddess of Reason. She was the wife of Momoro the printer, one of the friends of Vincent, Ronsin, Chaumette, Hébert, and the like. She was dressed in a white drapery; a mantle of azure blue hung from her shoulders; her flowing hair was covered with the cap of liberty. She sat upon an antique seat, entwined with ivy, and borne by four citizens. Young girls dressed in white, and crowned with roses, preceded and followed the goddess. Then came the busts of Lepelletier and Marat, musicians, troops, and all the armed sections. Speeches were delivered and hymns sung in the Temple of Reason; they then proceeded to the Convention, and Chaumette spoke in these terms:

"Legislators! Fanaticism has given way to reason. Its bleared eyes could not endure the brilliancy of the light. This day an immense concourse has assembled beneath those Gothic vaults, which for the first time re-echoed the truth. There the French have celebrated the only true worship, that of liberty, that of reason. There we have formed wishes for the prosperity of the arms of the republic. There we have abandoned inanimate idols for reason, for that animated image, the masterpiece of Nature." As he uttered these words, Chaumette pointed to the living goddess of Reason. The young and beautiful woman descended from her seat and went up to the president, who gave her the fraternal kiss amidst universal bravoes and shouts of *The republic forever! Reason forever! Down with fanaticism!* The Convention, which had not yet taken any part in these representations, was hurried away, and obliged to follow the procession, which returned to the Temple of Reason, and there sang a patriotic hymn.

From Vol. III, trans. Frederick Shoberl (Philadelphia: J. B. Lippincott Co., 1894).

ACKNOWLEDGMENTS

The editor wishes to thank the following for their kind permission to reprint excerpts from the works listed below:

Richard Aldington and Routledge & Kegan Paul, Ltd., London, translations from *Candide and Other Romances* by Voltaire and *Letters of Voltaire and Frederick the Great.*

George Allen & Unwin, Ltd., London, *Philosophical Dictionary* by Voltaire, translated by H. I. Woolf.

Mrs. Alan Conder, Birmingham, England, and Cassell & Company, Ltd., London, translation of Voltaire by Alan Conder in *A Treasury of French Poetry.*

Dodd, Mead & Company, New York, and William Heinemann, Ltd., London, translation of Chénier by Arthur Symons in *Knave of Hearts.*

E. P. Dutton & Co., Inc., New York, and J. M. Dent & Sons, Ltd., London, translation of Voltaire by J. G. Legge in *Chanticleer: A Study of the French Muse.*

The Golden Cockerel Press, London, *Maxims and Considerations* by S. R. N. Chamfort, translated by E. Powys Mathers.

Harcourt, Brace and Company, Inc., New York, *The Misanthrope* by Molière, translated by Richard Wilbur, copyright 1954, 1955, by Richard Wilbur.

The President and Fellows of Harvard College, Cambridge, Mass., *John Adams and the Prophets of Progress* by Zoltan Haraszti.

Alfred A. Knopf, Inc., New York, translation of Dumarsais by F. L. Baumer in *Main Currents of Western Thought,* copyright 1952 by Alfred A. Knopf, Inc.

Lawrence & Wishart, Ltd., London, *Diderot, Interpreter of Nature,* translated by Jean Stewart and Jonathan Kemp.

The Macmillan Company, New York, translation of the

Declaration of the Rights of Man and the Citizen by J. H. Stewart in *A Documentary Survey of the French Revolution;* and *Berenice* by Racine, translated by John Masefield in *Esther and Berenice: Two Plays.*

Oxford University Press, Inc., New York, *Reflections and Maxims* by Luc de Clapiers, Marquis of Vauvenargues, translated by F. G. Stevens.

Pantheon Books, Inc., New York, *Pensées* by Pascal, translated by H. F. Stewart.

Routledge & Kegan Paul, Ltd., London, *Persian Letters* by Montesquieu, translated by John Davidson.

The University of Chicago Press, Chicago, *Foundations of the Metaphysics of Morals* by Immanuel Kant, translated by Lewis White Beck.

The Viking Press, Inc., New York, *The Fables of La Fontaine,* translated by Marianne Moore, copyright 1952, 1954 by Marianne Moore.

George Weidenfeld & Nicolson, Ltd., London, *Sketch for a Historical Picture of the Human Mind* by Condorcet, translated by June Barraclough.